Little Champ

LITTLE CHAMP ADVENTURES: The Fight of His Life

LOOKING UP

WILLIE TAYLOR

Mission: To Proclaim Transformation and Truth
Publisher: Transformed Publishing, Cocoa, FL
Website: www.transformedpublishing.com
Email: transformedpublishing@gmail.com

Illustrations retrieved from Storyblocks.com (subscription plan March 2023).

ISBN: 978-1-953241-49-8

Little Champ loved hanging out with his dad (his champion) as a little kid.

They watched their favorite sport on T.V. - boxing, every Tuesday, Wednesday, and Friday night.

As Little Champ saw the excitement in his dad's eyes, he said, "Dad! Dad, look! I can do that," as he beat the air.

"I know you can, Little Champ. Come here," Dad requested.

Little Champ looked up, "Dad, why do you call me Little Champ?"

"Because I know you will never give up. You will give it your all and you will not stop until the task is completed. Now, let me see you do that," Dad demonstrated a punch combination for Little Champ to follow.

Little Champ gave it a try.

"Wow, you are good, Little Champ!"

"Dad, this is tiring," Little Champ said with exhaustion.

Dad encouraged Little Champ, "I know it is Little Champ, but I know you can do it. Keep it up and one day you can be the best."

One day, Dad walked into the house after work and shouted, "Where's my Little Champ?"

Little Champ looked up, "Here I am, Dad!"

"I have something for you," Dad said with a twinkle in his eye.

"Really Dad, what is it?"

"A new pair of boxing gloves,"
Dad replied as he extended
his arm and held out the gift.

"It's okay. One day,
you will fit them just fine,"
Dad reassured Little Champ.

Little Champ looked up
and asked, "Really, Dad?" as
a smile spread across his face.

"Yes, my Little Champ," Dad said
as he touched his son's hands.

Little Champ put the gloves on.

"Okay now, let's see what
you got, Little Champ!"

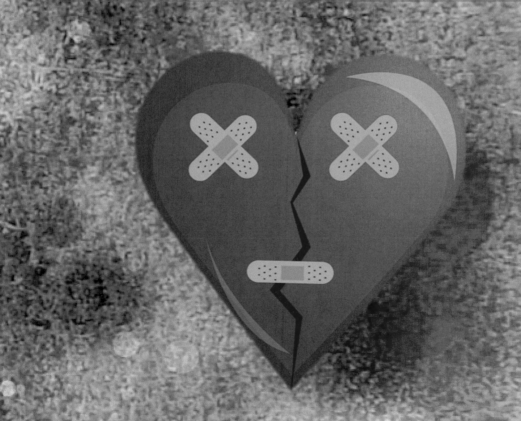

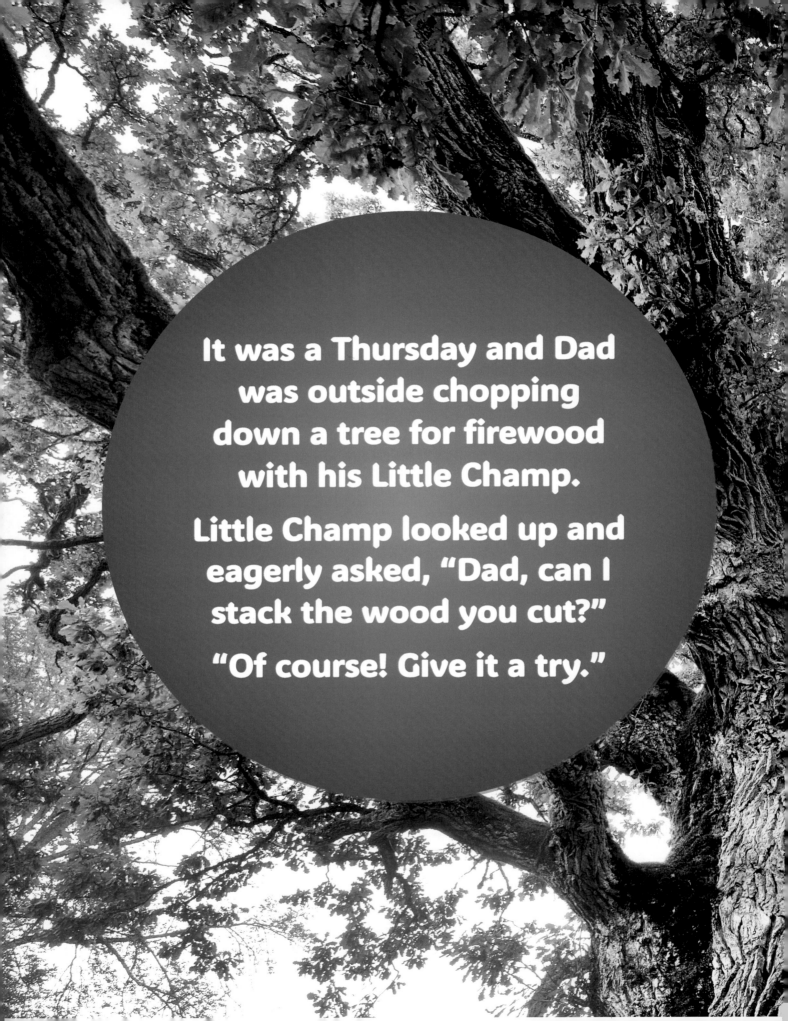

It was a Thursday and Dad was outside chopping down a tree for firewood with his Little Champ.

Little Champ looked up and eagerly asked, "Dad, can I stack the wood you cut?"

"Of course! Give it a try."

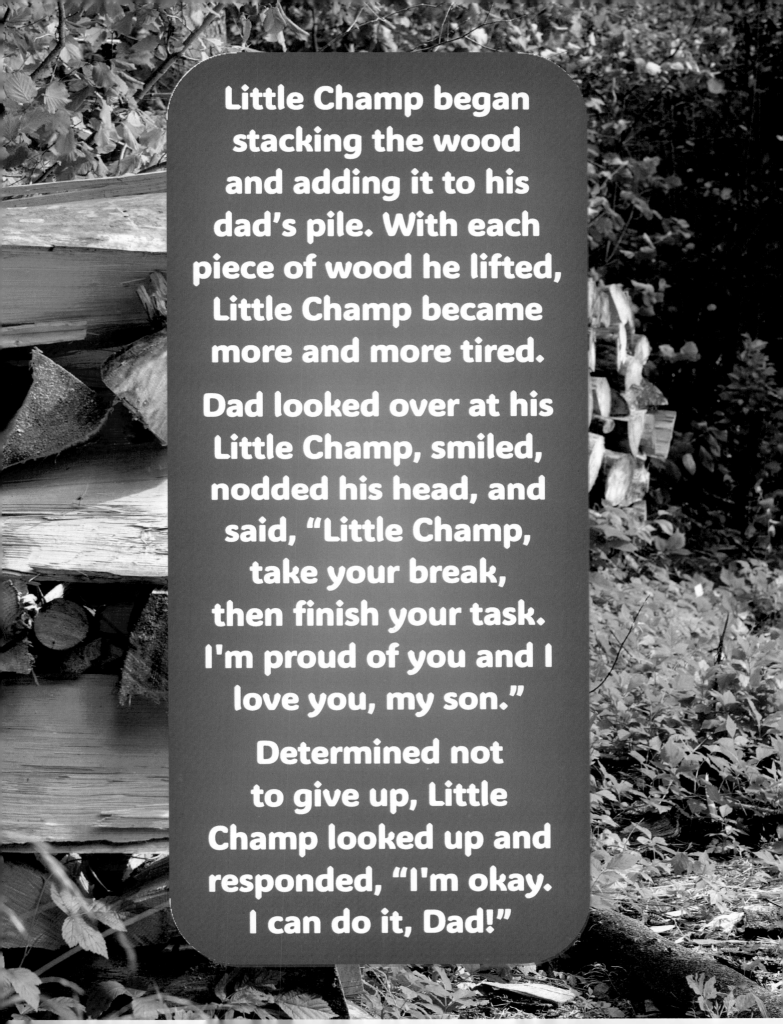

Little Champ began stacking the wood and adding it to his dad's pile. With each piece of wood he lifted, Little Champ became more and more tired.

Dad looked over at his Little Champ, smiled, nodded his head, and said, "Little Champ, take your break, then finish your task. I'm proud of you and I love you, my son."

Determined not to give up, Little Champ looked up and responded, "I'm okay. I can do it, Dad!"

The next day, Little Champ was waiting for his dad to come home. After all, it was time for them to watch Friday Night Boxing on TV.

Just as he hoped, Dad walked into the house and shouted, "Where's my Little Champ?"

Little Champ looked up and exclaimed, "Here I am!" as he ran into his dad's arms wearing his oversized boxing gloves. Little Champ was ready to watch the great boxers compete for the night.

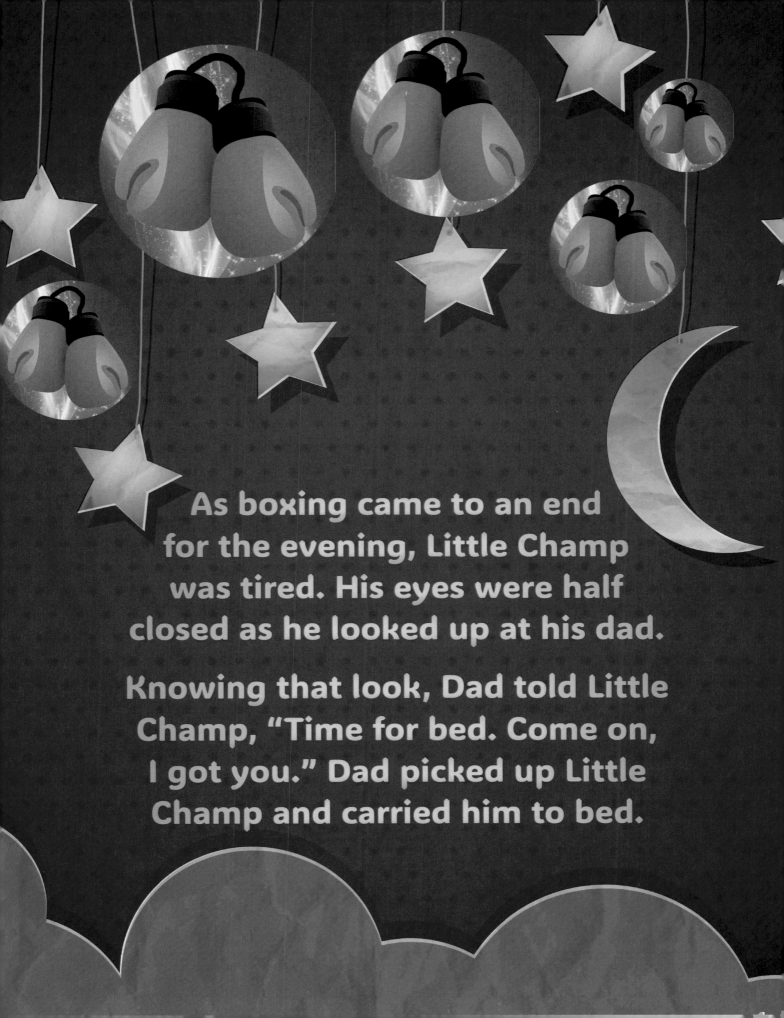

As boxing came to an end for the evening, Little Champ was tired. His eyes were half closed as he looked up at his dad.

Knowing that look, Dad told Little Champ, "Time for bed. Come on, I got you." Dad picked up Little Champ and carried him to bed.

The next morning Little Champ woke up and started to get ready for his day. He took a shower, brushed his teeth, and put on his clothes. As soon as Little Champ left his room, he heard, "Where's my Little Champ?"

Little Champ looked up and blurted out, "Here I am, Big Champ!" seeing his father at the end of the hallway. Little Champ ran and jumped into his dad's arms, "What are we doing today, Big Champ?"

"Little Champ, we are going to take a drive today after we eat breakfast. I have a surprise for you today!"

Little Champ could hardly contain his excitement, "Really, Dad, what is it?"

"You will see Little Champ," Big Champ responded with a sly grin.

When they got into the kitchen, Little Champ's mom already had breakfast ready. Glad to see her two champs, Mom greeted them with a smile, "It sounds like you two have an adventure ahead, but first you must eat."

"Really, Mom?"

"Yes, my son. Now let's eat so you and Dad can go on your adventure."

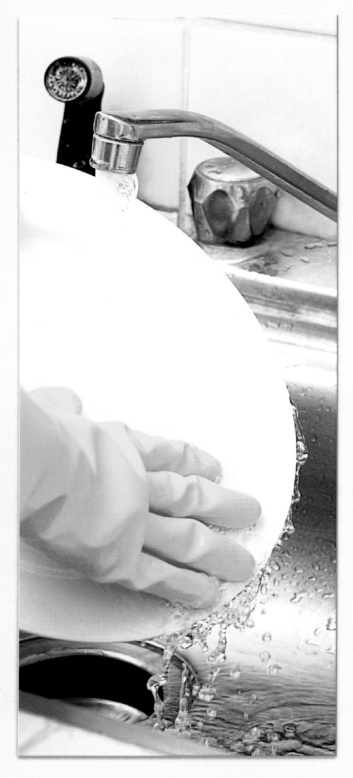

Little Champ and his dad finished their meals. "Please help Mom wash the dishes and dry them."

Little Champ looked up at his champion and declared, "I can do it!"

His champion looked at him with a smile and said, "I know you can my Little Champ!"

As soon as the dishes were done, Little Champ asked his dad, "Are you ready?"

"Let's go!" responded Big Champ.

They got into the car and drove away from their house listening to music and singing together.
Dad lovingly looked at his Little Champ and playfully asked, "So, you really like BOXING, don't you?"

Little Champ looked up inquisitively at his dad and responded, "More than anything! Well, not more than you and mom, though."

Suddenly, the car stopped in front of a building Little Champ had never seen before. Dad looked at his Little Champ and announced, "We are here!"

Little Champ looked up, "What is this place, Dad?"

"It is a BOXING gym!"

"Really, Dad!" Little Champ shouted with amazement radiating from all over his face.

They got out of the car and walked to the door hand in hand.

When they got in front of the door,
Little Champ paused. Dad looked down
and caringly asked, "Is something
the matter, Little Champ?"

Little Champ looked up at his dad
and shyly confessed, "I'm a little scared."

His dad looked at him and reminded his son,
"I'm right here with you. You got this,
Little Champ! I know you can do it!"

At that moment, looking up at his champion,
Little Champ boldly responded,
"Let's go, Dad. I'm ready!"

ABOUT THE AUTHOR

Willie Taylor is excited to share his journey in the form of motivational children's books. Looking up to his father and their shared love for boxing has driven him to demonstrate perseverance in every area of his life. Willie is a law enforcement officer in his community and the owner and operator of Fighting Edge.

Big Champ

Little Champ

FIGHTING EDGE IS A NON-PROFIT ORGANIZATION 501(C)(3)

Our Mission Statement:

"Don't talk about it, be about it." That is the motto of Fighting Edge. Starting out as a humble amateur boxing team and fitness program Fighting Edge is now a non-profit organization 501(c)(3) in support of programs geared towards growing our youth and improving our community. Whether it be our boxing, martial arts and fitness programs, organizing volunteers for events in our community, growing our youth through mentoring, or partnering with organizations to help those in need, Team Fighting Edge isn't here to "Talk about it"... we're here to "Be about it!"

Printed in the USA
CPSIA information can be obtained
at www.ICGtesting.com
LVRC090747311223
767725LV00039B/95

* 9 7 8 1 9 5 3 2 4 1 4 9 8 *

THE BOOK OF I^{2}C

A Guide for Adventurers

by Randall Hyde

no starch press

San Francisco

THE BOOK OF I²C. Copyright © 2023 by Randall Hyde.

Printed in the United States of America

First printing

26 25 24 23 22   1 2 3 4 5

ISBN-13: 978-1-7185-0246-8 (print)
ISBN-13: 978-1-7185-0247-5 (ebook)

Publisher: William Pollock
Managing Editor: Jill Franklin
Production Manager: Rachel Monaghan
Production Editor: Miles Bond
Developmental Editors: Abigail Schott-Rosenfield, Athabasca Witschi, and Jill Franklin
Cover Illustrator: Gina Redman
Interior Design: Octopod Studios
Technical Reviewer: Anthony Tribelli
Copyeditor: Kim Wimpsett
Compositor: Happenstance Type-O-Rama
Proofreader: Sadie Barry

For information on distribution, bulk sales, corporate sales, or translations, please contact No Starch Press, Inc. directly at info@nostarch.com or:

No Starch Press, Inc.
245 8th Street, San Francisco, CA 94103
phone: 1.415.863.9900
www.nostarch.com

Library of Congress Cataloging-in-Publication Data

Names: Hyde, Randall, author.
Title: The book of I²C : a guide for adventurers / Randall Hyde.
Description: San Francisco : No Starch Press, [2022] | Includes index. |
Identifiers: LCCN 2022018708 (print) | LCCN 2022018709 (ebook) | ISBN 9781718502468 (print) |
  ISBN 9781718502475 (ebook)
Subjects: LCSH: I2C (Computer bus) | Microcomputers--Programming. | Microcontrollers--Programming.
Classification: LCC TK7895.B87 H94 2022 (print) | LCC TK7895.B87 (ebook)
  | DDC 621.39/16--dc23/eng/20220627
LC record available at https://lccn.loc.gov/2022018708
LC ebook record available at https://lccn.loc.gov/2022018709

This book is dedicated to Limor
"Lady Ada" Fried of Adafruit and
Nathan Seidle of SparkFun.
Without these two great companies,
I never would have thought about
creating a book such as this one.

About the Author

Randall Hyde is the author of *The Art of 64-Bit Assembly*; *The Art of Assembly Language*; and *Write Great Code*, Volumes 1, 2, and 3 (all from No Starch Press); as well as *Using 6502 Assembly Language and P-Source* (Datamost). He is also the coauthor of *Microsoft Macro Assembler 6.0 Bible* (The Waite Group). Over the past 40 years, Hyde has worked as an embedded software and hardware engineer developing instrumentation for nuclear reactors, traffic control systems, and other consumer electronics devices. He has also taught computer science at California State Polytechnic University, Pomona, and at the University of California, Riverside. His website is *https://www.randallhyde.com*.

About the Technical Reviewer

Anthony Tribelli has more than 35 years of experience in software development. This experience ranges, among other things, from embedded device kernels to molecular modeling and visualization to video games. The latter includes 10 years at Blizzard Entertainment. He is currently a software development consultant and is privately developing applications utilizing computer vision.

BRIEF CONTENTS

CONTENTS IN DETAIL

PART IV: I²C PERIPHERAL PROGRAMMING EXAMPLES   251

ACKNOWLEDGMENTS

I would like to briefly mention the people at No Starch Press who made this book possible: Abigail Schott-Rosenfield, Athabasca Witschi, Jill Franklin, Bill Pollock, the production team, and anyone else I've missed.

I would also like to thank Anthony Tribelli for the great job he did as the technical reviewer for this book. The amount of effort he put into searching through datasheets, reviewing code, writing sample programs to test the book's concepts, and otherwise ensuring this book was of the highest technical quality was amazing.

I would like to thank Adafruit and Limor "Lady Ada" Fried for allowing me to use the Adafruit I^2C Address Compilation. This is an incredible resource for I^2C programmers, and its presence in this book is no small asset.

Finally, I would like to mention No Starch Press's original *The Book of SCSI: The Adventure Begins* by David Deming (2nd edition by Field, Ridge, et al.), the inspiration for this book's title.

INTRODUCTION

Welcome to *The Book of I²C*. This book provides the resources you need to design and program systems using the Inter-Integrated Circuit Bus (IIC, I2C, or I²C), a serial protocol for connecting various integrated circuits (ICs) together in computer systems. This book will teach you how to expand your embedded system design by adding I²C peripherals with minimal wiring and software.

To paraphrase from *https://i2c.info*, I²C uses only two wires to easily connect devices such as microcontrollers, A/D and D/A converters, digital I/O, memory, and many others, together in an embedded system. Although it was originally developed by Philips (now NXP Semiconductors), most major IC manufacturers now support I²C. I²C is popular because it is ubiquitous—most CPUs destined for embedded systems include support for I²C—and its peripheral ICs are inexpensive. It is present in hobbyist systems like Arduino and Raspberry Pi, as well as in most professional single-board computers (SBCs) intended for use in embedded systems.

The I²C bus is especially important on hobbyist-level embedded systems employed by "makers" working on personal projects, which typically use a commercially available off-the-shelf (COTS) SBC like an Arduino Uno, Teensy 4.*x*, or Raspberry Pi as the brains for the system. Such SBCs generally have limited I/O capability or other limitations, so the addition of peripheral ICs may be necessary to realize a given design. The I²C bus is one of the most popular and common ways to expand such systems, since it's easy, convenient, and inexpensive to use. Furthermore, there are hundreds of different devices available as individual ICs with a wide range of capabilities that connect directly to the I²C bus. Combined with a huge library of open source code to control these devices (especially for Arduino devices), it's almost trivial to expand small systems using the I²C bus.

NOTE *The SPI bus is another popular option for hobbyist systems, but discussing it will have to wait for a different book.*

Although higher-end custom SBCs intended for professional embedded systems often include many of the peripherals missing in hobbyist-grade SBCs, the I²C bus is still a cost-effective way to design such systems. Often, peripherals that don't have high-performance requirements connect to the CPU on the SBC using the I²C bus.

Because of the ubiquity of the I²C, it is difficult to work on embedded systems these days without at least a passing familiarity with the I²C bus. Sadly, most programmers are expected to figure out how to use the I²C bus on their own by searching the internet and piecing together design and programming information. This book rectifies that situation, collecting into one comprehensive book the resources needed to fully understand how to design and program systems using the I²C bus.

Expectations and Prerequisites

Working with I²C peripherals requires some hardware and software expertise. In theory, an electrical engineer with no software experience could design some hardware and hand it off to a software engineer with no hardware experience, and the two of them could get something working. However, this book is not intended to be read by such teams. Rather, it's meant for software engineers who aren't afraid to get their hands dirty by working directly with the hardware, or for hardware engineers who aren't afraid to sit down with a text editor and write software.

The Book of I²C assumes you are capable of reading schematics and wiring a COTS SBC (such as an Arduino, Pi, or other commercially available SBC) to various peripheral devices using breadboarding or point-to-point wiring on prototyping boards. You should be comfortable using tools such as DVMs, oscilloscopes, logic analyzers, and more to examine and debug such circuits.

This book also assumes you are familiar with the C/C++ programming language and are capable of creating, testing, and debugging decent-sized programs on the aforementioned SBCs. Although I²C code can be written in many different languages (including assembly language, Java, and Python), C/C++ is the universal language for embedded systems. Almost every COTS SBC's development software supports using C/C++, so the book assumes prior knowledge of this language.

Most of the examples in this book use the Arduino library due to its widespread use and simplicity. Therefore, it assumes at least a passing familiarity with the Arduino system. The Raspberry Pi examples obviously use the Raspberry Pi OS (Linux) and the Pi OS I²C library code; the book provides links to the documentation for those libraries as appropriate. For other systems (for example, μC/OS running on a NetBurner module or MBED running on an STM32 module), this book assumes no prior knowledge and provides either the necessary information or links to the associated documentation.

The software tools for embedded system programming generally run on Windows, macOS, or Linux. You should be familiar with the particular system running these tools (for example, the C/C++ compilers) and capable of running those tools on your own system, including learning how to use, install, and configure those tools with their accompanying documentation. As necessary, this book will describe how to find those tools and their documentation; however, its focus is the I²C bus, not running C/C++ compilers and integrated development environments (IDEs), so it leaves you to learn more about tools on your own.

Source Code in This Book

This book contains considerable C/C++ source code that comes in one of three forms: code snippets, modules, and full-blown programs.

Code snippets are fragments of a program, provided to make a point or provide an example of some programming technique. They are not standalone, and you cannot compile them using a C/C++ compiler. Here is a typical example of a snippet:

```
while( inputPin() == 0 )
{
    .
    .
    .
}
```

The vertical ellipses in this example denote some arbitrary code that could appear in their place.

Modules are small C/C++ code sections that are compilable but won't run on their own. Modules typically contain a function that some other program will call. Here is a typical example:

```
// inputPin function

int inputPin( void )
```

```
{
    int p = readPort( 0x48 )
    return p & 1;
}
```

Full-blown programs are called *listings* in this book, and I refer to them by listing number or filename. For example, the following example listing for an Arduino "blink" program is taken from the file *Listing1-1.ino*. The name indicates that it is the first listing in Chapter 1, and I refer to it as Listing 1-1 in the surrounding text, labeling the code itself with the filename in the comments:

```
// Listing1-1.ino
//
// An Arduino "Blink" program.

int led = 13;

void setup()
{
    pinMode( led, OUTPUT );
}

void loop()
{
    digitalWrite( led, HIGH );   // Turn on the LED
    delay( 500 );                // Wait for 1/2 second
    digitalWrite( led, LOW );    // Turn off the LED
    delay( 500 );                // Wait for a second
}
```

Note that the *Listing1-1.ino* filename format applies only to code of my own making. Any other source code retains its original filename. For example, I refer to Chapter 16's code from the TinyWire library as *attiny84_Periph.ino*. Certain non-Arduino systems (Pi OS and MBED, for example) use a standard *main.cpp* filename for their main programs; this book will generally place such programs in a subdirectory with a name such as *Listingx-x* and refer to that whole directory as the "listing." Many listings in this book are sufficiently long that I've broken them up into sections with text annotation between the sections. In such instances, I will place a comment such as // Listing10-1.ino (cont.) at the beginning of each section to provide continuity.

All listings and modules are available in electronic form at my website *https://bookofi2c.randallhyde.com*, either individually or as a ZIP file containing all the listings and other support information for this book, including errata, electronic chapters, and more.

Unless otherwise noted, all source code appearing in this book is covered under the Creative Commons 4.0 license. You may freely use that code in your own projects as per the Creative Commons license. See *https://creativecommons.org/licenses/by/4.0* for more details.

Typography and Pedantry

Computer books have a habit of abusing the English language, and this book is no exception. Whenever source code snippets appear in the middle of an English sentence, there is often a conflict between the grammar rules of the programming language and English. In this section, I describe my choices for differentiating syntactical rules in English versus programming languages, in addition to a few other conventions.

First, this book uses a monospace font to denote any text that appears as part of a program source file. This includes variable and procedure function names, program output, and user input to a program. Therefore, when you see something like get, you know that the book is describing an identifier in a program, not commanding you to get something.

There are a few logic operations whose names also have common English meanings. These logic operations are AND, OR, and NOT. When using these terms as logic functions, this book uses all caps to help differentiate otherwise confusing English statements. When using these terms as English, this book uses the standard typeset font. The fourth logic operator, exclusive-OR (XOR), doesn't normally appear in English statements, but this book still capitalizes it.

In general, I always try to define any acronym or abbreviation the first time I use it. If I haven't used the term in a while, I often redefine it when I use it next. I've added a glossary where I define most of the acronyms (and other technical terms) appearing in this book.

Finally, hardcore electrical engineers will often use the term *buss* when describing a collection of electronic signals, especially when describing buss bars. However, I use the spellings *bus* and *buses* simply because they are more prevalent in literature discussing the I^2C bus.

A Note About Terminology

In 2020, several major electronics firms and other members of the Open Source Hardware Association (OSHWA) proposed changing the names of various SPI bus terms to eliminate terms that some find morally questionable. The electronics industry has long used the terms *master* and *slave* to describe the operating hierarchy of various devices in the system. There is no technical justification for these names; they don't even precisely describe the relationship between devices, so better terms would be desirable even if other issues weren't a factor.

Although this is a book about the I^2C bus, not the SPI bus, I^2C is probably next on the list (as SparkFun notes at *https://www.sparkfun.com/spi_signal _names*). Though the I^2C bus does not have pins using the names master or slave, the terms *master, slave, multimaster,* and *multislave* are common in I^2C literature. This book substitutes the following more descriptive and less offensive terms, as per the OSHWA guidelines for the SPI bus:

- Master becomes *controller*
- Multimaster becomes *multicontroller*

- Slave becomes *peripheral*
- Multislave becomes *multiperipheral*

Of course, *controller* and *peripheral* have their own meanings and may not always correspond to an I²C bus controller or peripheral device. However, context within this book will make it clear which meaning I intend. Considerable historical documentation continues to use the terms *master* and *slave*, but you can simply mentally convert between *master/controller* and *slave/peripheral*. To avoid confusion with such historical documentation, this book uses *master* and *slave* only when referring to external documentation that uses those terms.

Organization

This book is organized into four parts as follows, in addition to appendixes and online chapters:

Part I: Low-Level Protocols and Hardware

This part describes the signals and hardware for the I²C. Though you don't necessarily need to know this information in order to design systems using the I²C bus or to write code to program peripherals, this knowledge is handy when debugging hardware and software that use the I²C bus. Part I also includes a software implementation of the I²C bus for those software engineers who relate more to code than electrical specifications, as well as a section on analyzing and debugging I²C bus transactions. Finally, the section concludes by discussing various real-world extensions to the I²C bus.

Part II: Hardware Implementations

This part describes several real-world implementations of the I²C bus. In particular, it reviews the I²C implementation of the following pieces of hardware:

- Arduino systems (and compatibles)
- The Teensy 3.*x* and 4.*x* SBC I²C implementations
- The Raspberry Pi, BeagleBone Black, PINE64 and ROCKPro64, Onion, and other Linux systems
- The STM32/Nucleo-144/Nucleo-64 I²C implementation
- The NetBurner MOD54415 I²C implementation

Part II also describes the following I²C bus implementations:

- The Adafruit Feather bus
- The SparkFun Qwiic bus
- The Seeed Studio Grove bus

Part III: Programming the I²C Bus

This part discusses programming devices on the I²C bus. It covers various generic programming techniques, such as real-time OS I²C programming, as well as providing specific real-world programming examples for Arduino, Raspberry Pi, Teensy, MBED, and NetBurner. Part III also describes how to implement an I²C using bare-metal programming techniques—those that work at the hardware level rather than calling library code.

Part IV: I²C Peripheral Programming Examples

This part provides programming examples for some common real-world I²C peripheral ICs, including the MCP23017 GPIO expander, ADS1115 16-bit A/D converter, MCP4725 D/A converter, and TCA9548A I²C multiplexer. Part IV also describes how to use a SparkFun Atto84 module as a custom I²C peripheral.

Appendixes

Appendix A is a snapshot of the Adafruit I²C Address Compilation, which lists the addresses of hundreds of commerically available I²C peripheral ICs.

Appendix B contains an overview of the online content. No matter how many pages I add to this book, it will be woefully incomplete. There are just too many I²C controllers and peripherals available. Furthermore, new peripherals will certainly appear after this book is published. To resolve this conundrum (and reduce the price you have to pay for this book), additional chapters are available online at *https://bookofi2c.randallhyde.com*.

The online content will cover (among other things) the following topics:

- The MCP4728 quad DAC
- The Maxim DS3502 digital potentiometer
- The DS3231 precision real-time clock
- The MCP9600 thermocouple amplifier
- I²C displays
- The SX1509 GPIO interface
- The PCA9685 PCM/servo interface
- The INA169 and INA218 current sensors
- The MPR121 capacitive touch interface
- The Raspberry Pi Pico SBC
- Espressif ESP32 (and ESP8266) SBCs

Glossary

A list of the terms and acronyms appearing in this book.

In addition to the online chapters, the website will contain help on constructing the circuitry appearing in this book and other information of interest to someone programming I^2C peripherals. It will also contain a parts list for all the electronic projects appearing within this book. My goal is to continuously update this information as new (important) peripherals and controllers appear that utilize the I^2C bus.

PART I

LOW-LEVEL PROTOCOLS
AND HARDWARE

1

I²C LOW-LEVEL HARDWARE

The I²C bus is a worldwide standard for communication between integrated circuits (ICs) on printed circuit boards (PCBs) and across multiple PCBs within a system. According to NXP Semiconductors, I²C is in use on more than 1,000 different ICs made by more than 50 different manufacturers. Without question, I²C is one of the more popular inter-IC data communication schemes available (Serial Peripheral Interface [SPI] being another).

The popularity of the I²C bus increased with the introduction of hobbyist-level single-board computers (SBCs) such as the Arduino and Raspberry Pi that include I²C support. Today, tens of thousands of programmers have learned the basics of the I²C bus because they wanted to interface some device to an Arduino- or Pi-class system. Because of the vast amount of open source library code available, it is possible to use and program devices on the I²C bus without really understanding its low-level signal protocols. However, to truly make the most of a design employing I²C peripherals, you need to understand those protocols, both hardware and software. This chapter introduces the low-level hardware aspects of the I²C, which you'll need to understand before learning about the signal protocols.

1.1 I²C Overview

Before buses such as the I²C bus, different components of a computer system communicated with one another using traditional CPU-style buses. These buses typically used 8 to 32 data lines and some number of address signals. Connecting a single 8-bit parallel I/O device to a CPU required a fair amount of PCB space to hold all the signal traces. Of course, adding additional I/O increased signal, space, and noise accordingly. In addition to space, those lines also increased the amount of noise that system engineers had to deal with in their designs.

The I²C bus was invented to alleviate these problems. With the I²C bus, a single pair of signal lines (PCB traces) can connect a wide variety of different I/O peripherals to a CPU. This reduces cost and eliminates many problems when building complex (embedded) computer systems (see the text box "Advantages of the I²C Bus" for more information).

I²C devices are divided into two general categories: controller devices (formerly known as masters) and peripheral devices (formerly slaves). A *controller device*, as its name suggests, controls the communication between the controller and the peripheral device. The *peripheral device* does not initiate any communication on its own and relies on the controller to manage the communication process.

The I²C protocol is a synchronous serial communication using two signal lines: *SCL*, which stands for "serial clock," and *SDA*, which stands for "serial data." The controller drives the clock line. When the peripheral is sending data to the controller, it puts the data bits on the data line; when the peripheral is receiving data, the controller places the serial data bits on the data line. Except for one special case—clock stretching, discussed later in this chapter—the peripheral never controls the clock line.

A typical system has a single controller and one or more peripheral devices. Each peripheral device has an address unique to a given I²C bus, which the controller uses to differentiate multiple peripherals on the same bus. In theory, a single I²C bus supports up to 127 or even 1,024 different peripheral devices, though practical matters limit the number of peripheral devices to a much smaller number.

Although a typical system has only a single controller, the I²C bus supports multiple controllers on the same bus. This allows multiple controllers to share a common set of peripheral devices. A given system can also support multiple I²C buses, so peripheral devices with the same address, which cannot be used together on the same I²C bus, can still be deployed in a given system.

The controller-peripheral relationship is fundamental to the I²C protocol. While, in theory, it is possible for a single IC to behave either as a controller or as a peripheral and even switch between these two functions in a given system, such activity is rare; in general, a device functions either as a peripheral or as a controller within a system.

1.2 Open-Drain (Open-Collector) Logic and Four-Wire Mode

One of the most fundamental electrical aspects of the I²C bus is that it is based on an open-drain (or open-collector) logic system. That is, a device connected to the I²C bus does not *drive* the signal lines high or low; instead, it can only *pull* these lines low using an open-drain (FET) connection. Pullup resistors that connect the signal lines on the I²C bus to a power supply pull the two bus lines, SDA and SCL, high by default. This design allows multiple controllers and peripherals to control the data and clock lines without running into problems associated with connecting multiple output pins to the same signal line.

To place a logic 1 on one of the lines, a device puts its open-drain (or open-collector, if using bipolar devices) into the high-impedance state. This allows the default logic 1 to appear on the line, placed there by the pullup resistor. To place a logic 0 on one of the lines, the device activates its open-drain device, which shorts the line to ground.

Most I^2C devices provide open-drain signals to connect to the I^2C bus, so you don't need to have any additional hardware to interface such devices to the bus. However, it is also possible to connect arbitrary logic devices to the I^2C bus by routing them through a bipolar transistor (open-collector), JFET, MOSFET, or other open-drain device to control the electrical access to the I^2C bus. The following subsection provides an example of this.

The SDA and SCL lines, by definition, are bidirectional on the controller device and are often bidirectional on peripheral devices. Certain single-board computers or CPUs might not support digital I/O pins that can operate in a bidirectional mode—that is, they can be programmed only as an input pin or an output pin. To resolve this, some system designers implement I^2C in *four-wire mode*. In four-wire mode the I^2C bus still has two wires, but the controller uses two wires to implement each of the signals: two output pins and two input pins. Figure 1-1 diagrams this four-wire controller connection.

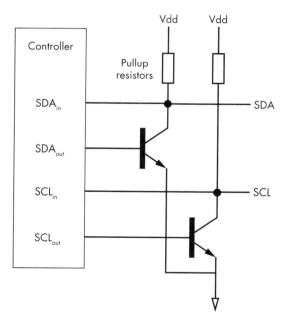

Figure 1-1: Four-wire controller connection

To prevent electrical conflicts (connecting two outputs together), the output pins drive the base of a transistor (gate on a FET or MOSFET), and the collector (drain) connects to the appropriate bus line. Then the controller CPU can simultaneously read the data on the bus lines using the input pins while writing data on the output pins with no electrical conflict and without support for bidirectional I/O pins.

1.3 I²C Signal Levels

When the I²C was designed in the early 1980s, 5 V logic was the prevalent design technology, so the original I²C assumed the use of 5-V logic signals. However, as the I²C bus is based on open-drain connections, the high voltage level is completely determined by the power supply that the pullup resistors connect to when designing the system. As computer systems started using 3.3 V or even down to 1.8 V, system designers began hooking up those pullup resistors to power supplies other than 5 V.

From the perspective of the I²C bus, as long as the controllers and peripherals can handle and properly work with the voltage levels appearing on the bus, any voltage *should* work fine. In reality, however, some voltages may cause problems. For this reason, recent I²C standards state that the voltage on the bus must be at least 2 V (so 1.8-V logic won't work). They also specify that a logic high is defined as greater than 70 percent of the power supply voltage and a logic low is defined as less than 30 percent of the power supply voltage. Today, generic I²C devices almost always expect 5-V or 3.3-V logic.

1.3.1 Level Shifting

What happens if you want to mix 3.3-V and 5-V I²C devices on the same bus? Sending a 3.3-V signal into a 5-V device probably won't damage it, but the device may not interpret 3.3 V as a logic 1, because the standard calls for a logic 1 are equal to 3.5 V on a 5-V system (70 percent of 5 V is 3.5 V). Sending a 5-V signal into a 3.3-V device is far worse; often, this will destroy the device. Clearly, you should avoid this situation at all costs.

When mixing 3.3-V and 5-V (or other different voltage range) devices on the same I²C bus, you must use *voltage translation*, or *level shifting*, to convert the actual voltage on the bus to something that is compatible with the device(s). NXP Semiconductors provides a technical note describing how to do this using discrete MOSFETs (see "For More Information" at the end of this chapter). Another solution is to purchase a commercial-off-the-shelf (COTS) part such as the Adafruit, four-channel, I²C-safe, bidirectional logic level converter (BSS138). The Adafruit BSS138 device provides a bridge between two I²C buses operating at 3.3 V and 5 V—or, if you need a larger voltage range, it's rated down to 1.8 V and up to 10 V. As I'm writing this, these Adafruit devices cost about $4 each (US) and support two independent I²C bus level shifters (the I²C bus requires two level shifters, one for the SDA line and one for the SCL line).

A third option is to level-shift with the TCA9548A I²C multiplexer device. This IC will split the I²C bus into eight separately controlled I²C buses. Each independent bus can have its own pullup resistor to an independent power supply (for example, 3.3 V or 5 V). Therefore, you can put the 3.3-V devices on one bus and the 5-V devices into another. The incoming bus (from the CPU to the TCA9548A) can be either voltage. See Chapter 12 for more information.

1.4 Choosing Pullup Resistor Sizes

Choosing resistor sizes for the SDA and SCL pullup resistors requires a bit of thought. While I won't go into the heavy math behind this choice, keep in mind that pullup resistors should be somewhere in the range of 1 kΩ to about 20 kΩ based on the supply voltage and bus capacitance. The higher the bus capacitance (in particular, the longer your I^{2}C bus lines are), the lower the resistor should be. The minimum value is generally determined by the power supply voltage. For 3.3-V systems, you can go to slightly below 1 kΩ, if you have to. For 5-V systems, 1.5 kΩ is probably as low as you should go.

NOTE *To dive into the math behind choosing resistor sizes, see* UM10204: I^{2}C Bus Specification and User Manual *in "For More Information."*

Generally, most systems start out with 4.7-kΩ pullups and go down from there if necessary. Note that if you are using commonly available COTS parts, such as breakout boards from Adafruit, SparkFun, or Seeed Studio, the boards often have pullup resistors already installed. If you attach two or more of these devices to your system, you have to compute the final resistance using a parallel resistance calculation ($1/R = 1/R_1 + 1/R_2 + \ldots + 1/R_n$). This means if you install two boards, each with a 4.7-kΩ pullup, you've actually got 2.35-kΩ pullups on the two lines. If you add too many of these boards on the same bus, you can wind up with pullup values below the minimum suggested resistances.

1.5 Bus Capacitance and Pullup Resistor Values

The speed of the I^{2}C bus, which I'll discuss further in the next section, is largely determined by the value of the pullup resistors (R_p) and the bus capacitance (C_p). Although the system designer has direct control over the value of the pullup resistors, bus capacitance is mostly a function of two things: input capacitance of the devices connected to the bus, and the length of the bus itself. Capacitance increases with bus length, as does resistance, though only by a small and generally insignificant amount. Why do these two parameters affect bus speed?

From electronics theory you know that the product of resistance and capacitance is time. In particular, 1 Ω × 1 farad = 1 second. When a device pulls one of the bus lines low or releases a bus line so that the pullup resistor returns the signal high, the bus capacitance and resistance affect the amount of time it takes for the signal to rise or fall. If this time exceeds a certain value, the I^{2}C bus will not be able to operate at its full rated speed.

The I^{2}C standard limits bus capacitance to 400 pF (*picofarads*, each of which is one trillionth of a farad). A typical pullup resistor on the I^{2}C bus is between 1 kΩ and 10 kΩ. This produces rise times in the range of 0.4 μsec (*microseconds*) to 4 μsec. If the I^{2}C bus is operating at 100 kHz (that is, a 10-μsec period), a 10-kΩ pullup (4-μsec rise time) will likely not work out well. The solution is to reduce the capacitance or the resistance.

The primary way to reduce bus capacitance is to keep the bus as short as possible. Longer bus lines dramatically increase the bus capacitance. You can also reduce bus capacitance by putting fewer I^{2}C devices on the bus. If you must put a fixed number of devices on the bus, you can reduce the number of devices on a given bus by using two separate buses.

Of course, another solution to reducing the rise time is to reduce the value of the pullup resistor. Using a 4.7-kΩ resistor rather than a 10-kΩ resistor, for example, cuts the rise time by about one half.

1.5.1   *What If the Bus Capacitance Is Too High?*

Reducing bus capacitance can be a difficult process. Shortening the I^{2}C bus length is the primary approach. You can also use better cabling if the I^{2}C signals are transmitted across wires, or you can reduce the number of devices on the bus (for example, move half the devices to a second I^{2}C bus).

If these solutions are impossible or insufficient, reduce the bus speed. If you're running at 400 kHz, drop down to 100 kHz; if you're already at 100 kHz, drop down to 50 kHz, and so on. If this doesn't solve the problem, a major circuit redesign may be necessary. Another solution to consider at this point is a differential bus driver like the SparkFun QwiicBus Kit: *https://www.sparkfun.com/products/17250.*

1.6   I^{2}C Bus Speeds

As discussed, the I^{2}C bus has two signal lines: serial data and serial clock. Controllers transmit data to and from peripherals on the SDA line. The SCL line controls the speed at which this serial data transfer takes place. The frequency of the signal on the SCL line controls how fast data moves between the controller and peripheral devices. The I^{2}C bus standard defines the following data transfer rates:

- *Standard mode*: 100-kHz SCL frequency, transferring data between devices at 100 kbit/sec
- *Fast mode*: 400-kHz SCL frequency, transferring data between the controller and peripherals at 400 kbit/sec
- *Fast mode plus*: 1-MHz SCL frequency, transferring data between the controller and peripherals at 1 Mbit/sec

- *High-speed mode*: Up to 3.4-MHz SCL frequency, transferring data between the controller and peripherals at up to 3.4 Mbit/sec
- *Ultra-fast mode*: 5-MHz SCL frequency, though data transmission is unidirectional only

In practice, the upper bound on the I^{2}C bus frequency is largely determined by the bus capacitance pullup resistors on the bus. However, there generally isn't a lower bound on the frequency. Indeed, many peripheral devices will actually freeze data transmission using *clock stretching* (see section 1.9, "Clock Stretching," later in this chapter) to provide the peripheral time to process data coming from the controller, which effectively reduces the clock speed and average data transmission speed. Furthermore, there is no requirement that the controller device place a 100-kHz signal (or whatever frequency) on the SCL line. It could run SCL at 50 kHz or any other frequency less than the usual clock speed, if desired.

The SCL signal is *not* a free-running clock. The I^{2}C controller explicitly toggles this line when it shifts a bit onto the SDA line. When the controller is not transmitting or receiving data on the SDA line, the controller leaves the SCL line programmed high. The I^{2}C bus frequency, therefore, is the SCL frequency during data transactions on the I^{2}C bus.

Probably the main limitation on the I^{2}C bus speed is that you have to run the bus at the speed of the slowest devices on the bus. If there is a 100-kbit/sec peripheral on the bus, you must run the bus at 100 kHz, even when communicating with 400-kbit/sec (or faster) peripherals on the same bus. Because most I^{2}C-compatible ICs are 100- or 400-kbit/sec devices, systems rarely run the I^{2}C bus above 400 kHz except for some very special hardware-specific cases. Typically, if you want to run above 400 kHz, you switch to the SPI bus.

NOTE *This book will mainly stick to standard and fast mode I^{2}C bus operation. In theory, this material also covers fast mode plus operation, as it is nearly the same as fast mode with tighter hardware specifications. High-speed mode and ultra-fast mode require special hardware to implement. See the I^{2}C Bus Specification and User Manual for more information about these two modes, via the link provided in "For More Information."*

1.7 Multicontroller I^{2}C Bus Clock Synchronization

The I^{2}C bus optionally supports multiple controllers on the same bus, which is known as a *multicontroller configuration*. In such cases the SCL frequencies of the two controllers must match, and they must both support multicontroller operation. However, running at the same frequency is not a sufficient condition for a multicontroller environment; their clocks must also be synchronized. Two controllers operate asynchronously with respect to one other. That is, if the bus is currently not being used by either controller, both controllers could decide to use the bus at the same time. However, it's unlikely that both controllers will decide to activate their SCL lines at exactly the same instant. The I²C protocol requires the two controllers' clock signals to rise and fall at roughly the same time to maintain appropriate timing. To achieve this, the I²C protocol introduces a clock synchronization operation that delays the start of one of the signals so they rise and fall approximately together after the synchronization operation.

Clock synchronization relies on a feature of an open-drain bus known as *wired-AND operation* that simulates a logical-AND circuit without additional hardware. The (two-input) logical-AND function produces a true result if and only if its two inputs are true. If either or both are false, the logical-AND function produces a false result. If you consider two open-drain devices connected to the SCL line, the result is equivalent to a logical-AND circuit. If both devices are programmed with a 1, so their outputs are in a high-impedance state, the pullup resistor on the SCL line pulls the bus high. If either or both devices are programmed such that the open-drain output is active, this pulls the SCL line to Gnd, resulting in a 0 on the SCL line.

Clock synchronization uses the wired-AND capabilities of the bus to synchronize the two clocks between controllers competing for the bus. The first controller to pull the SCL line low begins counting off its low period, approximately one half of the clock period. Sometime later (still within the low period), the second controller pulls the SCL line low. When the first controller reaches the end of its low period, it releases the SCL line. However, as the second controller is still pulling the SCL line low, it remains low. Later, when the second controller releases the SCL line, it goes high since both controllers have released the SCL line, as shown in Figure 1-2.

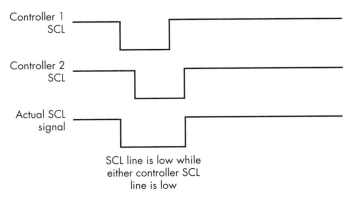

Figure 1-2: SCL driven low by multiple controllers

The first controller should note that the SCL line has not gone high and will delay counting off a one-half clock period (with SCL high, its *high period*) until it notices that the SCL line has actually gone high, as shown in Figure 1-3. Then both controllers will start counting off the high period with the SCL line high. The first to count off the one-half clock period will pull the SCL line low; the second should follow shortly.

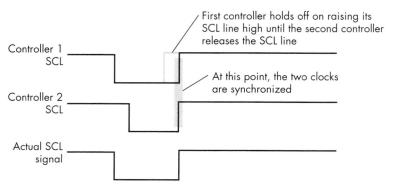

Figure 1-3: SCL clock synchronization by multiple controllers

At this point, the clocks should be fairly synchronized, with the low SCL period being the longest of the two controllers and the high SCL period being the shortest of the two. The two controllers will have similar, but not perfectly identical, timing for their clock periods.

1.8 Multicontroller I²C Bus Arbitration

Although synchronizing clocks is a necessary condition to allow multicontroller access to the I²C bus, it is not a sufficient condition. Even if two controllers have synchronized clocks, they could both be writing different data to the SDA line; that would corrupt the data on the bus and yield unreliable results. *Arbitration* is the process by which two (or more) controllers decide who can actually control the bus.

Before grabbing the I²C bus for its own use, a controller first checks to see if the bus is already in use. It does this by looking at the SDA and SCL lines for more than one half of a clock period and verifying that both signals remain high during this time. If so, it emits an I²C bus *start sequence* (see Chapter 2) and begins transmitting data.

Of course, there is no guarantee that the bus is actually free after this sequence, because a second controller could have started this same process at almost the same time. Therefore, the data the two controllers are placing on the bus could be in conflict. To detect this problem, the I²C bus arbitration system takes advantage of the wired-AND operation of the bus. If both devices write a 1 to the SDA line or both devices write a 0 to SDA, this line will correctly reflect the data signals being written by both controllers. However, if one controller writes a 0 while the other writes a 1, the controller writing the 0 will "win the war" on the SDA line—that is, the SDA line will be pulled low. To handle bus arbitration, the two controllers always look at the data they write on the SDA line to verify it contains what they've written. If a controller writes a value to the bus and then reads back a different value, then the two controllers have lost the arbitration and must stop controlling the bus.

In theory, two controllers could write the same data sequence to the bus, in which case they will both use the bus simultaneously. Unless the peripheral device is counting accesses, in which case these two controller activities would look like a single access, there is no reason this rare situation would create any problems.

Note that while the controllers are checking the data on the SDA line, they are also looking at the information appearing on the SCL line to synchronize the clocks while arbitrating for the bus.

1.9 Clock Stretching

Clock signals are always generated by controller devices on the I^2C bus. Controllers expect peripheral devices to operate properly at whatever clock frequency the controller signals on the SCL line. If the peripheral is incapable of operating at that frequency, the controller must be reprogrammed to talk to the peripheral at a lower clock speed.

As you'll see in the next chapter, data communication on the I^2C bus consists of a string of 8-bit bytes transmitted to a peripheral with the peripheral acknowledging each byte, using an *acknowledge bit*. When transmitting the acknowledge bit back to the controller, the peripheral has the option of holding the clock line inactive for an arbitrary period of time. As noted in a couple of earlier sections, this is known as *clock stretching* (see sections 1.6 and 1.1, "I^2C Bus Speeds" and "I^2C Overview," respectively). It effectively pauses the controller while the peripheral deals with the data that was transmitted to it (that is, clock stretching adds wait states to the I^2C clock).

As with arbitration and clock synchronization, clock stretching takes advantage of the wired-AND operation of the I^2C bus. If the peripheral is pulling the SCL line low when the controller sets it high, the SCL line remains low. The controller looks for this behavior and pauses data and clock output until the peripheral releases the SCL line.

Clock stretching is an optional feature of the I^2C protocol, meaning controllers don't have to support this feature. Obviously, if a peripheral uses clock stretching, that device will be incompatible with controllers that don't support this feature.

1.10 Cross Talk

Another problem that can befall I^2C communications is cross talk. If you run the SDA and SCL lines in parallel, especially over a long distance, signal changes on one line can affect the other. The SCL line affecting the SDA line is the most common problem. To reduce the problem of cross talk, the simple solution is to run a ground trace between the SCL and SDA lines on a PCB. Likewise, on a ribbon cable, running a ground line—or better yet, a power and a ground line—between the SDA and SCL conductors can reduce the incidence of cross talk.

Although cross talk between the SCL and SDA lines represents the most common cross talk problems on the I^{2}C bus, keep in mind that other signals can also induce noise on these two signal lines. When laying out PCBs, try to keep other high-frequency or high-current lines away from the SDA and SCL traces. Following good PCB design rules can really help. Likewise, when running I^{2}C signals or ribbon cables (or other wiring), interleaving a ground wire between the SDA and SCL signals can reduce noise in the system.

One solution to the cross talk problem is to use differential line drivers on the I^{2}C. SparkFun provides the QwiicBus Kit to solve cross talk and other issues with bus length. See "For More Information."

1.11 Chapter Summary

In this chapter, you learned that the I^{2}C bus solves several problems that designers of early embedded systems encountered when adding I/O to their designs. The two-wire (serial data and clock) interface reduces PCB size, noise, and design effort. The I^{2}C bus features the following specifications:

- Open-drain (open-collector) bus signals allowing multiple controllers and bidirectional communication on a single data line

- 100-kHz, 400-kHz, 1-MHz, 3.4 MHz, and 5-MHz bus speeds

- 2 V to 5 V operation (via pullup resistors)

- Bus arbitration and clock stretching to resolve timing issues

- A wide variety of I^{2}C peripheral ICs that can be connected to any I^{2}C bus

---

FOR MORE INFORMATION

UM10204 I^{2}C Bus Specification and User Manual: *https://www.nxp.com/docs/en/user-guide/UM10204.pdf*

The I^{2}C Bus: *https://www.i2c-bus.org*

Level-shifting the I^{2}C bus: *https://cdn-shop.adafruit.com/datasheets/AN10441.pdf*

I^{2}C voltage translator FETs: *https://www.nxp.com/products/interfaces/ic-spi-serial-interface-devices/ic-voltage-level-translators:MC_43683*

Adafruit bidirectional level-shifter breakout boards: *https://www.adafruit.com/product/757*

SparkFun Qwiic bus differential line drivers: *https://www.sparkfun.com/products/17250*

2

I²C PROTOCOL

The I²C bus definition is quite a bit more than electrical levels appearing on a bus. Equally important is the definition of the signals appearing on those two lines. This chapter discusses the data protocols associated with the I²C bus—that is, the speed at which the data transmission takes place, how a device can force the controller to wait for it, and how controllers do the following:

- Transmit bits to and from devices
- Specify the device's address
- Specify the data direction
- Specify the end of the data transmission

The order and definition of the bits appearing on the bus, and how they are clocked on the bus, are determined by the I^2C *protocol*. This chapter describes that protocol and discusses some useful topics such as resetting the I^2C bus and detecting peripherals on the bus.

2.1 Data on the I^2C Bus

The I^2C bus transmits data serially on the SDA line, clocked by the SCL signal (see Figure 2-1). The data on the SDA line must be stable (0 or 1) when SCL is high (1); data may change on the SDA line only while SCL is low (see Figure 2-1).

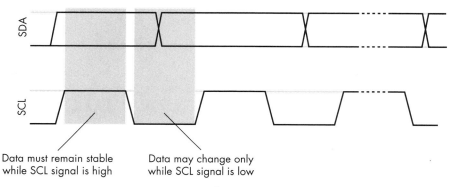

Data must remain stable while SCL signal is high

Data may change only while SCL signal is low

Figure 2-1: Serial data transmission on the I^2C bus

Data transmissions on the I^2C bus consist of a start signal, followed by one or more bytes of data, and end with a stop signal. Between data transmissions, the SDA and SCL lines are in their unasserted state (that is, both signals are pulled high). As noted in the previous chapter, if the SCL line is high for longer than a one-half clock period, the bus is currently unused.

NOTE *A one-half clock period value determines whether the bus is being used because if the bus is being used, the SCL line will switch low after about a one-half clock period, as a full clock period consists of 50 percent SCL high and 50 percent SCL low.*

A start condition consists of a controller pulling the SDA line low while the SCL line has been high for some period of time (see Figure 2-2). As mentioned earlier (see Figure 2-1), the SDA line normally must be stable while the clock line is high. This is to allow devices on the I^2C bus to detect a start (and as you will soon see, a stop) condition.

Generally, SCL must be high for the duration of between one-quarter and one-half clock period before SDA can go low to signal a start condition. Specifically, this start setup time is one of the following:

- For standard mode (10-μsec clock period): 4.7 μsec
- For fast mode (2.5-μsec clock period): 0.6 μsec
- For fast-plus mode (1-μsec clock period): 0.26 μsec

Once the data line has gone low, signifying the start condition, the controller can pull the SCL line low to begin clocking in data after the following startup hold times:

- For standard mode: 4.0 μsec
- For fast mode: 0.6 μsec
- For fast-plus mode: 0.26 μsec

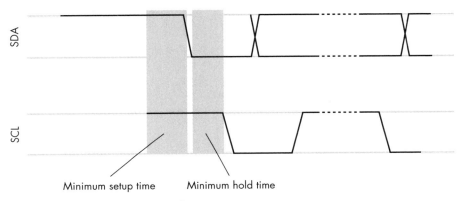

Figure 2-2: Start condition on the I²C bus

A byte transmission consists of 8 data bits and an acknowledgment bit (see Figure 2-3). The 8-bit data byte is shipped with the most significant bit (MSB) appearing first on the SDA line and the least significant bit (LSB) following eight clock periods later. Immediately following the byte data is a single acknowledgment bit. This bit is always 0 if the receiving device is acknowledging the data. It is a 1 (NAK, or negative acknowledgment) if there was a transmission error.

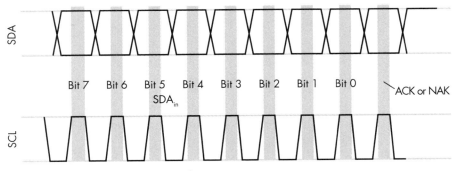

Figure 2-3: Byte transmission on the I²C bus

Note that either the controller or the peripheral could be placing the data on the data bus. For a write operation, the controller is responsible for placing the data on the SDA line; for a read operation, the peripheral is responsible for placing the data on the SDA line. For the acknowledgment, the roles are reversed: for reads, the controller pulls the SDA low to acknowledge the read from the peripheral, while for writes, the peripheral pulls the SDA line low to acknowledge the write operation. If the transmission is bad for whatever reason, the device accepting the data does not pull the SDA line low for the acknowledgment. This leaves the SDA line high (which is a NAK). The next section, "I²C Addresses and Read/Write Control," will discuss how the controller specifies whether a read or write operation is taking place.

A stop condition consists of changing the SDA line from low to high while the SCL line is held high (remember, data normally must be stable while the clock line is high). This typically consists of setting the SDA line low before the last rising edge of the SCL line at the end of the data transmission and then pulling the SDA line high afterward, as Figure 2-4 shows. Similar to the start condition, the SCL line must be high for a certain amount of time (the *setup time for the stop condition*) before transitioning the SDA line from low to high. These setup times are the same as for the start condition, specifically:

- For standard mode: 4.7 μsec
- For fast mode: 0.6 μsec
- For fast-plus mode: 0.26 μsec

Once the controller generates the stop condition, the I²C bus is free, and after an appropriate start setup time, a controller can obtain it and use it again.

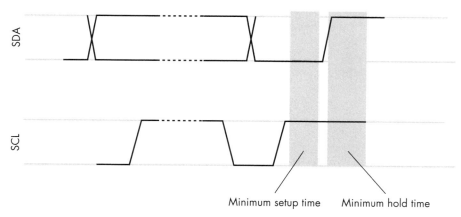

Figure 2-4: I²C stop condition (S_p)

A stop condition does not occur after every byte. Instead, a stop condition marks the completion of a string of byte transmissions over the I²C bus. Specifically, a single (atomic) transmission consists of a start condition, followed by one or more byte transmissions (each with their own ACK or NAK bit), and a stop condition at termination. This transmission is considered atomic because the controller driving the transmission has complete control of the I²C bus for the entire duration of the transmission; during this time, no other controller can take possession of the I²C bus.

2.2 I²C Addresses and Read/Write Control

The first byte appearing on the I²C bus after a start condition is special. This byte contains the I²C device address and the read/write state. Figure 2-5 shows the format for the peripheral address and R/W (read/write) byte (the overbar on the W indicates that the write signal is active low [0]).

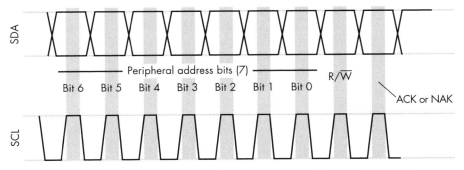

Figure 2-5: First byte following a start condition (peripheral address and R/W bit)

The upper 7 bits of this byte contain the address of the peripheral for whom this transmission is intended. Because there are 7 bits, you can specify a maximum of 128 peripheral addresses in this peripheral address byte (though see section 2.5, "Special Addresses," later in this chapter for information about a 10-bit address on the I²C bus). The LO bit of the byte contains an R/W flag. A 0 in this bit position specifies a write operation, and a 1 in this position specifies a read operation.

The R/W bit determines the data transfer directions of all the bytes following the peripheral address byte. If this bit is 0 (write operation), then the controller will supply all the data on the SDA line in the following bytes; if this bit is 1 (read operation), then the peripheral will place the data on the SDA line during the transmission. Regardless of the data direction, the controller is still responsible for driving the SCL line (though see section 2.4, "Clock Stretching," later in this chapter).

Generally, this book will write I²C addresses as 7-bit binary or hexadecimal values (using C notation, 0x*nn* or 0b*nnnnnnn*). The full address and R/W byte will normally be written in 8-bit hexadecimal form.

2.3 Repeated Start Conditions

In some special cases, a controller might need to write data to some particular peripheral and then immediately read data back from that peripheral as an atomic operation, without the possibility of some other controller accessing the peripheral between the write and read operations. Because the data direction is specified by the LO bit of the first byte after a start condition, a controller must send another start condition to change the direction. However, if the controller completes the current transfer by issuing a stop condition before sending another start condition, this gives a different controller the opportunity to seize the bus before the second transmission. This means the controller needs a way to hold onto the bus by not sending a stop condition. This is accomplished with a repeated start condition.

A *repeated start condition*, as its name implies, is a second start condition (SDA high-to-low while SCL is high) without an intervening stop condition on the I^2C bus. Until a stop condition comes along (which is what waiting controllers look for while waiting for the I^2C bus), the current controller owns the bus. Therefore, a controller can use a sequence of repeated starts during a data transmission to reverse the data direction, or even to communicate with multiple peripherals, without giving up the I^2C bus. When the atomic operations are complete, the controller can yield the bus by issuing a stop condition.

In a multicontroller environment, a controller should take care not to monopolize the I^2C bus. For operations that do not require atomicity, the controller should use stop conditions between transfers so that different controllers can gain access to the bus in a fair manner.

2.4 Clock Stretching

As mentioned in the previous chapter, clock stretching is a technique whereby a peripheral device can force the controller to wait while the peripheral is processing data. For example, a simple peripheral device polling the SDA and SCL lines and manually processing incoming data might need a small amount of time after each byte. During that time the controller might ship additional data that could be lost while the peripheral is busy processing the data. To resolve this problem, the peripheral can use clock stretching to force the controller to pause while the peripheral's CPU deals with the incoming data. This effectively adds *wait states* to the data transmission.

A peripheral can stretch the clock by pulling the SCL line low. Technically, this can occur at any time. However, when transmitting data from the controller to the peripheral, the peripheral usually pulls the SCL line low when the SCL line is also low just after the acknowledge bit, as this is when the peripheral has received the entire byte and will need to process it. Transmitting data from the peripheral to the controller is also a good time for the peripheral to pull the SCL line low after a complete byte transmission if the peripheral needs additional time to produce the next byte to transmit.

Note that clock stretching is an optional feature in the I^2C standard. In fact, most peripheral devices don't support clock stretching, as they can handle the data transmissions as fast as the controller sends them. Although it should be rare, a controller might not support clock stretching in certain situations, such as when someone uses a simple microcontroller device to build a multifunction I^{2}C controller that has to handle many different activities, which results in performance problems. See "For More Information" at the end of this chapter for details on how to deal with this situation.

2.5   Special Addresses

With 7 address bits you would get the impression that the I^{2}C bus supports up to 128 devices. In fact, this is not the case, for two reasons. First, the I^{2}C standard reserves two groups of 8 addresses (0 through 7 and 120 through 127) for special purposes. Second, I^{2}C uses a couple of those reserved addresses to allow extended addresses up to 10 bits in length. In theory, this allows an additional 1,024 devices on the bus.

Table 2-1 lists the special addresses currently defined for the I^{2}C bus. Don't-care bits (*xx*) appearing in these addresses can be 0b00, 0b01, 0b10, or 0b11. Most of the time, programs supply 0b00 for these bits.

Table 2-1: Special I^{2}C Addresses

Address bits	R/W	Description
0000-000	0	General call address
0000-000	1	Start byte
0000-001	x*	CBUS addresses
0000-010	x	Reserved for different bus format
0000-011	x	Reserved for future purposes
0000-1xx	x	High-speed mode controller code
1111-0aa	R/W	10-bit peripheral addressing (see section 2.5.6, "10-Bit Peripheral Addressing," later in this chapter for discussion of aa bits)
1111-1xx	1	Device ID

*x = "don't care" and can be 0 or 1

The following subsections describe the general call address (including hardware general calls), start byte, CBUS, high-speed controller mode, 10-bit addressing, and device ID special addresses in greater detail. Several addresses are also reserved for future device expansion. Existing controllers should not use these addresses until their use is defined within the I^{2}C standard.

2.5.1   The General Call Address

The *general call address* (0x00 with R/W = 0) is a special broadcast address that can address all devices on the bus. The R/W bit is always 0 (write) because you can never read from all the devices at the same time, as their return values would scramble one another.

The general call operation always consists of at least two bytes: the general call address (0x00) followed by a command byte (see Figure 2-6). Generally, systems use this command to initialize all the peripherals that respond to the general call operation with a single bus command.

| S | 0 | 0 | 0 | 0 | 0 | 0 | 0 | 0 | ACK | C | C | C | C | C | C | C | B | ACK | S_p |

General call command   Command byte

Figure 2-6: General call command format

When bit B is 0, the I²C protocol currently defines the following commands (ccccccc bits):

ccccccc = 0b0000011: Reset and set peripheral programmable address.

ccccccc = 0b0000010: Set peripheral programmable address but do not reset.

ccccccc = 0b0000000: Illegal command code, not allowed as second byte.

A *peripheral programmable address* is an address that can be set by hardware pins on the peripheral device. Many devices include pins on the IC package that can specify one of several different I²C addresses to which the device responds. This allows a designer, for example, to put several of the same ICs on the I²C bus and have them respond to different addresses by setting these pins high or low. For example, the MCP4725 DAC contains a pin that allows you to select one of two different I²C addresses by tying the pin to Vcc or Gnd. The general call commands 0x00/0x07 (ccccccc = 0b0000011, B = 0) and 0x00/0x05 (ccccccc = 0b0000010, B = 0) instruct such chips to load the address from these pins, as appropriate (the 0x00/0x06 command also instructs the peripheral to reset itself).

Most peripheral ICs set their programmed addresses on a power-up operation, and the address never changes after that point, so most peripheral devices will ignore this command or simply do a reset operation for the (0x00, 0x06) command.

Note that peripheral devices do not have to support the general call command—that is, its implementation is optional. If a device does not support the general call command, it must ignore it.

Because of the open-drain nature of the I²C SDA line, if any device acknowledges the general call address and the command byte, the controller will see an ACK. Only if none of the devices acknowledge the general call command will the controller see a NAK response.

The commands other than (0x00, 0x00), (0x00, 0x04), and (0x00, 0x06) are reserved for future use and devices must ignore them. However, if you are creating your own custom peripherals for a custom system, you could create your own general call commands. You could even pass along additional data after the command byte to broadcast to all the devices you've created that respond to the commands. Just keep in mind that future revisions of the I²C protocol may conflict with your definitions. Also keep in mind that you can write data only with the broadcast (general call) command.

2.5.2 Hardware General Calls

Hardware general calls are a special form of the general call that support peer-to-peer communication. If the B bit in Figure 2-6 is a 1, the 2-byte sequence is a *hardware general call*. The ccccccc bits specify the controller's address that it is broadcasting to all the devices, which could be followed by 0 or more bytes of additional data. Some other device on the bus could read this data and interpret it accordingly. Generally, a hardware general call is a way for one controller device to communicate with a different controller device and pass it a block of data. However, for this scheme to work, the second controller device receiving the data must be looking for the first controller's address within the hardware general call.

You won't find too many commercially available devices that support the hardware general call. Typically, custom-programmed controllers that communicate with one another in the system would use these messages.

To be honest, rather than design this protocol into your system, you'd probably be better off using the CANBUS or some other peer-to-peer networking scheme to transmit data between controllers in a system. As you might expect, very few devices take advantage of this feature in the I²C protocol. Most devices ignore hardware general calls.

2.5.3 Start Byte

The start byte (adrs = 0, R/W = 1) is a software mechanism for introducing delays in an I²C communication between a fast controller and a slow-responding peripheral. Some low-cost peripheral devices poll only the SDA line occasionally to see if a start condition exists. If the peripheral is otherwise preoccupied when the actual start condition arrives, the peripheral could miss a message intended for it. A start byte is the sequence 0x01 (that is, address 0 with the R/W bit high). These seven 0 bits, which will be spread over 70 µsec when using a 100-kHz clock, should give the peripheral sufficient time to detect that the SDA line has gone low.

Start bytes are always followed by a repeated start condition and the actual peripheral address byte (see Figure 2-7). Note that start bytes are never acknowledged—a NAK always follows in the ninth bit after the start byte. Also note that the start byte shares the same address as the general call function (see Figure 2-6). The difference is in the R/W bit; the start byte sequence always has a 1 in the R/W position, and the general call operation has a 0 in this position.

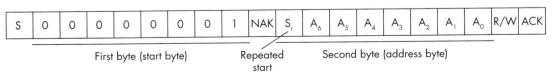

Figure 2-7: Start byte sequence

If a peripheral device is slow and requires a start byte prefix, the controller must explicitly transmit the start byte before communicating with the peripheral. Likewise, if the peripheral device is slow, its software must recognize the tail end of a start sequence and be ready to read the following address from the bus.

Be aware that not all peripheral ICs support the start byte. This means that if you send a start byte on the I^2C bus to communicate with a slow device, other devices on the bus may misinterpret this signal. If you're going to use this feature in the I^2C protocol, ensure that all the devices on the bus will respond properly (meaning, at the very least, they ignore the start byte).

2.5.4 CBUS and Reserved Addresses

The CBUS (adrs = 1, R/W = x [don't care]) is an old, obsolete variant of the I^2C bus. The CBUS address was originally used to activate CBUS devices on the I^2C bus. However, this address is no longer used for this purpose, and modern controllers should not place this address on the bus.

2.5.5 High-Speed Mode Controller Code

High-speed mode controller codes (adrs = 4 through 7, R/W = x) are special addresses that the I^2C protocol uses to switch between high-speed and slower (standard, fast, fast+) modes. Because very few devices operate on the I^2C bus in high-speed mode, this book largely ignores the high-speed and ultra-fast modes. For more information on the high-speed controller modes, consult the I^2C bus specification and user manual (see "For More Information").

2.5.6 10-Bit Peripheral Addressing

To many people, the 7-bit addressing scheme on the I^2C bus, which supports up to 112 devices, seems limiting. For a variety of reasons, this turns out to be far more than sufficient. However, the I^2C bus does define a special extension that allows the use of a 10-bit address on the bus, allowing up to 1,024 additional addresses on a single bus (adrs = 0x78 through 0x7B).

When one of the special addresses 0b1111000 (0x78), 0b1111001 (0x79), 0b1111010 (0x7A), or 0b1111011 (0x7B) appears as the first byte after a start condition, this is the start of a 2-byte address sequence. The LO two bits of this address become the most significant (HO) 2 bits of the result. A second byte follows this byte that contains the remaining (LO) 8 bits of the address. See Figure 2-8 for the details.

| S | 1 | 1 | 1 | 1 | 0 | A_9 | A_8 | R/W | ACK | A_7 | A_6 | A_5 | A_4 | A_3 | A_2 | A_1 | A_0 | ACK |

First byte (1111 0aa byte)   Second byte (LO address bits)

Figure 2-8: 10-bit address format

The peripheral device constructs the 10-bit address from the two bytes that begin with 0b11110aa. The remainder of the transmission starting with the third byte is identical to an I^{2}C transmission with a 7-bit address, following the first byte.

Although having a 10-bit address scheme seems reasonable, in the real world it's almost useless. First, few commercially available peripheral devices support 10-bit addresses. In theory, you could create your own custom peripheral device that looks for a 10-bit address. However, this would buy you almost nothing, as it's probably just as easy to find an unused 7-bit address in your system and use that. This saves the extra 100 μsec (at 100 kHz) required to transmit the extra address information, and I^{2}C transmissions are slow enough as it is.

Another issue is the fact that 112 unique addresses are far more than enough for the I^{2}C bus. Because of bus capacitance limitations, it would be nearly impossible to put that many devices on the same physical bus lines. Forget about adding another 1,024 devices; that's way beyond the electrical capabilities of the bus.

The only argument for 10-bit addresses is that it expands the peripheral designer's ability to put several copies of the same device on the bus with less chance of creating address conflicts with other devices. For example, you might want to put four copies of a digital-to-analog converter on the I^{2}C bus, but doing so might create address conflict with other chips you'd like to use. Using 10-bit addresses gives you more breathing room to spread out the addresses of the peripherals. However, as almost no peripheral ICs support extended addressing, this isn't useful.

Note that if you really want to include multiple copies of the same IC in your design with possible address conflicts, there is another solution: the I^{2}C multiplexer. See Chapter 12 for more information.

2.5.7   Device ID

The device ID is another really good idea that, unfortunately, a large percentage of devices don't support. The concept is to have a controller transmit the "device bus ID" (0xF8, which is address 0x7C plus R/W = 0), followed by the peripheral address. Then the controller does a restart, transmits 0xF9 (0x7C plus R/W = 1), and then reads 3 bytes back from the peripheral device: 12 bits that specify the manufacturer (a value specified by NXP Semiconductors), 9 bits that specify the part number (assigned by the manufacturer), and 3 bits that specify the die (IC) revision.

In theory, this would be a nice feature to use to identify devices on the bus. In practice, because so few chips support it, it's a nearly useless feature. Nevertheless, if a particular part does support it, obtaining the die revision information can be useful as it may help you program work-arounds for bugs in various revisions of the chip.

For more information about the device ID command, see the I^{2}C bus specifications and user manual in "For More Information."

2.6 Resetting the I²C Bus

Because of bugs in application software, device drivers, or firmware or hardware on the device, some peripheral chips have been known to "latch up" and enter an unknown, that is, illegal state. Sometimes this means you lose the functionality of that chip until it is reset. Even worse, sometimes that chip stops while pulling the SDA or SCL line low, meaning the I²C bus is useless from that point forward. In such situations, you'll want to reset the device.

Of course, you can use the general call command to send a reset command to all the devices in the system. However, this approach suffers from a couple problems:

- Not all devices respond to the general call/reset command.

- The general call/reset command resets *every* device that is listening for it. You may not want to do this as you'd have to reinitialize all the devices on the bus.

- If the device itself is hung up, it may not respond to a software command sent over the I²C bus. This is especially true if it is pulling the SDA or SCL line low, which means the command would never arrive.

Resetting the I²C bus calls for a hardware solution. A few devices support a *reset pin* on the IC. Typically, pulling such a pin low will reset the device and initialize it to a power-up state. The device may require further initialization once it has reached that state, but this is better than having to reset the whole system to make the chip recover. Connecting the device's reset pin to an available *general-purpose I/O (GPIO)* pin on the main CPU would allow you to programmatically reset the device under program control.

Of course, you could run a single reset line to all the devices that provide a reset pin. However, this runs into the same problem as the general call/reset command—you reset all the devices and have to reinitialize all of them to correct the problems with a single IC.

The biggest problem with the hardware reset approach is that not every I²C peripheral device out there has a reset pin on it. For those devices that don't have a reset chip, another solution is to temporarily turn off the power to the IC for a bit and then reapply power. This will certainly reset the chip to its power-on state. You could wire some transistors to do this. Another solution is an off-the-shelf device like the SparkFun Qwiic Power Switch (*https://www.sparkfun.com/products/16740*). This is an I²C peripheral that lets you turn on and off the power to other I²C devices, either for resetting or for low-power standby operation.

2.7 Detecting I²C Peripherals on the Bus

One common desire programmers have is to determine whether a peripheral is present at some address on the I²C bus. In theory, the Device ID operation (see section 2.5.7, "Device ID," earlier in this chapter) would provide this capability. A controller could send the Device ID special address (0xF8) on the bus followed by the device address to check. If the response is a NAK, then no device is at that address; if an ID response comes back, then the controller knows a device is present at that address, and the ID information exactly specifies the device.

The only problem with using the Device ID approach is that supporting the Device ID command is optional in a peripheral. If a peripheral does not support the Device ID command, it simply doesn't acknowledge the request. Therefore, although the peripheral is actually present, the Device ID command suggests that it is not. As a large percentage of I^2C peripheral ICs do not support the Device ID command, this isn't a practical way to detect such peripherals.

A common solution is to send a start condition, an address byte with the R/W bit high (a read operation), and then immediately send a stop condition without waiting for any data from the peripheral. The peripheral will acknowledge the address byte. However, the stop condition will prevent the peripheral device from actually transmitting data back to the controller. The controller can check for an ACK or NAK and use that response to determine if a peripheral is present at the specified address. This won't tell the controller which peripheral is present, but it will, at least, give a "something is there" or "nothing is there" response. This is how many utilities, such as the Linux i2cdetect utility, work.

There are a couple show-stopper problems with this approach to detection. One issue is that SMBus peripherals (SMBus is a variant of the I^2C bus; see section 5.1, "SMBus," in Chapter 5), according to the standard, can use the R/W bit as a data element. For example, the R/W bit can turn some external device on or off based on whether you read the address or write to it. If you send a read command immediately followed by a stop condition to such a peripheral, it could change the state of that device. If the state had previously been off, sending the read command might change the state to on (assuming the peripheral copies the value of the R/W bit directly to the state where 1 = on = R and 0 = off = W). Clearly, using a read command to detect the presence of the device is bad because the detection could also change its state.

One solution to this problem is to use both the Device ID and "read with immediate stop condition" commands. The SMBus standard requires all devices to support the Device ID command. If you *first* issue a Device ID command and an SMBus device is present, it will respond with appropriate identification information. If you get a NAK from the Device ID, then an SMBus device does not appear at that address, and you can try the read operation to see if you get a response. If you still get a NAK, you can probably assume that there is no device at the given address.

This assumes, of course, that only the devices that use the R/W bit as data will also support the Device ID command. The only place I've ever seen using the R/W bit as data has been in the SMBus documentation, so it's probably a safe assumption. Of course, if you create your own peripheral device and use the R/W bit as data, you should probably support the Device ID command to allow detection software to work around this issue.

Existing detection software may not use this two-phase (trying Device ID and then the read command) approach to device detection. For example, the Linux i2cdetect *utility does not use this approach.*

Another problem with putting a read command on the bus and checking for a response is that *write-only* devices may not respond to a read command. The Linux i2cdetect utility solves this problem by doing reads to certain addresses and writes to others, as well as providing command line options to force certain types of detection algorithms. Check out the source code for the i2cdetect application for more information on their technique (see "For More Information" for additional details on i2cdetect).

The bottom line is that there is no *perfect* way to detect peripheral devices on the I²C bus. Some schemes will fail to detect a device that is present; others may change the state of a device that is present. Ultimately, the best way to detect things is by design: know what devices are installed in your system and intentionally program for them.

2.8   Creating Custom Devices

For most real-world applications, you can probably find an IC that interfaces to the I²C bus and does just what you need. However, it's also possible that you have such a specialized application that no such peripheral could possibly exist. Fortunately, you don't have to rely solely on off-the-shelf parts: you can create your own I²C peripheral devices instead. There are several ways to do this, and this book covers a couple of them. The next chapter, for example, will discuss how to implement I²C controller and peripheral devices totally in software. Later chapters will discuss how to use the I²C hardware present on various SBCs to create such devices. You're limited only by your imagination.

2.9   Chapter Summary

This chapter discussed the format of the data on the I²C bus—the I²C protocol. This includes a description of data on the I²C bus, I²C addresses and R/W control, and special patterns to start and end I²C transmissions (start and stop conditions). This chapter also described a small optimization, repeated start conditions, and how to introduce wait states in an I²C transmission via clock stretching.

The I²C bus supports several features using special addresses. This includes the general call address, hardware general calls, the start byte, high-speed control, 10-bit peripheral addressing, and device ID. See the appropriate sections in this chapter for more details.

This chapter concluded with a discussion of resetting the I²C bus and detecting peripherals on the I²C bus, along with a brief discussion of creating custom I²C peripherals.

The next chapter uses the information from this chapter to describe how to implement the I^{2}C protocol using software. The code present in that chapter also provides another view of the I^{2}C protocol, clarifying it for those who prefer to see a formal (code) description of the protocol.

FOR MORE INFORMATION

Clock stretching: *https://www.silabs.com/documents/public/application-notes/an1095-i2c-master-does-not-support-clock-stretching.pdf*

i2cdetect documentation: *https://linux.die.net/man/8/i2cdetect*

i2cdetect source code: *https://kernel.googlesource.com/pub/scm/utils/i2c-tools/i2c-tools/+/v3.1.2/tools/i2cdetect.c*

High-speed and ultra-fast I^{2}C modes in the *I^{2}C Bus Specification and User Manual*: *https://www.nxp.com/docs/en/user-guide/UM10204.pdf*

UM10204 I^{2}C Bus Specification and User Manual: *https://www.nxp.com/docs/en/user-guide/UM10204.pdf*

The I^{2}C Bus: *https://www.i2c-bus.org*

3

A SOFTWARE IMPLEMENTATION OF THE I²C BUS

Although the vast majority of widely used I²C functionality comes as part of a peripheral IC or a CPU on an SBC, occasionally you may need to develop firmware for hardware that does not provide I²C support. In that case, you'll have to implement the I²C protocol in software.

This chapter shows how to implement both controller and peripheral devices using nothing more than GPIO pins on a standard microcontroller (MCU). I will use the Teensy 3.2 as an example, though the same principles apply to almost any device with at least two programmable I/O pins. If you want to use this code for some other MCU, you'll probably have to tweak and optimize it a bit, particularly on MCUs with lower performance and less memory than the Teensy 3.2. Chapter 17 (online at *https://bookofi2c .randallhyde.com*) provides an example of just such an optimization.

This chapter does not provide a drop-in, ready-to-use, software-based I^{2}C library. Almost any MCU you will use in an environment where you need I^{2}C will provide hardware support—the Teensy 3.2 itself provides two independent hardware I^{2}C buses. That said, a software implementation makes it clearer exactly what is happening in the hardware, so you'll benefit from studying this code.

3.1   A Software I^{2}C Implementation on the Teensy 3.2

The Teensy 3.2 is a 32-bit ARM (Cortex M4) that runs at 72 MHz, though it is often overclocked to 96 MHz. It features 256KB of flash storage for code, 64KB of RAM for data, 2,048KB of EEPROM for nonvolatile storage, and a huge amount of I/O, including three UARTs, two I^{2}C buses, and one SPI bus, all on a tiny—er, *teensy,* approximately 1.4 inch by 0.7 inch—PCB. Teensy has its own 3.3-V regulator on board, so the processor runs off 3.3 V, but all the I/O pins are 5-V tolerant. Typically, you program the Teensy using the Arduino IDE, and most Arduino code runs just fine on the Teensy 3.2.

Software implementation of I^{2}C on the Teensy 3.2 is primarily an educational exercise: since the Teensy 3.2 supports two hardware I^{2}C interfaces, there are few reasons to run a software-based I^{2}C system. The Teensy is very powerful, and it's possible to write the I^{2}C module in C/C++ without often having to drop down into hardware-specific code. Most of the code in this chapter is stock Arduino code, which should be much more approachable and understandable than I^{2}C optimized for lower-powered MCUs.

The following subsections describe two variants of a software-based I^{2}C system on the Teensy: a controller implementation and a peripheral implementation. For those interested in a hardware-based I^{2}C implementation, see Chapter 6 and section 11.1, "Teensy 4.*x* Controller Programming," in Chapter 11.

3.1.1   A Software-Based I^{2}C Controller for the Teensy 3.2

The code in Listing 3-1 implements a software-based I^{2}C controller running on a Teensy 3.2 by using Arduino library calls. I discuss each function and various code segments in the text between various sections of the listing.

This code is just meant to demonstrate how to implement an I^{2}C controller in software, so don't treat it as an I^{2}C library module for production use. It's intended to clarify the I^{2}C protocol in a concrete and formal manner for purely educational purposes.

As a test example, this particular program reads a value from an Adafruit ADS1115 I^{2}C ADC module from input A0, translates the binary input to the comparable range on the MCP4725, and then writes the result to a SparkFun MCP4725 DAC module (see Figure 3-1 for the wiring diagram).

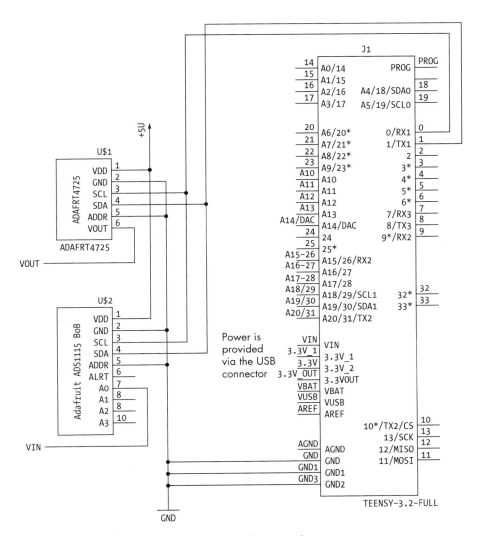

Figure 3-1: Circuit for the Teensy-based controller example

Inputting a voltage in the range of 0 V to 4.1 V should produce a similar voltage on the DAC output. This example program tests both reading from and writing to I^2C peripherals using the software-based I^2C controller software.

The MCP4725_ADDR and ADS1115_ADDR symbols specify the addresses of these modules. The DAC address should be 0x60 or 0x61, depending on the address jumper on the SparkFun board (the schematic in Figure 3-1 wires ADDR to Gnd, selecting address 0x60). Note that although the code in Listing 3-1 writes to a SparkFun board, you could also write to an Adafruit MCP4725 breakout board. In that case, the DAC address would be 0x62 or 0x63, depending on the on-board address setting. The ADS1115 address would be 0x48, 0x49, 0x4A, or 0x4B, depending how the address pin is jumpered on the breakout board; the schematic in Figure 3-1 assumes you've wired the ADDR pin to Gnd to use address 0x48. See the Adafruit documentation for more details (in "For More Information" at the end of this chapter).

The following code fragment begins Listing 3-1, which continues throughout this section with interspersed comments and annotations. You can find the full code file, *Listing3-1.ino*, at *https://bookofi2c.randallhyde.com*.

```
// Listing3-1.ino
//
// Software-based I2C controller device for
// the Teensy 3.2.
//
// Copyright 2020, Randall Hyde.
// All rights reserved.
// Released under Creative Commons 4.0.

#include <arduino.h>

// I2C address of the SparkFun MCP4725 I2C-based
// digital-to-analog converter.

#define MCP4725_ADDR 0x60
#define ADS1115_ADDR 0x48

// Pins on the Teensy 3.2 to use for the
// software SCL and SDA lines:

❶ #define SCL 0
#define SDA 1

// digitalWriteFast is a Teensy-specific function. Change
// to digitalWrite for standard Arduino.

❷ #define pinWrite digitalWriteFast
```

The SCL and SDA symbols define the Arduino-based pin numbers to use for the I^{2}C clock and data lines ❶. Pins 0 and 1 were arbitrary choices. Any available digital I/O pins will work fine here.

The pinWrite symbol maps to an Arduino-compatible digitalWrite() function ❷. Under normal circumstances, this would be the digitalWrite() function itself. However, the Teensy library has a special function, digitalWriteFast(), that is call-compatible with the Arduino digitalWrite() function but runs about three times faster by mapping pinWrite() to the Teensy function. If you're going to run this code on a different MCU, change the definition to digitalWrite().

The I^{2}C SDA and SCL lines are *bidirectional*; that is, the controller must be able to read data from these two lines as well as write data to them. As a general rule, Arduino GPIO pins are inputs or outputs, but not both at the same time. To simulate bidirectional I/O, the Teensy 3.2 software-based I^{2}C module takes advantage of the fact that Arduino-compatible GPIO pins can be dynamically switched between inputs and outputs. For the most part, the controller always knows when the signal line must be input or output so it can switch the pin's mode on the fly to accommodate the I^{2}C bus's needs.

```
// Listing3-1.ino (cont.):
//
// Pin set functions.
//
// setSCL-
//
// Sets the SCL pin high (1) by changing the pin mode to
// input and relying on the I2C bus pullup resistor to
// put a 1 on the bus.

❶ void setSCL( void )
  {
      pinMode( SCL, INPUT );
  }

// clrSCL-
//
// Sets the SCL pin low by changing the pin mode to output and
// writing a 0 to the pin. This will pull down the SCL line.

❷ void clrSCL( void )
  {
      pinMode( SCL, OUTPUT );
      pinWrite( SCL, 0 );
  }

// setSDA, clrSDA-
//
// Same as setSCL and clrSCL except they set/clr the SDA line.

❸ void setSDA( void )
  {
      pinMode( SDA, INPUT );
  }

❹ void clrSDA( void )
  {
      pinMode( SDA, OUTPUT );
      pinWrite( SDA, 0 );
  }
```

The setSCL() ❶, clrSCL() ❷, setSDA() ❸, and clrSDA() ❹ functions are responsible for writing a 0 or a 1 on the SCL and SDA lines. Writing a 1 to either line consists of switching the corresponding pin to the input mode. This puts the pin in a high-impedance state (open-collector or tri-state) without putting an actual signal on the line. The pullup resistor on the line then pulls the line high (1). Writing a 0 to either pin consists of changing the pin's mode to output and then writing a 0 to that pin. This pulls the line low, even in the presence of the pullup resistor.

It is important to leave the SCL and SDA lines high when you are not actively writing a 0 to these lines. This is a requirement not only of this software but also of the I²C bus in general—remember, other devices may be trying to pull the lines low.

```
// Listing3-1.ino (cont.):
//
// Reading the SCL and SDA pins.
//
// readSCL-
//
// Reads SCL pin until it gets the same value twice in
// a row. This is done to filter noise.

❶ inline byte readSCL( void )
  {
      byte first;
      byte second;
      do
      {
          first = digitalRead( SCL );
          second = digitalRead( SCL );
      }while( first != second );

      return first;
  }

❷ // readSDA-
  //
  // Reads SDA pin until it gets the same value twice in
  // a row. This is done to filter noise.

  inline byte readSDA( void )
  {
      byte first;
      byte second;
      do
      {
          first = digitalRead( SDA );
          second = digitalRead( SDA );
❸     }while( first != second );
      return first;
  }
```

The readSCL() function ❶ reads the data currently on the SCL line. The readSDA() function ❷ reads the data currently on the SDA line. The I²C standard requires filtering on the inputs to remove any glitches less than or equal to 50 nsec (nanoseconds) in duration ❸. Typically, this is done with an active filter (hardware) design. Although it is possible to attach such hardware to the pins on your microcontroller, this software-only I²C package performs this glitch filtering in software by reading all inputs twice and returning only once it has read the same value twice in a row. On most microprocessors, this will filter out glitches that are significantly greater than 50 nsec in length. However, as this software implementation handles only standard-speed I^{2}C operation (100 kHz), anything less than a microsecond could easily be considered noise.

These functions do not switch the pin to input mode before reading them. Most of the time these functions get called several times in a row, so it's more efficient to have the caller set the pin mode rather than having these functions set the mode every time they get called. Beyond that, some code calls these functions to verify that the signal lines have actually reached their final state after being set to 0 (handling delays due to bus capacitance, and so on).

```
// Listing3-1.ino (cont.):
//
// Setting the start condition on the SCL and SDA lines.
//
// setStartCond-
//
// First checks to see if the bus is being used, which requires
// a full 10 usec. If the bus is being used by some other bus
// controller, this function returns false.
//
// If the bus is not being used, this function issues a start
// condition for 5 usec (SDA = 0, SCL = 1) and then raises SDL
// in preparation for an address byte transmission. If it
// successfully sends a start condition, this code returns true.
//
// Postcondition:
//       SDA and SCL will both be low if this function is
//       successful. They will be unaffected if this function
//       returns false.

❶ int setStartCond( void )
  {
      byte bothPins;

      pinMode( SDA, INPUT ); // Going to be reading pins
      pinMode( SCL, INPUT );
      bothPins = readSDA() && readSCL();

❷     delayMicroseconds(1);
      bothPins &= readSDA() && readSCL();
      delayMicroseconds(1);
      bothPins &= readSDA() && readSCL();
      delayMicroseconds(1);
      bothPins &= readSDA() && readSCL();
      delayMicroseconds(1);
      bothPins &= readSDA() && readSCL();
      delayMicroseconds(1);
      bothPins &= readSDA() && readSCL();
      delayMicroseconds(1);
      bothPins &= readSDA() && readSCL();
      delayMicroseconds(1);
      bothPins &= readSDA() && readSCL();
      delayMicroseconds(1);
      bothPins &= readSDA() && readSCL();
      delayMicroseconds(1);
```

```
bothPins &= readSDA() && readSCL();
if( bothPins )
{
    // Both pins have remained high for around 10 usec
    // (one I2C clock period at 100 kHz). Chances
    // are, the bus isn't currently being used.
    // Go ahead and signal the start condition
    // by setting SDA = 0.

  ❸ clrSDA();
    delayMicroseconds( 4 );
    clrSCL();
    return 1; // In theory, this code has the bus

}
return 0;      // Bus is busy

}
```

The setStartCond() ❶ function allows the caller to take control of the I^2C bus. This function handles two primary tasks: it makes sure the bus isn't currently in use, and then if the bus is available, it transmits a start signal on the bus to claim the bus for its own use.

To see if the bus is already in use, the setStartCond() ❷ function checks the SCL and SDA lines every microsecond for 10 μsec. If either line is (or goes) low during these 10 μsec, the bus is in use, and this function returns failure (0). If both lines remain high for the duration, the bus is free, and the code can acquire the bus for its own purposes.

To acquire the bus, the code places the start condition on it ❸. This start condition begins with both lines high for 5 μsec (one-half clock cycle). This is followed by a transition on the SDA line from high to low and then a half clock period with SDA low and SCL high (see Figure 3-2).

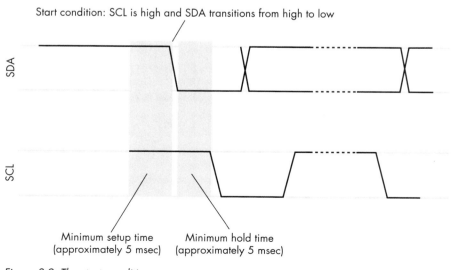

Figure 3-2: The start condition

If the setStartCond() function successfully places the start condition on the bus, it returns 1 as the function result. When this function returns to the caller, the caller tests the return result to determine whether it can begin using the I²C bus or whether it must wait and try to obtain the bus another time.

NOTE *This code generally does not supply the exact time specified by the I²C standard as an argument to the delayMicroseconds() function. For example, you will often see calls such as delayMicroseconds(3) or delayMicroseconds(4) when specifying a half clock cycle. The code uses these smaller numbers because surrounding statements consume the other time in the half cycle. During development, I used a logic analyzer to choose appropriate values that were greater than or equal to 5 μsec when the standard called for a half cycle (typically 4.7 μsec in the I²C standard).*

```
// Listing3-1.ino (cont.):
//
// Outputting a stop condition on the SCL and SDA lines.
//
// setStopCond-
//
// Generates an end-of-transmission stop sequence.
//
// Precondition:
//      SCL must be low when this is called.
// Postcondition:
//      SCL and SDA will be high.

❶ void setStopCond( void )
{
    clrSDA();                   // Initialize for stop condition
    delayMicroseconds( 1 ); // Give SDA time to go high
    setSCL();
    while( !readSCL() )
    {
        // Clock stretching-
        //
        // Wait while the peripheral is holding the clock
        // line low.
    }
    delayMicroseconds( 4 ); // SCL = 1, SDA = 0 for 5 usec
    setSDA();                   // Signal stop condition
}
```

When the software is done transmitting or receiving data and is ready to give up the I²C bus, it must put a stop condition on the bus, as shown in the setStopCond() code ❶.

Figure 3-3 shows the stop condition appearing on the I²C bus. The setStopCode() function brings the SCL line high (while SDA is low) and then pulls SCL high 5 μsec later.

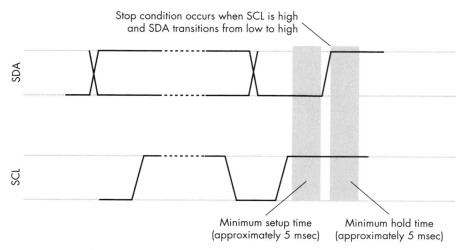

Figure 3-3: An I²C stop condition

The following code demonstrates how to detect and wait for a stop condition.

```
// Listing3-1.ino (cont.):
//
// Waiting for the stop condition to occur.
//
// waitForStop-
//
// If the bus is busy when this controller
// tries to use the I2C bus, this code
// must wait until a stop condition occurs
// before trying to use the bus again.
//
// Stop condition is:
//      SCL is high.
//      SDA goes from low to high.

void waitForStop( void )
{
    setSCL();   // Just make sure these are high;
    setSDA();   // they already should be

    do
    {

        while( !(readSCL() && !readSDA()) )
        {
                // Wait until the SCL line is high
                // and the SDA line is low
        }

        // Stop condition might have begun. Wait
        // for the data line to go high while
```

```
        // the SCL line remains high:

        while( !readSDA() && readSCL() )
        {
                // Wait for data line to go high
        }

        // Is the SCL line still high?
        // If not, you are just getting
        // some data and the code needs to
        // repeat until SCL is high again.

    }while( !readSCL() );
}
```

If some other controller is already using the I^{2}C bus, this software must wait until the other controller is done with the bus. That occurs when the other controller places a stop condition on the bus. The waitForStop() function watches the bus and waits for the stop condition to appear (SCL is high and SDA transitions from low to high).

```
// Listing3-1.ino (cont.):
//
// Transmitting a single bit on the I2C bus.
//
// sdaOut-
//
// bit:
//      Bit to transmit.
//      Transmits a single bit over the SDA/SCL lines.
//
// Returns:
//      1: If successful.
//      0: If arbitration failure or other error.
//
// Note:
//      Caller is responsible for setting SCL and SDA
//      high if there is an arbitration fault.

int sdaOut( byte bit )
{
    bit = !!bit;     // Force 0/1

    // Take SCL low so you can write to the
    // data line. Wait until SCL is actually
    // low before proceeding:

  ❶ clrSCL();
    while( readSCL() );

    // Set the SDA line appropriately:

  ❷ if( bit )
    {
```

```
        setSDA();
    }
    else
    {
        clrSDA();
    }

    // Wait for 1/2 of the I2C clock period
    // while SCL is low:

❸ delayMicroseconds( 3 );

    // Check to see if the value put on
    // the SDA line can be read back. The code
    // needed to delay before this call in order
    // to allow signal time to rise on the
    // SDA line.

❹ if( readSDA() != bit )
    {
        // If the bit just written does not
        // match the bit just read, then
        // the code must have written a 1 and
        // some other controller has written
        // a 0 to the SDA line. In this
        // case, the controller loses the
        // arbitration test.

        return 0;
    }

    // Raise the SCL line to indicate to the
    // peripheral that the data is valid:

❺ setSCL();

    // Must hold SCL line high for 5 usec:

    delayMicroseconds( 4 );

    // Clock stretching or synchronization
    // is handled here. Wait for the SCL
    // line to go high (it can be held
    // low by the peripheral or by another
    // controller):

❻ while( !readSCL() )
    {
        // Wait for SCL to go high
    }

    // Return success

    return 1;
}
```

The sdaOut() function writes a single bit to the I²C bus. Writing a bit to the I²C bus consists of the following sequence:

1. Set the SCL line low and verify that it is low ❶. Except for the start and stop conditions, the SDA line can change only while SCL is low.
2. Put the bit on the SDA line ❷.
3. Wait about a one-half clock period ❸.
4. Verify that the data on the SDA line matches the data just written (that is, verify that bus contention is not occurring). Fail (return 0) if the data does not match ❹.
5. Set the SCL line high ❺.
6. Wait for the SCL line to go high (clock stretching and synchronization) ❻.

Bus contention occurs if two controllers are trying to access the bus at the same time. This code detects bus contention if it writes a 1 to the SDA line and reads back a 0, which means the other controller is writing a 0. The I²C arbitration rule is "whoever writes the zero wins." If this code returns failure to the caller, it must cease the transmission and restart it when the next stop condition comes along.

```
// Listing3-1.ino (cont.):
//
// Transmitting a byte on the I2C bus.
//
// xmitByte-
//
// Transmits a byte across the I2C bus.
//
// Returns:
//      1: If ACK received after the transmission.
//      0: If NAK received after the transmission or
//         if there was bus contention (and this code
//         has to give up the bus).
//
// Precondition:
//      SCL must be low.
//
// Postcondition:
//      If arbitration failure, SDA and SCL will
//      both be high (to avoid conflicts with some
//      other controller).
//
// If successful:
//      SCL will be low.

int xmitByte( byte xmit )
{
  ❶ int result = sdaOut( xmit & 0x80 ); // MSB first!
    if( result )
```

```
            result = sdaOut( xmit & 0x40 ); // Bit 6
    if( result )
            result = sdaOut( xmit & 0x20 ); // Bit 5
    if( result )
            result = sdaOut( xmit & 0x10 ); // Bit 4
    if( result )
            result = sdaOut( xmit & 0x8 );  // Bit 3
    if( result )
            result = sdaOut( xmit & 0x4 );  // Bit 2
    if( result )
            result = sdaOut( xmit & 0x2 );  // Bit 1
    if( result )
            result = sdaOut( xmit & 0x1 );  // Bit 0

    if( result )
    {
        // And now the code must wait for
        // the acknowledge bit:

      ❷ clrSCL();
        delayMicroseconds( 1 );
        pinMode( SDA, INPUT );  // It's an input
        delayMicroseconds( 3 ); // 1/2 clock cycle

        // Raise the clock line and wait for it
        // to go high, which also handles clock
        // stretching and synchronization.

        setSCL();                   // Raise clock line
        while( !readSCL() );

        // Note that the clock line is high, so
        // this code can read the SDA bit (acknowledge).

        delayMicroseconds( 3 ); // Data valid for 5 usec
        result = readSDA();

      ❸ clrSCL();                   // Exit with SCL = 0
        while( readSCL() );
        return !result;
    }

    // If there is an arbitration failure,
    // then try to transmit a 1 bit while the
    // other controller transmits a 0 bit.
    // The 0 bit always wins, so this function
    // sets SDA and SCL to 1 to avoid creating
    // other problems for the other controller.

    setSCL();
    setSDA();
    return 0;   // Arbitration failure
}
```

The xmitByte() function transmits a whole byte across the I²C bus. Obviously, this function calls sdaOut() eight times to transmit the 8 bits ❶. As per the I²C standard, this code ships the bits out from the MSB down to the LSB. If at any time a call to sdaOut() returns failure, this function also returns failure.

At the end of the byte transmission, this code sets the SDA line high and issues an additional pulse on the SCL line ❷. While SCL is high, this code reads the SDA line. This retrieves either the acknowledge bit (0) from the peripheral, or, if there is not acknowledgment, a default NAK of 1. This function returns true if the transmission was properly acknowledged, and false otherwise.

After reading the acknowledgment bit, this code sets SCL low and continuously reads the line, waiting for it to actually go low ❸.

```
// Listing3-1.ino (cont.):
//
// Transmitting a sequence of bytes on the I2C bus.
//
// xmitBytes-
//
// Transmit a block of bytes (in write mode)
// via the I2C bus. adrs is the I2C device
// address. bytes is the array of bytes
// to transmit (after the address byte).
// cnt is the number of bytes to transmit
// from the bytes array. addStop is true
// if this function is to add a stop condition
// at the end of the transmission.
//
// Note that, including the address byte,
// this function actually transmits cnt + 1
// bytes over the bus.

int xmitBytes
(
    byte adrs,
    byte bytes[],
    int cnt,
    int addStop
)
{
    int result;

    // Send the start condition.

    result = setStartCond();
    if( result )
    {
        // If bus was not in use, transmit
        // the address byte:

        result = xmitByte( adrs << 1 );
        if( result )
        {
            // If there wasn't bus contention,
            // ship out the bytes (as long as
```

```
        // bus contention does not occur):

        for( int i=0; i < cnt; ++i )
        {
            result = xmitByte( bytes[i] );
            if( !result ) break;
        }
    }
    // If the transmission was correct to this
    // point, transmit the stop condition.
    // Note: if addStop() is false, don't send a
    // stop condition after this transmission
    // because a repeated start is about
    // to happen.

    if( result && addStop )
    {
        setStopCond();
    }
}
return result;
}
```

The xmitBytes() function handles a complete I²C write transmission.
The caller passes it the I²C address of the peripheral, an array of bytes
(along with a count), and a special "stop" flag, and this function sends out
the appropriate start condition and address byte and writes all the data bytes.
If the addStop flag is true, this function also attaches a stop condition to the
end of the transmission. If addStop is false, this function transmits the data
without the stop condition—presumably because you want to hold the I²C
bus and issue a repeated start condition shortly thereafter.

This function returns true or false based on success or failure of the
transmission. If this function returns false, either the bus is already in
use or there was bus contention, and this code lost the arbitration battle.
Whatever the reason, if this function returns false, the caller must retry
the transmission later.

```
// Listing3-1.ino (cont.):
//
// Receiving a single bit on the I2C bus.
//
// sdaIn-
//
// Retrieves a single bit from the SDA line.

byte sdaIn( void )
{

    // Take SCL low before writing to the
    // data line. Wait until SCL is actually
    // low before proceeding:

    clrSCL();
```

```
    while( readSCL() );

    // Wait for 1/2 clock period for
    // the peripheral to put the data
    // on the SDA line:

    delayMicroseconds( 4 );

    // Bring the clock line high.

    setSCL();

    // Wait until it actually goes high
    // (stretching or syncing might be
    // happening here).

    while( !readSCL() );

    // Wait for 1/2 of the I2C clock period
    // while SCL is high:

    delayMicroseconds( 3 );

    // Read the data from the SDA line:

    byte input = readSDA();

    // Hold SCL line high for the
    // remainder of this 1/2
    // clock period:

    delayMicroseconds( 2 );

    // Return result.

    return input;
}
```

The sdaIn() function reads a single bit from the I^{2}C bus. This function is similar to sdaOut(), except that it reads the data from SDA rather than writing data. Also, there is no need to check for arbitration failure when reading, though this function still handles clock stretching and synchronization. Although the data is coming from the peripheral, it is still the controller's responsibility to drive the clock signal on the SCL line.

```
// Listing3-1.ino (cont.):
//
// Receiving a byte on the I2C bus.
//
// rcvByte-
//
// Receives a byte from the I2C bus.
//
```

```
// Precondition:
//     SCL must be low.
// Postcondition:
//     SCL will be low.

byte rcvByte( void )
{
    setSDA();             // Before reading inputs
    byte result = sdaIn()  7;
    result |= sdaIn() << 6;
    result |= sdaIn() << 5;
    result |= sdaIn() << 4;
    result |= sdaIn() << 3;
    result |= sdaIn() << 2;
    result |= sdaIn() << 1;
    result |= sdaIn();

    // Generate the ACK bit:

    clrSCL();
    while( readSCL() ); // Wait until it's low
    delayMicroseconds( 2 );
    clrSDA();
    delayMicroseconds( 2 );
    setSCL();
    while( !readSCL() )
    {
        // Wait until SCL goes high (could be
        // waiting for stretching or syncing).
    }
    delayMicroseconds( 4 );

    // Leave SCL low for the next byte
    // or the beginning of the stop
    // condition:

    clrSCL();
    return result;

}
```

The rcvByte() function reads an 8-bit byte from the I^{2}C bus by calling the sdaIn() function eight times. After the function reads those 8 bits, the controller is responsible for putting the ACK signal (a 0) on the SDA line to inform the peripheral that everything has gone well. This function returns the byte read as the function result.

```
// Listing3-1.ino (cont.):
//
// Receiving a sequence of bytes on the I2C bus.

int rcvBytes( byte adrs, byte bytes[], int cnt, int addStop )
{
```

```
        int result;

        // Send the start condition.

        result = setStartCond();
        if( result )
        {
            // If bus was not in use, transmit
            // the address byte:

            result = xmitByte( (adrs << 1) | 1 );
            if( result )
            {
                // Read the specified number of
                // bytes from the bus:

                for( int i=0; i < cnt; ++i )
                {
                    bytes[i] = rcvByte();
                }
            }

            // If no errors at this point, transmit
            // the stop condition.
            // Note: if addStop is false, don't send
            // a stop condition after this transmission
            // because a repeated start is about
            // to happen.

            if( result && addStop )
            {
                setStopCond();
            }
        }
        return result;
}
```

The rcvBytes() function is the input analog to the xmitBytes() function. It acquires the I^{2}C bus, transmitting a start condition; transmits the address byte with a high R/W bit; and then receives some specified number of bytes from the peripheral device. Optionally, this function will transmit a stop condition after receiving the bytes.

The code, up to this point, for *Listing3-1.ino* is the complete set of routines needed to implement a software-based I^{2}C controller. The remainder of *Listing3-1.ino* contains the usual Arduino initialization (setup) and main loop functions.

```
// Listing3-1.ino (cont.):
//
// Arduino setup() function for Listing3-1.ino.
//
// Standard Arduino initialization code:

void setup( void )
```

```
{
    pinMode( SCL, INPUT ); // Begin with SCL/SDA = 1
    pinMode( SDA, INPUT );

    Serial.begin( 9600 );
    delay( 1000 );
    Serial.println( "teensyTest" );
}
```

The setup() function sets up the SCL and SDA pins as inputs so they are left in the high condition to avoid interfering with other controllers.

```
// Listing3-1.ino (cont.):
//
// Arduino main loop() function for Listing3-1.ino.
//
// Arduino main loop:

void loop( void )
{
    static  int    result;
    static  word   adcValue;
    static  byte   bytes[16];

    // Read a 12-bit value from
    // an Adafruit ADS1115 breakout
    // board. The following configuration
    // is for:
    //
    // * AIN[0]
    // * 0-4.096 V operation
    // * 1600 samples/second
    // * Disabled comparator

    adcValue   = 0;
    bytes[0]   = 1;        // Point at config reg
    bytes[1]   = 0xc2;     // MSB of config
    bytes[2]   = 0x03;     // LSB of config

    // adcValue = ADS1115.readADC_SingleEnded( 0 );
    // Serial.print( "ADC: " );
    // Serial.println( adcValue, 16 );

    result  = xmitBytes( ADS1115_ADDR, bytes, 3, true );
    if( result )
    {
    // Point at the conversion register. Note that
    // this is a repeated start condition command
    // but ends with a stop condition.

        bytes[0] = 0;
        result = xmitBytes( ADS1115_ADDR, bytes, 1, true );

        // Read the ADC value from the ADS1115.
```

```
        if( result )
        {
            // This really should go into a loop
            // testing bit 16 of the config (status)
            // register, but this is easier:

            delay( 1 );

            result = rcvBytes( ADS1115_ADDR, bytes, 2, true );
            if( result )
            {
                adcValue = (bytes[0] << 8) | bytes[1];
            }
        }
    }

    // Start by writing 64 (0x40) to
    // the DAC register (command byte
    // which states that the next two
    // bytes go into the DAC register).

    bytes[0] = 64;

    // The next two bytes to write are the
    // 12 bits of the DAC value. The HO
    // 4 bits are put in the first byte
    // and the LO 8 bits appear in the
    // second byte.

    float volts = (((float) adcValue) * 4.096 / 32768.0 );
    Serial.print( "Volts: " ); Serial.print( volts, 3 );
    adcValue    = (word) (volts * 65536.0/5);
    bytes[1]    = (adcValue >> 8) & 0xff;
    bytes[2]    = (adcValue & 0xf0);

    // Transmit the data to the DAC IC:

    if( !xmitBytes( MCP4725_ADDR, bytes, 3, true ) )
    {
        // If there was an arbitration failure,
        // wait for a start condition to come along.

        waitForStop();
    }
    Serial.println();
    delay( 100 );

}
```

The main loop() function reads data from an ADS1115 analog-to-digital converter (ADC), translates the input, and writes the data to an MCP4725 digital-to-analog converter (DAC). Though the conversion isn't perfect, this effectively copies the input voltage present on A0 of the ADC to the analog output on the DAC.

NOTE   *For more information on the MCP4725, see Chapter 15. For more information on the ADS1115, see Chapter 14.*

As explained earlier, this code is just an example to demonstrate how you would implement an I^{2}C controller in software, so it's not really intended to be used. For one thing, it's written using standard functions rather than classes and methods, which makes it easier to understand but harder to use. It also may not port directly to other MCUs; although I wrote this code using mostly standard Arduino calls, I ran it through a logic analyzer to hand-tune all the delays to produce reasonable timing on a 96-MHz Teensy 3.2. I suspect the timing values might vary a bit too much on other faster or slower MCUs.

The other problem with this code is that it uses a single pair of I/O pins for the SDA and SCL lines. Constantly changing the data direction on the pins to make them bidirectional is the standard way of doing things in software I^{2}C implementations. While this approach probably works just fine in single-controller environments and when working with peripherals that don't implement too many optional features, I'm not confident it will work flawlessly in multicontroller environments. Unfortunately, the race conditions that might exist—possible errant calculations based on the timing of your program's execution—are difficult to create (for testing).

3.1.2   A Software-Based I^{2}C Peripheral for the Teensy 3.2

The previous section provided a software implementation of an I^{2}C controller device. This section provides the companion to that implementation: a software-controlled I^{2}C peripheral device. The code in this section turns a Teensy 3.2 into an I^{2}C peripheral with the following features:

- It saves any byte value written to it.
- When the controller reads a byte from it, it returns the last value written, or 0 if there was no previously written byte.

Effectively, this code turns the Teensy into a 1-byte I^{2}C memory unit. Although this is a lame I^{2}C peripheral, it completely demonstrates everything you need in order to develop your own software-based I^{2}C peripheral.

In many respects, the peripheral software is easier to write. The peripheral doesn't have to worry about bus contention, clock synchronization, and many other issues. On the other hand, the peripheral should respond to several optional messages that controllers don't have to worry about.

The following code ignores all the reserved address values. For the general call address reset function, it might be reasonable to set the stored memory value to 0 (though it's easy enough to write a 0 to this peripheral if you want). You could also create a device ID for this peripheral; I will leave that exercise to you.

Listing 3-2 provides the source code for this simple peripheral.

```
// Listing3-2.ino
//
// Software-based I2C peripheral device for
// the Teensy 3.2.
//
// Copyright 2020, Randall Hyde.
// All rights reserved.
// Released under Creative Commons 4.0.

#include <arduino.h>

// Pins on the Teensy 3.2 to use for the
// software SCL and SDA lines:

#define SCL 0
#define SDA 1

// PeriphAddress is the address of this PeripheralAddress.

#define PeriphAddress (0x50)
#define PeripheralAddress ((PeriphAddress) << 1)

// digitalWriteFast is a Teensy-specific function. Change
// to digitalWrite for standard Arduino.
// Likewise, digitalReadFast changes to digitalRead for
// standard Arduino.

#define pinWrite digitalWriteFast
#define pinRead  digitalReadFast
```

As for the controller code, the two identifiers SCL and SDA define the pin numbers on the Teensy 3.2 that this code will use for the SCL and SDA lines. The PeriphAddress definition specifies the I^2C address to which this peripheral will respond. To finish the definitions, pinRead and pinWrite expand to Teensy-specific (fast) versions of the Arduino digitalRead() and digitalWrite() functions.

```
// Listing3-2.ino (cont):
//
// Pin control functions.
//
// setSCL-
//
// Sets the SCL pin high (1) by changing the pin mode
// to input and relying on the I2C bus pullup resistor
// to put a 1 on the bus.

❶ void setSCL( void )
{
    pinMode( SCL, INPUT );
}
```

```
       // clrSCL-
       //
       // Sets the SCL pin low. Changes the pin mode to output and
       // writes a 0 to the pin to pull down the SCL line. Used
       // mainly for clock stretching.

❷ void clrSCL( void )
   {
       pinMode( SCL, OUTPUT );
       pinWrite( SCL, 0 );
   }

       // setSDA, clrSDA-
       //
       // Same as setSCL and clrSCL except they set or clr the SDA line.

❸ void setSDA( void )
   {
       pinMode( SDA, INPUT );
   }

❹ void clrSDA( void )
   {
       pinMode( SDA, OUTPUT );
       pinWrite( SDA, 0 );
   }

❺ // readSCL-
   //
   // Reads SCL pin until it gets the same value twice in
   // a row. This is done to filter noise.

   inline byte readSCL( void )
   {
       byte first;
       byte second;
       do
       {
           first = pinRead( SCL );
           second = pinRead( SCL );
       }while( first != second );
       return first;
   }

❻ // readSDA-
   //
   // Reads SDA pin until it gets the same value twice in
   // a row. This is done to filter noise.

   inline byte readSDA( void )
   {
       byte first;
       byte second;
       do
       {
```

```
            first = pinRead( SDA );
            second = pinRead( SDA );
        }while( first != second );
        return first;
}
```

The setSCL() ❶, clrSCL() ❷, setSDA() ❸, and clrSDA() ❹ functions were copied straight over from the controller code; they set or clear the SCL and SDA lines. Likewise, the readSCL() ❺ and readSDA() ❻ functions (also copied from the controller code) read the current values on the SDA and SCL lines. Refer back to the sections of *Listing3-1.ino* that begin with the comments Pin set functions and Reading the SCL and SDA pins for more details.

```
// Listing3-2.ino (cont.):
//
// Transmitting a single bit on the I2C bus.
//
// sdaOut-
//
//      bit: Bit to transmit.
//      Transmits a single bit over the SDA/SCL lines.
//
// Returns:
//      1: If successful.
//      0: If arbitration failure or other error.

void sdaOut( byte bit )
{
    unsigned long time;

    bit = !!bit;      // Force 0/1

    // Wait until SCL is low.
    // It's okay to change SDA
    // when SCL is low:

❶ while( readSCL() );

    // Set the SDA line appropriately.

❷ if( bit )
    {
        setSDA();
    }
    else
    {
        clrSDA();
    }

    // Wait for the SCL line to go high and
    // then back to low. After that, release
    // the SDA line by setting it to 1.

❸ while( !readSCL() );
```

```
        time = micros() + 15;
        while( readSCL() )
        {
            // If stuck in this loop for
            // more than 15 usec, then bail.
            // Need a timeout so it doesn't
            // hold SDA low for an extended
            // period of time.

          ❹ if( micros() > time ) break;
        }

        // Release the SDA line by setting it high.

        setSDA();
}
```

The sdaOut() function places a single bit, passed as an argument, on the SDA line in response to an SCL clock transition. Unlike the controller code, the peripheral code does not control the SCL line. Instead, the controller must pulse the clock line.

1. The sdaOut() function must wait until the clock line is low ❶.
2. Then it can write the data to the SDA line ❷.
3. Finally, it waits for the SCL line to go high and then back low again before returning ❸.

Note that this code has a timeout while waiting for the SCL line to go high. If for some reason the controller doesn't bring the SCL line back high, this code will break out of the wait loop after about 15 μsec rather than just hang up ❹.

```
// Listing3-2.ino (cont.):
//
// Transmitting a byte on the I2C bus.
//
// xmitByte-
//
// Transmits a whole byte by call sdaOut
// eight times.

void xmitByte( byte xmit )
{
    unsigned long time;

  ❶ sdaOut( xmit & 0x80 );
    sdaOut( xmit & 0x40 );
    sdaOut( xmit & 0x20 );
    sdaOut( xmit & 0x10 );
    sdaOut( xmit & 0x8 );
    sdaOut( xmit & 0x4 );
    sdaOut( xmit & 0x2 );
    sdaOut( xmit & 0x1 );
```

```
        // The controller will generate the ACK
        // bit. This code will ignore it.
        // However, it does have to wait for
        // the clock pulse (low->high->low)
        // to come along.

    ❷ while( readSCL() ); // Wait for low clock

        time = micros()+25;
        while( !readSCL() )
        {
            // Wait until SCL goes high (could be
            // waiting for stretching or syncing).
            // Bail if there is a timeout, though.

          ❸ if( micros() > time ) break;
        }

        // Okay, SCL is (probably) high; wait for it
        // to go low again:

        while( readSCL() );
}
```

The xmitByte() function transmits an 8-bit byte on the SDA line by calling sdaOut() eight times ❶. This code also consumes the clock cycle for the
ninth bit—the acknowledge bit ❷—though it ignores that bit's state, since
some controllers don't bother putting the ACK bit on the SDA line. This
code also has a timeout ❸ in case the SCL line never goes high while it is
waiting for the acknowledge bit.

```
// Listing3-2.ino (cont.):
//
// Receiving a single bit on the I2C bus.
//
// sdaIn-
//
// Retrieves a single bit from the SDA line.
// Note: no timeout on the loops because this
// code doesn't mess with the SDA line.

byte sdaIn( void )
{
    byte input;

  ❶ while( readSCL() );

        // Wait until the SCL line is high.
        // That is when data will be valid
        // on the SDA line:

  ❷ while( !readSCL() );
```

```
    // Wait for a small amount of time for the
    // controller's data to be stabilized
    // on the SDA line:

  ❸ delayMicroseconds( 1 );

    // Read the data from the SDA line:

    input = readSDA();

    // Return result:

    return input;
}
```

The sdaIn() function reads a bit appearing on the SDA line. It begins by waiting until the SCL line is low ❶, if it wasn't already. Then it waits for the SCL line to go high (the start of the read cycle) because SDA data is valid only while the clock line is high ❷. Once the clock line goes high, this function delays for a microsecond to give the data time to settle, and then this function reads the data from the SDA line ❸.

```
// Listing3-2.ino (cont.):
//
// Receiving a byte on the I2C bus.
//
// rcvByte-
//
// Receives a byte from the I2C bus.

byte rcvByte( void )
{
    unsigned long time;

    pinMode( SDA, INPUT );

    // Read 8 bits from the SDA line:

  ❶ byte result7 = sdaIn() << 7;
    byte result6 = sdaIn() << 6;
    byte result5 = sdaIn() << 5;
    byte result4 = sdaIn() << 4;
    byte result3 = sdaIn() << 3;
    byte result2 = sdaIn() << 2;
    byte result1 = sdaIn() << 1;
    byte result0 = sdaIn();
    byte result = result7
            |    result6
            |    result5
            |    result4
            |    result3
            |    result2
            |    result1
            |    result0;
```

```
    // Generate the ACK bit.
    // Wait for the SCL line to go low,
    // pull SDA low, then wait for the
    // SCL line to go high and low:

    while( readSCL() );

❷ clrSDA();
    time = micros()+25;
    while( !readSCL() )
    {

    // Wait until SCL goes high (could be
    // waiting for stretching or syncing).
    // Bail if there is a timeout, though.

        if( micros() > time ) break;
    }

    // Okay, SCL is (probably) high; wait for it to go
    // low again and then release the SDA line:

    while( readSCL() );
    setSDA(); // Set SDA high (releases SDA)

    return result;
}
```

The rcvByte() function calls sdaIn() eight successive times to read a byte from the I²C bus ❶. At the end of those 8 bits ❷, this function must pull the SDA line low to acknowledge the data: the ACK bit. The function pulls the SDA line low while SCL is low and leaves the SDA line while SCL is high, with the usual timeout check in case the controller leaves SCL high for too long.

```
// Listing3-2.ino (cont.):
//
// Waiting for a start condition, while allowing other work.
//
// waitForStart-
//
// Wait until a start condition arrives.
// The peripheral address byte will follow.
//
// Start condition is:
//
//     SCL is high.
//     SDA goes from high to low.
//
// An address byte immediately follows the
// start condition. Read it. Return
// one of the following values:
//
```

```
// Negative:
//          Address does not match or
//          start condition yet to be
//          received.
//      0: Address match, R/W = 0 (W)
//      1: Address match, R/W = 1 (R)
//
// This function is a state machine that
// rapidly returns. It has the following
// states:
//
// -1: Waiting for SCL and SDA to both
//     be high.
// -2: SCL and SDA are both high, waiting
//     for SDA to go low.

int waitForStart( void )
{
    static int  state = -1;
    byte        sdaVal;
    byte        sclVal;

    switch( state )
    {
        case -1:

            // Wait until the SCL line is high and the
            // SDA line is high.

            if( readSCL() && readSDA() )
            {
                state = -2;
            }
            return state;

        case -2:

            // Start condition may have begun. Wait
            // for the data line to go low while
            // the SCL line remains high:

            sdaVal = readSDA();
            sclVal = readSCL();
            if( !sdaVal && sclVal )
            {
                break;
            }

            // If code sees anything other than
            // SCL = 1 and SDA = 1 at this point,
            // it has to reset the state machine
            // to -1.

            if( !( sclVal && sdaVal ) )
            {
```

```
            state = -1;
        }
        return state;

    // Just a fail-safe case:

    default:
        state = -1;
        return state;

    }   // Switch

    // Reset the state machine for the next invocation:

    state = -1;

    // Okay, there is a start condition.
    // Read the address byte.

    byte address = rcvByte();
    if( (address & 0xFE) == PeripheralAddress )
    {
        return address & 1;
    }
    return -1;  // Not our address
}
```

The waitForStart() function doesn't actually wait for a start condition to happen. Instead, it is a state machine that traverses between states on each call based on the state of the SDA and SCL lines. This function returns 0, 1, or some negative number.

A 0 return result indicates an address match with a write operation. A return value of 1 indicates an address match with a read operation. A negative return value indicates that nothing of interest has come along just yet and the caller should repeat the call in the near future, fast enough to catch an incoming start condition.

The waitForStart() function was written this way—rather than not returning until a start condition and valid address have come along—because it allows the CPU to do other work while waiting for a start condition.

```
// Listing3-2.ino (cont.):
//
// Standard Arduino setup() function.
//
// Standard Arduino initialization code:

void setup( void )
{
    pinMode( SCL, INPUT ); // Begin with SCL/SDA = 1
    pinMode( SDA, INPUT );

    Serial.begin( 9600 );
```

```
        delay( 1000 );
        Serial.println( "teensy Peripheral Test" );
}
```

The standard Arduino setup() function just initializes the SDA and
SCL lines as inputs, putting a 1 on these lines, so that this peripheral
does not interfere with any other activity taking place on the bus. This
particular code also prints a message to the Serial output for debugging
purposes.

```
// Listing3-2.ino (cont.):
//
// Standard Arduino loop() function.
//
// Arduino main loop:

void loop( void )
{
    static byte memory = 0; // Holds I2C memory byte

    // Wait for a start condition to arrive.
    // If not a start condition yet, just
    // keep looping.
    //
    // Assumption: Arduino code outside this
    // loop takes less than about 5 usec
    // to execute. If that is not the case,
    // then waitForStart() should be called
    // in a hard loop to continuously poll
    // for a start condition.

    int gotStart = waitForStart();

 ❶ if( gotStart == 0 )          // Write request
    {
        // On write operation, read the next byte
        // coming from the I2C bus and store it
        // into the memory location.

        memory = rcvByte();

        Serial.print( "Memory=" );
        Serial.println( memory, 16 );
    }
 ❷ else if( gotStart == 1 )     // Read request
    {
        // On a read request, transmit the
        // value in memory across the I2C bus.

        xmitByte( memory );
        Serial.print( "Transmitted " );
        Serial.println( memory );

    }
```

```
❸ // else: not of interest to us.

}
```

The Arduino loop function is the main body of the peripheral program. It calls the `waitForStart()` function and checks the return value. It handles the following three cases:

0   A write operation (from controller to peripheral) is taking place. In this case the code reads the next byte available from the I^{2}C bus and stores this value into the memory location ❶.

1   A read operation (controller is reading the peripheral) is taking place. In this case the code writes the value of the memory variable onto the I^{2}C bus as the controller clocks out the next byte ❷.

A negative value   The main loop does nothing in this case; it just returns to the caller, which, after some possible internal bookkeeping work, calls the `loop()` function again ❸.

Listing 3-3 is a short Teensy 3.2/Arduino program I used to test the software-based I^{2}C peripheral code appearing in Listing 3-2.

```
// Listing3-3.ino
//
// Software-based I2C test program.

#include <Wire.h>
#define LED 13

void setup( void )
{
    Serial.begin( 9600 );
    delay( 1000 );
    Serial.println( "test.ino" );
    Wire.begin();
    pinMode( LED, OUTPUT );
}

void loop( void )
{
    static byte value = 0;

    digitalWrite( LED, 0 );
    Serial.print( "Writing: " );
    Serial.print( value, 16 );
    Wire.beginTransmission( 0x50 );
    Wire.write( value );
    Wire.endTransmission();
    delay( 250 );

    digitalWrite( LED, 1 );
    Wire.requestFrom( 0x50, 1 );
    while( Wire.available() )
```

```
    {
        byte data = Wire.read();
        Serial.print( ", read=" );
        Serial.print( data, 16 );
        Serial.print( ", value=" );
        Serial.print( value, 16 );
    }
    Serial.println();
    ++value;
    delay( 250 );
}
```

The code in Listing 3-3 can run on a Teensy 3.2 or just about any Arduino-compatible system. It repeatedly writes a value to the peripheral and then reads that value back. See Chapter 8 for more details about how this sample program works.

3.1.3   Some Final Comments on the Teensy 3.2 Software I²C Code

The software in the previous two sections was hand-tuned to work on a Teensy 3.2. It may not work on different systems, and it likely won't work on significantly faster or slower systems. If you want to use this code for some other MCU, you'll probably have to tweak and optimize it a bit, particularly on MCUs with lower performance and less memory than the Teensy 3.2. To provide an example of just such an optimization, Chapter 17 (online at *https://bookofi2c.randallhyde.com*) describes how to implement a controller and peripheral using an ATtiny84 CPU running at only 8 MHz.

There are a couple of issues with the Teensy software implementation of the I²C bus. First, this code is relatively fragile with respect to timing. It uses software delay loops to measure the I²C clock cycles. Interrupts and other activities that can suspend the execution of such delay code may produce incorrect timings, resulting in improper operation. Although there are a few timeout checks on various loops, a real-world project would require more of these checks to prevent the code from hanging up if an errant controller or peripheral is on the bus. While this chapter avoids too many timeout checks because they would have cluttered up the code and made it harder to understand, if you intend to use this code as the basis for a real-world project, you should address that shortcoming.

3.2   Basic ATtiny84 and ATtiny85 Hardware

The example code given thus far runs on a high-performance Teensy microcontroller. While that code is useful as an educational tool, in reality you usually won't have to implement the I²C protocol on such a powerful processor—such processors will include built-in I²C hardware. Software-based I²C packages are far more common on low-end CPUs, such as the ATtiny84.

The ATtiny84 is a typical 8-bit AVR microcontroller similar to those found on low-end Arduino boards. These microcontrollers typically cost less than $3 (US) from vendors such as SparkFun (*https://www.sparkfun.com/products/11232*), and you can find them in small quantities (25 or so) for much less on Amazon or eBay. They have the following features:

- 8-KB flash memory
- 512-bytes EEPROM
- 512 bytes of RAM
- 12-MHz operation using internal clock, 20 MHz using external crystal
- One 8-bit and one 16-bit counter
- 10-bit ADCs
- On-chip analog comparator
- 12 I/O pins (in 14-pin dual-in-line [DIP] package)
- Nearly 12 MIPS operation at 12 MHz (1 MIPS/MHz)

This CPU is great for handling 100-kHz I^{2}C operations, assuming non-I^{2}C activities are not especially compute intensive.

The ATtiny85 microcontroller IC is a similar device in an 8-pin DIP package with six GPIO pins. It has fewer peripheral devices built in (due to packing constraints), and the timers are both 8 bits, but otherwise it does the same job as the ATtiny84. Most source codes that don't use the extra ATtiny84 features will run on both MCUs.

NOTE   *Technically, the ATtiny84 and ATtiny85 MCUs have a Universal Serial Interface (USI) port that you can program to support hardware I^{2}C operations. However, that port might not be available; if it's being used for SPI or other serial communication, this forces you to implement the I^{2}C protocol in software.*

You can find the complete code for a SparkFun Atto84 device programmed as an I^{2}C controller in Chapter 17 online. This code isn't identical to the Teensy code in this chapter, but much of it is similar; the code was placed in the online chapter to avoid redundancy in this chapter.

3.2.1   Atto84 Software-Based I^{2}C Peripheral

Unfortunately, the Atto84 is just slightly too underpowered to support a reliable I^{2}C peripheral mode in software. I spent several days attempting this with the following compromises:

- Dropping filtering on the SDA and SCL input lines
- Removing timeout checks on loops
- In-lining most of the functions that manipulate I/O port bits (including reading bits, waiting for the clock line to go high or low, and many other functions)
- Dropping down into AVR assembly language for time-critical code

In the end, the Atto84 managed to support peripheral mode once in a while but was not at all consistent. The Atto84 can act as a controller because it controls the clock frequency; if one-half clock periods wind up being stretched to 5.5 μsec, 6.0 μsec, or even 7.1 μsec, any normal peripheral can handle that just fine. However, as a peripheral, the Atto84 must be capable of always keeping up with a 100-kHz clock (5-μsec one-half clock periods), and even using straight-line assembly language code with all the compromises listed earlier is not quite good enough to do the job. The Atto84 still misses putting the ACK bit on the SDA line every now and then. Of course, once you remove all the timeouts from the loops, the code gets out of sync when it misses a bit, and things go very badly after that point.

This is not to say that you cannot use the Atto84 (or generic ATtiny84) as an I^{2}C peripheral device. The generic ATtiny84 can run at up to 20 MHz with an external crystal, which might be fast enough to work. More importantly, the ATtiny84 has built-in hardware (the USI) that provides hardware support for I^{2}C operations. I'll return to this subject in Chapter 16.

3.3   Chapter Summary

This chapter provided a software implementation of the I^{2}C protocol running on a Teensy 3.2 microcontroller as an educational tool. It began by describing a small hardware setup using a Teensy 3.2, an Adafruit ADS1115 ADC breakout board, and a SparkFun MCP4725 DAC breakout board. After the basic hardware introduction, it presented a software implementation of an I^{2}C controller and an I^{2}C peripheral. Finally, it briefly reviewed issues with software-based I^{2}C protocol implementation on an ATtiny84 microcontroller.

Carefully studying a software implementation of the I^{2}C protocol will help solidify your understanding of its low-level details. That information becomes particularly important when you begin debugging I^{2}C signals using logic and protocol analyzers. The next chapter will delve into that subject with a discussion of I^{2}C debugging tools.

FOR MORE INFORMATION

Another Arduino-compatible software-based I^{2}C library: *https://www .arduinolibraries.info/libraries/soft-wire*

Adafruit ADS1115 documentation: *https://www.adafruit.com/product/1085*

Adafruit MCP4725 documentation: *https://www.adafruit.com/product/935*

Information about AVR assembly language, for those brave enough to try to best my attempts at a software-based I^{2}C peripheral system using the Atto84:

AVR Assembler documentation: *https://ww1.microchip.com/downloads/en/ devicedoc/40001917a.pdf*

More AVR Assembler documentation: *https://academy.cba.mit.edu/classes/ embedded_programming/doc1022.pdf*

4

TOOLS FOR ANALYZING AND DEBUGGING I²C TRANSMISSIONS

When designing I²C hardware and writing software to work with I²C hardware, you will often discover that software-based debuggers and printf statements are insufficient for quickly tracking down problems in the hardware and software. If you're going to program I²C devices regularly, you will want to invest in some proper hardware tools to reduce debugging and testing effort.

This chapter discusses several of those tools, including multimeters, oscilloscopes, logic analyzers, bus monitors, and protocol analyzers. Although such tools cost money, using them will reduce the time you spend debugging code.

4.1 Generic Hardware Testing and Debugging Tools

If you're working with hardware devices (generic, not just I^{2}C), there are a few tools you should have available in your tool chest:

- A digital multimeter (DMM)
- An oscilloscope
- 5-V, 3.3-V, and variable power supplies (0 V to 10 V, at the very least)

The DMM comes in handy for checking the power supply pins on I^{2}C devices, as well as any other DC signals. Most DMMs are worthless for measuring signals on pins whose voltage is changing, such as the SDA and SCL lines, because the DMM will average the voltage over a relatively long time frame, producing an inaccurate picture if the signal is not stable.

DMMs are also useful for measuring the pullup resistance on the I^{2}C lines. In theory, you should be able to read the color codes or SMT resistor codes and figure out the resistance on the bus. However, if multiple pullups are scattered around the system, the resistor might be lower than what you expect. A quick ohm check between Vcc and the SDA or SCL lines could prove handy.

Some DMMs have a capacitance meter built into them. These are rarely good enough to measure the bus capacitance. Unless you have a *really expensive* DMM, don't even bother trying to make such a measurement. The capacitance is usually too low for your average meter. On the other hand, capacitance meters that can handle low capacitances, and that might give you an idea of how bad the bus capacitance is in your system, are available for as little as $100. Fortunately, you can observe the signals with an oscilloscope and determine if there is too much bus capacitance, so a capacitance meter isn't necessary. It's not worth buying one if you don't already have one and can't justify the purchase for other reasons.

In theory, an oscilloscope isn't absolutely necessary for debugging I^{2}C signals, but it's still a useful device for quickly determining whether signals are active and what the voltage levels are on those signals. As just noted, however, one useful reason for having an oscilloscope is that it allows you to monitor the analog condition of the signals appearing on the I^{2}C bus. You can easily see if the voltage levels are reasonable—that is, not too high—and whether you're getting huge voltage drops. An oscilloscope will also let you determine whether the bus capacitance has gotten out of control by showing you the rise times of the SCL and SDA signals. If it's taking too long for these signals to rise, the devices on the bus might not register those signals as a logic 1. For example, Figure 4-1 shows the SCL line in a reasonable system. This image is on a 100-kHz system with a Teensy 3.2 acting as the controller and an Adafruit ADS1115 as the peripheral. It was wired together on a "wireless" breadboard (which are famous for having a high capacitance).

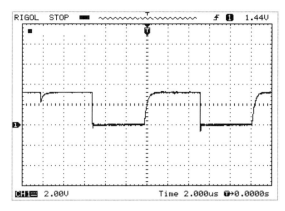

Figure 4-1: Oscilloscope image of the SCL line

Figure 4-2 shows a really bad version of the clock signal, with a very slow rise time. In this particular case I attached a 470-pF capacitor across the SCL and Gnd lines to simulate an excessive bus capacitance. As you can see, the signal suffers considerable degradation. By the time the signal has risen enough to register as high, around 2 µsec have passed. This doesn't leave the device that is putting a bit on the SDA line much time to do its job. These types of issues are most easily spotted using an oscilloscope, so oscilloscopes are handy to have around.

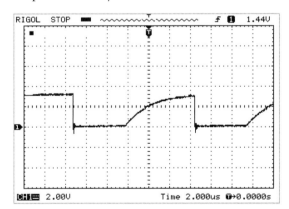

Figure 4-2: Oscilloscope image of the SCL line with high bus capacitance

A "decent" oscilloscope, one that is good enough for debugging I²C signals, will probably cost you around $300 to $600. Of course, a good, brand-name oscilloscope will cost you several thousand dollars. However, such devices are probably overkill for observing I²C bus signals. Unless you have other projects requiring the speed and features of such devices—or you really want to impress your friends—you can stick with one of the "advanced hobbyist" devices.

Some really cheap devices (sub-$100 to around $200) use a low-end LCD display or connect to your computer. They might work for someone on an extreme budget, but at some point or another you'll wind up buying a real oscilloscope if you actually use it regularly. As they say: "buy once, cry once."

4.2 Logic Analyzers

Without question, the most important tool you should obtain when working with I^2C hardware and software is a logic analyzer. Like oscilloscopes, logic analyzers come in all different shapes and sizes, with widely varying feature lists, and ranging in price from less than $30 to thousands of dollars.

At the low end are two interesting devices that, despite their low price, are actually quite useful: the I^2C Driver and the Bus Pirate. These two devices are probably more correctly called *bus monitors* or *bus drivers* rather than logic analyzers. While they have some of the features of an actual logic analyzer, the software support attached to these (open hardware or open software) projects isn't quite up to par with that you would find on true logic analyzers.

In the $300 to $500 range, things start to get more interesting. Total Phase offers several different I^2C and SPI debugging modules. These devices connect to a PC (Windows, Linux, or macOS), and software running on those machines allows you to capture and manipulate the I^2C data. (See "For More Information" at the end of this chapter for links to the Total Phase and other debugging modules this section describes.)

Another interesting device, from Analog Devices (the IC manufacturer, which makes several I^2C ICs), is the ADALM2000 Active Learning Module. This device is intended for student laboratories and supports a wide range of measurement and control options, I^2C monitoring among them.

If you really want to spend some money, the BusPro-I from Corelis is a professional-level I^2C bus analyzer available for around $1,700. Corelis also has an advanced version (at greater cost, no doubt) that can emulate I^2C controller and peripheral devices.

The devices I've described up to this point have been tools that were largely built for I^2C and SPI measurement. For the most part, these devices are simple versions of what is known as a logic analyzer. A *logic analyzer* is similar to an oscilloscope insofar as it takes a sequence of readings over time and displays the state of those readings (typically on some sort of LCD display, which is either built into the logic analyzer or on a PC to which the logic analyzer connects). There are a couple of major differences between oscilloscopes and logic analyzers, however:

- Logic analyzers are inherently *digital* devices, whereas oscilloscopes are *analog* devices.
- Logic analyzers tend to store data and display it after the fact, whereas oscilloscopes tend to be more real time.

- Logic analyzers often interpret the digital information they record according to some protocol (such as the I^2C protocol), whereas oscilloscopes tend to display just raw analog data.

- Logic analyzers tend to capture many pieces (bits) of data simultaneously (often 4 to 16 channels), whereas oscilloscopes are generally limited to 1 to 4 channels.

Not all of these differences are absolute; for example, some storage oscilloscopes can also store data, and certain logic analyzers can display their data and analysis in real time. It is even possible to get a logic analyzer and oscilloscope built into the same box. For example, the Siglent SDS1104X-E is a 100-MHz scope with a 4-channel logic analyzer, and the Owon MSO8102T and Rigol MSO1104Z-S offer 16 channels along with oscilloscope functionality.

Of course, if you're spending someone else's money, you can get some really fancy logic analyzers from Tektronix, Keysight Technologies, NCI Logic Analyzers, National Instruments, and other high-end professional instrumentation companies. However, if you don't need gigahertz sampling rates, scores of input channels, and a fancy name, or if you're having to foot the bill for this device from your own pocket, then you'll probably need to look at something a little lower end.

In the $100 to $1,000 range, a wide variety of decent logic analyzers that are USB-based and connect to a PC are available; see "For More Information" for details.

Ultimately, you'll want to ask the following questions when looking for a logic analyzer:

- Does it support the protocols you're interested in (I^2C for the time being, but you'll probably use it to debug SPI, CAN, and other bus protocols, too)?

- Is the software high quality, and does it run on your development machine?

- Is it well documented?

- Is there ongoing support (for example, software updates)?

I own a Saleae Logic 8 and can vouch for the fact that it is a high-quality unit with great support. That is not to say that these other units I've listed aren't also excellent (I don't know, I've never used them) or that some other unit not listed here would also work out well for you. However, the Saleae units have been well-received by the engineering community. Perhaps the only complaint is that they are a bit pricey ($400 to $1,000), but that's the price associated with high-quality hardware and software.

The remainder of this chapter will concentrate on three of the devices mentioned to this point: the I^2C Driver, the Bus Pirate, and the Saleae Logic 8.

4.3 The I²C Driver

The I²C Driver is a small board with a small-format color LCD display. It has three sets of I²C probes coming off the board; I'm not sure why it has more than one set, as the connectors all have the same signals and are wired together. It has a micro-USB port to connect to a Linux, Mac, or Windows PC.

When the unit comes up, it displays any I²C activity on the little LCD display. While this is pretty, it's not all that useful: I²C data transfer may be slow compared to other protocols, but it is still much faster than you can see on a display in real time.

The real functionality lies in the software that runs on the PC at the other end of the USB cable. Excamera Labs, the outfit that developed the I²C Driver, supplies some Python code to support the I²C Driver. The software is crude and bare bones but about what you can expect for $30.

The main Python software provides an interface like a command line (within Python). You perform various activities by manually calling Python functions. For example, if you want to do a bus scan to see what peripheral devices respond on the bus, enter the command `i2c.scan()` after the Python > prompt. The i2c.scan() function call displays something like the following:

```
-- -- -- -- -- -- -- --
-- -- -- -- -- -- -- --
-- -- -- -- -- -- -- --
-- -- -- -- -- -- -- --
-- -- -- -- -- -- -- --
-- -- -- -- -- -- -- --
-- -- -- -- -- -- -- --
-- -- -- -- -- -- -- --
48 -- -- -- -- -- -- --
-- -- -- -- -- -- -- --
-- -- -- -- -- -- -- --
-- -- -- -- -- -- -- --
-- -- -- -- -- -- -- --
-- -- -- -- -- -- -- --
[72]
```

where -- indicates that a device did not respond at the particular I²C address and a hexadecimal numeric value (48 being the only example here that corresponds to a responsive device address). In this case, I have a single Adafruit ADS1115 ADC breakout board configured for address 0x48 installed on the I²C bus.

The I²C Driver Python software provides many additional commands you can execute or call from Python code you write. The call `help(i2cdriver)` displays the Python application programming interface (API). Some useful commands you can execute directly include the following:

> `setspeed(speed)`   Argument is 100 or 400 (corresponding to 100 kHz or 400 kHz, respectively)

> `setpullups(bitmask)`   Argument is a 6-bit value specifying pullup values for the three I²C connectors (2 bits each, for SCL and SDA) on the I²C Driver

reset()   Sends a bus reset (general call address)

scan()   Scans the bus and displays addresses that respond

monitor(flag)   Turns on monitor mode if flag is true (nonzero); turns it off if flag is false (0)

getstatus()   Displays status information

There are also commands for starting an I^{2}C bus transaction, writing data to the bus, reading data from the bus, and sending a stop command. However, those are operations you'd normally do within a Python program.

The I^{2}C Driver software also has a GUI application that brings up the window shown in Figure 4-3. Click the **Monitor mode** button to activate monitor mode on the I^{2}C Driver's built-in LCD. Click the button again to turn monitor mode off. While not in monitor mode, select one of the addresses (if there is a device attached at that address) and read or write data to that device using the edit boxes at the bottom of the window.

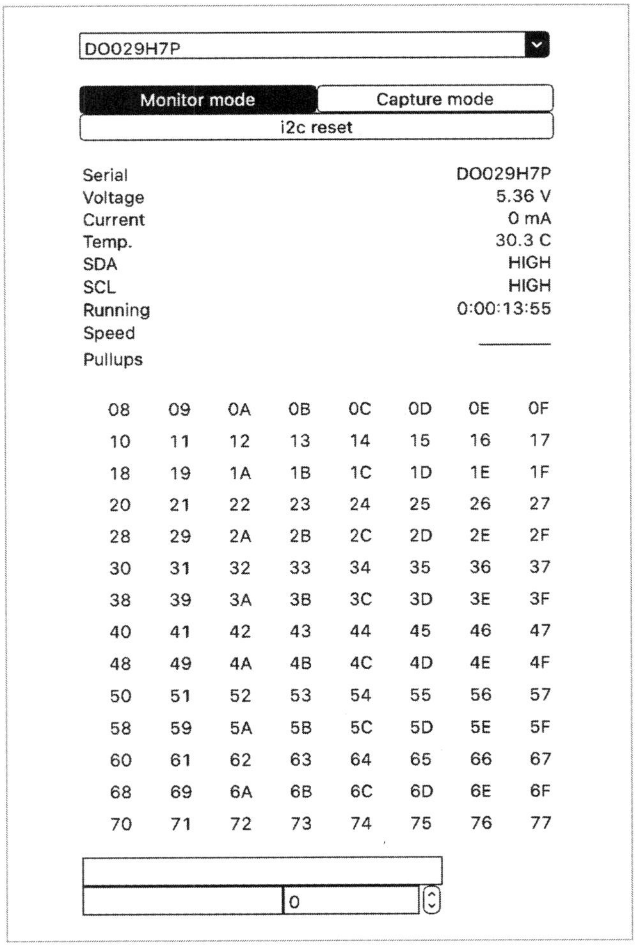

```
DO029H7P                                      ▾

  ┌──────────────────────┬──────────────────────┐
  │    Monitor mode      │     Capture mode      │
  ├──────────────────────┴──────────────────────┤
  │                  i2c reset                    │
  └───────────────────────────────────────────────┘

Serial                               DO029H7P
Voltage                                5.36 V
Current                                 0 mA
Temp.                                  30.3 C
SDA                                     HIGH
SCL                                     HIGH
Running                            0:00:13:55
Speed
Pullups                            _____

    08    09    0A    0B    0C    0D    0E    0F
    10    11    12    13    14    15    16    17
    18    19    1A    1B    1C    1D    1E    1F
    20    21    22    23    24    25    26    27
    28    29    2A    2B    2C    2D    2E    2F
    30    31    32    33    34    35    36    37
    38    39    3A    3B    3C    3D    3E    3F
    40    41    42    43    44    45    46    47
    48    49    4A    4B    4C    4D    4E    4F
    50    51    52    53    54    55    56    57
    58    59    5A    5B    5C    5D    5E    5F
    60    61    62    63    64    65    66    67
    68    69    6A    6B    6C    6D    6E    6F
    70    71    72    73    74    75    76    77

  ┌───────────────────────────────────────────────┐
  └───────────────────────────────────────────────┘
  ┌──────────────────────────────────┬────────┐
  │                  0                │     ⌄  │
  └──────────────────────────────────┴────────┘
```

Figure 4-3: I^{2}C Driver GUI display on a Mac

While there is activity on the I²C bus, click the **Capture mode** button to redirect I²C to a comma-separated values (*.csv*) file. Here's a small sample of the data from one such file:

```
START,WRITE,72,ACK
BYTE,WRITE,0,ACK
STOP,,,
START,READ,72,ACK
BYTE,READ,12,ACK
BYTE,READ,23,NACK
STOP,,,
START,WRITE,72,ACK
BYTE,WRITE,1,ACK
BYTE,WRITE,193,ACK
BYTE,WRITE,131,ACK
STOP,,,
START,WRITE,72,ACK
BYTE,WRITE,0,ACK
STOP,,,
START,READ,72,ACK
BYTE,READ,12,ACK
BYTE,READ,43,NACK
STOP,,,
START,WRITE,72,ACK
BYTE,WRITE,1,ACK
BYTE,WRITE,193,ACK
BYTE,WRITE,131,ACK
STOP,,,
```

While the I²C Driver was capturing data on the bus, I had a Teensy 3.2 talking to an Adafruit ADS1115 breakout board. Sadly, all the numbers this program displays are in decimal format, rather than the more useful hexadecimal format. The value 72_{10} is 0x48—the address of the ADS1115.

It would be easy enough to write some software to parse each of these lines and display the data in a more appropriate fashion. Unfortunately, timing information is missing from this display. However, it's open source software, so feel free to go in and modify it if you would like a different output.

Perhaps the most interesting use of the I²C Driver capture mode is for generating test result data. You can run some tests with your I²C software for a controller or peripheral, capture the output, and then compare the output against known data or run the output through a filter program that examines it for correctness. This way of generating test results is a useful tool for semi-automating complex test procedures.

Because the I²C Driver also lets you read and write data to an I²C peripheral, it's also useful for checking the operation of a peripheral device you've created. You can manually write bytes to the device, read the response from the device, and verify the results are what you expect.

Although the I²C Driver is not the be-all and end-all of I²C debugging tools, it's an interesting tool. Furthermore, it provides a USB interface to the I²C bus, which you can program from your PC; see their website for details (link provided in "For More Information"). For less than $30, having this device in your toolbox is a no-brainer.

4.4 The Bus Pirate

The Bus Pirate is another open-hardware, less-than-$30 device you can use to analyze signals on the I^2C bus. Whereas the I^2C Driver is basically a USB-to-I^2C device with a display bolted to it, the Bus Pirate is actually a small microcontroller (a PIC) that is programmed to read and write various digital I/O pins. Using bit-banging software, it emulates (slowly) the I^2C protocol. Because it's open hardware and software, is low cost, and has been around forever, the Bus Pirate has gained a tremendous following for people who want low-cost hardware hacking, analyzing, or testing capabilities.

The Bus Pirate is different from most of the other devices mentioned in this chapter because it doesn't really have any PC-related software. The Bus Pirate looks like a serial device (USB-to-serial), so you operate the Bus Pirate using a serial terminal emulation program. You enter commands into the terminal and the Bus Pirate responds appropriately. In operation, this is similar to the command-line mode of the I^2C Driver.

Most of the Bus Pirate commands are single character inputs. The most important command for you to know is the ? command. This is the help command that displays a list of all the commands to the terminal.

By default, the Bus Pirate comes up in a special *Hi-Z* (high-impedance) mode, which basically turns all the outputs off to prevent any damage to the Bus Pirate or to any device connected to the Bus Pirate. You switch to a new mode by pressing **M**. This will present you with a menu to select the new operation mode (such as I^2C mode). If you select I^2C, it will ask you to input a bus frequency.

NOTE *The Bus Pirate uses a software-only bit-banging implementation of the I^2C protocol. While it can, in theory, operate as fast as 400 kHz, it probably wouldn't hurt to operate at a sub-100 kHz speed, especially if the devices you want to monitor don't require the high speed.*

Once the Bus Pirate is running in I^2C mode, you can write data to the bus, read data from the bus, or monitor data on the bus (similar to the I^2C Driver). See the Bus Pirate documentation for more details (link provided in "For More Information").

4.5 The Saleae Logic Analyzers

Although the I^2C Driver and Bus Pirate are useful devices for certain types of I^2C monitoring, testing, and debugging, they aren't true logic analyzers. They aren't great at monitoring and displaying I^2C information in near real time. Furthermore, although both devices can monitor—and to a certain extent, capture—data on the bus, they're nearly useless for timing analysis like, for example, verifying each bit happens within a certain amount of time. This is where a real logic analyzer excels.

The Saleae Logic 8, Logic 8 Pro, and Logic 16 Pro devices are fully featured logic analyzers with 8 or 16 channels. The Logic 8 unit operates at 100 million samples per second (Msps), and the Logic 8 Pro or Logic 16 Pro units operate at 500 Msps. Generally, you want your logic analyzer to run five to ten times faster than the fastest signal you need to capture, so the Logic 8 (100 Msps) is easily good for signals in the 10 MHz to 20 MHz range. This certainly covers all I^2C frequencies.

The devices themselves provide 8 or 16 probes to connect to your circuitry. For standard I^2C measurements, you really need to connect only two of these probes, plus a ground wire. Having additional channels is useful because they let you check the status of other pins in your system during an I^2C transmission. For example, if you're sending data to a GPIO expander, you can connect some of the probes to input or output pins to see their levels change before, during, and after the I^2C transmissions.

The Logic software that runs on a PC looks something like that appearing in Figure 4-4 (macOS version). The left side of the screen defines the signals; you can specify the names appearing here. The middle section of the screen displays the timing and protocol information, and the right side of the screen lets you choose the protocols to decode.

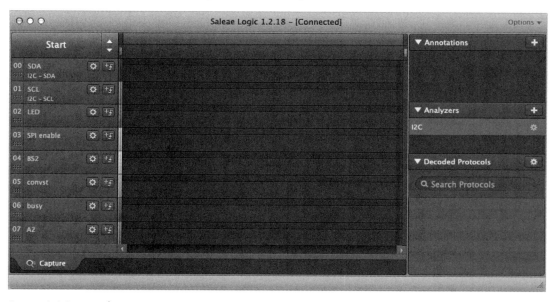

Figure 4-4: Logic software running on macOS

Clicking the **Start** button on the left side of the window initiates a capture operation. You can specify how much data to capture; I have my personal copy set up to capture data for two seconds. Figure 4-5 shows a typical data capture. As usual for this chapter, the logic analyzer is capturing the communication between a Teensy 3.2 and an ADS1115.

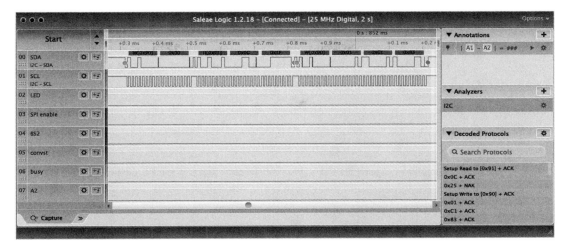

Figure 4-5: Logic software timing display

Logic has been programmed to analyze an I²C data stream. As such, it displays the address byte and R/W command and each data byte passing on the bus. It's not clear in this black-and-white image, but the display also marks the start and stop conditions with green and red dots on the data waveforms.

I've shrunk this timing diagram so you can see a complete I²C transmission. However, Logic allows you to expand or shrink the timing diagram so you can adjust the level of detail. Figure 4-6 shows the expansion of the first (address) byte transmission from Figure 4-5.

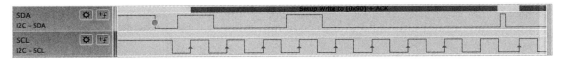

Figure 4-6: A timing expansion in Logic

Another nice feature in Logic is that you can move the cursor over a section of one of the timing signals and get timing information. Figure 4-7 shows what happened when I moved the cursor over one of the SCL clock pulses. Logic responded by displaying the width of the pulse and the frequency (5.12 µsec and 96.9 kHz). I made considerable use of this feature when working on the software-based I²C controller and peripheral implementations in the previous chapter. This is how I fine-tuned the delays to get the software I²C emulation running close to 100 kHz.

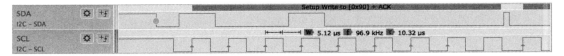

Figure 4-7: Extracting timing information from Logic

Logic also lets you set cursors within the timing diagrams so you can measure the time between any two arbitrary points, not just the width of some signal pulse. This comes in handy, for example, when measuring the time of a whole transmission rather than a single bit of a transmission.

At just under $400, the least expensive Saleae unit isn't super cheap, but having one of these devices is a sound investment if you're going to be debugging lots of I^2C code and hardware.

4.6   A Final Comment on I^2C Monitors and Logic Analyzers

Because this is *The Book of I^2C*, the discussion of the analyzers in this chapter has centered on their use for debugging and analyzing I^2C signals. In fact, most of the devices in this chapter support several other protocols as well, including SPI, CANBUS, MIDI, DMX, 1-Wire, and just about any typical protocol you can imagine. (The I^2C Driver is the exception to this; it supports only I^2C monitoring.) Therefore, the purchase of a device such as the Saleae Logic 8 is actually a good investment because you can use it for testing and debugging all kinds of hardware, not just I^2C signals.

4.7   Chapter Summary

Writing software to work with I^2C devices invariably requires testing and debugging said software. Such work is much easier accomplished using hardware testing and debugging tools. This chapter discussed several types of devices you can use for this purpose, including oscilloscopes, logic analyzers, and bus sniffers. It highlighted several commercially available options, including the I^2C Driver, the Bus Pirate, and the Salae Logic Analyer. It also mentioned various combination oscilloscope and logic analyzer options and concluded by noting that these devices are useful for debugging other protocols, not just I^2C devices, which makes them more universally applicable.

FOR MORE INFORMATION

For more information on logic analyzers, Google is your friend. Just search for "logic analyzers" or "USB-based" logic analyzers, and you should be set. You can also visit the websites of the products mentioned in this chapter:

Tech Tools DigiView: *https://www.tech-tools.com/logic-analyzer.htm*

Digital Discovery's Digilent: *https://store.digilentinc.com/digital-discovery -portable-usb-logic-analyzer-and-digital-pattern-generator*

Intronix LogicPort: *https://www.pctestinstruments.com*

Perytech Logic Analyzer: *https://www.perytech.com/Logic-Analyzer.htm*

BitScope: *https://bitscope.com*

DSLogic U3Pro16: *https://www.dreamsourcelab.com/shop/logic-analyzer/ dslogic-u3pro16*

Saleae Logic 8, Logic 8 Pro, and Logic 16 Pro: *https://www.saleae.com*

Bus Pirate: *http://dangerousprototypes.com/docs/Bus_Pirate*

Total Phase debugging modules: *https://www.totalphase.com/solutions/apps/ i2c-guide*

Analog Devices ADALM2000 active learning module: *https://wiki.analog .com/university/tools/m2k*

BusPro-I from Corelis: *https://www.corelis.com/products/serial-bus-analyzers/ i2c-bus-analyzer-exerciser-products/buspro-i2c-bus-analyzer*

I^{2}C Driver: *https://i2cdriver.com*

5

I²C VARIANTS

This chapter briefly describes several variants of the I²C bus, including the System Management Bus (SMBus), VESA DDC and E-DDC, ACCESS.bus, and two-wire interface. For the most part, these variants apply a protocol on top of the physical two-wire interface of the I²C bus, defining messages and other data flowing across the bus.

Going into detail on such protocol extensions is generally beyond the scope of this book. Nevertheless, this chapter gives an overview of those protocols (and information for other specific bus variants) and explains where you can find more information about these variants. We begin with the SMBus protocol, which deserves the most in-depth discussion, since it is widely used in computer systems.

5.1   SMBus

The *SMBus* was originally developed by Intel and Duracell as a means for managing battery power in computer-based systems. SMBus v1.0 and v1.1 dealt with low-power devices such as battery power management systems, while SMBus v2.0 added high-power devices to the specification.

It might seem unnecessary to devote a whole section to the SMBus implementation of the I^{2}C bus, since there are few SMBus peripherals and most embedded software designers don't spend much time on battery management, the SMBus's main use. However, Linux I^{2}C support, including the Raspberry Pi, provides API functions based on the SMBus protocol. For that reason alone, this slightly more-than-brief coverage of the SMBus is worthwhile. Furthermore, of all the I^{2}C extensions and variants, the SMBus is by far the most common.

Most of the few peripheral ICs that support the SMBus protocol will behave like standard I^{2}C peripherals if you ignore the information in this chapter and simply program them according to their datasheets. Many devices support some aspects of the SMBus protocol even though they do not support the full protocol. Many of the MCP23017 GPIO expander's command sequences, for example, follow the SMBus protocol in this chapter (see Chapter 13). Therefore, having an understanding of the SMBus can help you with many peripherals out there, even if they don't fully support the SMBus specification.

5.1.1   Differences Between SMBus and Standard I^{2}C

Though it's based on the I^{2}C bus, the SMBus places some additional requirements on the I^{2}C signals:

- The clock—SMBCLK, the SMBus name for SCL—must be between 10 kHz and 100 kHz. In particular, note that SMBus does not support arbitrary clock stretching (below 10 kHz). Later versions of the SMBus specification also support 400-kHz and 1-MHz signals.

- SMBus v3.0 supports signal voltages in the range of 1.8 V to 5 V. Also, SMBus explicitly states that a logic 0 is less than 0.8 V and a logic 1 is greater than 1.35 V.

- SMBus specifies a clock low timeout of 35 msec (about 15 Hz, assuming a 50 percent duty cycle). The I^{2}C standard specifies no such timeout.

- SMBus specifies both rise and fall times for bus signals; the I^{2}C standard provides no such specifications (other than bus capacitance, which affects rise and fall times).

- NAK behavior is different between I^{2}C and SMBus.

- SMBus devices must always acknowledge the receipt of their address on the I^{2}C bus; standard I^{2}C protocol doesn't require this (for example, if the device is busy doing something else).

- The SMBus supports three types of devices on the bus: controllers, peripherals, and a single, special version of a controller known as the *host*.

- All devices on the SMBus must have a unique ID associated with them.
- SMBus v2.0 introduced the concept of a dynamically assigned device address.
- SMBus supports optional hardware signals, SMBAlert and SMBSuspend, that can create interrupts or suspend operations for low-power operation.

The SMBus also reserves certain device addresses for purposes such as prototype devices, far beyond the number that the I^2C bus reserves for special use. The SMBus also supports dynamically specified device addresses, allowing devices to choose their addresses during operation.

On top of the hardware differences, the SMBus specification calls out several protocol changes, including features for transferring blocks of data, bus-specific commands, and device enumeration. The SMBus specification provides more details (link provided in "For More Information" at the end of this chapter).

5.1.2   SMBus Electrical Specifications

As noted previously, the SMBus SMBCLK signal must operate between 10 kHz and maximum bus speed (100 kHz, 400 kHz, or 1 MHz). In reality, most modern SMBus implementations operate at 50 kHz or faster. NXP's documentation (see the SMBus quick start guide in "For More Information") states that a system must not reduce the clock frequency to the minimum speed even in response to clock stretching on the part of peripheral devices. In addition, SMBus devices must be ready to operate within 500 msec after power is applied.

The SMBus has better electrical specifications than the standard I^2C bus. It defines a logic 0 on the clock or data lines as 0.8 V or less and a logic 1 as 1.35 V or greater.

5.1.3   SMBus Reserved Addresses

The SMBus reserves several addresses above and beyond the I^2C reserved addresses (see section 2.5, "Special Addresses," in Chapter 2). In addition to these addresses, the SMBus reserves 7-bit addresses 0x08 for SMBus host devices, 0x0C for SMBus alert responses, and 0x61 for the SMBus device default address. The SMBus specification also reserves certain device address for specific purposes, as described in Table 5-1.

Table 5-1: Reserved SMBus Device Addresses

Address bits	Description
0001-000	SMBus host
0001-001	Smart battery charger
0001-010	Smart battery selector or smart battery system manager

(continued)

Table 5-1: Reserved SMBus Device Addresses *(continued)*

Address bits	Description
0001-011	Smart battery
0001-100	SMBus alert response
0101-000	ACCESS.bus host
0101-100	Originally reserved for LCD contrast controllers (may be reassigned in future versions of the SMBus)
0101-101	Originally reserved for CCFL backlight controllers (may be reassigned in future versions of the SMBus)
0110-111	ACCESS.bus default address
1000-0xx	Originally reserved for PCMCIA socket controllers (may be reassigned in future versions of the SMBus)
1000-100	Originally reserved for VGA graphics controllers (may be reassigned in future versions of the SMBus)
1001-0xx	Unrestricted addresses
1100-001	SMBus device default address

Please consult the SMBus documentation to see if there are any additions to this list. Later versions of the SMBus standard may add device addresses to this list.

5.1.4   SMBus Protocol Commands

The standard I^{2}C bus protocol specifies only the address byte, and R/W bit, format. It does not define any further data appearing on the bus. In contrast, the SMBus protocol defines several different command formats including Quick Command, Send Byte, Receive Byte, Write Byte, Write Word, Read Byte, Read Word, Process Call, Block Read, and Block Write.

NOTE *The SMBus specification also provides for a Block Write-Block Read Process Call. This book will not cover that particular command. See the SMBus specification for more details (the link is in "For More Information").*

SMBus devices do not have to implement all the SMBus protocol commands—only those that are relevant to the particular device. If a device supports the Quick Command, it likely supports only that command. Similarly, if the device supports the Read Byte command and the Send Byte command, it likely supports only those two commands. The remaining SMBus protocol commands include an extra *command byte*; this byte can specify the particular command protocol to use. The following subsections define each of these command types.

5.1.4.1 SMBus Quick Commands

SMBus Quick Commands are simple 1-bit commands built into the R/W bit of the address byte (see Figure 5-1). The Quick Commands transmit a single bit to the peripheral device that can be used to turn the device on or off or perform some other operation based on a single bit of binary data.

Figure 5-1: Quick Command format

There is no additional data beyond the address byte sent to the device with a Quick Command.

5.1.4.2 SMBus Send Byte and Read Byte Commands

The SMBus Send Byte and Read Byte commands include 1 byte of data after the address byte. The R/W bit of the address byte specifies the particular command (read or write; see Figure 5-2).

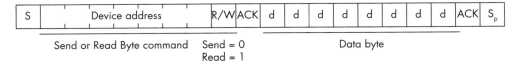

Figure 5-2: Send or Read Byte command format

With a Send Byte command, the host/controller device transmits the second byte to the peripheral; with the Read Byte command, the peripheral places the data on the SMBDAT (SDA) line to be read by the host/controller device.

5.1.4.3 SMBus Read Byte and Read Word Commands

The SMBus Read Byte command allows you to read a single byte of data from a peripheral device with no way to specify what byte data you're reading. That command is useful for simple devices that return a single byte value, such as reading a single set of eight digital I/O pins. The SMBus Read Byte and Word commands, on the other hand, include a special command byte that allows you to specify parameter information to select the particular byte you want to read. This could be, for example, a register or memory address or other selection or control information. The sequence for a Read Byte command appears in Figure 5-3.

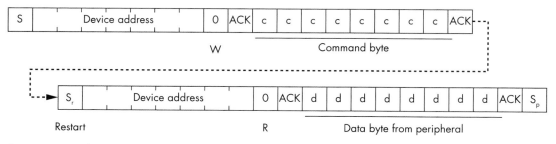

Figure 5-3: Read Byte command format

The sequence for a Read Word command appears in Figure 5-4.

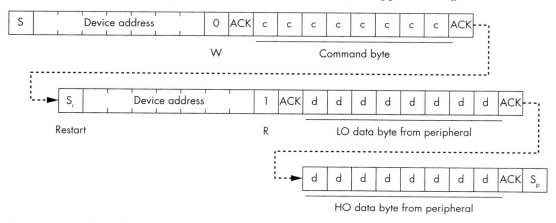

Figure 5-4: Read Word command format

Because the controller must first write the command byte to the peripheral device, the Read Byte and Read Word commands begin with a write operation (bit 0 of the address byte contains a 0). Then the sequence must include a restart operation followed by a second address byte with bit 0 containing a 1 (for read). Then the controller reads the next byte or word (depending on the command) from the peripheral device.

Not all devices support both Read Byte and Read Word commands. The peripheral device's design determines whether the controller can read a single byte, a word, or both. If the device supports reading both bytes and words using this command, then the controller must somehow specify whether it wants to read a byte or a word from the device, typically using a bit within the command byte.

5.1.4.4 SMBus Write Byte and Write Word Commands

The SMBus Write Byte and Write Word commands also include a command byte that allows you to specify parameter information to select the particular byte or word you want to write to the peripheral. This could be a register or memory address or other selection or control information. The sequence for a Write Byte command appears in Figure 5-5.

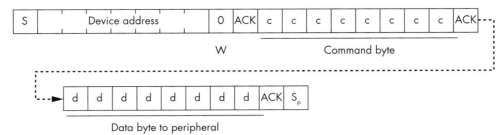

Data byte to peripheral

Figure 5-5: Write Byte command format

The sequence for a Write Word command appears in Figure 5-6.

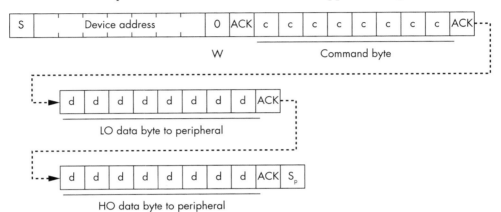

Figure 5-6: Write Word command format

Because the controller is strictly writing to the peripheral device, there is no need for the restart command and the extra address-R/W byte in these sequences. As for the Read Byte and Read Word commands, the device's design determines whether it supports the Write Byte, Write Word, or both commands. If the device supports both byte and word writes, then presumably the controller must somehow specify the size to write within the command byte.

5.1.4.5 SMBus Block Read Command

Although most SMBus transactions involve reading or writing a single byte or word, a few devices support larger data transfers. The SMBus Block Read command handles reading blocks of data. As for the Read Byte and Read Word command, the controller transmits an address byte (with the LO bit equal to 0 to denote a write operation) followed by a command byte. Then the controller sends a repeated start operation followed by an address byte with the LO bit equal to 1 (to denote a read). The peripheral responds by sending a byte containing the byte count followed by that many data bytes, as shown in Figure 5-7.

The peripheral specifies how many bytes it is returning in the byte count value. In theory, it is possible for the controller to specify how many bytes it wants to read by providing this count as part of the command byte field. However, the peripheral's design determines who specifies the number of bytes returned; it could be a fixed value or a programmed value.

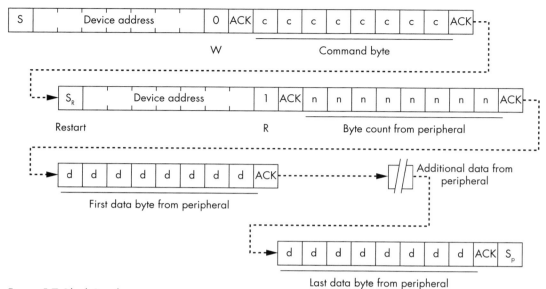

Figure 5-7: Block Read sequence

5.1.4.6   SMBus Block Write Command

Of course, the SMBus provides a Block Write complement to the Block Read command. The command is a bit simpler than the Block Read command, as you don't have to reverse the data direction after sending the command byte. Figure 5-8 provides the write sequence.

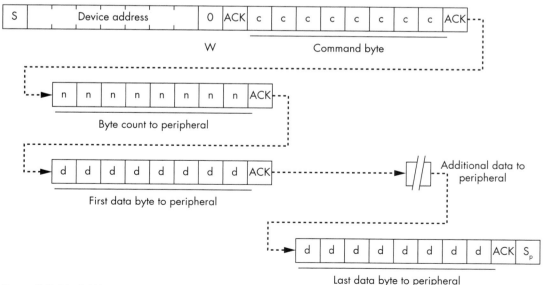

Figure 5-8: Block Write sequence

Because there is no need to resend the device address with a new R/W bit, this sequence is shorter (and more efficient) than the Block Read command operation.

5.2   VESA DDC and E-DDC

The VESA DDC (obsolete) and E-DDC (modern) interfaces allow communication between a host (computer) system and a display monitor (the VESA device). The DDC/E-DDC (hereafter E-DDC) is a two-wire communication bus built on the I^2C bus. The E-DDC protocol allows the host system to determine monitor information, set display parameters such as brightness, and perform other operations.

Displays that are compatible with VESA E-DDC look like I^2C peripherals on the I^2C bus. In particular, compatible devices can respond to the (8-bit) addresses 0xA0, 0xA1, 0xA4, or 0xA5 and a command register at address 0x60. The host (computer) exchanges information with the display through these addresses. For the most part, this is display identification and parameter information.

VESA specifies I^2C signaling only in the VGA, HDMI, and DVI interfaces. DisplayPort interfaces use a different mechanism for transferring data between the host computer and the display device. See the VESA E-DDC specifications for more details (link in "For More Information").

5.3   ACCESS.bus

The ACCESS.bus system was an early, pre-USB attempt to allow the attachment of low-speed peripheral devices such as keyboards and mice to a computer system. The intent was to support hot-pluggable devices that could be attached and removed without powering down the system, unlike AT and PS-2 keyboards of that era. ACCESS.bus was based on the I^2C bus, supporting up to 125 devices.

As USB arrived about a year later, interest in ACCESS.bus quickly diminished, though it did become the basis for the VESA DDC communication system (and the obsolete Apple Desktop Bus).

5.4   Two-Wire Interface and Two-Wire Serial Interface

Two-wire interface (TWI) and *two-wire serial interface (TWSI)* are names that various manufacturers use to avoid trademark and compliance issues with I^2C. Some manufacturers will often use TWI when their devices don't completely support the full I^2C standard—if a device doesn't support the START byte, for example. Some people use this term if the bus doesn't support multiple controllers, clock stretching, or other I^2C features. In general, if you see this term being used, you can probably assume that the device doesn't fully support the I^2C standard, though it will likely work fine in your application if you aren't relying on cutting-edge features.

5.5 Chapter Summary

This chapter briefly covered various protocol extensions to the I^{2}C bus including the SMBus, VESA (DDC and E-DDC), ACCESS.bus, and the TWI. Of these, the SMBus and VESA bus are commonly used today. The SMBus is largely employed for system power management, and the VESA variants are used to control video displays.

The SMBus protocol is significant because Linux's I^{2}C support is based on it. Therefore, this chapter spent considerable time discussing several SMBus commands, including Quick Commands, Send and Read Byte commands, Read Byte and Read Word commands, Write Byte and Write Word commands, and Block Read and Block Write commands.

Unless you are dealing with the specific device categories these higher-level protocols support, it's unlikely you'll need more than a passing familiarity with these protocols. Nevertheless, it is important to understand that, at their core, these protocols are still based on the venerable I^{2}C bus.

FOR MORE INFORMATION

SMBus website: *http://smbus.org*

SMBus specification: *http://smbus.org/specs*

SMBus Quick Start Guide: *https://www.nxp.com/docs/en/application-note/AN4471.pdf*

VESA homepage: *https://vesa.org*

VESA EDDC v1.2 standard: *https://glenwing.github.io/docs/VESA-EDDC-1.2.pdf*

VESA EDID description: *https://media.extron.com/public/download/files/articles/understandingedid.pdf*

VESA DDC description: *https://en.wikipedia.org/wiki/Display_Data_Channel*

ACCESS.bus wiki page: *https://en.wikipedia.org/wiki/ACCESS.bus*

ACCESS.bus v3.0 specification: *https://www.mcc-us.com/abspec30.htm*

PART II

HARDWARE IMPLEMENTATIONS

6

I²C ON COMMON SINGLE-BOARD COMPUTERS

Several common single-board computers provide at least one I²C port for interfacing with I²C peripherals. While some low-end boards might use a software implementation (or a quasi-hardware implementation, like that of the ATtiny84), I²C support is near universal on most hobbyist-level and professional SBCs. This chapter provides a brief introduction to the I²C implementations found on many common SBCs.

The list of SBCs in this chapter is far from exhaustive and focuses on more commonly used, low-cost SBCs. I intend not to provide low-level details of the I²C interfaces on these SBCs but to give an overview of the various boards that support I²C communications. I include links to the various web pages (see "For More Information" at the end of this chapter) that describe each of these boards in more detail for those who are interested in following up on them.

Of course, many new single-board computers that support the I²C interface will appear after this book's publication. The online chapters (available at *https://bookofi2c.randallhyde.com*) will include continuously updated information on many new SBCs that do not appear in this chapter.

6.1 The Arduino Family

The Arduino family is one of the more popular choices for connecting I²C devices. Whenever someone exhausts the limited I/O ports (analog or digital) on the Arduino board or wants to connect something that doesn't have a simple digital or analog interface (such as a thermocouple or a small display), the I²C interface often provides the solution.

The Arduino is not a single computer board. True, when most people use the term *Arduino*, they're probably referring to the Arduino Uno Rev3 SBC. However, a wide variety of Arduino boards exists with many different types of I²C interfaces on them.

First, Arduino® is a registered trademark of Arduino. However, the Arduino design is open source and open hardware, so there are many different single-board computers out there that are, more or less, compatible with the Arduino system. This book will adopt the attitude that any SBC you can program using the Arduino IDE and Arduino libraries is an Arduino or, more correctly, is *Arduino compatible*. For example, because you typically program it using the Arduino IDE, this book considers the SparkFun ATTO84 board used in Chapter 3 (see section 3.2, "Basic ATtiny84 and ATtiny85 Hardware," in Chapter 3) as Arduino compatible even though it lacks many of the features found on common Arduino-compatible devices, including a fully supported hardware I²C interface.

NOTE *The Arduino trademark lawyers would disagree with the idea that any SBC you can program using the Arduino IDE and Arduino libraries is an Arduino. An SBC product may not include the word* Arduino *as part of the product name, at least in most parts of the world. See* https://www.arduino.cc/en/Trademark/HomePage *for all the legal stuff.*

Because a large number of Arduino-compatible boards is available, discussing "the I²C port on an Arduino" as though it were a standard connection is difficult. I²C ports on Arduino-class devices may differ from one another in the following ways:

- Some ports are 3.3 V; some are 5 V.
- Different Arduino-class devices can have zero, one, two, or more hardware I²C ports available.
- Some devices might not support hardware-based peripheral mode.
- Some devices might not support multiple controllers on the same I²C bus.
- Some devices might not support other I²C bus features, such as clock stretching.

The bottom line is that you must look carefully at the documentation for your particular "Arduino" board to determine which I²C features it supports (if it supports I²C at all).

Even from Arduino, you have a wide variety of Arduino models to choose from. The following subsections describe some popular models and their support for I²C.

6.1.1   The Arduino Uno Rev3 and Leonardo

The Uno Rev3 is the classic Arduino unit. It has a 16-MHz, 8-bit ATmega328P with the following features:

- 5-V operation
- Standard Arduino pinout and expansion bus (for shields)
- Single I²C interface (5 V)
- 32-KB flash ROM for program storage
- 2-KB RAM
- 1-KB EEPROM (nonvolatile storage)

Figure 6-1 shows the location of the I²C lines on the Arduino bus.

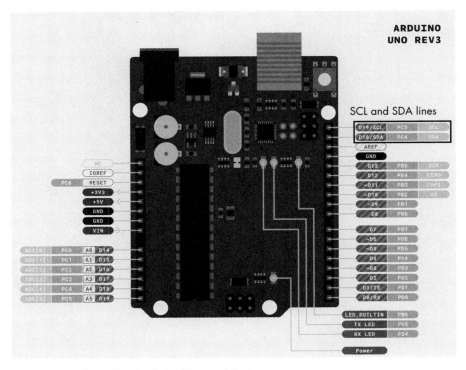

Figure 6-1: Arduino Uno Rev3 (and Leonardo) pinouts

The Arduino Leonardo uses (mostly) the same CPU and pinouts that the Arduino Uno Rev3 uses. The major difference is that the Leonardo was the first Arduino to include a built-in USB port that could be programmed to act as a keyboard or other USB device; it also has an ATmega32u4 with 2.5-KB RAM. Of course, the Uno Rev3 (versus the original Uno) also has a built-in USB, so there is little benefit to the Leonardo over the Uno Rev3 (though the Leonard does have more analog I/O pins). See "For More Information" for more details.

Note that the Arduino pinouts appearing in this chapter come from the Arduino website (*https://www.arduino.cc*). These images are covered under the Creative Commons 4.0 license (free to use with attribution). See *https://www.arduino.cc/en/Main/FAQ* and *https://www.arduino.cc/en/Trademark/HomePage* for more legal rigmarole from Arduino.

6.1.2   The Arduino Nano

The Arduino Nano uses the same CPU as that of the Arduino Uno Rev3, which means their tech specs are the same, but the Arduino Nano is packaged into a much smaller footprint for use in space-critical applications. Figure 6-2 shows the pinouts for the Nano.

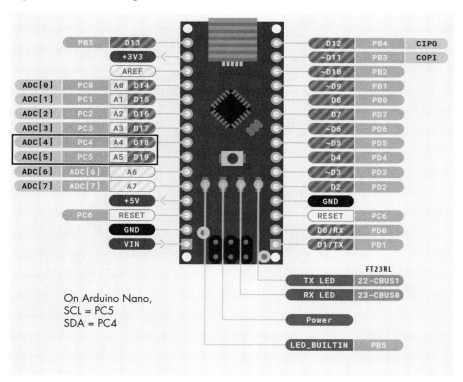

Figure 6-2: Arduino Nano pinouts

The Arduino Nano uses pins A4 and A5 for the SDA and SCL lines, respectively; these are the standard pins for I^{2}C on many Arduino units.

6.1.3 The Arduino Micro

The Arduino Micro is another small form factor Arduino unit. It has a slightly beefier CPU than that of the Nano:

- ATmega32U4 CPU at 16 MHz
- 32-KB flash for program storage
- 2.5-KB RAM
- 1-KB EEPROM

Figure 6-3 shows the Arduino Micro pinouts.

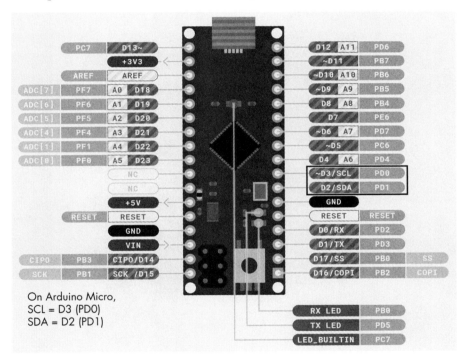

Figure 6-3: Arduino Micro pinouts

The I^{2}C bus appears on pins D2 (SDA) and D3 (SCL).

6.1.4   The Arduino Nano Every

The Arduino Nano Every is a much beefier version of the Nano (and Micro) while still using a compact form factor. The Arduino Nano Every has the following features:

- ATMega4809 at 20 MHz
- 5-V operation
- 48-KB flash storage
- 6-KB RAM
- 256-byte EEPROM

Figure 6-4 shows the Arduino Nano Every pinouts.

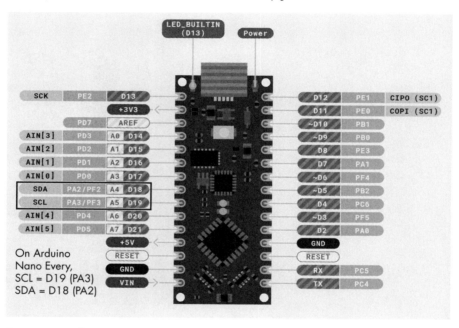

Figure 6-4: Arduino Nano Every pinouts

The Nano Every supports a single I^{2}C port on pins D18 (PA2) and D19 (PA3).

6.1.5   The Arduino Mega 2560 Rev3

The Arduino Mega 2560 Rev3 (or just "Arduino Mega") is physically the largest of the common Arduino boards. It has the following feature set:

- 5-V operation
- 8-bit CPU running at 16 MHz
- Mega expansion shield capabilities (which is mostly an upwards-compatible variant of the standard Arduino Shield connections)

- Single I^{2}C interface (5 V)
- 256-KB flash ROM for program storage
- 8-KB RAM
- 4-KB EEPROM (nonvolatile storage)

Because of the large number of I/O pins, the Arduino Mega board is laid out differently from the Uno. However, most standard Uno shields will fit on the corresponding connectors on the Mega board (see Figure 6-5).

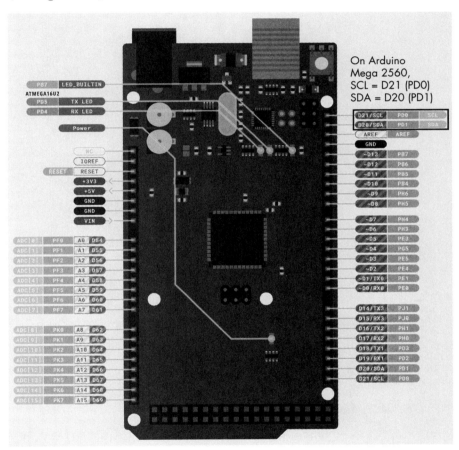

Figure 6-5: Arduino Mega 2560 Rev3 pinouts

The Arduino Uno Rev3 is upwards compatible with the Arduino Mega 2560 Rev3's bus. Therefore, the I^{2}C pins appear at the same physical locations as they do on the Uno Rev3; however, note that electrically, these signals appear on the D20 and D21 signals rather than on the D18 and D19 signals of the Rev3.

6.1.6 The Arduino Zero

The Arduino Zero is a high-performance, 32-bit board based on the ARM Cortex M0+. It has 256KB of flash memory for program storage and 32KB of RAM (no EEPROM). Electrically, there is one huge difference between the Arduino Zero and its 8-bit brothers: all pins on the Zero are 3.3 V, including its I²C pins. See Figure 6-6 for the Arduino Zero pinouts.

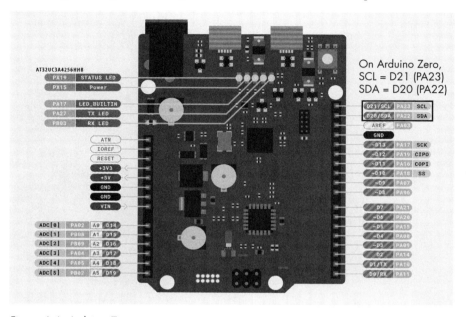

Figure 6-6: Arduino Zero pinouts

The pins on the board are laid out to be physically compatible with the Arduino Uno. However, keep in mind they are not *electrically* compatible, as they are 3.3-V logic.

6.1.7 The Arduino Due

The Arduino Due is currently the highest-performance official Arduino board. It has the following features:

- 32-bit CPU at 84 MHz, based on the Atmel SAM3X8E ARM Cortex M3
- 512-KB flash memory for program storage
- 96-KB RAM
- Massive number of I/O pins (comparable to Mega 2560)
- 3.3-V operation

Figure 6-7 provides the pinouts.

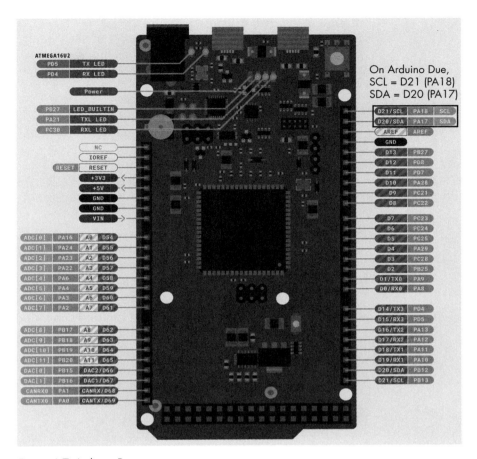

On Arduino Due,
SCL = D21 (PA18)
SDA = D20 (PA17)

Figure 6-7: Arduino Due pinouts

The Arduino Due is basically the 32-bit version of the Arduino Mega 2560 (but with 3.3-V pins). It drops four ADC inputs and replaces them with DAC and CANBUS ports.

6.1.8 Other Arduino-Brand Single-Board Computers

This section has covered the main SBCs available from Arduino. However, this chapter ignores several additional boards intended for the Internet of Things (IoT), and Arduino is constantly producing new products. Visit its website at *https://www.arduino.cc* to check out the latest offerings.

6.2 Adafruit Single-Board Computers

Adafruit produces many SBCs that provide I^2C capability and Arduino compatibility. Perhaps number one on this list is the Adafruit Metro 328 (*https://www.adafruit.com/product/50*), which is a clone of an Arduino Uno with a few improvements. Adafruit also provides several small form factor Arduino IDE–compatible boards. Here are some of the SBCs Adafruit offered as this chapter was being written. You can find technical information for each at the links provided:

- Adafruit Metro Mini 328: a "stick of gum"-sized version of the Metro 328: *https://www.adafruit.com/product/2590*
- Adafruit METRO M0 Express: a 32-bit version of the Metro 328: *https://www.adafruit.com/product/3505*
- Adafruit Metro M4 Express AirLift and Metro M4 Feat: 32-bit versions (AirLift has built-in Wi-Fi) and high speed (120 MHz) with hardware floating-point support: *https://www.adafruit.com/product/4000* and *https://www.adafruit.com/product/3382*
- Adafruit Grand Central M4 Express: similar to the Arduino Due with a high-performance, 32-bit CPU and lots of I/O pins: *https://www.adafruit.com/product/4064*
- Arduino Pro Mini 328: another small unit (3.3-V and 5-V versions): *https://www.adafruit.com/product/2378*
- Adafruit FLORA, GEMMA M0, and Circuit Playground (or Circuit Playground Express) Miniature wearable electronic platform devices:

  - Circuit Playground Express: *https://www.adafruit.com/product/3333*
  - Circuit Playground Classic: *https://www.adafruit.com/product/3000*
  - Flora: *https://www.adafruit.com/product/659*
  - Gemma v2: *https://www.adafruit.com/product/1222*
  - Gemma M0: *https://www.adafruit.com/product/3501*

- Adafruit Trinket M0: a very small form factor, 32-bit SBC: *https://www.adafruit.com/product/3500*
- Adafruit ItsyBitsy M0 Express and ItsyBitsy 32u4: modern versions of the Trinket with lots of I/O pins: *https://www.adafruit.com/product/3727* and *https://www.adafruit.com/product/3677*
- Adafruit Bluefruit LE Micro: a mini-SBC with built-in Bluetooth: *https://www.adafruit.com/product/2661*

Because of the wide variety of available boards, this chapter doesn't include the pinouts for each of these boards. See the Adafruit website for that information.

In addition to these SBCs, Adafruit offers a large line of Adafruit Feather SBCs. See section 7.1.2, "I^2C on the Feather Bus," in Chapter 7 for more information about the Feather bus.

Adafruit is constantly creating new SBCs that support the I^2C bus, particularly Feather-based units. Almost all Adafruit SBCs fully support I^2C in hardware. By the time you're reading this, Adafruit has probably introduced many other boards that do not appear here, and no doubt I've missed a few while fishing for information on the Adafruit website. Visit *https://www .adafruit.com/category/17* to check out any new Arduino IDE–compatible units Adafruit may have developed.

6.3   SparkFun Single-Board Computers

SparkFun is the "little brother" to Adafruit. Both companies cater to electronics and software hobbyists and makers by supplying a wide variety of SBCs and modules that plug into those SBCs. Whereas Adafruit is famous for its Feather modules, SparkFun is known for the creation of the Qwiic ("quick") bus based on I^2C technology. SparkFun provides a wide variety of SBCs that support I^2C, quite often using a Qwiic connector. The following are some of its most recent offerings:

- SparkFun RedBoard: SparkFun's variant of the Arduino Uno: *https://www.sparkfun.com/products/13975* and *https://www.sparkfun.com/ products/15123*

- SparkFun Qwiic Pro Micro, USB-C: small form factor Arduino-compatible module: *https://www.sparkfun.com/products/15795*

- SparkFun RedBoard Turbo: 32-bit Cortex M0+ (ARM) variant of the RedBoard: *https://www.sparkfun.com/products/14812*

- SparkFun Pro nRF52840 Mini: a mini board with Bluetooth capabilities: *https://www.sparkfun.com/products/15025*

- SparkFun Thing Plus, ESP32 WROOM: an ESP-32–based module that supports Bluetooth and Wi-Fi: *https://www.sparkfun.com/products/15663*

- SparkFun RedBoard Artemis Nano: a small-footprint, high-performance SBC with four on-board I^2C ports: *https://www.sparkfun.com/products/ 15443*

- SparkFun RedBoard Artemis: a high-performance, 32-bit CPU with up to six independent I^2C buses in an Arduino Uno form factor: *https:// www.sparkfun.com/products/15444*

- SparkFun RedBoard Artemis ATP: a mega-footprint version of the Artemis with up to six I^2C buses: *https://www.sparkfun.com/products/15442*

- SparkFun Thing Plus, Artemis: an Artemis module in a Feather form factor (see section 7.1.2, "I^2C on the Feather Bus," in Chapter 7) that supports two I^2C buses: *https://www.sparkfun.com/products/15574*

- SparkFun Thing Plus, SAMD51: Cortex M4 (ARM)-based high-performance module in a very small footprint: *https://www.sparkfun .com/products/14713*

- FreeSoC2 Development Board: Freescale Cortex M3 (ARM)-based board: *https://www.sparkfun.com/products/13714*

- SparkFun RED-V RedBoard: a RISC-V–based Arduino Uno form factor board. Note that this board is not programmed using the Arduino IDE (at least, as this was being written): *https://www.sparkfun.com/products/15594*

- SparkFun RED-V Thing Plus: small form factor version of the RED-V: *https://www.sparkfun.com/products/15799*

- SparkFun Edge Development Board, Apollo3 Blue: a Cortex M4–based development module for edge (AI) computing: *https://www.sparkfun.com/products/15170*

- Alchitry Au FPGA Development Board: not a single-board *computer* at all. This is a Field Programmable Gate Array (FPGA) module with I^2C support. Two versions are available: Alchitry Au (Gold) at *https://www.sparkfun.com/products/16527* and Alchitry Cu (Copper) at *https://www.sparkfun.com/products/16526*.

Because of the wide variety of available boards, this chapter will not include the pinouts for each of these boards. See the SparkFun website for that information. For more on the Qwiic bus in this book, see section 7.2, "I^2C on the SparkFun Qwiic Bus," in Chapter 7.

As usual, you can expect that this list has expanded since this chapter was written. Visit the SparkFun website (*https://www.sparkfun.com*) to check out what is currently available.

6.4 The Teensy Family

The Teensy series from PJRC is a popular set of microcontroller boards that you can program using the Arduino IDE with a set of libraries that PJRC provides. The Teensy series is popular with designers who want to program high-performance embedded systems using very small (dare I say, *teensy*) MCU modules.

As this was being written, PJRC was selling eight different SBC modules:

- Teensy 2.0: based on an 8-bit CPU (soon to be deprecated). Provides a single I^2C port.

- Teensy++ 2.0: an expanded (I/O) version of the Teensy 2.0 (also soon to be deprecated). Provides a single I^2C port.

- Teensy LC: a low-cost, 32-bit version of the Teensy, 3.3 V only. Provides two I^2C ports.

- Teensy 3.2: a 32-bit, Cortex M4 (ARM) CPU running at 72 MHz (over-clockable to 96 MHz), 3.3 V with 5-V–tolerant pins. About the size of two postage stamps. Provides two I^2C ports.

- Teensy 3.5: a 32-bit, Cortex M4 CPU running at 120 MHz, 3.3 V with 5-V–tolerant pins. About the size of a big stick of gum. Provides three I^2C ports.

- Teensy 3.6: a 32-bit, Cortex M4 CPU running at 180 MHz, 3.3 V only (no 5-V–tolerant pins). About the size of a big stick of gum. Provides four I^2C ports.

- Teensy 4.0: a 32-bit, Cortex M7 (ARM) CPU running at 600 MHz (overclockable to 1 GHz), 3.3 V only. About the size of two postage stamps. Provides three I^2C ports.

- Teensy 4.1: a 32-bit, Cortex M7 (ARM) CPU running at 600 MHz (overclockable to 1 GHz), 3.3V only. Expanded I/O version of Teensy 4.0 with Ethernet and SD card support. About the size of a big stick of gum. Provides three I^2C ports.

All Teensy I^2C interfaces are hardware controlled. With Teensy-specific library code, you can operate these I^2C interfaces at 400 MHz. Read about these SBCs at *https://www.pjrc.com/store/index.html*.

6.5 Other Arduino-Compatible Single-Board Computers

Because the Arduino design is open source and open hardware, many different companies produce Arduino-compatible boards. You can find some Chinese knock-offs for less than $10 online if you look hard enough. One vendor to look at is Seeed Studio, which is advertising Arduino-compatible boards for less than $8 on its website as I was writing this (*https://www .seeedstudio.com/Seeeduino-V4-2-p-2517.html*). Seeed Studio also promotes the Grove interconnection bus (see section 7.4, "I^2C on the Seeed Studio Grove Bus," in Chapter 7), which has a large ecosystem of sensors and other devices that connect to Grove-compatible boards.

If you're interested in other sources of Arduino-compatible boards, check out the following Wikipedia page that lists Arduinos and Arduino-compatible devices: *https://en.wikipedia.org/wiki/List_of_Arduino_boards _and_compatible_systems*.

Many various boards are compatible with the Arduino IDE that cover many different performance levels, memory capabilities, and I/O capabilities. Almost all Arduino-compatible boards include at least one hardware I^2C interface, as I^2C is one of the most common ways to expand the I/O capabilities of an Arduino device.

6.6 The Raspberry Pi

After the Arduino SBCs, the Raspberry Pi is perhaps the next most popular SBC used for interfacing to real-world devices via I^2C. Figure 6-8 shows the pins on the Raspberry Pi GPIO connector where the *hardware* I^2C pins are located. I emphasize hardware because the Pi also supports software-controlled I^2C ports (more about that a little later).

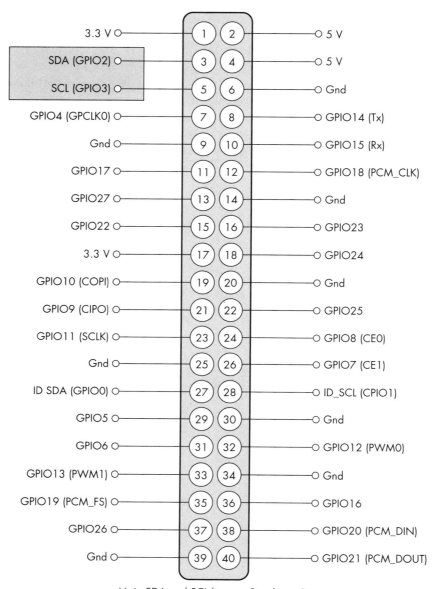

Main SDA and SCL lines on Raspberry Pi

Figure 6-8: GPIO pinouts on the Raspberry Pi (40-pin connector). This image is copyrighted by the Raspberry Pi Foundation. Use here is allowed by the Creative Commons 4.0 license.

The Raspberry Pi is a 3.3-V device. Therefore, you must connect only 3.3-V I²C devices to the Pi's GPIO connector. Connecting 5-V devices could damage the Raspberry Pi. If you need to use 5-V devices with the Pi, be sure to use a level converter, such as the TXB0104 Bi-Directional Level Shifter (*https://www.adafruit.com/product/1875*).

There are a couple of known issues with the Raspberry Pi I^{2}C interface. In particular, it does not support (at least at the time of writing) hardware clock stretching, so you cannot connect devices that add wait states by stretching the clock. However, you can specify a lower clock frequency; in some cases, this will solve the problem. It is also possible to use a software-based I^{2}C system (using a pair of the GPIO pins as SDA and SCL). Software-based solutions can support clock stretching. See *https://github.com/fivdi/i2c-bus/ blob/master/doc/raspberry-pi-software-i2c.md* for details on setting up a software-based I^{2}C port on the Raspberry Pi. Also see *https://forums.raspberrypi.com/ viewtopic.php?t=302381* for information concerning clock stretching on the Pi 4.

6.7   The Raspberry Pi Pico

In 2021, the Raspberry Pi folks introduced their own embedded microcontroller, the RP2040, along with a small single-board computer, the Raspberry Pi Pico. This device was built to compete with the likes of Arduino boards in small, real-time embedded applications. The RP2040 has the following feature set:

- Dual-core Arm Cortex M0+ at 133 MHz
- 264KB of on-chip RAM
- Support for up to 16MB of off-chip flash memory via a dedicated QSPI bus (the Pico board provides 2MB of flash ROM)
- DMA controller
- Interpolator and integer divider peripherals
- 30 GPIO pins, 4 of which can be used as analog inputs
- Two UARTs, two SPI controllers, and two I^{2}C controllers
- 16 PWM channels
- One USB 1.1 controller and PHY, with host and device support
- Eight Raspberry Pi Programmable I/O (PIO) state machines
- USB mass-storage boot mode with UF2 support, for drag-and-drop programming
- Cost of only $4 at the time of writing

The Raspberry Pi Pico supports two independent I^{2}C ports, which can be assigned to any pair of digital I/O pins on the device (see Figure 6-9). The Raspberry Pi Pico is a 3.3-V device, which means you can connect only 3.3-V I^{2}C devices to the Pico's I^{2}C pins. Connecting 5-V devices could damage the Raspberry Pi Pico. If you need to use 5-V devices with the Pico, use a level converter.

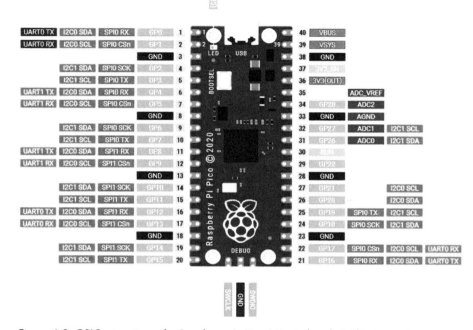

Figure 6-9: GPIO pinouts on the Raspberry Pi Pico (40-pin header). This image is copyrighted by the Raspberry Pi Foundation. Use here is allowed by the Creative Commons 4.0 license.

Although the Raspberry Pi Pico isn't the speediest little board around (the Teensy 4.*x* probably holds that honor among the more popular low-cost boards), at 133 MHz, it's no sloth. Furthermore, unlike most Arduino-class SBCs, the Pico actually has two CPU cores on board, which you can program using the Pico SDK (C/C++) or Micro Python. At the time of writing, some enterprising individuals had actually hacked the Arduino IDE to program the Pico. Shortly afterward, Arduino provided official support (*https://www.tomshardware.com/news/raspberry-pi-pico-arduino-official*).

6.8　The BeagleBone Black

The BeagleBone Black is a low-cost, open source, and open hardware alternative to the Raspberry Pi. Technically, it provides three separate I^2C interfaces, although only one pair of lines (I2C2) is available in the standard (default) configuration. The SCL and SDA lines appear on pins 19 and 20, respectively, of the P9 connector on the BeagleBone Black (see Figure 6-10).

Unlike the Raspberry Pi, the BeagleBone Black seems to support clock stretching just fine. The I^2C interface(s) can run at 100 kHz or 400 kHz.

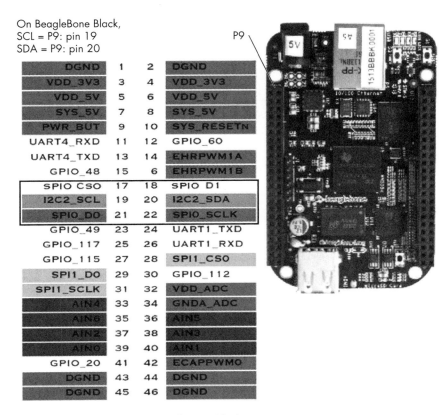

On BeagleBone Black,
SCL = P9: pin 19
SDA = P9: pin 20

P9

DGND	1	2	DGND
VDD_3V3	3	4	VDD_3V3
VDD_5V	5	6	VDD_5V
SYS_5V	7	8	SYS_5V
PWR_BUT	9	10	SYS_RESETN
UART4_RXD	11	12	GPIO_60
UART4_TXD	13	14	EHRPWM1A
GPIO_48	15	6	EHRPWM1B
SPIO_CSO	17	18	SPIO_D1
I2C2_SCL	19	20	I2C2_SDA
SPIO_DO	21	22	SPIO_SCLK
GPIO_49	23	24	UART1_TXD
GPIO_117	25	26	UART1_RXD
GPIO_115	27	28	SPI1_CSO
SPI1_DO	29	30	GPIO_112
SPI1_SCLK	31	32	VDD_ADC
AIN4	33	34	GNDA_ADC
AIN6	35	36	AIN5
AIN2	37	38	AIN3
AINO	39	40	AIN1
GPIO_20	41	42	ECAPPWM0
DGND	43	44	DGND
DGND	45	46	DGND

Figure 6-10: P9 pinouts on BeagleBone Black

6.9   The PINE A64 and ROCKPro64

The PINE A64 and ROCKPro64 SBCs were an attempt to make a very low-cost, 64-bit, Raspberry Pi–like system. The original Pine A64 sold for $15. The ROCKPro64 was a higher-end unit featuring on-board EMMC (flash) memory, six compute cores, USB-C/3.0, a PCI-e slot, and much more. Both boards include a 40-pin connector that is compatible with the Raspberry Pi GPIO connector, including the I²C interface.

For more information about the PINE64 products, visit *https://www .pine64.org*.

6.10   The Onion Omega

The Onion Omega series is composed of some very tiny, low-cost SBCs running Linux variants. The Onion Omega2+ features an MT7688 SoC that incorporates a 580-MHz MIPS CPU, Wi-Fi, and 10/100 Mbs Ethernet. It includes 128MB of DDR2 DRAM memory and 32MB of on-board flash storage—and it supports I^{2}C. A typical Onion Omega2+ module sells for under $15, though the purchase of other modules in the system might raise the price depending on what features you add.

Although the Onion Omega2+ modules are very small (about 1 inch × 1.7 inches, or 2.5 cm × 4.4 cm), the actual system size is a bit larger because the Onion system consists of a series of stackable modules. For example, to gain easy access to the I^{2}C pins, you'll likely want to use an Onion Dock module (though this is optional, as the Omega Onion2+ module has some breadboard-friendly I^{2}C pins that you can wire directly into a circuit). The Omega2 pinout appears in Figure 6-11.

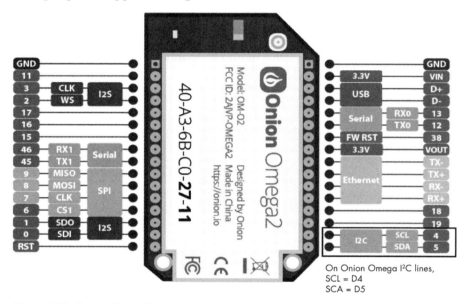

Figure 6-11: Onion Omega2+ pinout

You can find more information about the Onion products at *https:// onion.io/omega2*. SparkFun sells the Onion Omega line; visit its site at *https://www.sparkfun.com/search/results?term=onion*.

6.11   The STM32 Single-Board Computer Family

STMicroelectronics produces a wide set of development boards for its ARM microcontrollers. These SBCs provide different evaluation environments for CPUs operating at different speeds and with varying amount of I/O. Many of the units are programmable using the Arduino IDE, although STMicroelectronics provides its own development software for more professional use, as well as the MBED real-time operating system running on various STM32 boards.

Although the list of STMicroelectronics boards is too long to include here, the following sections provide details on a few of the boards used in this book.

6.11.1 STM32F767/Nucleo-144

The STM32F767/Nucleo-144 is based on an ARM Cortex M7 at 216 MHz. It comes with 2-MB flash memory, 512-KB RAM, USB and Ethernet interfaces, and other I/O. It provides a set of headers that are compatible with Arduino Uno V3 (though 3.3 V only).

Because the STM32F767/Nucleo-144 provides a (3.3 V) set of connections that is mostly compatible with Arduino Uno, you can find the I^2C pins in the usual place, which turns out to be pins PB8 (SCL) and PB9 (SDA) on the device (also corresponding to Arduino A4 and A5 pins). For more information on this board, see *https://www.st.com/en/evaluation-tools/nucleo-f767zi.html*.

6.11.2 STM32F746G-Disco

The STM32F746G-Disco (as in discovery kit, not disco music) is another 216-MHz, M7 device with an Arduino-compatible pinout (though still only 3.3 V), a color LCD display, Ethernet, USB, audio, camera interface, and other I/O. As it contains an Arduino-compatible shield connector, you can find the I^2C pins in the usual place. For more information, visit the STMicroelectronics website for this module at *https://www.st.com/en/evaluation-tools/32f746gdiscovery.html*.

6.11.3 STM32 Boards Galore

STMicroelectronics makes a wide variety of evaluation boards with different amounts and types of I/O. If you're interested in these boards, visit the product evaluation website at *https://www.st.com/en/evaluation-tools/mcu-mpu-eval-tools.html#products*.

6.12 The NetBurner MOD54415

Most of the SBCs appearing in this chapter could probably be labeled hobbyist, discovery, or evaluation devices. Although plenty of real-world professional systems use these boards, professional embedded engineers might question the pedigree of such SBCs. Personally, I avoid religious or elitist arguments about what is "professional" and what is "hobbyist." If a board does the job, that's a sufficient argument for using it. Nevertheless, a big world exists beyond Arduino and Raspberry Pi single-board computers, and I would be remiss not to mention at least one example of a serious SBC commonly used in real-world professional embedded applications.

One such board is the NetBurner MOD54415 SBC, a small board built around a 250-MHz Coldfire CPU running the μC/OS real-time operating system (NetBurner also has the MODM7AE70, a Cortex M7 variant running at 300 MHz). The well-written TCP/IP stack and the use of an RTOS differentiate the NetBurner offerings from many of the hobbyist-level products. I'll provide several programming examples using the MOD54415 later in this book.

For more information on NetBurner products, see *https://www.netburner.com*.

6.13 I²C on the Personal Computer

Although most PCs (Windows, macOS, and Linux) support I²C communication for internal reasons (for example, SMBus for power management and VESA E-DDC on displays), few user programs have access to these I²C controllers. Even if they did, you couldn't easily attach I²C peripherals to these buses. Wouldn't it be nice if there were an I²C port on your PC to interface to I²C peripherals directly?

Well, there are several ways to do this. Of course, you could use an Arduino or other SBC as a coprocessor connected to a PC to handle I²C communications. However, that's a lot of work. Another way to do this is to grab a Bus Pirate or I²C Driver device (see section 4.3, "The I²C Driver," and section 4.4, "The Bus Pirate"). These devices allow you to send commands from the PC to an I²C bus using various commands (from a terminal window with the Bus Pirate or from an application with the I²C Driver). While using these devices makes it possible to control I²C from a PC application, it's not very convenient.

Fortunately, FTDI (*https://www.ftdichip.com*) has created an IC that does most of the work for you. The folks at Adafruit have built a little board with this chip on it to allow you to control I²C from a PC's USB port. This device is the Adafruit FT232H Breakout – General Purpose USB to GPIO, SPI, I2C – USB C & Stemma QT/Qwiic (*https://www.adafruit.com/product/2264*). As its name suggests, it connects the USB to the I²C bus, to the SPI bus, or to generic GPIO pins. Along with some libraries that FTDI provides, you can easily control I²C peripherals directly from a PC application.

In addition to the FT232H Breakout, Adafruit sells a little board, the Adafruit MCP2221A Breakout – General Purpose USB to GPIO ADC I2C – Stemma QT/Qwiic (*https://www.adafruit.com/product/4471*) that is also capable of driving an I²C bus from a USB. While it doesn't provide as many GPIO pins as the FT232H Breakout, it is about half the price. It also includes a Qwiic connector (*Stemma QT* in Adafruit-speak) for easy connection to Qwiic-compatible devices.

6.14 Chapter Summary

This chapter provided a generic overview of numerous hobbyist- and professional-level SBCs that support I²C communication and concluded with a brief mention of controller I²C devices using a traditional PC. Its list of SBCs is by no means exhaustive. If you want more information about the products this chapter discusses, see the web links associated with each item. To delve into the many SBCs not discussed here, see "For More Information" next.

FOR MORE INFORMATION

Hundreds, if not thousands, of SBCs in the real world support I²C communication. If none of the boards listed in this chapter suits your needs, a simple web search should turn up many additional candidates. If you're building your own SBC and you want to incorporate I²C communication on the board, consult the datasheet for the MCU you are intending to use for more details.

As a starting point, here are some URLs that can help you locate various single-board computers that support I²C communications:

Raspberry Pi alternatives: *https://www.seeedstudio.com/blog/2020/10/20/raspberry-pi-alternatives-17-best-single-board-computers-in-2020*

Raspberry Pi Pico: *https://www.raspberrypi.org/products/raspberry-pi-pico*

Arduino-compatible systems: *https://en.wikipedia.org/wiki/List_of_Arduino_boards_and_compatible_systems*

BeagleBone Black: *https://beagleboard.org/black*

SBC reviews: *https://www.slant.co/topics/1629/~best-single-board-computers*

Low-cost SBCs: *https://all3dp.com/2/cheapest-single-board-computer*

Seeed Studio Arduino-compatible SBCs: *https://www.seeedstudio.com*

Teensy documentation: *https://www.pjrc.com*

Arduino Leonardo documentation: *https://www.arduino.cc/en/Guide/ArduinoLeonardoMicro* and *https://store-usa.arduino.cc/products/arduino-leonardo-with-headers*

7

I²C ON VENDOR BUSES

This chapter describes three popular vendor buses that support I²C signals: the Adafruit Feather bus, the SparkFun Qwiic bus (which Adafruit calls Stemma QT), and the Seeed Studio Grove bus. Hundreds of peripheral devices can connect to these buses, so it's essential to familiarize yourself with them if you want to use a large number of existing peripheral devices in your systems. You're also likely to encounter these buses in existing systems.

To connect a pair of I²C devices, you need only three wires: SCL, SDA, and Gnd. Outfits like Adafruit, Seeed Studio, and SparkFun sell a wide variety of I²C breakout boards that connect to systems using pins with these three signals.

Unfortunately, breakout board designers tend to bring out the IC's signals to arbitrary header pins on the board. Two breakout boards, even from the same manufacturer, might bring out SCL and SDA signals to different sets of pins. This makes it difficult to swap different breakout boards. A few companies have attempted to organize these signals, along with ground and power supply lines, using a consistent interconnection scheme. Sadly, none of those systems was widely adopted, so you can't mix and match modules from different vendors using the same connector.

In some respects, the Arduino, Raspberry Pi, and BeagleBone GPIO connectors provide a de facto standard for connecting I^2C devices to embedded systems. It was not uncommon to see *shields* (Arduino add-on boards), *hats* (Raspberry Pi add-on boards), and *capes* (BeagleBone add-on boards) connecting I^2C peripherals to these computer systems. However, these add-on boards are physically large and proportionately expensive. It's a waste of space and money to build an I^2C peripheral on one of these platforms when you typically need only four wires (SDA, SCL, Gnd, and power) for the actual connection.

For this reason, vendors created the Feather, Qwiic, Grove, and other buses that incorporate I^2C signals, and sometimes other signals as well, into more compact form factors. These buses provide a well-defined mechanical connector for I^2C devices, allowing you to easily connect peripherals and controllers, typically by simply plugging in a cable between the two devices, no soldering required. Many controller and peripheral devices support these buses, making it easy to prototype systems with them.

7.1 The Adafruit Feather Bus

Adafruit developed the Feather bus to meet industry demands for a consistent platform that had a smaller form factor and was *CPU and peripheral agnostic*, pairable with any mix of appropriate CPUs and peripherals. As the Arduino devices became more popular, some designers wanted smaller devices that could easily fit in small spaces or even be included as part of a costume. The standard Arduino Uno and Mega 2560 boards were way too big for this purpose. To solve this problem, the Arduino company developed the Arduino Micro and Nano devices. Likewise, third parties developed devices like the Adafruit Trinket series. However, all these new devices used different pinouts for the signals coming off the PCBs. As such, a vibrant ecosystem of add-on boards similar to the Arduino shields for the Uno never developed. This made it difficult to design products that could easily swap out different CPUs, peripherals, battery packs, and other devices as with the standard Arduino Uno platform.

The Feather bus solved this problem by defining a standardized physical connection between an arbitrary CPU and an arbitrary set of peripheral devices using a fixed set of signals on 28 header pins (16 pins on one header, 12 on another). Because the signal lines exist in fixed positions on the Feather bus, Adafruit and many other vendors were able to create a whole set of add-on boards that could be used on a wide variety of SBCs that support the Feather bus.

NOTE *Read more about the history of the Feather bus and its design goals here:* https:// learn.adafruit.com/adafruit-feather/feather-history.

The Feather bus has become very popular with costume designers and other system engineers who need compact, low-power designs. While it contains quite a few signals beyond I^2C, its small form factor makes it a reasonable platform even if you're hooking up only the I^2C lines, power, and Gnd. Many vendors have produced Feather bus components, creating a large Feather ecosystem.

The Feather bus supports two basic component types: Feathers and FeatherWings. The *Feather* is a small SBC that brings out various analog, digital, and other signals, including I^2C. Different Feather implementations include 8-bit and 32-bit CPUs with a wide degree of performance, memory, and power consumption features, allowing a system designer to pick a CPU or other Feather feature ideal for the task at hand while still connecting the wide range of Feather peripherals to that SBC.

A *FeatherWing* is an add-on board, like an Arduino shield, Pi HAT, or BeagleBone cape, holding the peripheral to connect to the controller. Although it is common to have only a single FeatherWing connected to a single Feather, it is possible to connect several FeatherWings to a single Feather (SBC) by stacking FeatherWings or by using FeatherWing expansion boards. This allows you to, for example, connect both OLED display and Ethernet FeatherWings to the same Feather.

A particular FeatherWing board might not use all the I/O pins on the bus; indeed, many FeatherWings use only the I^2C and Gnd pins on the bus and don't connect to any of the other pins. Many FeatherWings also don't use the I^2C signals at all—they might use just some of the digital or analog pins, or perhaps the SPI pins on the Feather bus. This book discusses only those FeatherWings that use the I^2C pins on the bus.

Adafruit provides formal specifications for Feathers and FeatherWings; see the Adafruit Feature bus specification for more details (link provided in "For More Information" at the end of this chapter). For Feathers, the basic specifications are the following:

- Standard Feathers and Wings are 0.9 inches × 2.0 inches with 0.1-inch holes at each corner. The Feather length can vary a bit, but it should always maintain a width of 2.0 inches.

- A 16-pin header strip appears on the bottom side, centered 1.0 inch from the left edge.

- A 12-pin header strip appears on the top side, 1.2 inches from the left side.

- The spacing between the two strips must remain 0.8 inches to ensure compatibility with FeatherWings.

- All Feathers and FeatherWings use 3.3-V logic for all digital inputs and outputs. Analog inputs may vary, but they are usually 3.3 V as well.

SparkFun calls its Feather-compatible boards *Thing Plus* boards. Particle also has a set of Feather-compatible boards it calls *Photon*. See their websites for details (links provided in "For More Information").

7.1.1 Feather Bus Pinouts

Figure 7-1 shows a typical pinout organization for the Feather bus. I say "typical" because the pin assignments are not absolute. Not all Feathers support all the pin types present on the Feather bus. For example, not all devices support six analog inputs. Whenever a particular CPU does not support a particular pin type, that Feather will attempt to map some other appropriate CPU function in its place. For example, if a CPU doesn't support six analog inputs, its Feather may substitute a digital I/O pin in its place.

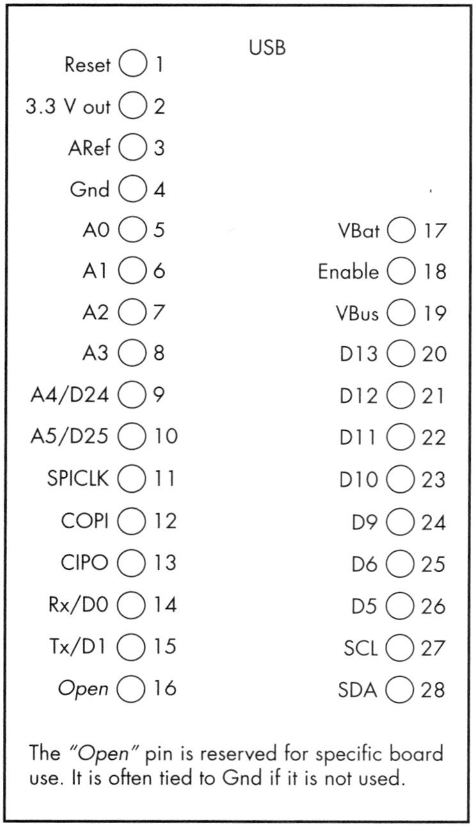

```
                      USB
        Reset  ◯ 1
      3.3 V out ◯ 2
          ARef  ◯ 3
          Gnd  ◯ 4
            A0 ◯ 5            VBat  ◯ 17
            A1 ◯ 6          Enable  ◯ 18
            A2 ◯ 7            VBus  ◯ 19
            A3 ◯ 8            D13  ◯ 20
       A4/D24 ◯ 9            D12  ◯ 21
      A5/D25 ◯ 10            D11  ◯ 22
       SPICLK ◯ 11           D10  ◯ 23
         COPI ◯ 12            D9  ◯ 24
         CIPO ◯ 13            D6  ◯ 25
       Rx/D0 ◯ 14            D5  ◯ 26
       Tx/D1 ◯ 15            SCL  ◯ 27
        Open ◯ 16            SDA  ◯ 28

The "Open" pin is reserved for specific board
use. It is often tied to Gnd if it is not used.
```

Figure 7-1: Typical Feather bus pinouts

In Figure 7-1 I attached pin numbers to the 16-pin and 12-pin headers. This is not a standard Feather bus feature, however. Feather pins are generally identified by their function, not by a pin number.

Figure 7-1 uses the modern names Controller Out, Peripheral In (COPI) and Controller In, Peripheral Out (CIPO) for the SPI signals MOSI and MISO. See "A Note About Terminology" in the Introduction for the reason I've changed these names.

Often, the pins on the Feather bus can take on other functions based on the CPU's feature set. For example, most Arduino-class CPUs allow you to redefine analog pins as digital I/O pins if you don't require the analog input functionality, so many Feathers support digital I/O on pins A0 through A5. Similarly, a few CPUs provide a digital-to-analog output facility. By convention, most Feathers that have this feature attempt to map the DAC output to the A0 pin, so various FeatherWings that require this functionality can find it on a common pin.

The A0 through A5 pin designations do not necessarily correspond to Arduino analog pin numbers. For example, the Adafruit Feather 32u4 Basic maps the Arduino analog pins shown in Table 7-1.

Table 7-1: Arduino-to-Feather Pin Mapping

Arduino pin	Feather pin
ADC 7	A0
ADC 6	A1
ADC 5	A2
ADC 4	A3
ADC 1	A4
ADC 0	A5

Feathers usually maintain the Arduino pin numbering for digital pins, since the I^2C and SPI FeatherWings often use these pins as interrupt inputs and as chip selects. For example, D10 is the common chip select signal for the SPI bus.

7.1.2 I^2C on the Feather Bus

This book is about the I^2C bus, not the Feather bus. While many Feather bus pins might prove useful to someone wanting to use an I^2C FeatherWing—for example, to provide a reset line or an interrupt input—the main pins of interest to us in this book are the SCL (pin 27 in Figure 7-1) and SDA (pin 28) lines. Because the SDA and SCL lines are *always* brought out to the same pins on the Feather bus, any I^2C-based FeatherWing peripheral will automatically work.

The Feather bus provides only one set of I^2C lines. If the particular CPU on the Feather supports multiple I^2C interfaces, only the first of these is brought out to the Feather bus. Technically, the other signals could come out on a pair of the other Feather bus pins if they just happen to map to those signals as an alternate function. However, this is not something you can count on. Furthermore, unless you built the FeatherWing yourself, it would not recognize the alternate I^2C bus pins.

Because the Feather bus is a 3.3-V–only bus, the SDA and SCL lines have pullup resistors to the 3.3-V supply. If FeatherWings were to put 5 V on these lines, they could damage the underlying Feather CPU.

Feathers generally provide their own pullup resistors, as do most FeatherWings. If you attach multiple FeatherWings to a single Feather, each having its own set of pullup resistors, the cumulative pullup resistance could drop to a low value that interferes with I^2C bus operation. FeatherWings that supply their own I^2C pullups will often provide solder jumpers you can cut to remove the resistance from the lines (or, at the very least, the documentation will describe which resistors you remove). Consult your FeatherWing documentation for more details.

7.1.3   Multicontroller Operation

The Feather bus assumes there is a single Feather (the controller) controlling one or more FeatherWings (peripherals). Multicontroller operation is not generally possible with the Feather bus. You might be able to wire a separate controller device to the SDA and SCL lines, but the Feather's CPU may not support this. Generally, you should assume single-controller operation with the Feather bus. Of course, multiple peripherals are perfectly fine.

7.1.4   Feathers and FeatherWings

Adafruit and several other manufacturers produce a wide variety of Feather CPU modules and an even wider variety of FeatherWings peripherals. Although every Feather module supports I^2C, not all FeatherWings use I^2C: some use the SPI bus, and some use just the digital and analog pins on the Feather bus. Table 7-2 lists many of the Feathers available from multiple vendors.

Table 7-2: Common Feather Modules

Name	Manufacturer	Description	Link
nRF52840 Express	Adafruit	Bluetooth LE with Cortex M4 CPU	https://www.adafruit.com/product/4062
32u4 Bluefruit LE	Adafruit	Bluetooth LE with ATmega32u4 CPU	https://www.adafruit.com/product/2829
M0 Bluefruit LE	Adafruit	Bluetooth LE with Cortex M0 CPU	https://www.adafruit.com/product/2995
M0 WiFi	Adafruit	WiFi with Cortex M0+ CPU	https://www.adafruit.com/product/3010
HUZZAH32ESP32	Adafruit	WiFi plus Bluetooth with ESP 32 CPU	https://www.adafruit.com/product/3405
Feather 32u4 RFM95	Adafruit	LoRa Radio plus ATmega32u4 CPU	https://www.adafruit.com/product/3078
M0 RFM69HCW Packet Radio	Adafruit	Packet radio transceiver plus Cortex M0 CPU	https://www.adafruit.com/product/3176

Name	Manufacturer	Description	Link
STM32F405 Express	Adafruit	High-performance Cortex M4 CPU	*https://www.adafruit.com/ product/4382*
WICED WiFi	Adafruit	WiFi plus Cortex M3 CPU	*https://www.adafruit.com/ product/3056*
Teensy 3.x Feather Adapter	Adafruit	Puts Teensy 3.2 on Feather bus	*https://www.adafruit.com/ product/3200*
Thing Plus SAMD51	SparkFun	Cortex M4 CPU	*https://www.sparkfun.com/ products/14713*
Thing Plus Artemis	SparkFun	Artemis module (Cortex M4F, for machine learning)	*https://www.sparkfun.com/ products/15574*
Thing Plus ESP32 WROOM	SparkFun	WiFi with ESP32 module	*https://www.sparkfun.com/ products/15663*
RED-V Thing Plus	SparkFun	RISC-V CPU	*https://www.sparkfun.com/ products/15799*
Particle Boron LTE	Particle	Cellular modem plus nRF52840 SoC (Cortex M4) CPU	*https://www.adafruit.com/ product/3998*
Particle Argon	Particle	WiFi plus Bluetooth with nRF52840 and ESP32 processors	*https://docs.particle.io/ argon*

Table 7-3 lists some FeatherWings that interface via the I^{2}C bus.

Table 7-3: Examples of I^{2}C-Based FeatherWing Modules

Name	Manufacturer	Description	Link
128×64 OLED	Adafruit	Small OLED display for Feather	*https://www.adafruit.com/ product/4650*
RTC plus SD Add-on	Adafruit	I^{2}C-based real-time clock and SPI-based SD card interface	*https://www.adafruit.com/ product/2922*
DS3231 Precision RTC	Adafruit	High-precision real-time clock	*https://www.adafruit.com/ product/3028*
8-Channel PWM or Servo	Adafruit	Eight-channel motor (servo) controller	*https://www.adafruit.com/ product/2928*
4-Digit 7-Segment LED Matrix Display	Adafruit	Seven-segment display driver	*https://www.adafruit.com/ product/3088*
AMG8833 IR Thermal Camera	Adafruit	Infrared thermal imaging camera	*https://www.adafruit.com/ product/3622*

(continued)

Table 7-3: Examples of I²C-Based FeatherWing Modules *(continued)*

Name	Manufacturer	Description	Link
14-Segment Alphanumeric LED	Adafruit	14-segment display driver	*https://www.adafruit.com/ product/3089*
8×16 LED Matrix	Adafruit	Driver for 8×16 LED matrix	*https://www.adafruit.com/ product/3090*
Joy FeatherWing	Adafruit	Joystick and game button adapter	*https://www.adafruit.com/ product/3632*
LSM6DSOX plus LIS3MDL FeatherWing Precision 9-DoF IMU	Adafruit	Nine degrees of freedom sensor	*https://www.adafruit.com/ product/4565*
ADXL343 plus ADT7410 Sensor	Adafruit	Motion and temperature sensing	*https://www.adafruit.com/ product/4147*
Qwiic Shield for Thing Plus	SparkFun	Breakout Qwiic connectors from Feather bus	*https://www.sparkfun.com/ products/16790*

See "For More Information" for links to a more complete and up-to-date list of Adafruit Feather modules, SparkFun modules, and vendors selling Feathers (SBCs) and FeatherWing (peripheral) boards.

7.2 I²C on the SparkFun Qwiic Bus

Unlike the Feather bus, the SparkFun Qwiic bus is strictly an I²C bus. The idea behind Qwiic was to create a standard plug and receptacle for connecting I²C devices. As with the Adafruit Feather bus, the Qwiic connectors have become immensely popular with many compatible products employing the Qwiic bus, both peripherals and CPU modules.

Qwiic connectors are four-pin JST SH connectors with very tiny pins (1-mm pitch). The connectors have a standardized pinout given in Table 7-4.

Table 7-4: Qwiic Connector Pinout

Pin	Function
1	Gnd
2	Vcc
3	SDA
4	SCL

Figure 7-2 shows the connector layout.

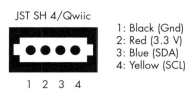

JST SH 4/Qwiic

1: Black (Gnd)
2: Red (3.3 V)
3: Blue (SDA)
4: Yellow (SCL)

1 2 3 4

Figure 7-2: Qwiic pinout

The Qwiic bus is 3.3 V only. Connecting a 5-V device onto the Qwiic bus could damage the device, other devices on the bus, or the controller on the bus.

Though it was designed for a single controller, the Qwiic bus can, in theory, support multiple controllers. However, like the Feather bus, physical constraints prevent this. For example, the controller is generally responsible for putting 3.3 V on the Qwiic bus. If two different controllers each supply different values for 3.3 V to the bus, this could create some problems. In theory, you could cut the 3.3 V from multiple controllers and use an independent 3.3-V supply or allow a single controller to provide the voltage. In practice, you'd likely run into problems.

Adafruit also makes several controller and peripheral devices that connect to the Qwiic bus. While it has some "pure" Qwiic devices, for the most part its modules use the name STEMMA/QT rather than Qwiic. STEMMA/QT is upward compatible from Qwiic, the major difference being that it supports 5-V devices as well as 3.3-V devices. STEMMA/QT peripherals contain level-shifting circuitry on every board to allow them to work properly with either 3.3-V or 5-V signal lines. In theory, this is a great idea, allowing 5-V parts to be used on the bus alongside the 3.3-V part. In practice, almost all Qwiic bus peripherals and controllers are 3.3 V today, so this extension seems to have gone to waste.

As with the Feather bus, a fair number of different manufacturers have created Qwiic bus–compatible products: SparkFun has dozens of boards, Adafruit makes several, and Smart Prototyping makes a bunch (such as Zio; the link is provided in "For More Information"), as do many other outfits. See the next section, "Qwiic Bus Peripherals," for a small sampling of the Qwiic-compatible products available.

7.3 Qwiic Bus Peripherals

At the time of writing, SparkFun had created more than 150 different Qwiic-compatible modules (SBCs and peripheral devices). Many other vendors also produce Qwiic-compatible boards. Table 7-5 provides a tiny sampling of the Qwiic peripherals you can purchase.

Table 7-5: Qwiic Peripheral Devices

Name	Manufacturer	Description	Link
Zio Qwiic MUX	Smart Prototyping	Eight-channel I^{2}C multiplexer	https://www.smart-proto typing.com/Zio-Qwiic -Mux.html
Zio OLED Display	Smart Prototyping	128×32 OLED display	https://www.smart-proto typing.com/Zio-OLED -Display-0-91-in-128-32 -Qwiic.html
Zio 16 Servo Controller	Smart Prototyping	16-channel servo controller	https://www.smart-proto typing.com/Zio-16 -Servo-Controller.html
Zio Qwiic IO Expander	Smart Prototyping	16-channel GPIO expander	https://www.smart-proto typing.com/Zio-Qwiic -IO-Expander.html
Zio 4 DC Motor Controller	Smart Prototyping	Two-channel bidirectional motor control	https://www.smart-proto typing.com/Zio-4-DC -Motor-Controller.html
Zio TOF Distance Sensor RFD77402	Smart Prototyping	Time of flight distance measurement (10 cm to 200 cm)	https://www.smart-proto typing.com/Zio-TOF -Distance-Sensor -RFD77402.html
Zio 9DoF IMU BNO055	Smart Prototyping	Nine degrees of freedom position measurement	https://www.smart-proto typing.com/Zio-9DOF -IMU-BNO055.html
9DoF Sensor Stick	SparkFun	Nine degrees of freedom position measurement	https://www.sparkfun .com/products/13944
6 Degrees of Freedom Breakout LSM6DS3	SparkFun	Six degrees of freedom position measurement	https://www.sparkfun .com/products/13339
Atmospheric Sensor Breakout BME280	SparkFun	Barometric pressure, humidity, and temperature	https://www.sparkfun .com/products/13676
I^{2}C DAC Breakout	SparkFun	12-bit digital-to-analog converter	https://www.sparkfun .com/products/12918
16 Output I/O Expander Breakout SX1509	SparkFun	16-channel GPIO expander	https://www.sparkfun .com/products/13601
GPS Breakout XA1110	SparkFun	Global Positioning Satellite module	https://www.sparkfun .com/products/14414
RFID Qwiic Reader	SparkFun	Radio Frequency ID tag reader	https://www.sparkfun .com/products/15191
Qwiic Thermocouple Amplifier MCP9600	SparkFun	Read temperatures with a thermocouple	https://www.sparkfun .com/products/16295

Name	Manufacturer	Description	Link
Qwiic Quad Solid State Relay Kit	SparkFun	Four-channel high-current/high-voltage SSRs	https://www.sparkfun.com/products/16833
Qwiic Twist RGB Rotary Encoder Breakout	SparkFun	Rotary encoder with RGB LED	https://www.sparkfun.com/products/15083
BH1750 Light Sensor	Adafruit	Ambient light sensor	https://www.adafruit.com/product/4681
LPS25 Pressure Sensor	Adafruit	Atmospheric pressure sensor	https://www.adafruit.com/product/4530
PCF8591 Quad 8-bit ADC plus 8-bit DAC	Adafruit	Four-channel 8-bit ADC and single-channel 8-bit DAC	https://www.adafruit.com/product/4648
DS3502 I^{2}C Digital 10K Potentiometer Breakout	Adafruit	10 kΩ digital potentiometer	https://www.adafruit.com/product/4286
MCP4728 Quad DAC with EEPROM	Adafruit	Four-channel 12-bit DAC	https://www.adafruit.com/product/4470
PMSA003I Air Quality Breakout	Adafruit	Air quality monitor	https://www.adafruit.com/product/4632

See "For More Information" for links to information on Zio devices, SparkFun devices, and Adafruit STEMMA/QT devices.

7.4   I^{2}C on the Seeed Studio Grove Bus

The Grove bus, created by Seeed Studio in 2010, was one of the earliest attempts at a standardized hobbyist interconnection system. It uses a proprietary four-pin locking connector on 2-mm centers, though it's easy enough to force a JST PH four-pin female connector into the Grove socket.

The Grove system looks like somebody went to the expense of creating a custom connector and then tried to utilize that connector for as many different things as possible. Grove uses a single connector to carry 3.3-V and 5-V versions of digital signals, analog signals, I^{2}C signals, and UART signals. This means it's easy to damage a device by plugging it into a connector with a different set of signals or voltages on the same pins. You must be careful to ensure you're mating compatible devices because the connector offers no protection or indication of the types of signals present.

Figure 7-3 shows the pin layout for the Grove connector.

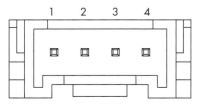

Figure 7-3: Grove connector

This book will not consider the UART, digital, or analog functions of the Grove connection system; Table 7-6 simply lists the different possible functions for each Grove pin to show that the I^2C signals share the same pins as other functions in the Grove system. Be aware that different devices might expect different voltages on the Vcc pin (that is, 3.3 V or 5 V).

Table 7-6: Grove Connector Pin Functions

Pin	I^2C function	UART function	Digital function	Analog function
1	SCL	Rx	Dn	An
2	SDA	Tx	Dn+1	An+1
3	Vcc	Vcc	Vcc	Vcc
4	Gnd	Gnd	Gnd	Gnd

Although a few manufacturers have placed Grove receptacles on their CPU boards, Seeed Studio seems to be the primary (if not only) manufacturer of Grove modules. The Seeed Studio Wiki gives specs for the Grove interconnection system and a list of the Grove products the company currently manufactures (link provided in "For More Information").

7.5 Chapter Summary

This chapter discussed three common vendor-defined buses that support the I^2C bus: the Adafruit Feather bus, the SparkFun Qwiic bus, and Seeed Studio's Grove connection.

The Adafruit Feather bus is probably the most popular of the three, in terms of the number of Feathers (CPU boards) and Featherwings (peripheral boards) available. The SparkFun Qwiic bus is also very popular. The main difference between the two is that the Qwiic bus is I^2C (plus power) only, whereas the Feather bus also contains other signals. The Qwiic connection system is more convenient for attaching and detaching small devices to a breadboard system.

The Grove connection system is similar to Qwiic insofar as it is a four-wire system. Different variants of the Grove connector support I^2C, SPI, serial, analog, and digital signals, though you must take care not to confuse signal types when using the Grove bus.

The main advantage of these vendor buses is the *ecosystem* support they provide. Several different manufacturers provide small boards that attach to these buses, making it easy to add functionality to systems you are assembling.

FOR MORE INFORMATION

The Arduino (Uno) connector: *https://content.arduino.cc/assets/Pinout-UNOrev3 _latest.pdf*

Pinouts for various Arduino boards: *https://arduino.pinout.guide*

The Raspberry Pi GPIO connector: *https://www.raspberrypi.org/documentation/ usage/gpio*

The Adafruit Feather bus: *https://learn.adafruit.com/adafruit-feather/ feather-specification*

Complete and up-to-date list of Adafruit Feather modules: *https://www.adafruit .com/feather*

SparkFun: *https://sparkfun.com*

SparkFun modules: *https://www.sparkfun.com/search/results?term=Feather*

Vendors selling Feathers (SBCs) and FeatherWing (peripheral) boards: *https:// github.com/adafruit/awesome-feather*

The SparkFun Qwiic system: *https://www.sparkfun.com/qwiic*

Particle: *https://www.particle.io*

Adafruit's STEMMA/QT (their variant of Qwiic): *https://learn.adafruit.com/ introducing-adafruit-stemma-qt/technical-specs*

The Grove interconnect: *https://wiki.seeedstudio.com/Grove_System*

Zio: *https://www.smart-prototyping.com/Zio*

Particle Photon: *https://docs.particle.io/datasheets/wi-fi/photon-2-datasheet*

Smart Prototyping Zio modules: *https://www.smart-prototyping.com/blog/ Introducing-I2C-with-ZIO-and-Qwiic*

PART III

PROGRAMMING THE I^{2}C BUS

8

ARDUINO I²C PROGRAMMING

This first chapter on I²C programming will start by discussing the Arduino platform, since it's probably safe to say that more lines of I²C code have been written for the Arduino than for any other.

This chapter covers the following information:

- An introduction to basic I²C programming
- A discussion of the Wire programming model that the Arduino library and IDE uses
- Arduino I²C read and write operations
- Accessing multiple I²C ports on various Arduino devices

This book tends to use Arduino *sketches* (programs) as the basis for generic examples, so a good understanding of Arduino I²C programming will be invaluable as you continue through subsequent chapters.

THE MCP4725 DIGITAL-TO-ANALOG CONVERTER

This book uses the MCP4725 DAC to demonstrate programming various control devices (SBCs), since the MCP4725 is easy to program and understand. It has the following features:

- 12-bit resolution
- On-board nonvolatile memory (EEPROM)
- External A0 address pin
- Normal or power-down mode
- Single-supply operation: 2.7 V to 5.5 V
- Standard (100 kbit/sec), fast (400 kbit/sec), and high (3.4 Mbit/sec) speeds
- Eight available I²C addresses (though any given MCP4725 IC supports only two different addresses, a full range of eight addresses is possible since there are four different variants of the MCP4725, each supporting a different pair of addresses)

For Part III of this book, there are two I²C operations of interest: writing a 12-bit digital value to the DAC and reading the current DAC output and EEPROM values from the chip.

The MCP4725 will respond to one of the following I²C addresses: 0x60/0x61, 0x62/0x63, 0x64/0x65, or 0x66/0x67. An address pin on the MCP4725 provides the LO bit (bit 0) of this address. Bits 1 and 2 are determined by the particular IC you purchase. For example, the Adafruit MCP4725 breakout board uses an IC that responds to addresses 0x62 and 0x63; the SparkFun variant responds to addresses 0x60 and 0x61. If you purchase boards from Adafruit and SparkFun, you can put four of these boards on the same I²C bus without having to resort to using an I²C multiplexer. (There is a sneaky way to hook more of these boards to the same bus by using the address selection bit as a "chip select" line; see *https://mitchtronic.blogspot .com/2017/03/addressing-multiple-mcp4724s-in-same.html* for an example.) If you want to use chips with addresses 0x64/0x65 or 0x66/0x67, you could search for various boards on Amazon or build your own breakout board.

Both Adafruit and SparkFun have made their boards open hardware via the Creative Commons license, so you could build these boards and substitute in the appropriate MCP4725 IC. Note that these designs use surface-mounted parts and are not easy to assemble by hand. Check out the Adafruit and SparkFun designs at *https://github.com/sparkfun/MCP4725_Breakout/tree/ v14* and *https://github.com/adafruit/Adafruit-MCP4725-PCB*. For more information about the MCP4725, see Chapter 15.

8.1 Basic I²C Programming

In Chapter 2, you learned that an I²C transmission begins with the output of a start condition followed by an address-R/W byte, followed by zero or more bytes of data, and, finally, end with a stop condition. The controller places these data bytes on the I²C bus, either by bit banging or by some hardware registers.

The only parts of this transmission that are common to all I²C devices are the start condition, the very first address byte, and the stop condition. Any bytes the controller transmits after the address byte until a stop condition comes along are specific to the peripheral responding to the address in the address byte.

The MCP4725 supports several command formats based on data you transmit immediately after the address byte. The programming examples in this part of the book will use only one of those commands: the *Fast Mode Write command*. This command requires 3 bytes on the I²C bus, as shown in Table 8-1.

Table 8-1: Fast Mode Write Command

First byte	Second byte	Third byte
Address	HO DAC value	LO DAC value
aaaa aaax	0000 hhhh	1111 1111

In Table 8-1, the aaaa aaa bits are the MCP4725 address. These will be 1100cba where bits c and b are hard-coded into the IC itself and a comes from the address line on the chip. This corresponds to addresses 0x60 through 0x67. (Keep in mind that the I²C protocol shifts these address bits one position to the left and expects the R/W bit in bit 0. For this reason, the address byte will actually contain the values 0xC0 through 0xCF, depending on the IC address and the state of the R/W line.) The hhhh 1111 1111 bits are the 12 bits to write to the digital-to-analog conversion circuitry. The HO 4 bits of the second byte must contain zeros (they specify the Fast Mode Write command and power-down mode). Assuming a 5-V power supply to the chip, the 3-byte sequence *0xC0, 0x00, 0x00* (the 3 bytes from Table 8-1) will write the 12-bit value 0x000 to the DAC at address 0x60, which will cause 0 V to appear on the DAC's output. Writing the 3-byte sequence *0xC0, 0x08, 0x00* will put 2.5 V on the output pin. Writing the 3-byte sequence *0xC0, 0x0F, 0xFF* will put 5 V on the analog output pin. In general, a value between 0x000 and 0xFFF (linearly) maps to a voltage between 0 V and 5 V on the DAC analog output. All you need is some way of placing these 3 bytes on the I²C bus.

Whereas the DAC uses the HO 4 bits of the second byte to specify the command (0b0000 is the Fast Mode Write command), the DAC read command is simpler still. The R/W bit in the address byte is all the MCP4725 needs to determine how to respond. It responds by returning 5 bytes: the first is some status information (which you can ignore until Chapter 15, where I discuss the MCP4725 in detail), the second byte contains the HO 8 bits of the last value written to the DAC, and the third byte contains the LO 4 bits of the last value written in bits 4 through 7 (and bits 0 through 3 don't contain any valid data). The fourth and fifth bytes contain some status information and the 14 bits held in the on-chip EEPROM (see Chapter 15 for more information about the EEPROM).

How you place bytes on the I^2C bus and how you read data from the I^2C bus entirely depends on the system, library functions, and operating system (if any) you're using. This chapter discusses I^2C on the Arduino; therefore, we're going to consider how to read and write data on the I^2C bus using the Arduino library code.

8.2   Basic Wire Programming

The Arduino library responsible for I^2C communication is the Wire library. I^2C communication functions are not built into the Arduino language (which is really just C++ with some default include files). Instead, you have to enable the Arduino I^2C library code by including the following statement near the beginning of your program's source file:

```
#include <Wire.h>
```

Note that *Wire.h* must have an uppercase *W* on certain operating systems (Linux, in particular).

The *Wire.h* header file creates a singleton class object named Wire that you can use to access the class functions. You do not have to declare this object in your programs; the header file automatically does this for you. The following sections describe the various available Wire functions.

8.2.1   *Wire Utility Functions*

The Wire.begin() function initializes the Arduino Wire (I^2C) library. You must call this function once before executing any other functions in the Wire library. The convention is to call this function in the Arduino setup() function.

Without a parameter, Wire.begin() will initialize the library to work as a controller device on the I^2C bus. If you specify a 7-bit integer as an argument, this will initialize the library to operate as a peripheral device on the I^2C bus.

The Wire.setClock() function allows you to change the I^2C clock frequency, supplied as an integer parameter. This call is optional; the default clock speed is 100 kHz. Most Arduino boards will support 100,000 or 400,000 as the argument. A few high-performance boards might support 3,400,000 (high-speed mode). A few will also support 10,000 (low-speed mode on the SMBus).

Keep in mind that all peripherals and CPU(s) on the I^2C bus must be capable of supporting the clock speed you select. That is, you must set a clock speed that is no faster than the slowest peripheral on the bus.

8.2.2 Wire Read Operations

The `Wire.requestFrom()` function reads data from an I²C peripheral device. There are two forms of the `Wire.requestFrom()` function call:

```
Wire.requestFrom( address, size )
Wire.requestFrom( address, size, stopCond )
```

In each of these calls, `address` is the 7-bit peripheral address, `size` is the number of bytes to read from the device, and the optional `stopCond` argument specifies whether the function issues a stop condition (if true) after receiving the bytes. If false, then the function sends a restart condition. If the optional `stopCode` argument is not present, the function uses `true` as the default value (to issue a stop condition after receiving the data).

NOTE   *The Arduino library maintains a 32-byte buffer for incoming I²C data reads. Because `Wire.requestFrom()` reads all incoming data before returning to its caller, an I²C peripheral can transfer a maximum limit of 32 bytes in one operation using this call.*

Once the controller receives the data from the peripheral, an application can read that data using the `Wire.read()` and `Wire.available()` functions. The `Wire.available()` function returns the number of bytes left in the internal receive buffer, while the `Wire.read()` function reads a single byte from the buffer. Typically, you would use these two functions to read all the data from the internal buffer using a loop such as the following:

```
while( Wire.available() )
{
    char c = Wire.read(); // Read byte from buffer

    // Do something with the byte just read.
}
```

There is no guarantee that the peripheral will actually transmit the number of bytes requested in the call to the `Wire.requestFrom()` function—the peripheral could return *less* data. Therefore, it is always important to use the `Wire.available()` function to determine exactly how much data is in the internal buffer; don't automatically assume it's the amount you requested.

The peripheral determines the actual amount of data it returns to the controller. In almost all cases, the amount of data is fixed and is specified in the datasheet for the peripheral (or by the peripheral's design). In theory, a peripheral could return a variable amount of data. How you retrieve such data is determined by the peripheral's design and is beyond the scope of this chapter.

To read data from a peripheral device, a controller must transmit the peripheral address and an R/W bit equal to 1 to that peripheral. The `Wire.requestFrom()` function handles this. After that, the peripheral will transmit its data bytes. The Arduino controller will receive those bytes and buffer them to be read later. Note, however, that the full read operation takes place with the execution of the `Wire.requestFrom()` function.

8.2.3 Wire Write Operations

A controller can write data to a peripheral using the `Wire.beginTransmission()`, `Wire.endTransmission()`, and `Wire.write()` functions. The beginTransmission() and endTransmission() functions bracket a sequence of write operations.

The `Wire.beginTransmission()` function takes the following form:

```
Wire.beginTransmission(address)
```

where address is the 7-bit peripheral address. This function call builds the first byte of the data transmission consisting of the address and a clear R/W bit.

There are three forms of the `Wire.write()` function:

```
Wire.write( value )
Wire.write( string )
Wire.write( data, length )
```

The first form appends a single byte to an internal buffer for transmission to the peripheral. The second form adds all the characters in a string (not including the zero-terminating byte) to the internal buffer for transmission to the peripheral. The third form copies some bytes from a byte array to the internal buffer (the second argument specifies the number of bytes to copy).

NOTE *In addition to its aforementioned 32-byte buffer for incoming I^2C data reads, the Arduino library maintains a 32-byte buffer for outgoing I^2C writes. Although you can have multiple calls to the various write functions between a* `Wire.beginTransmission()` *call and a* `Wire.endTransmission()` *call, the cumulative length must be 32 bytes or less.*

The `Wire.endTransmission()` function takes the address byte and data bytes from the internal buffer and transmits them over the I^2C bus. This function call takes two forms:

```
Wire.endTransmission()
Wire.endTransmission( stopCond )
```

The first form transmits the data in the internal buffer and follows that transmission with a stop condition. The second form uses the single Boolean argument to determine whether it should send a stop condition (true) after transmitting the data (the next read or write operation will begin with a restart if stopCond is false).

Remember that the actual data transmission does not take place until the execution of the `Wire.endTransmission()` function call. The other calls simply build up an internal buffer for later transmission.

8.2.4 Wire Peripheral Functions

The Arduino functions up to this point have assumed that the Arduino is acting as an I^{2}C bus controller device. You can also program an Arduino to act as a peripheral device. The Arduino library provides two functions for this purpose:

```
Wire.onReceive( inHandler )
Wire.onRequest( outHandler )
```

In the first function, inHandler is a pointer to a function with the following prototype: void inHandler(int numBytes). In the second, outHandler is a pointer to a function with the following prototype: void outHandler().

The Arduino system will call outHandler whenever the (external) controller device requests data. The outHandler function will then use the Wire.beginTransmission(), Wire.endTransmission(), and Wire.write() functions to transmit data from the peripheral back to the (external) controller. The inHandler function will use the Wire.begin(), Wire.available(), and Wire.read() functions to retrieve data from the controller device.

8.3 Arduino I^{2}C Write Example

The program in Listing 8-1 demonstrates using the I^{2}C bus to talk to a SparkFun MCP4725 DAC breakout board. This program was written for and tested on a Teensy 3.2, though it should work with any compatible Arduino device (with slightly different timings).

The program generates a continuous triangle wave by continuously incrementing the DAC output from 0x0 to 0xfff (12 bits) and then decrementing from 0xfff back to 0x0. As you will see, this program produces a triangle wave with slightly less than a 2.4-second period (around 0.42 Hz) when running on my setup (your mileage may vary). This frequency is determined by the amount of time it takes to write 8,189 12-bit values to the DAC. Since each transmission requires 3 bytes (address, HO byte and command, and LO byte), plus start and stop condition timings, it takes around 35 bit times at 100 kHz (10 μsec per bit time) to transfer each value.

```
// Listing8-1.ino
//
// A simple program that demonstrates I2C
// programming on the Arduino platform.

#include <Wire.h>

// I2C address of the SparkFun MCP4725 I2C-based
// digital-to-analog converter.

#define MCP4725_ADDR 0x60

void setup( void )
```

```
{
    Serial.begin( 9600 );
    delay( 1000 );
    Serial.println( "Test writing MCP4725 DAC" );
    Wire.begin(); // Initialize I2C library
}

void loop( void )
{
    // Send the rising edge of a triangle wave:

    for( int16_t dacOut = 0; dacOut < 0xfff; ++dacOut )
    {
        // Transmit the address byte (and a zero R/W bit):

      ❶ Wire.beginTransmission( MCP4725_ADDR );

        // Transmit the 12-bit DAC value (HO 4 bits
        // first, LO 8 bits second) along with a 4-bit
        // Fast Mode Write command (00 in the HO 2 bits
        // of the first byte):

      ❷ Wire.write( (dacOut >> 8) & 0xf );
        Wire.write( dacOut & 0xff );

        // Send the stop condition onto the I2C bus:

      ❸ Wire.endTransmission( true );

        // Uncomment this delay to slow things down
        // so it can be observed on a multimeter:
        // delay( 5 );
    }

    // Send the falling edge of the triangle wave:

    for( int16_t dacOut = 0xffe; dacOut > 0; --dacOut )
    {
        // See comments in previous loop.

        Wire.beginTransmission( MCP4725_ADDR );
        Wire.write( (dacOut >> 8) & 0xf );
        Wire.write( dacOut & 0xff );
        Wire.endTransmission( true );

        // Uncomment this delay to slow things down
        // so it can be observed on a multimeter:
        // delay( 5 );
    }
}
```

Wire.beginTransmission() initializes the Wire package to begin accepting data for (later) transmission on the I^{2}C bus ❶. The Wire.write() function copies data to transmit to the internal Wire buffers for later transmission on the I²C bus ❷. After that, `Wire.endTransmission()` instructs the device to actually begin transmitting the data in the internal `Wire` buffers onto the I²C bus ❸.

Figure 8-1 shows one of the DAC 3-byte transmissions appearing on the I²C bus during the execution of the program in Listing 8-1 (this particular transmission was writing 0x963 to the DAC).

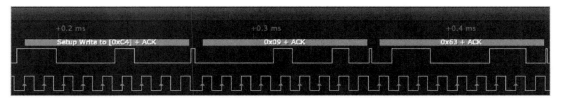

Figure 8-1: Sample I²C output during triangle wave transmission

As you can see in the oscilloscope output appearing in Figure 8-2, it takes approximately 2.4 seconds for a full cycle (one rising edge and one falling edge) of the triangle wave. Using the logic analyzer, I was able to determine that each 3-byte transmission took slightly less than 300 μsec, which roughly matches what you see on the oscilloscope output in Figure 8-2. Note that the timing between transmissions isn't constant and will vary by several microseconds between transmissions. This means 300 μsec is not a hard transmission time for 3 bytes.

The maximum frequency this software can produce based on a 100-kHz bus speed is approximately 0.4 Hz. To produce a higher frequency value, you would need to run the I²C bus at a higher clock frequency (for example, 400 kHz) or reduce the number of values you write to the DAC per unit time (for example, you can double the frequency by incrementing the loop counter by two rather than one).

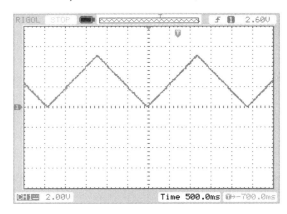

Figure 8-2: Triangle wave output from MCP4725

The code in Listing 8-1 gives up the I²C bus after each DAC transmission. If there were other controllers on the same bus talking to different peripherals, this would further reduce the maximum clock frequency of the triangle wave (not to mention that it would add some distortion to the triangle wave if there were many pauses in the output sequence to the DAC). In theory, you could prevent this distortion by refusing to yield the I^{2}C bus during the transmission; however, given the vast number of transmissions required here, the only reasonable solution to producing an undistorted triangle wave would be to ensure that the MCP4725 was the only device on the I^{2}C bus.

8.4 Arduino I^{2}C Read Example

Fundamentally, a DAC is an (analog) output-only device. You write a value to the DAC registers and an analog voltage magically appears on the analog output pin. Reading from a DAC doesn't make much sense. That said, the MCP4725 IC does support I^{2}C read operations. A read command returns 5 bytes.

To read a value from the MCP4725, simply place the device's address on the I^{2}C bus with the R/W line high. The MCP4725 will respond by returning 5 bytes: the first byte will be status information, the next two will be the last DAC value written, and the last pair of bytes will be the EEPROM value. The EEPROM stores a default value to initialize the analog output pin when the device powers up, before any digital value is written to the chip. See Chapter 15 for more details.

The program in Listing 8-2 demonstrates an I^{2}C read operation.

```
// Listing8-2.ino
//
// This is a simple program that demonstrates
// I2C programming on the Arduino platform.
//
// This program reads the last written DAC value
// and EEPROM settings from the MDP4725. It was
// written and tested on a Teensy 3.2, and it also
// runs on an Arduino Uno.

#include <Wire.h>

// I2C address of the SparkFun MCP4725 I2C-based
// digital-to-analog converter.

#define MCP4725_ADDR 0x60

#define bytesToRead (5)
void setup( void )
{
    int     i = 0;
    int     DACvalue;
    int     EEPROMvalue;
    byte    input[bytesToRead];

    Serial.begin( 9600 );
    delay( 1000 );
    Serial.println( "Test reading MCP4725 DAC" );
```

```
Wire.begin();  // Initialize I2C library

Wire.requestFrom( MCP4725_ADDR, bytesToRead );
while( Wire.available() )
{
    if( i < bytesToRead )
    {
        input[ i++ ] = Wire.read();
    }
}

// Status byte is the first one received:

Serial.print( "Status: " );
Serial.println( input[0], 16 );

// The previously written DAC value is in the
// HO 12 bits of the next two bytes:

DACvalue = (input[1] << 4) | ((input[2] & 0xff)  4);
Serial.print( "Previous DAC value: " );
Serial.println( DACvalue, 16 );

// The last two bytes contain EEPROM data:

EEPROMvalue = (input[3] << 8) | input[4];
Serial.print( "EEPROM value: " );
Serial.println( EEPROMvalue, 16 );

while( 1 ); // Stop
}

void loop( void )
{
    // Never executes.
}
```

The following is the output from the program in Listing 8-2. Note that the output is valid only for my particular setup. Other MCP4725 boards may have different EEPROM values. Furthermore, the previous DAC value output is specific to the last write on my particular system (this was probably the last output written from Listing 8-1, when I uploaded the program in Listing 8-2 while the previous program was running).

```
Test reading MCP4725 DAC
Status: C0
Previous DAC value: 9B
EEPROM value: 800
```

The only thing interesting in this output is that I had programmed the MCP4725's EEPROM to initialize the output pin to 2.5 V on power-up (the halfway point with a 5-V power supply).

8.5 Arduino I²C Peripheral Example

The previous two sections described read and write operations from the perspective of a controller device. This section describes how to create an Arduino system that behaves as an I²C peripheral device. In particular, the source code appearing in Listing 8-3 simulates an MCP4725 DAC device using a Teensy 3.2 module. The Teensy 3.2 has an on-board, 12-bit DAC connected to pin A14. Writing a value between 0x000 and 0xfff produces a voltage between 0 V and +3.3 V on that pin. The code in Listing 8-3 associates rcvISR (and ISR) with the data received interrupt. When data arrives, the system automatically calls this routine and passes it the number of bytes received on the I²C bus.

The rcvISR interrupt service routine (ISR) fetches the bytes transmitted to the peripheral from the controller, constructs the 12-bit DAC output value from those bytes, and then writes the 12 bits to the DAC output (using the Arduino analogWrite() function). Once the output is complete, the code waits for the next transmission to occur. Just like a debug and test feature, this program writes a string to the Serial output every 10 seconds so you can verify that the program is still running.

```
// Listing8-3.ino
//
// This program demonstrates using an
// Arduino as an I2C peripheral.
//
// This code runs on a Teensy 3.2
// module. A14 on the Teensy 3.2 is
// a true 12-bit, 3.3-V DAC. This program
// turns the Teensy 3.2 into a simple
// version of the MCP4725 DAC. It reads
// inputs from the I2C line (corresponding
// to an MCP4725 fast write operation)
// and writes the 12-bit data to the
// Teensy 3.2's hardware DAC on pin A14.

#include <Wire.h>

// I2C address of the SparkFun MCP4725 I2C-based
// digital-to-analog converter.

#define MCP4725_ADDR 0x60

// Interrupt handler that the system
// automatically calls when data arrives
// on the I2C lines.

void rcvISR( int numBytes )
{
    byte LObyte;
    byte HObyte;
    word DACvalue;
```

```
    // Expecting 2 bytes to come
    // from the controller device.

    if( numBytes == 2 && Wire.available() )
    {
        HObyte = Wire.read();
        if( Wire.available() )
        {
            LObyte = Wire.read();

            DACvalue = ((HObyte << 8) | LObyte) & 0xfff;
            analogWrite( A14, DACvalue );
        }
    }
}

// Usual Arduino initialization function:

void setup( void )
{
    Serial.begin( 9600 );
    delay( 1000 );
    Serial.println( "I2C peripheral test" );

    // Initialize the Wire library to treat this
    // code as an I2C peripheral at address 0x60
    // (the SparkFun MCP4725 breakout board):

    Wire.begin( MCP4725_ADDR );

    // Set up the Teensy 3.2 DAC to have
    // 12-bit resolution:

    analogWriteResolution(12);

    // Define the I2C interrupt handler
    // for dealing with incoming I2C
    // packets:

    Wire.onReceive( rcvISR );
}

void loop( void )
{
    Serial.println( "MCP4725 emulator, waiting for data" );
    delay( 10000 ); // Delay 10 seconds
}
```

I connected the SCL, SDA, and Gnd pins of two Teensy 3.2 devices together (using a Teensy and an Arduino also works). On one of the units, I programmed the DAC output code similar to that found in Listing 8-1. On the other, I programmed the code in Listing 8-3. I put an oscilloscope on the A14 pin on the Teensy running the peripheral code (Listing 8-3). The output appears in Figure 8-3. Note that the peaks on the triangle waves are between 0.0 V and 3.3 V (rather than 0 V and 5 V in Figure 8-2) because the Teensy is a 3.3-V device.

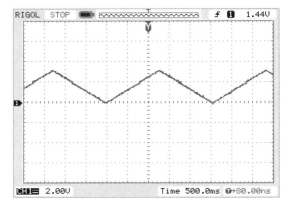

Figure 8-3: Triangle wave output from the Teensy 3.2 A14 pin

Figure 8-4 shows a small section of the output when some clock stretching occurs.

Figure 8-4: A stretched clock signal reduces the triangle wave frequency.

As you can see in Figure 8-4, the clock is stretched to 8.4 μsec after the transmission of the byte.

8.6   Multiple I²C Port Programming

The standard Arduino library assumes that only a single I²C bus is on the board (based on the hardware of the Arduino Uno). Many Arduino-compatible boards provide multiple I²C buses. This allows you to spread your I²C devices across multiple buses, allowing them to run faster, or to, perhaps, include two devices with the same address without having to resort to using an I²C bus multiplexer.

The standard Arduino library does not support multiple I²C buses; however, devices that do provide them will often provide some special library code that lets you access the additional I²C buses in the system. The Arduino convention when there are multiple instances of a device is to use a numeric suffix after the name to designate a particular device. In the case of the I²C bus, those device names are Wire (for the first, or 0th, port), Wire1, Wire2, and so on.

For example, to write a sequence of bytes to the second I^{2}C port, you might use code like the following:

```
Wire1.beginTransmission( 0x60 );
Wire1.write( (dacOut << 8) & 0xf );
Wire1.write( dacOut & 0xff );
Wire1.endTransmission( true );
```

The mechanism for achieving this is hardware and system specific. Check the documentation for your particular SBC to see how this is done.

8.7 Chapter Summary

The Arduino library provides the Wire object to support I^{2}C bus transactions. This chapter described the basic Wire functions available in the Arduino library, including those to initialize the I^{2}C library, choose the I^{2}C clock frequency, initiate a read from an I^{2}C peripheral, read peripheral data placed in the internal buffer, initialize a buffer for transmission to a peripheral, and more.

This chapter also included several real-world examples of I^{2}C communication using the SparkFun MCP4725.

FOR MORE INFORMATION

To learn more about Wire programming on the Arduino, you should first stop at the Arduino Wire library reference page: *https://www.arduino.cc/en/Reference/Wire*.

Simon Monk's book, *Programming Arduino Next Steps: Going Further with Sketches,* 2nd edition (McGraw-Hill Education TAB, 2018), contains a chapter on Arduino I^{2}C programming.

Of course, you can find about a bazillion different websites with Arduino I^{2}C programming examples. A quick web search for "Arduino I^{2}C examples" will probably turn up more hits than you are willing to read. Here are some additional resources:

Adafruit tutorials on Arduino I^{2}C programming: *https://learn.adafruit.com/circuitpython-basics-i2c-and-spi/i2c-devices*

SparkFun I^{2}C tutorials on Arduino I^{2}C programming: *https://learn.sparkfun.com/tutorials/i2c/all*

Datasheets for the MCP4725 DAC: *https://cdn-shop.adafruit.com/datasheets/mcp4725.pdf*

More information about the Teensy 3.2: *https://www.pjrc.com/store/teensy32.html*

9

RASPBERRY PI (AND LINUX) I²C PROGRAMMING

After the Arduino, the Raspberry Pi probably ranks second highest in I²C bus usage. In some respects, the I²C bus is probably even more important to Raspberry Pi hardware hackers than Arduino users because the Pi provides nothing in the way of analog-to-digital converters. Most often, Pi users add such capabilities to their systems using the I²C bus.

This chapter discusses the following:

- The I^{2}C bus on the Raspberry Pi's GPIO header
- How to activate the I^{2}C bus on the Raspberry Pi (by default, it is deactivated)
- How to set the I^{2}C bus speed, which may be necessary for slow peripherals as the Pi does not support clock stretching
- How to use the I^{2}C utility package on the Pi
- Programming I^{2}C devices on the Pi
- I^{2}C on other Linux-based systems
- A bit-banging implementation of I^{2}C on the Raspberry Pi to overcome some of the Pi's limitations

Although this chapter specifically discusses the Raspberry Pi single-board computer, Pi OS is really just a variant of the Linux operating system, so much of the information in this chapter covers generic Linux systems as well as the Raspberry Pi.

9.1 The I^{2}C Bus Pins on the Pi General-Purpose Input/Output Header

The Raspberry Pi has always supported at least one I^{2}C bus on the GPIO connector. Pins 3 and 5 (GPIO 2 and GPIO 3) provide the SDA and SCL lines, respectively. These pins were available on the original 26-pin GPIO header.

After the introduction of the Raspberry Pi B+, the GPIO header was extended to 40 pins, and a second hardware I^{2}C bus was added. This second I^{2}C bus (on pins 27 and 28 of the 40-pin header; see Figure 9-1) was originally intended to connect to EEPROM devices on Pi HATs—Raspberry Pi add-on boards whose name stands for "hardware attached on top." The I^{2}C EEPROM device provided identification information for the board so the operating system could identify it and load an appropriate device driver in a "plug-and-play" fashion.

The second I^{2}C lines were originally intended for EEPROM, camera, and DSI display use. Enabling these lines could cause the display, camera, and HAT units to malfunction, so most programmers and system designers leave these lines alone. However, if you are not using any of these devices, you could use the I^{2}C bus on pins 27 and 28 for your own purposes.

Technically, there is a third I^{2}C bus on the HDMI connector (a 5-V variant to support VESA E-DDC). In theory, you could use it with a bit of work. However, this book will not consider the use of that bus as it's really intended for use by the video display subsystem.

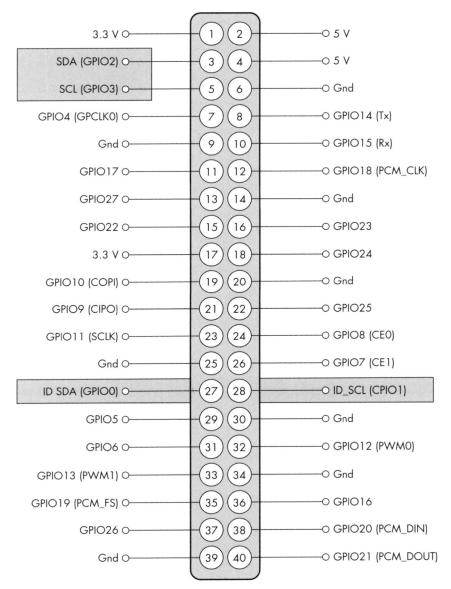

Figure 9-1: Main and alternate (HAT EEPROM) I²C pins on Raspberry Pi bus

With the arrival of the Raspberry Pi 4, the number of possible I²C buses increased yet again. Figure 9-2 shows the pinout of the 40-pin GPIO connector on the Raspberry Pi 4.

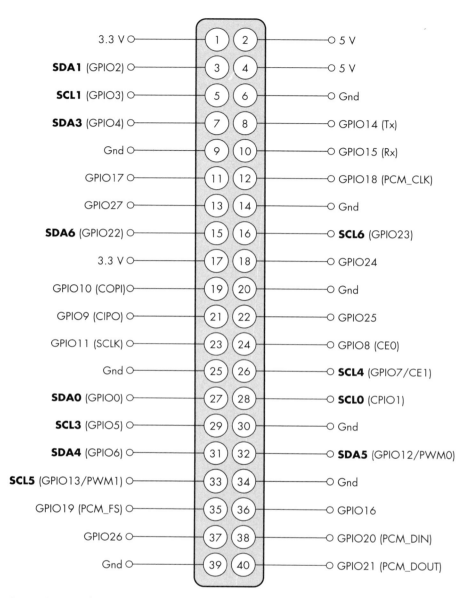

Figure 9-2: Raspberry Pi 4 GPIO pinout

Figure 9-2 shows six I²C buses on the Raspberry Pi 4:

i2c-0   SDA0 and SCL0 on pins 27 and 28

i2c-1   SDA1 and SCL1 on pins 3 and 5

i2c-3   SDA3 and SCL3 on pins 7 and 29

i2c-4   SDA4 and SCL4 on pins 31 and 26

i2c-5   SDA5 and SCL5 on pins 32 and 33

i2c-6   SDA6 and SCL6 on pins 15 and 16 (shares these pins with i2c-0)

Note that the i2c-1 bus on the Raspberry Pi provides pullup resistors to +3.3 V. The remaining I^2C ports do not. Therefore, if you activate any I^2C bus other than i2c-1, you will need to add pullup resistors for the bus to work properly.

9.2 Manually Activating the I^2C Buses

By default, the Raspberry Pi OS does not enable any of the I^2C buses on the GPIO connector—those pins default to their GPIO pin definitions. You can use the raspi-config application to activate the I^2C bus. This application will automatically edit appropriate system files to activate the I^2C bus. If you would like to manually make these changes yourself, you must edit a couple files on the Raspberry Pi to enable the appropriate I^2C bus(es).

If you want to activate i2c-1, you will need to edit the */boot/config.txt* text file as the superuser. In this file you will usually find the following line:

```
#dtparam=i2c_arm=on
```

The # at the beginning of this statement turns the whole line into a comment, making the statement invisible to the system and the I^2C bus inactivated. To activate the I^2C bus, simply delete the # character at the beginning of the line.

The i2c_arm label tells you that this particular I^2C port is part of the ARM processor (the CPU on the Raspberry Pi). The second I^2C port (pins 27 and 28, which is really Linux port i2c-0) is part of the video controller chip. You could activate that I^2C bus with the following statement:

```
dtparam=i2c_vc=on
```

However, the Raspberry Pi documentation is pretty clear that i2c-0 is reserved for HAT EEPROMs and you are not supposed to use it for other purposes (see *https://github.com/raspberrypi/hats/blob/master/designguide.md*). Abuse this suggestion at your own risk.

If you edit the dtparam=i2c_arm=on statement in */boot/config.txt* and reboot, you'll discover that the I^2C bus is still not available. This is because Raspberry Pi OS uses loadable kernel modules (LKMs) to handle I^2C processing. At this point the system hasn't loaded the appropriate module. To do that, execute the following two commands:

```
modprobe i2c-bcm2708 #Note:use i2c-bcm2835 on Pi zero W, 3, and 4
modprobe i2c-dev
```

Of course, manually loading these modules every time you boot the system can get old fast if you're using the I^2C all the time. If you edit the */etc/modules* file as superuser and add the following two lines to the file, the system will automatically load those modules when you boot the system:

```
i2c-bcm2708
i2c-dev
```

If you have a Raspberry Pi 4 system, you can enable additional I^{2}C buses by adding one or more of the following lines to the */boot/config.txt* text file:

```
dtoverlay=i2c1,pins_2_3
dtoverlay=i2c3,pins_4_5
dtoverlay=i2c4,pins_6_7
dtoverlay=i2c5,pins_12_13
dtoverlay=i2c6,pins_22_23
```

The pin numbers to which the pins_*xx*_*yy* parameters refer are the GPIO pin numbers, not the physical pin numbers on the Pi 40-pin connector. Table 9-1 lists the correspondence between GPIO pin numbers and physical pin numbers. See *https://www.raspberrypi.com/documentation/computers/os.html#gpio-and-the-40-pin-header* for more information.

Table 9-1: GPIO Pins to Physical Pin Numbers

GPIO pin number	Connector pin number
GPIO 2	Board pin 3
GPIO 3	Board pin 5
GPIO 4	Board pin 7
GPIO 5	Board pin 29
GPIO 6	Board pin 31
GPIO 7	Board pin 26
GPIO 12	Board pin 32
GPIO 13	Board pin 33
GPIO 22	Board pin 15
GPIO 23	Board pin 16

Finally, make sure the following line is present in *config.txt*:

```
enable_uart= 1
```

In theory, enabling the UART (serial port) shouldn't have anything to do with I^{2}C on the Pi. In practice (at least on a Pi 3), if you don't include this line, the system will run the SCL line at about 65 kHz rather than the nominal 100 kHz.

9.3   Changing the I^{2}C Clock Frequency

By default, Raspberry Pi sets the I^{2}C clock frequency to 100 kHz. To change the speed of the main I^{2}C bus (i2c-1), use the following statement in */boot/config.txt*:

```
dtparam=i2c_arm_baudrate=xxxxxx
```

where *xxxxxx* stands for the clock frequency (for example, 100000) that you want to use. Normally, you would place this statement immediately after dtparam=i2c_arm=on in that file.

The Raspberry Pi OS will choose an available clock frequency that is less than or equal to the value you specify.

On the Raspberry Pi 4, you can set the clock frequency of i2c-3, -4, -5, and -6 using the following statements:

```
dtoverlay=i2c3,pins_4_5
dtparam=baudrate=xxxxxx #sets clock frequency for i2c-3
dtoverlay=i2c4,pins_6_7
dtparam=baudrate=xxxxxx #sets clock frequency for i2c-4
dtoverlay=i2c5,pins_12_13
dtparam=baudrate=xxxxxx #sets clock frequency for i2c-5
dtoverlay=i2c6,pins_22_23
dtparam=baudrate=xxxxxx #sets clock frequency for i2c-6
```

Once again, Pi OS will choose a clock frequency that is less than or equal to the actual value you specify.

9.4 I²C Clock Stretching Issues and Solutions

At the time of writing, there has long been a known issue with the I²C protocol on the Raspberry Pi: the Pi does not support clock stretching. This issue seems to be with the hardware; it's been around so long (and across many different Raspberry Pi models) that you'd expect it to have been fixed by now if it were software. The bottom line is that if you have an I²C device that depends on adding wait states via clock stretching, that device may not work very well on a standard Pi I²C setup.

This problem has two solutions. The first is a big kludge: reduce the SCL clock frequency using the techniques from the previous section, hoping to slow the clock down enough that the clock period provides enough time for the peripheral to do its thing. Adafruit, for example, suggests setting the I²C clock frequency (*baudrate* in *config.txt* notation) to 10 kHz. Ideally, this is so slow that it gives your peripherals sufficient time to process the I²C data.

Slowing down the clock frequency is unsatisfactory for two main reasons. First, there is no guarantee that the new, slower clock frequency provides enough time for an arbitrary peripheral to do its work. Second, this technique slows down all bit transfers, including those to and from peripherals that don't use clock stretching as well as all the bits that don't need clock stretching on the devices that use it. In sum, this approach doesn't guarantee success and is very inefficient to boot.

The second solution is to use a *bit-banging* (software) I²C transmission. Software I²C processing can handle bit stretching properly. True, bit-banging is much slower and less efficient than a hardware implementation, but probably no more so than slowing down the hardware SCL frequency.

To set up a software-controlled I^{2}C bus using (arbitrary) GPIO pins, add the following statement to your */boot/config.txt* file:

```
dtoverlay=i2c-gpio,bus=x,i2c_gpio_sda=y,i2c_gpio_scl=z
```

where *x* represents a bus number, and *y* and *z* represent GPIO pins on the Raspberry Pi GPIO connector. This creates an I^{2}C device using the name i2c-*x* that operates on the specified GPIO pins (these are the GPIO pin number designations, not the physical pin numbers on the Pi GPIO connector).

If the i2c_gpio_sda parameter is not present, the system will use GPIO 23 as the default (physical pin 16 on the connector). If the i2c_gpio_scl parameter is not present, the system will use GPIO 24 (physical pin 18) as the default. If the bus parameter is not present, the system will dynamically assign a device number, so you really should explicitly provide the bus argument.

Note that the i2c-gpio device can use any arbitrary GPIO pins; you don't have to specify pins that have I^{2}C hardware associated with them. This means you can actually increase the number of supported I^{2}C buses in the system by using software-based I^{2}C devices (though, to be honest, if you need additional I^{2}C buses, an I^{2}C multiplexer is probably a better solution).

As a general rule, I would advise putting all I^{2}C devices that depend on clock stretching on an i2c-gpio device and place all other I^{2}C devices on hardware-based I^{2}C buses to make your system more efficient.

9.5 Raspberry Pi OS (Linux) I^{2}C Utilities

Several I^{2}C-specific utilities are useful on the Raspberry Pi. In addition to these, a few normal Linux and Raspberry Pi commands are also of interest when working with I^{2}C devices.

First, to determine whether the I^{2}C device drivers are even operational, enter the following Linux command:

```
ls /dev/i2c*
```

This command lists all the Linux I^{2}C devices you can currently access. For example, on my Raspberry Pi 4, I got the following output:

```
/dev/i2c-1 /dev/i2c-6
```

which tells me that I^{2}C interface 1 (i2c-1, on pins 3 and 5) and I^{2}C interface 6 (i2c-6, on pins 15 and 16) are currently active. Before even attempting to run an application that uses the I^{2}C signals, you should issue this command to verify that the I^{2}C buses are functioning.

The remaining four utilities I will discuss in this section are part of the i2c-tools package. Originally, Raspberry Pi OS did not include these tools by default, though later versions of Pi OS seem to include them. If they are not present on your system, you must download them using the following command:

```
sudo apt-get install i2c-tools libi2c-dev
```

This installs the four programs, i2cdetect, i2cdump, i2cget, and i2cset, on your system. The i2cdump utility is mainly useful for viewing the contents of I^2C EEPROM devices. We won't consider that application any further here; see the Linux man page for more information about this code.

The i2cget and i2cset programs allow you to read a byte or word from certain I^2C devices or write a byte or word to certain I^2C devices. Because of the way they operate, they will prove to be of marginal value to us in this chapter. Both applications assume that they write a register number to the I^2C address followed by additional data to write to that register (in the case of i2cset) or that they write a register number and then read data from the specified register number (in the case of i2cget). This works well for I^2C devices such as the MCP23017 GPIO expander IC. It does not work well for devices such as the MCP4725 DAC we're using as an example in this chapter.

To run the i2cget application, enter the following (the items in braces are optional):

```
i2cget {-y} i2cbus device_address {register {mode}}
i2cget -y i2cbus device_address register mode
```

where *i2cbus* is the number of an active I^2C bus (such as *1* for *i2c-1*), *device _address* is the 7-bit I^2C address of the device to read from, *register* is an 8-bit register number (specifying a particular register on the device), and *mode* is one of the letters b, w, or c (corresponding to byte, word, or R/W byte, respectively). If the *register* operand is present, this command will place the I^2C address on the bus and write the *register* value to the I^2C address. On a device such as the MCP23017, this sets the register inside the IC to read. The next operation is a read operation, with the system reading the specified register value from the IC. In the case of the MCP4725, there are no registers you can select by first writing a byte to the IC, so you should never specify the *register* argument when using this command. Doing so will write a value to the MCP4725 and affect the analog output.

Unfortunately, the i2cget application is poorly matched to the MCP4725. The MCP4725 returns 5 bytes of data when you read from the chip. The i2cget command will read a maximum of 2 bytes. There is no real way to use this command to read all the MCP4725 data, so we will ignore this command until Chapter 13.

The i2cset command is the output version of the i2cget program. It has the following syntax:

```
i2cset {-y} i2cbus device_address data_address {value} {mode}
```

where *i2cbus* and *device_address* have the same meanings as for the i2cget command. The *data_address* argument is effectively the same thing as the *register* operand in the i2cget command: it's a byte value that is written to the IC immediately after the address byte is placed on the bus with the assumption that this is selecting some register on the IC.

Again, the fact that it expects to be able to write a register (*data_address*) makes this program somewhat incompatible with the MCP4725 DAC. However, with some hackery, this one can actually be made to work with the DAC. The MCP4725 expects a 3-byte transmission (for the Fast Mode Write command). The first byte, of course, is the address and R/W bit, the second byte is the HO 4 bits of the 12-bit DAC value, and the third byte is the LO 8 bits of the DAC value. As it turns out, the i2cset command can be coerced to output this data using the following syntax:

```
i2cset -y i2cbus device_address HOByte LOByte
```

where *HOByte* is the upper 4 bits of the DAC output value and *LOByte* is the lower 8 bits of the DAC value.

Of the four utilities in the i2c-tools package, the i2cdetect program is, without question, the most useful of the batch. As its name suggests, this program detects I^{2}C devices on the I^{2}C bus. This program has three main forms, which the following paragraphs describe.

i2cdetect -l

The first form scans the system for all available I^{2}C buses and displays them. Note that the command-line option is l (the letter L, for *list*), not 1 (one). This command is similar to using ls /dev/i2c* to identify available I^{2}C buses. Executing this command on a Raspberry Pi 3 with I^{2}C enabled, I get the following output:

```
i2c-1 i2c bcm2835 (i2c@7e804000) I2C adapter
```

The second form of the i2cdetect command outputs status and capability information about the I^{2}C bus you specify as an argument:

i2cdetect -F bus

Here's some sample output on the Raspberry Pi for i2c-1:

```
Functionalities implemented by /dev/i2c-1:
I2C                     yes
SMBus Quick Command     yes
SMBus Send Byte         yes
SMBus Receive Byte      yes
SMBus Write Byte        yes
SMBus Read Byte         yes
SMBus Write Word        yes
SMBus Read Word         yes
SMBus Process Call      yes
SMBus Block Write       yes
```

SMBus Block Read	no
SMBus Block Process Call	no
SMBus PEC	yes
I2C Block Write	yes
I2C Block Read	yes

For a description of these Linux-kernel level functionalities, visit *https://www.kernel.org/doc/html/latest/i2c/functionality.html*.

The third form of the i2cdetect command scans the bus looking for valid I^2C devices and (if possible) reports their presence:

```
i2cdetect {-y} {-a} {-q|-r} bus {first last}
```

where *bus* is an I^2C bus specification (either an integer such as 1 or the bus name such as i2c-1). The optional *first* and *last* parameters are device addresses (with *first* < *last*) that limit the range of I^2C bus addresses that i2cdetect will scan.

Generally, use the command as follows or supply a different bus value as the argument:

```
i2cdetect 1
```

After entering the command, you'll get a warning prompt that this command may mess with I^2C devices on the bus. Knowing this, you'll be asked to verify that you want the command to probe the bus.

If you would prefer not to respond to this prompt when running i2cdetect (for example, from within a shell script), add the -y option, which tells the program "answer yes to the question":

```
i2cdetect -y 1
     0  1  2  3  4  5  6  7  8  9  a  b  c  d  e  f
00:          -- 04 -- -- -- -- -- -- -- -- -- -- --
10: -- -- -- -- -- -- -- -- -- -- -- -- -- -- -- --
20: -- -- -- -- -- -- -- -- -- -- -- -- -- -- -- --
30: -- -- -- -- -- -- -- -- -- -- -- -- -- -- -- --
40: -- -- -- -- -- -- -- -- -- -- -- -- -- -- -- --
50: -- -- -- -- -- -- -- -- -- -- -- -- -- -- -- --
60: -- -- 62 -- -- -- -- -- -- -- -- -- -- -- -- --
70: -- -- -- -- -- -- -- --
```

This matrix shows the valid I^2C addresses and whether i2cdetect has found a device at that address. The -- entries indicate that i2cdetect doesn't believe a device is at that address, and a hexadecimal number in the matrix indicates that a device exists at that address. In this case, i2cdetect found two devices at addresses 0x04 (probably the Broadcom I^2C hardware, as that address is reserved for high-speed controllers) and 0x62 (the Adafruit MCP4725 I currently have wired to the bus).

If a UU appears in one of the matrix entries, a device is installed at that address but is currently in use by the kernel, which commonly occurs, for example, when you've hooked a real-time clock (RTC) to the system to set the date and time automatically when the system boots.

As noted in Chapter 2, the I²C bus does not provide a standardized mechanism for detecting devices. SMBus devices, in particular, can react in a bad way with simple attempts to read or write the device without a data payload. Therefore, it is possible for the i2cdetect program to change the state of an I²C device on the bus just by probing for it, which is why i2cdetect asks you to verify that you really want to scan the bus before it transmits data.

Because i2cdetect can mess with certain types of peripherals on the bus, it offers an option to limit the scanning to a certain range of addresses. For example, if you know an MCP4725 DAC is installed but don't know what address it's connected to, use the following command to search for the DAC:

```
i2cdetect -y 1 0x60 0x67
```

The 0x60 and 0x67 arguments limit the scanning range of the program (we know that the MCP4725 must have an address in the range of 0x60 to 0x67 because of its hardware design).

The -q (quick write) and -r (quick read) arguments are advanced options, and using those options can corrupt EEPROMs or hang the system. See the i2cdetect man page for details and seriously consider what you are doing before using those options.

9.6 Reading and Writing I²C Data

Once you have installed and initialized the I²C drivers, transmitting and receiving data on the I²C bus is relatively straightforward. Like most devices, Raspberry Pi OS (Linux) treats the I²C bus like a file. You open the device driver as a file and then read and write data using the Linux read() and write() functions.

NOTE *Note that to write to the I²C bus, you must run the program using administrative or root privileges.*

First, call the Linux open() function to get a file handle associated with the I²C bus:

```
handle = open( busName, O_RDWR );
```

where *handle* is an integer (file descriptor) type and *busName* is a string containing the device name for the I²C bus you want to use. Bus names are the */dev/i2c** names for the buses you've defined in the */boot/config.txt* file. For example, the standard I²C bus is */dev/i2c-1*.

The open() function returns a negative number on an error and a non-negative file handle value if it is successful. Save the file handle value so you can read and write data later.

Before accessing the I²C bus, you must set the address of the peripheral device you want to access using the Linux ioctl() (I/O control) function, as follows:

```
result = ioctl( handle, I2C_SLAVE, i2cAddr );
```

where *result* is an integer variable that holds the error return result, *handle* is the handle the open() function call returns, and *i2cAddr* is the 7-bit address of the peripheral to access.

You can call ioctl() multiple times on the same file handle in order to access different peripherals on the same I²C bus. Raspberry Pi OS will continue to use the same peripheral address for all read and write operations until you explicitly change it.

To read data from an I²C peripheral, you use the Linux read() function using the following syntax:

```
result = read( handle, buffer, bufferSize );
```

where *result* is an integer variable that will hold the function return result (a negative if an error or number of bytes read if non-negative), *handle* is the I²C bus handle returned by open(), *buffer* is an array of bytes that will receive the data, and *bufferSize* is the number of bytes to read. If everything happens correctly, the function returns *bufferSize* as the result.

To write data to the peripheral, use the write function:

```
result = write( handle, buffer, bufferSize );
```

The arguments are the same as for read() except the buffer holds the data to be written (rather than being a storage location for the data read).

The program in Listing 9-1 demonstrates reading and writing data on the I²C bus using the open(), read(), write(), and ioctl() functions. As in the previous chapter, this program emits a triangle wave on the MCP4725 DAC outputs.

```cpp
// Listing9-1.cpp

// Demonstrates reading from and
// writing to an MCP4725 DAC.

#include <unistd.h>
#include <fcntl.h>
#include <sys/ioctl.h>
#include <linux/i2c-dev.h>

#include <stdio.h>
#include <string.h>
#include <errno.h>
```

```
        #define ever  ;;

❶ #define i2cDevname       "/dev/i2c-1"
  //#define i2cAddr (0x60) // Adafruit MCP4725 address
  #define i2cAddr (0x62)    // SparkFun MCP4725 address

  int main()
  {
      #define bufferSize (5)

      static unsigned char buffer[bufferSize + 1];

      // Open the I2C interface (i2c-1):

    ❷ int fd_i2c = open( i2cDevname, O_RDWR );

      if( fd_i2c < 0 )
      {
          printf
          (
              "Error opening %s, terminating\n",
              i2cDevname
          );
          return -1;
      }

      // Assign the device address of the MCP4725 to
      // the open handle:

    ❸ int result = ioctl( fd_i2c, I2C_SLAVE, i2cAddr );
      if( result < 0 )
      {
          printf
          (
              "Error attaching MCP4725: %d, %s\n",
              result,
              strerror( result )
          );
          return result;
      }

      // Just for fun, read the 5 data bytes from the
      // MCP4725.

    ❹ result=read( fd_i2c , buffer, bufferSize );
      if( result < 0 )
      {
          printf
          (
              "Error reading from %s, terminating: %s\n",
              i2cDevname,
              strerror( errno )
          );
```

```
        return -1;
    }

    printf( "Data from DAC:\n" );
    for ( int i = 0; i < bufferSize; i++ )
    {
        printf( "0x%02x ", (int) buffer[i] );
    }
    printf( "\n" );

    // Continuously send a triangle wave to the
    // MCP4725 until the user hits CTRL-C:

    for(ever)
    {
        // Output the rising edge:

        for( int i=0; i < 4095; ++i )
        {
            buffer[0] = (i >> 8) & 0xf; // HO 4 bits is first
            buffer[1] = i & 0xff;       // LO byte is second

            // Write the two bytes to the DAC:

          ❺ result = write( fd_i2c, buffer, 2 );
        }

        // Output the falling edge:

        for( int i=4095; i > 1; --i )
        {
            buffer[0] = (i >> 8) & 0xf; // HO 4 bits is first
            buffer[1] = i & 0xff;       // LO byte is second

            // Write the two bytes to the DAC:

            result = write( fd_i2c, buffer, 2 );
        }
    }

    return 0;
}
```

In Listing 9-1, the Linux filename for the main Raspberry Pi I^{2}C port is "/dev/i2c-1" ❶. To write to the Raspberry Pi I^{2}C port, open it like a file ❷. To read or write a particular I^{2}C address, you must first issue an ioctl() call with the I2C_SLAVE argument and the I^{2}C address to use. From that point forward (until another ioctl() call changes the address), reads and writes to the I^{2}C bus will use this address ❸. To read data from the I^{2}C bus, just call the read() function specifying the file handle returned by the earlier open() call for the I^{2}C port ❹. To write data to the I^{2}C bus, call the write() function and specify the I^{2}C file handle ❺.

Figure 9-3 shows the DAC output on an oscilloscope.

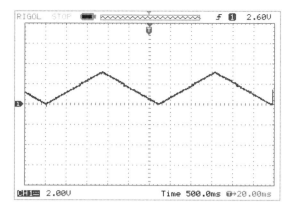

Figure 9-3: Triangle wave output from Raspberry Pi 3

The output is only 3.3 V (rather than 5 V) because the Pi is a 3.3-V machine (I'm running the MCP4725 at 3.3 V, though you could run it at 5 V as long as the SCL and SDA lines are 3.3 V).

9.7 Advanced I²C Kernel Calls

Although using open(), read(), write(), and ioctl() works reasonably well for simple I²C bus transactions, various forms of the ioctl() function provide more advanced operations called *kernel function calls*.

The kernel function calls take place through the Linux ioctl() API function. You marshal up some parameters in a data structure along with a function identifier and call ioctl(). The ioctl() function decodes its arguments and then passes the parameters along to the specified function. That function returns appropriate function results (via the ioctl() return value and the parameter list you pass to ioctl()). Consider the following i2c_smbus_access() function that sets parameters for various Linux SMBus (I²C) function calls:

```
#include <linux/i2c.h>

static inline __s32 i2c_smbus_access
(
    int file,
    char read_write,
    __u8 command,
    int size,
    union i2c_smbus_data *data
){
    struct i2c_smbus_ioctl_data args;

    args.read_write = read_write;
```

```
    args.command = command;
    args.size = size;
    args.data = data;
    return ioctl( file,I2C_SMBUS,&args );
}
```

This function copies its arguments into a local data structure (args) and then passes them on to the ioctl() function with the I2C_SMBUS argument that tells ioctl() to call one of the SMBus functions; the args.command parameter specifies the particular function to call. Most of the I2C_SMBUS functions use the same parameter list: the read_write, size, and data fields of the args structure.

Note that i2c_smbus_access() isn't actually a specific SMBus function. It's the function that marshals the arguments and passes them on to ioctl(), a *dispatcher function*: a single entry point (into the OS in this case) that transfers (dispatches) control to one of several different functions. An example of a specific SMBus function is i2c_smbus_read_byte():

```
static inline __s32 i2c_smbus_read_byte( int file )
{
    union i2c_smbus_data data;
    if
    (
        i2c_smbus_access
        (
            file,
            I2C_SMBUS_READ,
            0,
            I2C_SMBUS_BYTE,
            &data
        )
    ){
        return -1;
    }
    return 0x0FF & data.byte;
}
```

This function uses i2c_smbus_access() to marshal the parameters and make the actual call to ioctl().

The following subsections describe the SMBus functions available via the ioctl() dispatcher. While some of these functions are very SMBus specific, many of them are quite useful for normal I^{2}C operations.

9.7.1 The i2c-dev Functions

The *linux/i2c-dev.h* header file defines the SMBus functions that follow. The apt-get install libi2c-dev command entered earlier in this chapter installs this header file so you can use this library in your applications. You do not have to link a specific library against your code to use these functions, because the i2c-dev functions are installed as part of the kernel (or a loadable module) and accessed via the ioctl() API call. To access these functions, include the following statements at the beginning of your C/C++ applications:

```
extern "C" { // Required for CPP compilation
    #include <linux/i2c-dev.h>
    #include <i2c/smbus.h>
    #include <sys/ioctl.h>
}
```

The header file itself contains the function definitions that the following sections describe. They are all *static inline* functions, so the compiler expands them (as macros) directly in place of the calls you make.

This header file, through its own includes, defines the types shown in Table 9-2.

Table 9-2: Integer Types

Type	Meaning
__u8	Unsigned 8-bit integer
__u16	Unsigned 16-bit integer
__u32	Unsigned 32-bit integer
__s8	Signed 8-bit integer
__s16	Signed 16-bit integer
__s32	Signed 32-bit integer

You must pass the following functions a file handle specifying the I^2C bus to use. You obtain the file handle using the open() function (see section 9.6, "Reading and Writing I^2C Data," earlier in this chapter). You do not pass these functions a device address. Instead, specify the device address to use with an ioctl() call, for example, ioctl(*handle,* I2C_SLAVE, *i2cAddr*). Once you set the device address for a given I^2C bus (specified by the *handle*), that address remains in effect until you explicitly change it with another ioctl() call.

The following functions all return -1 if an error occurs. The write() functions return 0 if they are successful. The read() functions will either return the value read from the bus (when reading a single value) or return the number of bytes read when reading a block of bytes.

9.7.2   The i2c_smbus_write_quick Function

The i2c_smbus_write_quick() function writes a single bit value to an I^2C device:

```
__s32 i2c_smbus_write_quick( int file, __u8 value );
```

In this function, file is a file handle returned by the open function (generally specifying the I^{2}C device, such as i2c-1), while value is the bit value (0 or 1) to write to the I^{2}C bus specified by file.

This function writes a single bit to the I^{2}C bus. The data payload is buried in the R/W bit of the address byte transmitted on the bus. This function transmits the start condition, the address byte (with data payload in R/W), and a stop condition. There are no data bytes transmitted as part of this operation.

9.7.3   The i2c_smbus_read_byte Function

The i2c_smbus_read_byte() function reads a single byte from the I^{2}C bus. Here is the prototype:

```
__s32 i2c_smbus_read_byte( int file );
```

This function returns a single byte from the I^{2}C device on the bus specified by the file handle you pass as an argument (the device address was set up earlier with an ioctl() call). The function transmits a start condition and an address byte to the device. It then reads the response byte from the device. Finally, it transmits the stop condition.

Do not use this function to read a sequence of bytes from an I^{2}C device—for example, reading all the status information from an MCP4725. Because it brackets the address and data values with start and stop conditions, you'll likely wind up reading just the first byte of the data sequence twice in a row. The program in Listing 9-2 demonstrates this problem.

```
// Listing9-2.cpp
//
// Demonstration of two consecutive
// i2c_smbus_read_byte calls.
//
// gcc Listing9-2.c -li2c

#include <unistd.h>          // Needed for I2C port
#include <fcntl.h>           // Needed for I2C port
extern "C"                   // Needed for C++ compiler
{
    #include <linux/i2c-dev.h>  // Needed for I2C port
    #include <i2c/smbus.h>
}
#include <sys/ioctl.h>
#include <stdio.h>

#define i2cDevname      "/dev/i2c-1"
#define i2cAddr (0x62)       // Adafruit MCP4725 address
//#define i2cAddr (0x60)     // SparkFun MCP4725 address

int main()
{
    unsigned char buffer[2];
```

```
    int file;

    file = open( i2cDevname, O_RDWR );
    ioctl( file, I2C_SLAVE, i2cAddr );
    buffer[0] = i2c_smbus_read_byte( file );
    buffer[1] = i2c_smbus_read_byte( file );
    printf( "Buffer[0,1]=%02x, %02x\n", buffer[0], buffer[1] );
    return 0;

}
```

When connected to a SparkFun MCP4725 at address 0x60, the program in Listing 9-2 produced the following output:

```
Buffer[0,1]=c0, c0
```

The program just read the status information byte twice. When reading data from non-SMBus devices (such as the MCP4725), use standard I²C read operations; save this function for actual SMBus devices.

9.7.4   The i2c_smbus_write_byte() Function

The i2c_smbus_write_byte() function writes a single byte to an I²C device:

```
__s32 i2c_smbus_write_byte( int file, __u8 value );
```

The *file* argument is a handle specifying the bus (device), and *value* is the byte to transmit on the bus. This function transmits a start condition, an address byte, a data byte, and, finally, a stop condition.

As with the i2c_smbus_read_byte() function, do not use this function to write a sequence of bytes to an I²C device (such as writing the DAC value to an MCP4725). Because it brackets the address and data values with start and stop conditions, you'll likely wind up writing only the first byte of the data sequence twice in a row.

9.7.5   The i2c_smbus_read_byte_data() Function

The i2c_smbus_read_byte_data() function writes a register number to an I²C device and then reads a data byte (presumably from the register specified by the write operation). The prototype is

```
__s32 i2c_smbus_read_byte_data( int file, __u8 command );
```

where *file* is the file handle specifying the I²C device and *command* is a register number or command byte to write to the device before reading from it.

This function transmits the start condition, the address byte with the R/W set to 0 (write), and then the command byte. Then it sends a (re)start condition, followed by another address byte (this time with the R/W bit set to 1). The peripheral responds by transmitting a data byte and then the controller puts a stop condition on the bus. The program in Listing 9-3 demonstrates this call.

```
// Listing9-3.cpp
//
// Demonstration of i2c_smbus_read_byte_data call.
//
// gcc listing-9-3.c -li2c

#include <unistd.h>
#include <fcntl.h>
extern "C"                      // Needed for C++ compiler
{
    #include <linux/i2c-dev.h> // Needed for I2C port
    #include <i2c/smbus.h>
}
#include <sys/ioctl.h>
#include <stdio.h>

#define i2cDevname      "/dev/i2c-1"
#define i2cAddr (0x62)          // Adafruit MCP4725 address
//#define i2cAddr (0x60)        // SparkFun MCP4725 address

int main()
{
    unsigned char result;
    int file;

    file = open( i2cDevname, O_RDWR );
    ioctl( file, I2C_SLAVE, i2cAddr );
    result = i2c_smbus_read_byte_data( file, 0 );
    printf( "Result=%02x\n", result );
    return 0;
}
```

Figure 9-4 shows the logic analyzer output when running the program in Listing 9-3. As you can see from this image, the i2c_smbus_read_byte_data() function call emits two I²C operations: a write operation (writing the byte 0, which was the command argument in the call) and a read operation, which winds up reading 0xC0 from the DAC (the status byte). You can't see it because Figure 9-4 is not in color, but between the two transmissions is a restart condition: a start condition without a stop condition from the previous transmission (the dot between the commands).

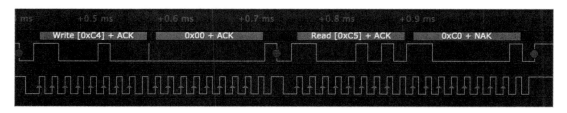

Figure 9-4: Logic analyzer output when running the program in Listing 9-3

Normally, you would not use this function on an MCP4725 DAC device. Writing a single byte wipes out the HO 4 bits of the output value (without affecting the LO byte). Of course, reading a single byte does very little good as well, unless you're interested only in the status byte from the MCP4725.

Generally, you would use this function to talk to a more sophisticated device that requires writing a command or register byte before reading a byte back from the device, which is a common sequence with SMBus devices. For example, the MCP23017 GPIO expander IC works in this fashion.

The big difference between this function call and a call to write a byte followed by a call to read a byte is that the latter form would emit a stop condition after writing the first byte. This stop condition would reset the state machine logic of devices, such as the MCP23017, and might cause it to treat the second write as an independent operation, leaving the bus vulnerable to a different controller sending data.

9.7.6   The i2c_smbus_write_byte_data() Function

The i2c_smbus_write_byte_data() function writes a byte to specify an I^2C device register and then writes a second byte to that register. This is its prototype:

```
static inline __s32 i2c_smbus_write_byte_data
(
    int file,
    __u8 command,
    __u8 value
);
```

Like the i2c_smbus_read_byte_data() function, this call is mainly intended for use when communicating with devices such as the MCP23017 GPIO expander that expect you to transmit a register number immediately before transmitting the data byte.

9.7.7   The i2c_smbus_read_word_data() Function

The i2c_smbus_read_word_data() function writes a register number to an I^2C device and then reads a pair of bytes from the device (presumably from the specified register). This is its prototype:

```
__s32 i2c_smbus_read_word_data( int file, __u8 command );
```

This function is similar to i2c_smbus_read_byte_data() except that it reads 2 bytes (a word) after writing the command byte to the I^2C bus.

When this function executes, the following I^2C bus transactions occur:

1.   A start condition is sent.
2.   The address byte with an R/W bit of 0 is sent.
3.   The command byte is sent.
4.   A (re)start condition is sent.
5.   The address byte with an R/W bit of 1 is sent.
6.   Two bytes are read from the peripheral device.
7.   A stop condition is sent.

This function reads the bytes back in little-endian order; that is, the first byte it reads from the bus is the LO byte, and the second byte it reads is the HO byte, which is often reversed from the way data actually arrives. For example, when using this function to read the MCP4725 DAC, the word comes back with the status byte in the LO 8 bits and the next byte read (which turns out, coincidentally, to be the HO 8 bits of the last DAC value written) in the HO byte. Be aware of that issue when using this function.

9.7.8 The i2c_smbus_write_word_data() Function

The i2c_smbus_write_word_data() function writes 3 bytes to an I²C device: the first byte specifies a register number, and the next 2 bytes are a word value that is written to that register. This is its prototype:

```
i2c_smbus_write_word_data( int file, __u8 command, __u16 value )
```

This function is similar to i2c_smbus_write_byte_data(), except that it writes 2 bytes (a word) after writing the command byte to the I²C bus. Note that this function writes the bytes in little-endian order. Be aware of this issue when using this function.

When this function executes, the following I²C bus transactions occur:

1. A start condition is sent.
2. The address byte with an R/W bit of 0 is sent.
3. The command byte is sent.
4. The LO byte of value is sent.
5. The HO byte of value is sent.
6. A stop condition is sent.

Note that, unlike the read word function, only a single address byte is sent with no restart conditions. This function simply writes 3 bytes (a command and 2 data bytes) after the address byte. The first byte, presumably, is a register or command byte followed by 2 data bytes.

9.7.9 The i2c_smbus_read_block_data() Function

The i2c_smbus_read_block_data() function reads a block of data from the specified device and places that data in the values array. This function first writes the register number or command byte to the device, and then the device responds with the data. Here is its prototype:

```
static inline __s32 i2c_smbus_read_block_data
(
    int file,
    __u8 command,
    __u8 *values
}
```

This command is useful for very specific I^{2}C devices. The bus transactions are the following:

1. A start condition is sent.
2. The address byte with an R/W bit of 0 is sent.
3. The `command` byte is sent.
4. A (re)start condition is sent.
5. The address byte with an R/W bit of 1 is sent.
6. The system reads a count byte (*n*) and then reads *n* bytes from the device (the particular device determines how many bytes are actually read).
7. A stop condition is sent.

NOTE   *The* `i2c_smbus_read_block_data()` *function requires SMBus block read functionality. On the Raspberry Pi, the I^{2}C device driver does not support this functionality, so this function will not work. Execute the* **i2cdetect -F 1** *command (or whatever bus you want to check in place of the* **1***) to verify whether this function—and, indeed, any of these functions—work.*

To read an arbitrary block of bytes from the I^{2}C bus, without a command or register byte, just use the Linux `read` function.

9.7.10 The i2c_smbus_write_block_data() Function

The `i2c_smbus_write_block_data()` function writes a block of data to the specified device. This function first writes the register number or command byte to the device followed by the data. This is its prototype:

```
static inline __s32 i2c_smbus_write_block_data
(
    int file,
    __u8 command,
    __u8 length,
    const __u8 *values
)
```

This function writes a `command` byte to the device and then a write of `length` bytes specified by the `values` array. The bus transactions are the following:

1. A start condition is put on the bus.
2. An address byte with the R/W bit set to 0 is written to the bus.
3. The `command` byte is written to the bus.
4. `length` bytes from `values` are written to the bus.
5. A stop condition is placed on the bus.

No extra address byte is written after the `command` byte. Indeed, this function is roughly equivalent to sticking the `command` byte at the beginning of the values array and calling the Linux `write` function with `length+1` as the number of bytes to write.

9.7.11 Miscellaneous Functions

There are a few other miscellaneous (SMBus-only), lesser-used functions that I'm not going to document here. For more information on those functions, check out the Linux kernel I^2C documentation at *https://www.kernel.org/doc/Documentation/i2c/smbus-protocol*.

9.8 Reentrancy Issues with I^2C Operations

Keep in mind that Linux (Raspberry Pi OS) is a multitasking operating system. Therefore, it is perfectly possible for two different threads or processes to attempt to access the I^2C bus concurrently. Linux will serialize access to the I^2C/SMBus device driver automatically. Therefore, if some thread is currently executing I^2C code inside the Linux kernel and another thread attempts to invoke some I^2C kernel code, the Linux system will block the second task until the first thread exits the `ioctl()` call. In that sense, you don't have to worry about reentrancy or anything like that.

That said, two different threads cannot talk concurrently to the same device, but two different threads can talk to two independent devices on the I^2C bus. Therefore, Linux will allow two threads, or even the same thread, to open the same bus multiple times. This means that, for example, two different threads could open the i2c-1 bus and both of them could write data to the same MCP4725 DAC. Of course, the output of the DAC will be really messed up if both threads are writing to the DAC independently. Unfortunately, Linux cannot solve this problem for you. You must exercise care when writing multiple threads or programs that might access the same I^2C device concurrently.

9.9 Multicontroller Operation Under Linux

As far as I can tell, the Raspberry Pi OS (and Linux in general) does not support multiple controllers on the same I^2C bus. Linux is a single-controller, multiple-peripheral I^2C interface.

I suspect the Raspberry Pi hardware will not support multiple controllers, given the aforementioned hardware issue with the Raspberry Pi I^2C controller, which doesn't handle clock stretching properly, and the fact that the same types of operations are necessary for clock synchronization and arbitration. Of course, this issue applies only to the Pi; other Linux systems will likely support multiple controllers on the same bus just fine.

9.10 Other Linux Systems

This chapter has largely focused on the Raspberry Pi, but in truth, the only really Pi-specific topic in this chapter is activating the I^2C bus. Most of the functions and utilities this chapter discusses are generic to Linux. The following subsections describe some other common Linux-based systems that support I^{2}C for general interfacing purposes.

9.10.1 PINE A64 and ROCKPro64

The ROCKPro64 is a 64-bit ARM SBC built to look and behave a whole lot like the Raspberry Pi. While it is a great little board (along with its smaller brother, the PINE A64), the folks at PINE64 rely on third parties to provide their Linux operating system ports. Multiple ports are available, which makes it a bit difficult to find a reasonable tutorial on getting the SBC to enable the I^{2}C lines. Here are some references (both describe I^{2}C programming on the ROCKPro64 SBC) I've found that might prove helpful if you're using one of these machines:

- *https://forum.armbian.com/topic/8792-i2c-and-i2s-on-rock64*
- *http://synfare.com/599N105E/hwdocs/rock64/index.html*

9.10.2 BeagleBone Black

The BeagleBone Black is an open source alternative to the Raspberry Pi. Because this device was designed with hardware hackers in mind, it's not surprising that it comes with the i2c-tools set already installed and I^{2}C buses pre-activated.

On the BeagleBone Black, bus i2c-2 (pins 19 and 20 on the P9 connector; see Figure 6-10 in Chapter 6) is generally available for external use. Use "/dev/i2c-2" as the filename when opening the bus to access the bus on the BeagleBone Black.

9.10.3 Onion Omega2+

The Onion Omega2+ is a small Linux-based module intended for IoT operation. This little module comes with I^{2}C communication installed and ready to run.

Onion provides an I^{2}C library you can link with to access I^{2}C devices. Check out Onion's I^{2}C documentation at *https://docs.onion.io/omega2-docs*.

9.11 Using the Raspberry Pi as an I^{2}C Peripheral Device

Although the standard Raspberry Pi hardware and device drivers do not support using the Pi as an I^{2}C peripheral device, it is possible to do so using bit-banging techniques. The pigpio free software library (*https://abyz.me.uk/rpi/pigpio*) provides an API for dealing with the GPIO pins on the Raspberry Pi. This library provides a software-based I^{2}C interface supporting both controller and peripheral modes.

The pigpio library also supports bit-banging controller operations. Using a software-controlled I^{2}C driver provides additional features not possible with the hardware I^{2}C system, including the following:

- Baud rates as low as 50
- Repeated starts
- Clock stretching
- I^{2}C on any pair of spare GPIO

See *https://abyz.me.uk/rpi/pigpio/cif.html#bbI2COpen* for more information on the bit-banging I^{2}C functions in the pigio library.

Finally, pigpio also provides a veneer (facade design pattern) over the existing ioctl() functions. See *https://abyz.me.uk/rpi/pigpio/cif.html#i2cOpen* for a list of these functions.

9.12 Chapter Summary

This chapter discussed I^{2}C programming on the Raspberry Pi, beginning with a discussion of the I^{2}C pins on the Pi 40-pin GPIO header. It showed how to activate the I^{2}C buses on the Pi and adjust the SCL clock frequency, and then it covered some issues with I^{2}C on the Pi, such as its lack of support for clock stretching. You also learned various generic Linux utilities you can use to probe the I^{2}C bus and access certain types of I^{2}C peripherals. However, the real meat of this chapter was its treatment of reading and writing data on the I^{2}C bus via Linux, including various advanced kernel calls. Unlike Arduino and other simple systems, Linux is a full multitasking/multiprocessing operating system. To address the problems in such systems, this chapter briefly discussed reentrancy issues and how to work around the problems when multiple threads or processes are accessing the same I^{2}C bus concurrently.

Although this chapter focused on the Raspberry Pi, the Pi is a generic Linux system, and most of the comments in this chapter that are not Pi-hardware-specific apply to other Linux-based systems as well. Therefore, the chapter also gave an overview of I^{2}C programming on the PINE A64 or ROCKPro64, the BeagleBone Black, and the Onion Omega2+. Finally, you learned to use the Raspberry Pi as an I^{2}C peripheral device with the pigpio library, as well as how to use the same library for generic bit-banging I^{2}C support.

FOR MORE INFORMATION

Enabling I^{2}C ports on Raspberry Pi:

> *https://www.raspberrypi-spy.co.uk/2014/11/enabling-the-i2c-interface-on -the-raspberry-pi*

> *https://www.instructables.com/id/How-to-enable-I2C-on-RaspberryPI*

> *(continued)*

I²C/SMBus functions under Linux: *https://www.kernel.org/doc/html/latest/i2c/smbus-protocol.html*

I²C on the BeagleBone Black: *http://beaglebone.cameon.net/home/i2c-devices*

I²C on the Onion Omega2+: *https://docs.onion.io/omega2-docs/communicating-with-i2c-devices.html*

10

I²C PROGRAMMING IN REAL-TIME OPERATING SYSTEMS

I²C transmissions are slow, typically 100 kHz. In systems like Arduino, your code must wait for each transmission or reception to complete before doing other work, which drastically reduces your application's performance. While waiting, the CPU is just executing a busy-waiting loop (also called a *spin loop*), wasting CPU cycles. In this chapter, you'll learn to use real-time operating systems (RTOSs) to put those CPU cycles to work.

This chapter introduces several different RTOSs—µC/OS, FreeRTOS, Teensy Threads, and Mbed—that you can run on typical SBCs, and it provides an example program using I²C for each. Some RTOSs, such as Mbed, provide full I²C support. Others, like FreeRTOS and Teensy Threads, are simple schedulers for which you must provide your own compatible I²C library code. The choice of RTOS is often dictated by the SBC you're using, since if you've chosen a particular SBC to use, you can run only an RTOS that has been ported to that board. Conversely, if you want to use a particular RTOS, you must choose an SBC to which it has been ported—unless you're willing to set up the port yourself, which is generally a lot of work.

This chapter begins with a description of some basic RTOS concepts and then introduces a few RTOSs, along with one or a few representative SBCs to use with the RTOS the section describes. This is not to suggest that the SBC I pair with a given RTOS is the only (or even the best) SBC to use with that RTOS—these are just the components I had available while writing this book. For most of these RTOSs, you'll generally have a much wider selection of platforms to choose from when designing your own systems.

10.1 Real-Time Operating System Basics

The purpose of an RTOS is to handle asynchronous events, such as the completion of an I^2C transmission, within a guaranteed amount of time. Another way to do this, of course, is via *polling*—the CPU simply waits in a spin loop, testing for the event until it occurs and then immediately handling it. While polling has some advantages (in particular, it can provide the fastest response time to an event), there's also a huge disadvantage: the CPU is tied up in the spin loop and cannot do other work.

This book will typically use the term *task* to denote some generic execution unit that is running (pseudo-)concurrently with other execution units. Threads and processes are examples of types of tasks, which I'll discuss shortly.

RTOSs allow other tasks to do work while the CPU is waiting for some event to occur. Some hardware support is needed to make this practical; in particular, the external event must be capable of generating an interrupt signal on the CPU. As its name suggests, an *interrupt signal* will cause the CPU to suspend execution of the currently executing task and transfer control to a special ISR that will handle the event. For some devices, the ISR completely handles the event, and the suspended task resumes control. With most RTOSs and ISRs, however, the ISR simply sets a flag that notes the event has occurred, and the RTOS will schedule the execution of the original code (which was waiting for the completion of an I^2C transaction or some other task) for some point in the future.

NOTE *The RTOS's guaranteed response time is the length of time between when the event occurs (the interrupt) and when the ISR starts executing. If the ISR sets a flag to execute some additional handler code in the future, there is no guarantee that such execution will take place within a specified time period. If some action must be immediately taken after the event, that action must take place in the ISR.*

In the context of an I^2C write, for example, a call to the write function will set up the I^2C hardware to begin the transmission of the data on the I^2C bus. Then the task that is writing the data will *suspend*, allowing other tasks to do some work. When the I^2C transmission is complete, the I^2C hardware will generate an interrupt, and the ISR will make a special system call to the RTOS telling it to wake up the suspended task that was writing data to the I^2C bus.

The RTOS moves the I^{2}C write task from a suspended queue to a ready-to-run queue. This, however, does not guarantee that the I^{2}C write task immediately begins execution (that depends on various RTOS scheduling policies). Control might transfer back to the task that was just suspended when the interrupt came along.

At some point in the future, the RTOS will decide to allow the I^{2}C write task to continue execution. It will then move the task off the ready-to-run queue and start it running, suspending the currently executing task. At that time, the I^{2}C write task can continue doing whatever it needs to do, such as writing additional data, reading data, or simply returning to the application that requested the I^{2}C write operation.

10.1.1 Processes and Threads

Operating systems theory defines multiple levels of tasks, including processes and threads. As noted earlier, this book will use the generic term *task* to describe both processes and threads.

A *thread* is a unit of execution that shares an address space with other concurrently executing threads. Because the threads share memory (the address space), one thread can change the memory that another thread reads. This provides an easy way for the threads to communicate with one another, but it also introduces some problems, as you'll see in the next section.

A *process* is a unit of execution that has its own address space and does not share that memory with other processes. Communication between processes is a little more difficult than with threads, since you typically have to use files or other OS-defined data structures for the communication. However, because the processes can't overwrite each other's memory spaces, there's less opportunity for them to interfere with one another.

An application may consist of one or more processes. Each process will contain one or more threads. The simplest application consists of a single process executing a single thread. One step up in complexity is an application executing a single process that has multiple threads of execution. Above that are applications with multiple processes, each with one or more threads of execution.

The easiest visualization of multiple processes and threads is to think of each process and thread corresponding to procedures or functions in a programming language. Each independent process or thread corresponds to a unique function that executes the code for that process or thread. While this is a simple model to visualize, it is actually common for different processes and threads to share the same code. For example, two threads of execution could run the same function in memory, perhaps being passed different parameters to allow them to do different operations.

10.1.2 Multithreading and Multitasking

The principal function of an RTOS is to allow multiple threads to run concurrently. A few microcontrollers include multiple CPUs (*multicore CPUs*), meaning two or more tasks really can run on different CPUs at exactly the same time. However, most embedded microcontrollers are limited to a single

CPU (core), allowing only a single task to run at any given time. To simulate multitasking (also known as *multithreading*), RTOSs rapidly switch between tasks to give the illusion that multiple tasks are executing concurrently.

Most modern RTOSs use preemption to suspend one task and then allow another to execute. Each RTOS uses a given policy to determine how to preempt a running task. Some RTOSs give each task a fixed amount of time to run and switch between tasks when the timer expires. This time period is known as a *time slice* or *time quantum*; the process of switching between tasks is called *time multiplexing*. Other RTOSs assign priorities to different tasks and allow higher-priority tasks to run unimpeded until they suspend or a higher-priority task is ready to run. Many RTOSs use a combination of these policies. For example, if two tasks with the same priority are ready to run, they use time slicing to switch between themselves, while lower-priority tasks remain suspended until both tasks suspend themselves.

In a pure priority-based system, lower-priority tasks may never run if some higher-priority task is always running. This could lead to *starvation*, meaning a given task never executes. Many RTOSs temporarily raise the priority of a low-priority task after some time period to ensure it gets some attention every now and then.

An RTOS's scheduling policy determines how it selects the next task to run. For example, if an RTOS assigns equal priority to tasks and gives each task a time slice of equal size, the scheduling policy decides how the CPU chooses the next task to run when one task completes its time slice (or suspends for some other reason). One obvious solution is a *round-robin* scheduling policy in which the RTOS maintains a queue of ready-to-run tasks and picks the task off the front of the queue when switching between tasks; it places the newly suspended task at the end of the queue. Most of the time, this ensures a fair allocation of CPU resources to each of the ready-to-run tasks. There are some degenerate cases where this scheme is not entirely fair. For example, if a particular task suspends more frequently than others, it must wait through the whole queue again even though it uses little CPU time while actually running. However, as a quick-and-dirty solution, round-robin scheduling works well.

Sometimes an application can control various aspects of the scheduling priority, but more often than not the application has to live with the scheduling policies provided by the operating system. Tuning RTOS policies is beyond the scope of this book, but to learn more, see "For More Information" at the end of this chapter or the manual for your particular RTOS. Fortunately, I^2C activities tend to be very slow (at least, when running at 100 kHz), so scheduling tuning generally won't affect the performance of an I^2C-based application by that much.

10.1.3 Reentrancy

Perhaps the biggest problem with programming I^2C devices in a multithreaded environment is *reentrancy*, which occurs when two separate threads attempt to run the same code concurrently. An I^2C device is a single, shared system resource. If a function called by two separate threads attempts to communicate with an I^2C device, a second thread reentering that same function will attempt to talk to that same device concurrently. If one thread started to write a 2- or 3-byte sequence to the device and was interrupted after transmitting the first byte, then from the device's perspective, the first byte from the second thread would look like the second byte from the first thread. If two threads are going to share the same I^{2}C device, proper operation will take very careful synchronization on the part of the two threads.

Even if two threads don't access the same device, two different threads cannot talk to two different devices simultaneously on the same bus. Once again, different threads must synchronize their use of the same I^{2}C bus. In some respects, this is similar to having two controllers sharing the bus; however, there is no protocol to handle conflicts—the individual threads must handle contention on their own.

10.1.4 Synchronization

Synchronization is typically handled by mutexes (mutual exclusion primitives), critical sections, semaphores, events, and other such OS synchronization primitives. The basic idea behind all of these operations is to allow access to some section of code by only one thread at a time. In a typical RTOS, a thread will request exclusive access to a critical section of code. If the RTOS grants this request, future requests by other threads will be blocked until the original thread holding the critical section releases it. This mechanism allows only a single thread to enter the critical section at a time, thus eliminating the problems with reentrancy.

While a thread is waiting for some other thread to release a critical section, the waiting thread is suspended (blocked) and does not consume any CPU cycles waiting for the release of the critical section. In the case of I^{2}C transmission, this blockage could last a considerable amount of time; the thread holding the critical section could be transmitting and receiving several bytes on the I^{2}C bus (typically requiring 100 μmsec to 1,000 μmsec per byte, plus more if clock stretching occurs). The good news is that the blocked thread does not interfere with the current transmission taking place on the I^{2}C bus.

10.1.5 Safety Critical Systems

Certain RTOSs such as μC/OS or FreeRTOS have been *safety qualified*, meaning that they have been thoroughly tested using stringent quality-assurance programs. This is a major advantage, since if you're developing medical equipment, nuclear instrumentation, or automotive applications, industry regulators will probably require that you use either a safety-qualified operating system or provide appropriate documentation and testing that makes the case for the system you've chosen before they allow you to deploy your system. For example, I've used μC/OS (running on a NetBurner) in the development of instrumentation for nuclear reactors.

Of course, if you're not developing mission-critical applications, you might not need a safety-qualified RTOS. Obviously, the choice is very application dependent, but be aware that quality assurance issues may restrict your choice of real-time OSs.

10.2 Real-Time Operating System I²C Programming

This chapter focuses on four RTOSs: μC/OS, FreeRTOS, Teensy Threads (not really an RTOS, just a multithreading package), and Mbed.

FreeRTOS and Teensy Threads are really just thread scheduling packages that provide basic multitasking and thread synchronization functions. They do not provide any other library code, such as I²C communication functions; you're expected to provide that code yourself. In particular, you are responsible for synchronizing access to shared resources like the I²C bus.

The second two RTOSs, μC/OS and Mbed, are full-featured RTOSs that include library support for many activities, such as I²C communication. These fancier RTOSs provide synchronized access to the resources they use.

The following subsections provide a brief discussion of each of these RTOSs. Where applicable, they also describe how to protect access to shared resources, such as the I²C bus.

10.2.1 μC/OS

In this chapter, I'm going to use the NBRTOS variant of μC/OS provided by NetBurner, Inc., running on their NetBurner MOD54415 SBC. NBRTOS is a variant of μC/OS I that includes several additional libraries to support the MOD54415, including a couple of I²C libraries.

The original μC/OS I RTOS was a purely priority-based RTOS with 64 different priority levels. It had the onerous restriction that each task (the μC/OS name for thread) had to run at a different priority so that you could not have two tasks running at the same priority while using round-robin/time multiplexed scheduling for those tasks at the same priority. Later versions of μC/OS, such as μC/OS III, introduced more priority levels (up to 256) and allowed multiple tasks to run at the same priority by using time multiplexing to switch between tasks of equal priority. However, as NBRTOS uses a version of μC/OS I, this book will stick with priority-based scheduling for μC/OS. Most of the other RTOSs in this book use time slicing (time multiplexing) rather than a priority-based scheme, so μC/OS is unusual in this respect.

The MOD54415 SBC supports up to four different I²C ports. A special library, MultiChannel_I2C, provides support in a multithreaded environment for these four channels. This library provides several different I²C functions you can call, though this chapter will use only two of them, MultiChannel _I2CInit() and MultiChannel_I2CSendBuf(), to demonstrate writing to the MCP4725 DAC:

```
void MultiChannel_I2CInit
(
    int     moduleNum = DEFAULT_I2C_MODULE,
    uint8_t slave_Addr = 0x08,
    uint8_t freqdiv = 0x3C
);

uint8_t MultiChannel_I2CSendBuf
(
```

```
    int     moduleNum,
    uint8_t addr,
    puint8_t buf,
    int     num,
    bool    stop = true
);
```

The first function, MultiChannel_I2CInit(), initializes the I^2C port you're going to use. This is usually a small integer in the range 0 to 3 (for ports i2c-0 through i2c-3). The second parameter specifies a peripheral address for the port; you specify this only if you're using the I^2C port in peripheral mode. If you're using the port in controller mode, you can ignore this argument (the default of 0x08 is fine). The last argument specifies the frequency divisor for the I^2C bus. The default of 0x3C is fine for 100-kHz operation; see the NetBurner documentation if you want to operate at a different clock frequency.

The second function, MultiChannel_I2CSendBuf(), writes data to the I^2C bus. The first argument is the I^2C port number (for example, 0 for i2c-0), the second argument is the I^2C address of the device, the third argument is an array of bytes containing the data to be written, the fourth argument specifies the number of bytes to write, and the last argument specifies whether a stop condition is written to the I^2C bus after the transmission (the default is true, which means to send the stop condition).

The NetBurner library provides a fair number of other functions you can use to manipulate the I^2C bus. For more detail, see the NetBurner documentation linked in "For More Information."

The program in Listing 10-1 is the usual triangle wave DAC output sample program. Other than a few μC/OS peculiarities (outside the scope of this book), this program is equivalent to the demonstration program from other chapters.

```
// Listing 10-1 (main.cpp)
//
// DAC output example for μC/OS.

#include "predef.h"
#include <stdio.h>
#include <startnet.h>
#include <autoupdate.h>
#include <multichanneli2c.h>

#define ever ;;

#define I2C_CHANNEL 0      // Going to use I2C0 on NetBurner
#define mcp4725     0x60   // DAC I2C address
extern "C"
{
    void UserMain( void * pd );
}

// DACout-
//
```

```
// Draws one cycle of a triangle waveform on
// the MCP4725 I2C DAC device (for example,
// Adafruit MCP4725 breakout board).
//
// Argument: I2C address for the DAC. For
// Adafruit MCP4725 breakout boards, this
// is either 0x62 or 0x63. For SparkFun
// boards, this is either 0x60 or 0x61.

void DACout( int adrs )
{
    uint8_t buf[2];

    // Send the rising edge of a triangle wave:

    for( uint16_t dacOut = 0; dacOut < 0xfff; ++dacOut )
    {
        // Note: MCP4725 requires that you write
        // the HO byte first and the LO byte second!

        buf[0] = (dacOut << 8) & 0xff;
        buf[1] = dacOut & 0xff;

        // Transmit the data from the buffer:

      ❶ MultiChannel_I2CSendBuf
        (
            I2C_CHANNEL,
            adrs,       // Device address
            buf,        // Data to write
            2,          // 2 bytes to write
            true        // Send stop condition
        );
    }

    // Send the falling edge of the triangle wave.

    for( uint16_t dacOut = 0xffe; dacOut > 0; --dacOut )
    {
        // HO then LO byte:

        buf[0] = (dacOut << 8) & 0xff;
        buf[1] = dacOut & 0xff;
        MultiChannel_I2CSendBuf
        (
            I2C_CHANNEL,
            adrs,       // Device address
            buf,        // Data to write
            2,          // 2 bytes to write
            true        // Send stop condition
        );
    }
}
```

```
void UserMain( void * pd )
{
    int cntr = 0;

    // Standard NetBurner initialization stuff:

    InitializeStack();
    EnableAutoUpdate(); // Allow Ethernet update of code

    // Initialize I2C0 on the NetBurner MOD54415:

  ❷ MultiChannel_I2CInit( I2C_CHANNEL );
    for( ever )
    {
        // Print status information to the serial console
        // every now and then to show that something is
        // happening:

        iprintf( "main loop, cntr=%d\n", cntr++ );

        // Draw one cycle of the triangle waveform
        // on the DAC:

        DACout( mcp4725 ); // MCP4725 output

    } // endfor
} // UserMain
```

The MultiChannel_I2CInit() ❷ and MultiChannel_I2CSendBuf() ❶ functions are the μC/OS I^{2}C initialization and I^{2}C output routines.

Figure 10-1 shows the oscilloscope output from the program in Listing 10-1. Note that the frequency is much closer to the Arduino example (see Figure 8-2 in Chapter 8) than the Raspberry Pi example (see Figure 9-3 in Chapter 9). The slower frequency in the Pi example is, undoubtedly, due to all the extra work happening under the multitasking Pi OS (Linux).

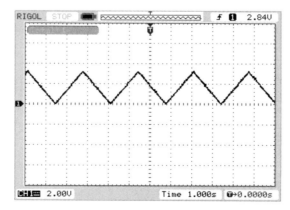

Figure 10-1: Oscilloscope output from Listing 10-1

Since μC/OS supports multitasking, you might wonder, why not write some code to generate two separate triangle waves concurrently? Of course, two tasks cannot access the same I²C device concurrently, but you might reason that you could fix that issue by putting two different DACs on the I²C bus. One task could write to the first DAC, and the second task could write to the second DAC.

Unfortunately, under a pure priority-based system such as μC/OS, this won't work out well. The higher-priority task always runs, and the lower-priority task never gets a chance to execute (unless you put in code to explicitly suspend the higher-priority task).

Listing 10-2 provides the source code to the version of the code that demonstrates one way to do this.

```cpp
// Listing 10-2 (main.cpp)
//
// Multi-threaded I2C demonstration #2.
// This program writes to two separate
// MCP4725 devices on the same I2C bus
// using separate threads for each of the
// DACs, with a semaphore to protect
// writes to the I2C port.

#include "predef.h"
#include <stdio.h>
#include <startnet.h>
#include <autoupdate.h>
#include <pins.h>
#include <multichanneli2c.h>

#define ever ;;

#define I2C_CHANNEL0 0            // Going to use I2C0

#define dac1 0x62                 // MCP4725 #1 address
#define dac2 0x63                 // MCP4725 #2 address

extern "C"
{
    void UserMain(void * pd);
}

// Stack for DACthread:

#define DACthread_STK_SIZE (4096)
static  DWORD   DACthread_stack[ DACthread_STK_SIZE ]
                        __attribute__((aligned(4)));

// Critical section protecting console I/O:

OS_CRIT ioCS;

❶ OS_SEM   threadSem;
```

```
OS_SEM  mainSem;

// DACout-
//
// Draws one cycle of a triangle waveform on
// the MCP4725 I2C DAC device (e.g., Adafruit
// MCP4725 breakout board).
//
// Argument: I2C address for the DAC. For
// Adafruit MCP4725 breakout boards, this
// is either 0x62 or 0x63. For SparkFun
// boards, this is either 0x60 or 0x61.

void DACout( int adrs, OS_SEM *enter, OS_SEM *leave )
{
    uint8_t buf[2];

    // Send the rising edge of a triangle wave:

    for( uint16_t dacOut = 0; dacOut < 0xfff; ++dacOut )
    {
        // Note: MCP4725 requires that you write
        // the HO byte first and the LO byte second!

        buf[0] = (dacOut << 8) & 0xff;
        buf[1] = dacOut & 0xff;

        // Transmit the data from the buffer:

    ❷ OSSemPend( enter, 0 );   // Protect call

        ❸ MultiChannel_I2CSendBuf
          (
              I2C_CHANNEL0,
              adrs,          // Device address
              buf,           // Data to write
              2,             // 2 bytes to write
              true           // Send stop condition
          );

    ❹ OSSemPost( leave );      // Enable other thread
    }

    // Send the falling edge of the triangle wave.

    for( uint16_t dacOut = 0xffe; dacOut > 0; --dacOut )
    {
        // HO then LO byte:

        buf[0] = (dacOut << 8) & 0xff;
        buf[1] = dacOut & 0xff;
        OSSemPend( enter, 0 );   // Protect call

            MultiChannel_I2CSendBuf
```

```
                    (
                        I2C_CHANNEL0,
                        adrs,            // Device address
                        buf,             // Data to write
                        2,               // 2 bytes to write
                        true             // Send stop condition
                    );

            OSSemPost( leave );     // Enable other thread
        }
    }

    void DACthread( void *parm )
    {
        int cntr = 0;

        for( ever )
        {
            // Print a message each time the thread
            // completes one cycle of the triangle
            // wave. Note that iprintf must be
            // protected by a critical section.

            OSCritEnter( &ioCS, 0 );

                iprintf( "thread loop, cntr=%d\n", cntr++ );

            OSCritLeave( &ioCS );

            // Draw one cycle of the triangle waveform
            // on the DAC at address 0x63:

            DACout( dac2, &threadSem, &mainSem );

        } // endfor
    }

    void UserMain( void * pd )
    {
        int cntr = 0;

        // Standard NetBurner initialization stuff:

        InitializeStack();
        EnableAutoUpdate(); // Allow Ethernet update of code

        // Initialize the critical sections used to protect
        // console I/O and the I2C output.

        OSCritInit( &ioCS );
        OSSemInit( &threadSem, 1 );
        OSSemInit( &mainSem, 0 );
```

```
             // Initialize I2C0 pins on the NetBurner MOD54415:

             MultiChannel_I2CInit( I2C_CHANNEL0 );

             // Start a thread running that will write to the
             // DAC at address 0x63. Give the thread a higher
             // priority than that of the main thread.
             //
             // The parameters are the following:
             //
             //  1. Address of function to invoke as the
             //     new thread ("task" in NBRTOS terminology).
             //
             //  2. Parameter to pass to the thread.
             //
             //  3. Address of the first byte beyond the
             //     stack space allocated for the thread.
             //
             //  4. Address of the start of the task.
             //
             //  5. Thread priority (lower number is
             //     higher priority).

     ❺ OSTaskCreate
          (
             DACthread,
             NULL,
             (void*)&DACthread_stack[DACthread_STK_SIZE],
             (void *)DACthread_stack,
             MAIN_PRIO + 1
          );

          for( ever )
          {
             // Print a message each time the main thread
             // completes one cycle of the triangle
             // wave. Note that iprintf must be
             // protected by a critical section.

             OSCritEnter( &ioCS, 0 );

                 iprintf( "main loop, cntr=%d\n", cntr++ );

             OSCritLeave( &ioCS );

             // Draw one cycle of the triangle waveform
             // on the DAC at address 0x62:

             DACout( dac1, &mainSem, &threadSem );
          } // endfor
     } // UserMain
```

Unfortunately, you cannot use μC/OS critical section variables (OS_CRIT) to protect access to the I²C bus. As noted earlier, because μC/OS is strictly a priority-based system, the lower-priority thread will not get a chance to run unless some system call explicitly blocks the main thread. To overcome this problem, the code in Listing 10-2 uses semaphores.

Semaphores are similar to critical sections insofar as you can use them to protect a section of code. They differ from critical sections in that they have a counter associated with them. When you enter a critical section (a μC/OS OSSemPend() call), the system first checks to see if this counter is 0. If so, the code blocks; if not, the code decrements the counter and enters the critical section. Note that if you initialize a semaphore with 1, it behaves like a critical section variable.

μC/OS semaphores use three main functions: OSSemInit(), OSSemPend(), and OSSemPost(). In addition to initializing internal data structures, the OSSemInit() function allows you to initialize the counter with the integer; for managing critical sections, the initial value is usually 0 or 1. As already noted, the OSSemPend() function checks the counter for 0 (and blocks if 0) and decrements the counter if it is nonzero, as well as allowing entry into the critical section. OSSemPost() increments the counter associated with the semaphore. This means you would normally use OSSemPend() to enter a critical section and OSSemPost() to leave a critical section.

The trick in Listing 10-2 is to use two semaphores, mainSem and threadSem, to protect access to the DACs by multiple tasks ❶. Whenever one of these semaphores contains 1, the associated task can execute; when the semaphore is 0, the task will block. The trick is to make sure that the two threads alternate setting the semaphores to 0 or 1 to allow execution to "ping-pong" between the two tasks.

If you look at the DACout() function in Listing 10-2, you'll see that a task enters its critical section by executing OSSemPend() on the semaphore associated with that task ❷. To exit the critical section, the code executes the OSSemPost() function on the semaphore associated with the other thread ❹. This might seem incorrect, but let's consider this sequence step-by-step:

1. Assume the mainSem (enter parameter) counter is 1 and the threadSem (leave parameter) is 0.

2. Upon executing OSSemPend(enter, 0);, the system decrements the counter to 0 and enters the critical section (because the counter wasn't already 0). Note that because the UserMain() task has a higher priority than the DACthread() task, the UserMain() task continues execution (and the DACthread() task is currently blocked).

3. The UserMain() task writes data to the I²C bus ❸.

4. The UserMain() task executes OSSemPend() on the threadSem semaphore (leave parameter) ❹. This increments the counter associated with threadSem; note that the mainSem counter is still 0.

5. The UserMain() task continues execution, which in this case means repeating the loop and re-executing the OSSemPend() function at ❸. Because the counter is now 0, the task blocks.

6. Once `UserMain()` blocks, the `DACthread()` task begins execution and eventually winds up in `DACout()` executing the `OSSemPend()` call. Because the `OSSemPost( leave );` call in the `UserMain()` task incremented the `threadSem` counter, the counter now contains 1 so the `DACthread()` task can enter its critical section.

7. The `DACthread()` task calls `DACout()` to write a value to the DAC.

8. The `DACthread()` task exits its critical section by calling `OSSemPost()` but passing the `mainSem` semaphore variable. This increments the `mainSem` counter; note that the `threadSem` counter is still 0.

9. Because the `UserMain()` thread has the highest priority, it immediately takes over, and this process repeats itself.

Note that both tasks in Listing 10-2 call the `DACout()` function to actually write the data to the DAC (the DAC address and the two semaphores are passed as arguments). The calls to `DACout()` swap the two semaphore arguments so that `UserMain()` passes `mainSem` as the first semaphore argument, whereas `DACthread()` passes `threadSem` as the first semaphore argument.

Figure 10-2 shows the oscilloscope output for the program in Listing 10-2.

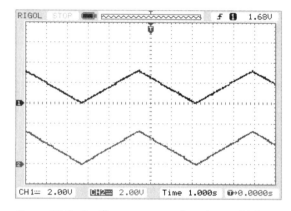

Figure 10-2: Oscilloscope output from Listing 10-2

As you can see, both tasks are producing proper triangle waves. The frequency of the triangle waves in Figure 10-2 is about half that of Figure 10-1 (note the time scale for the oscilloscope in the two figures). The reason for this discrepancy is that the frequency is completely determined by the speed at which the program transmits data to the MCP4725. In Listing 10-2, twice as much data is transmitted by sending roughly the same data to both MCP4725 devices, so the frequency is cut roughly in half.

10.2.2 FreeRTOS I^{2}C Programming

FreeRTOS is, in its developer's words, "the market leading, de facto standard, and cross platform RTOS kernel." You'll likely encounter this popular open source kernel if you work with many different RTOSs.

To use FreeRTOS, you'll need a port of the OS to your particular device (or you'll have to port it yourself). In this chapter I'm going to use the Teensy 4.0 port created by Julian Desvignes running under the PlatformIO IDE (*https://platformio.org/lib/show/6737/FreeRTOS-Teensy4*). The PlatformIO, FreeRTOS, and Teensy4 port uses the Arduino library and Teensyduino support to run FreeRTOS code in an Arduino environment. This makes it possible to create multithreaded applications while using Arduino-style programming.

NOTE   *Chapter 30 (online at* https://bookofi2c.randallhyde.com) *discusses using FreeRTOS with the ESP32 SBC module.*

Because FreeRTOS is just a scheduler that provides basic task switching functionality along with synchronization primitives, you'll have to provide your own I^{2}C library code. Fortunately, such code is easy to find from the Arduino libraries and elsewhere. However, the Arduino libraries are not reentrant, so you have to ensure that only one task is calling a particular library function (or family of functions) using mutexes, critical sections, semaphores, or other synchronization operations. See *https://www.freertos .org/a00113.html* for more details on FreeRTOS synchronization primitives.

Listing 10-3 presents the usual triangle wave output demo under FreeRTOS that creates two tasks; one of the tasks will blink the Teensy's LED, and the other will output the triangle wave data to the MCP4725 DAC device:

```
// Listing 10-3 (main.cpp)
//
// Simple demonstration of I2C programming
// under FreeRTOS running on a Teensy 4.0.

#include <FreeRTOS_TEENSY4.h>
#include <Wire.h>

#define ever ;;

// The LED is attached to pin 13 on the Teensy 4.0.

const uint8_t LED_PIN = 13;

// Thread1-
//
// This task blinks the Teensy 4.0's LED
// every second (1/2 second on, 1/2 second off).

static void Thread1( void* arg )
{
    for( ever )
    {

        // Turn LED on:
```

```
                digitalWrite( LED_PIN, HIGH );

                // Delay 1/2 second:

                vTaskDelay( (500 * configTICK_RATE_HZ) / 1000 );

                // Turn LED off:

                digitalWrite( LED_PIN, LOW );

                // Delay 1/2 second:

                vTaskDelay( (500 * configTICK_RATE_HZ) / 1000 );
        }
}

// Thread2-
//
// This task outputs a triangle wave
// to the MCP4725 device at address 0x62
// (i.e., an Adafruit MCP4725 breakout board).

static void Thread2( void* arg )
{

for( ever )
    {
        for( uint16_t dacOut = 0; dacOut < 0xfff; ++dacOut )
        {
            // Transmit the address byte (and a zero R/W bit):

            Wire.beginTransmission( 0x62 );

            // Transmit the 12-bit DAC value (HO 4 bits first,
            // LO 8 bits second) along with a 4-bit
            // "fast write" command (0000 in the HO 4 bits
            // of the first byte):

            Wire.write( (dacOut << 8) & 0xf );
            Wire.write( dacOut & 0xff );

            // Send the stop condition onto the I2C bus:

            Wire.endTransmission( true );
        }   // for

        // Send the falling edge of the triangle wave:

        for( uint16_t dacOut = 0xffe; dacOut > 0; --dacOut )
        {
            // See comments in previous loop.

            Wire.beginTransmission( 0x62 );
            Wire.write( (dacOut << 8) & 0xf );
            Wire.write( dacOut & 0xff );
```

```
                    Wire.endTransmission( true );
            }   // for
        }          // forever
    } // Thread2

    // In FreeRTOS for the Teensy 4.0, the
    // Arduino "setup" function is really the
    // equivalent of the main program.

    void setup()
    {
        portBASE_TYPE s1, s2;

        pinMode( LED_PIN, OUTPUT ); // LED is output
        Wire.begin();               // Initialize I2C library

        // Create task at priority two
        // Arguments:
        //
        //  1.  Address of function to serve as task code.
        //  2.  A descriptive name for the task (can be NULL).
        //  3.  Stack depth for the task.
        //  4.  Parameter to pass to task.
        //  5.  Task priority.
        //  6.  Task handle returned here (ignored if NULL).

        s1 =    xTaskCreate
                (
                    Thread1,
                    NULL,
                    configMINIMAL_STACK_SIZE,
                    NULL,
                    2,
                    NULL
                );

        // Create task at priority one
        // (see comments above concerning parms).

        s2 =    xTaskCreate
                (
                    Thread2,
                    NULL,
                    configMINIMAL_STACK_SIZE,
                    NULL,
                    1,
                    NULL
                );

        if ( s1 == pdPASS && s2 == pdPASS )
```

```
    {
        // Start scheduler:

        vTaskStartScheduler();
    }

    // Drop down here if there was
    // insufficient RAM to create
    // the tasks or if there was
    // any other problem in their
    // creation.

    for( ever );
}

// WARNING: idle loop has a very small stack
// (configMINIMAL_STACK_SIZE), so
// loop must never block.

void loop()
{
    // Not used.
}
```

The actual I²C code was taken straight out of Listing 8-1 (Arduino code), which is not reentrant code. The key thing to note is that the tasks do not call common library code. Thread1() calls only the Arduino digitalWrite() function, and Thread2() calls only the Wire class functions. Had this example tried to write to I²C devices from two separate tasks (even devices on separate I²C buses), it would have required mutexes to ensure that only one task at a time could actually execute those function calls. Here's an example:

```
SemaphoreHandle_t xSemaphore = NULL;
    .
    .
    .
xSemaphore = xSemaphoreCreateMutex();
    .
    .
    .
if( xSemaphoreTake( xSemaphore, portMAX_DELAY ) == pdTRUE )
{
        // Own the critical section.
    .
    . // In critical section, access I2C device here.
    .
    xSemaphoreGive( xSemaphore );
}
```

Figure 10-3 shows the oscilloscope output from the program in the FreeRTOS demonstration program.

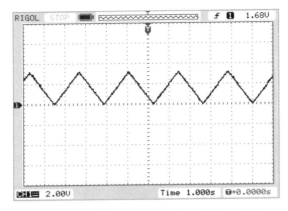

Figure 10-3: Oscilloscope output from Listing 10-3

Because this program is writing only one stream of data to the MCP4725, the frequency is back up to about 0.5 Hz (again, this is limited by the 100-kHz data transmission speed).

10.2.3 Teensy Threads I²C Programming

There are thread scheduling packages written for many low-end SBCs that you can grab off the Internet and use in simple applications. In this section, I'll demonstrate how to use one such package: the Teensy Threading Library, created by Fernando Trias. This section also uses the Teensy 4.0 I²C library by Richard Gemmell. (See "For More Information" for the links.) It supports the Teensy 3.x and 4.x CPU modules from PJRC and it has the ability to create multiple threads—up to eight, by default, though this can be changed—along with some simple synchronization primitives and various thread utilities. Because the Teensy Threads package uses the term *threads*, I will use that specific term in this section rather than *tasks*.

The Teensy Threading Library is an Arduino library that assumes code is being developed in the Arduino programming model; as such, when you work with Teensy Threads, use the standard Arduino (or Teensy-specific) I²C programming libraries to communicate with I²C devices. Remember that Arduino code is not reentrant and must be protected when called from various threads. The example in this section will avoid calling the same function in different threads so that synchronization is not required.

The program in Listing 10-4 demonstrates multithreading using the Teensy Threading Library. It creates three additional threads (plus the main thread that continues execution). One thread blinks the LED every second, two threads transmit triangle waves to MCP 4725 DAC devices (on separate I²C buses), and the main thread writes "loop" to the serial output every two seconds.

```
// Listing 10-4 (Listing10-4.ino)
//
// Simple demonstration of I2C programming
// using Teensy Threads running on a Teensy 4.0.

#include <TeensyThreads.h>
#include <i2c_driver_wire.h>

#define ever ;;

#define dac1 0x62
#define dac2 0x60

// The LED is attached to pin 13 on the Teensy 4.0.

const uint8_t LED_PIN = 13;

// Thread1-
//
// This thread blinks the Teensy 4.0's LED
// every second (1/2 second on, 1/2 second off).

❶ static void Thread1( int arg )
{
    for( ever )
    {

        // Turn LED on:

        digitalWrite( LED_PIN, HIGH );

        // Delay 1/2 second:

        delay( 500 );

        // Turn LED off:

        digitalWrite( LED_PIN, LOW );

        // Delay 1/2 second:

        delay( 500 );
    }
}

// Thread2-
//
// This thread outputs a triangle wave
// to the MCP4725 device at address 0x62 on
// I2C bus zero (SDA0/SCL0 on Teensy 4.0)
// (i.e., an Adafruit MCP4725 breakout board).

❷ static void Thread2( int arg )
```

```
{
    for( ever )
    {
        for( uint16_t dacOut = 0; dacOut < 0xfff; ++dacOut )
        {
            // Transmit the adrs byte (and a 0 R/W bit):

            Wire.beginTransmission( dac1 );

            // Transmit the 12-bit value (HO 4 bits first,
            // LO 8 bits second) along with a 4-bit
            // "fast write" command (0000 in the HO 4 bits
            // of the first byte):

            Wire.write( (dacOut << 8) & 0xf );
            Wire.write( dacOut & 0xff );

            // Send the stop condition onto the I2C bus:

            Wire.endTransmission( true );
        }   // for

        // Send the falling edge of the triangle wave:

        for( uint16_t dacOut = 0xffe; dacOut > 0; --dacOut )
        {
            // See comments in previous loop.

            Wire.beginTransmission( dac1 );
            Wire.write( (dacOut << 8) & 0xf );
            Wire.write( dacOut & 0xff );
            Wire.endTransmission( true );
        }   // for
    }           // forever
} // Thread2

// Thread3-
//
// This thread outputs a triangle wave
// to the MCP4725 device at address dac2 on
// I2C bus one (SDA1/SCL1 on Teensy 4.0)
// (i.e., an Adafruit MCP4725 breakout board).

❸ static void Thread3( int arg )
{
    for( ever )
    {
        for( uint16_t dacOut = 0; dacOut < 0xfff; ++dacOut )
        {
            // Transmit the adrs byte (and a 0 R/W bit):

            Wire1.beginTransmission( dac2 );

            // Transmit the 12-bit DAC value (HO 4 bits
            // first, LO 8 bits second) along with a
```

```
                   // 4-bit "fast write" command (0000 in the HO
                   // 4 bits of the first byte):

                   Wire1.write( (dacOut << 8) & 0xf );
                   Wire1.write( dacOut & 0xff );

                   // Send the stop condition onto the I2C bus:

                   Wire1.endTransmission( true );
               }   // for

           // Send the falling edge of the triangle wave:

           for( uint16_t dacOut = 0xffe; dacOut > 0; --dacOut )
           {
               // See comments in previous loop.

               Wire1.beginTransmission( dac2 );
               Wire1.write( (dacOut << 8) & 0xf );
               Wire1.write( dacOut & 0xff );
               Wire1.endTransmission( true );
           }   // for
       }           // forever
} // Thread3

// In TeensyThreads for the Teensy 4.0, the
// Arduino "setup" function is really the
// equivalent of the main program.

void setup()
{

    Serial.begin( 9600 );
    pinMode( LED_PIN, OUTPUT ); // LED is output
    Wire.begin();               // Initialize I2C port 0
    Wire1.begin();              // Initialize I2C port 1

    // Create thread
    // Arguments:
    //
    // 1.  Address of function to serve as thread code.
    // 2.  Optional argument passed to thread function.
    // 3.  Stack size (default is 1024).
    // 4.  Stack address (default is on heap).

❹ int id1 = threads.addThread( Thread1,  0 );
    if ( id1 == -1 )
    {

        Serial.println( "Thread 1 creation failed" );
        for( ever );
    }

    // Create task at priority one
    // (see comments above concerning parms).
```

```
❺ int id2 = threads.addThread( Thread2, 0 );
  if ( id2 == -1 )
  {

      Serial.println( "Thread 2 creation failed" );
      for( ever );
  }

  // Create task at priority three
  // (see comments above concerning parms).

❻ int id3 = threads.addThread( Thread3, 0 );
  if ( id3 == -1 )
  {

      Serial.println( "Thread 3 creation failed" );
      for( ever );
  }
}

// The loop function is, essentially, a fourth thread
// of execution.

❼ void loop()
{
    Serial.println( "loop" );
    delay( 2000 );
}
```

The Thread1() function executes for the first thread, blinking the LED on the Teensy ❶. The Thread2() function writes a triangle wave to the DAC at address dac1 (0x62) connected to the Teensy's I^{2}C port 0 ❷. The Thread3() function writes a triangle wave to the DAC at address dac2 (0x60) connected to the Teensy's I^{2}C port 1 ❸. Note that because the two DACs are on different I^{2}C ports, the code does not need to synchronize access to the devices.

The setup() function starts the three threads by calling threads.addThread() ❹, ❺, and ❻ and passing in the addresses of the three thread functions. The loop() function effectively becomes a fourth thread ❼.

Because the i2c_driver_wire library allocates separate memory objects for wire (SDA0 and SCL0) and wire1 (SDA1 and SCL1), calls through these two separate objects do not interfere with one another when called from different threads. Were two different threads to call wire simultaneously, the code would have needed to protect the calls using the Teensy Threads lock() and unlock() functions:

```
Threads::Mutex wire_lock;
    .

    .

    .
  wire_lock.lock();
```

```
                    Wire.beginTransmission( 0x62 );
                    Wire.write( (dacOut << 8) & 0xf );
                    Wire.write( dacOut & 0xff );
                    Wire.endTransmission( true );

    wire_lock.unlock();
```

Figure 10-4 shows the oscilloscope output for the program in Listing 10-4. The time base has changed for this display (two seconds per major division rather than one).

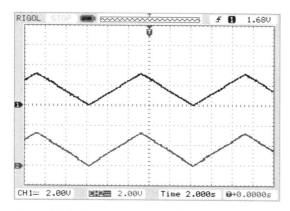

Figure 10-4: Oscilloscope output from Listing 10-4

As you can see, the frequency here is much slower than in previous examples (note the time scale on the oscilloscope). This is likely due to the interaction between the synchronous I^2C library calls and the Teensy Threads package, a typical issue when you bolt on a threading library to a nonthreading package (like Arduino) versus running a true RTOS.

10.2.4 Mbed I^2C Programming

Mbed is an RTOS developed by ARM Limited for use on ARM CPUs. It is marketed as an IoT development system, though it is certainly useful for normal embedded applications. Unlike many RTOSs, which tend to be very generic, Mbed fully supports features found on typical ARM MCUs, including I^2C and other peripherals. The Mbed RTOS provides a rich set of I^2C functions you can use in your applications. The library is thread safe, so you don't have to worry about protecting calls across various threads (of course, your applications must synchronize access to specific devices on the I^2C bus).

NOTE *This section uses the term* thread *rather than the generic term* task *used elsewhere in the chapter, in keeping with standard Mbed terminology.*

ARM also provides the Mbed Studio IDE that runs under Linux, macOS, or Windows (see "For More Information" for the link). Mbed Studio allows you to edit, compile, run, and debug your applications on any Mbed-enabled SBC.

Listing 10-5 provides the standard MCP4725 triangle wave output program running under Mbed. This program has two threads: the main thread and a second thread that it starts. Each thread produces a triangle wave output on separate MCP4725 devices. This particular program runs on an STMicroelectronics Nucleo-F767ZI board (*https://www.st.com/en/evaluation-tools/nucleo-f767zi.html*) that I found on Amazon for around $35; you can also use the NUCLEO-WB55RG available from SparkFun for around $40 (*https://www.sparkfun.com/products/17943*). Of the several I²C ports this board supports, I used ports one and two for the program in Listing 10-5.

```cpp
// Listing10-5.cpp
//
// Mbed RTOS I2C programming example.
//
// This program writes triangle wave
// data to two MCP4725 DAC devices at
// addresses 0x62 and 0x63 on I2C ports
// one and two on a Nucleo-F767ZI board.
// Or ports one and three on a
// Nucleo-WB55RG board.

#include "PinNames.h"
#include "mbed.h"
#include "mbed_wait_api.h"

#define ever ;;
#define mcp4725a (0x62 << 1)
#define mcp4725b (0x63 << 1)

// Thread1-
//
// Writes a triangle wave to the
// MCP4726 at address 0x62 on
// I2C port 1.

❶ void Thread1( void )
{
    int  cntr = 0;
    char data[2];
    I2C i2c1( I2C_SDA, I2C_SCL );

    // Set bus frequency to 100 kHz
    // (this is actually the default,
    // this call appears here for
    // testing purposes).

    i2c1.frequency( 100000 );

    // Create a continuous triangle
    // wave output:

    for( ever )
```

```
{
    // Create the rising edge of the
    // triangle wave:

    for( int tri=0; tri < 4095; ++tri )
    {
        // Note: MCP4725 requires that you
        // transmit the HO byte first, followed
        // by the LO byte of the 16-bit
        // DAC value (HO 4 bits are zeros).

        data[0] = (char) (tri >> 8) & 0xff;
        data[1] = (char) (tri & 0xff);
        i2c1.write ( mcp4725a, data, 2, false );
    }

    // Create the falling edge of the
    // triangle wave:

    for( int tri=4094; tri > 0; --tri )
    {
        data[0] = (char) (tri >> 8) & 0xff;
        data[1] = (char) (tri & 0xff);
        i2c1.write ( mcp4725a, data, 2, false );
    }
}
}

// Application main program and main thread.
// This starts Thread1 and then emits the
// triangle wave on the second MCP4725:

int main()
{
    int  cntr = 0;
    char data[2];
    Thread thread1;

    // Nucleo-F767ZI: PB_11, PB_10
    // Nucleo-WB55RG: A1, A0

    I2C i2c2( PB_11, PB_10 );

    i2c2.frequency( 100000 );

    // Start the thread:

    thread1.start( Thread1 );

    // Emit the second triangle wave to
    // the MCP4725 at address 0x63 on
    // I2C bus two:

    for( ever )
```

```
{
    ❷ // See comments in Thread1.

    for( int tri=0; tri < 4095; ++tri )
    {
        data[0] = (char) (tri >> 8) & 0xff;
        data[1] = (char) (tri & 0xff);
        i2c2.write ( mcp4725b, data, 2, false );
    }
    for( int tri=4094; tri > 0; --tri )
    {
        data[0] = (char) (tri >> 8) & 0xff;
        data[1] = (char) (tri & 0xff);
        i2c2.write ( mcp4725b, data, 2, false );
    }
}
}
```

The code for the first thread writes a triangle wave to the DAC on I^{2}C bus 1 ❶. It sets the I^{2}C clock frequency to 100 kHz and then writes out 4,000 increasing DAC values followed by 4K decreasing DAC values. The code for the second thread (the main program ❷) writes a triangle wave to the DAC on I^{2}C bus 2 using the same algorithm as employed by Thread1().

Once again, the sample program in Listing 10-5 avoids synchronization issues by writing to DAC devices on two separate buses. The triangle wave outputs on the oscilloscope appear in Figure 10-5.

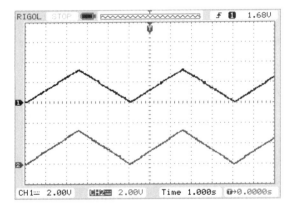

Figure 10-5: Triangle wave output from Listing 10-5

If you look closely at Figure 10-5, you'll notice that the frequency is about half of what you normally get for this application. Though two separate ports should be able to operate independently, these two ports alternate outputting data to the DACs, as shown by the logic analyzer output in Figure 10-6. The top two traces are from port one; the bottom two traces are from port two.

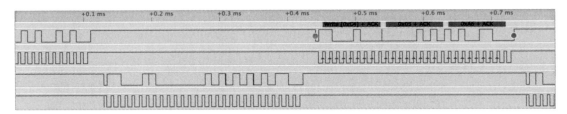

Figure 10-6: Logic analyzer output from the program in Listing 10-5

I can't say for sure whether the two ports operating at half speed is because of a limitation of the hardware (or the particular I^2C device driver for the hardware port) or the fact that Mbed's thread-safe code doesn't allow concurrent I^2C transmissions. Whatever the case, the result is that it's only about half the bandwidth on each bus that you'd expect, and you probably could have gotten the same performance by putting both devices on the same I^2C bus.

10.3   Other Real-Time Operating System I^2C Programming

Several RTOSs beyond those discussed in this chapter support I^2C devices. Due to limited space in this chapter and the lack of development systems on my part, I won't include example code for these operating systems, but they still deserve mention.

QNX   One of the older microcomputer RTOSs. Pronounced "cue-nix," it was originally named Qunix; although it changed its name to avoid trademark infringement, it started out as a "Unix-like" microkernel operating system running on the original IBM PC (an 8088 CPU). It then quickly morphed into an RTOS supporting embedded systems and became very popular in that field.

QNX was originally developed by Quantum Software Systems (QSS), who changed the company's name to QNX Software Systems. QNX Software Systems was bought out by BlackBerry, and QNX became the basis for BlackBerry's tablet and phone offerings after the rise of the Apple iPad. Though the BlackBerry phones and tablets eventually died out, QNX prospered as an OS specifically targeted at automotive and safety-based applications.

QNX provides I^2C communications "baked into" the OS. You can read about the I^2C API at the QNX website at *http://www.qnx.com/developers/ docs/6.5.0_sp1/index.jsp?topic=%2Fcom.qnx.doc.neutrino_technotes%2Fi2c _framework.html* (or just search for "QNX I^2C Programming").

VxWorks   Another early RTOS that appeared in the late 1980s from Wind River Associates. It was based on an earlier operating system, VRTX, which was created by Mentor Graphics (see *https://en.wikipedia.org/wiki/ VxWorks* for more history). VxWorks has been very popular in hardcore embedded systems requiring safety, including aerospace, medical, and nuclear applications. If QNX is best known for automotive applications, VxWorks is best known for aerospace applications.

As you can imagine, VxWorks is not a low-cost or open source system hobbyists often use. It does, however, have a no-cost license available for noncommercial or hobbyist use (see *https://labs.windriver.com/vxworks-sdk*) that runs on Raspberry Pi and other SBCs. Like QNX, VxWorks includes built-in support for I^2C device programming. For more information on the VxWorks I^2C library, see *https://docs.windriver.com/bundle/ vxworks_7_application_core_os_sr0630-enus/page/VXBUS/vxbI2cLib.html*.

eCos The embedded configurable operating system (eCos) was originally developed by Cygnus (of Windows and Unix shell fame) and was later bought out by Red Hat. Eventually, Red Hat abandoned eCos, releasing it as open source, and some of the original developers created eCos Pro as a commercial product. For a couple of years now, they've been promising to deliver a version that runs on Raspberry Pi systems. However, as I'm writing this, that version is yet to appear.

For more about eCos's built-in support for I^2C programming, see *https:// ecos.sourceware.org/docs-latest/ref/i2c-porting.html*. You can find additional eCos information at *https://doc.ecoscentric.com/user-guide*.

ChibiOS/RT A small-footprint, open source, real-time operating system. Although ChibiOS has been ported to a wide range of microcontrollers (see *https://en.wikipedia.org/wiki/ChibiOS/RT*), perhaps its biggest claim to fame is that it has been successfully ported to the Raspberry Pi, providing an honest-to-goodness RTOS for the Pi (see *https://www .stevebate.net/chibios-rpi/GettingStarted.html*).

See *http://chibios.sourceforge.net/docs3/hal/group___i2_c.html* for more details on ChibiOS's I^2C capabilities.

10.4 Chapter Summary

This chapter introduced I^2C programming under multithreaded, real-time operating systems. It began with a gentle introduction to RTOSs and then provided some simple I^2C examples using four different RTOSs: µC/OS, FreeRTOS, Teensy Threads, and Mbed. Finally, it concluded by briefly discussing four other RTOSs you might find in the real world.

FOR MORE INFORMATION

Real-time operating systems: *Hands-On RTOs with Microcontrollers: Building Real-Time Embedded Systems Using FreeRTOS, STYM32 MCUs, and SEGGER Debug Tools* by Brian Amos (Pakt Publishing, 2020)

NetBurner and μC/OS information: *https://www.netburner.com* and *https://netburner.com/NBDocs/Developer/html/index.html*

NetBurner I^{2}C library documentation: *https://netburner.com/NBDocs/Developer/html/group__group_i2_c-_m_c_f5441x.html*

FreeRTOS information: *https://www.freertos.org*

PlatformIO information: *https://platformio.org*

The Teensy Threading Library: *https://github.com/ftrias/TeensyThreads* and *https://github.com/Richard-Gemmell/teensy4_i2c*

Teensy 3.x and 4.x modules from PJRC: *https://www.pjrc.com/teensy*

Examples and Teensy Thread tutorial: *https://seansembeddedlinux.wordpress.com/2018/04/02/inter-thread-communications-with-teensythreads*

Mbed downloads and documentation: *https://os.mbed.com*

Introduction to Mbed OS: *https://os.mbed.com/docs/mbed-os/v6.15/introduction/index.html*

List of about 170 off-the-shelf boards that support Mbed: *https://os.mbed.com/platforms*

NUCLEO-WB55RG SBC: *https://os.mbed.com/platforms/ST-Nucleo-WB55RG*

11

BARE-METAL I^{2}C CONTROLLER PROGRAMMING

To this point, most of the sample programs in this book have relied on some third-party library code to interface with the I^{2}C hardware on the SBC. At the hardware level, I^{2}C communication normally consists of reading and writing hardware-dependent registers on the microcontroller. Having library code that hides these low-level details from you is convenient, but if you're the one tasked with writing that library code in the first place—or if you need better performance or features that the library doesn't provide—you'll have to learn to program low-level I^{2}C operations yourself.

Nearly every real-world MCU does things differently when it comes to low-level I^{2}C programming, even if they share some common peripheral hardware. Fortunately, the I^{2}C protocol isn't *that* complex, so the basic programming ideas apply no matter what the underlying hardware. If you learn how to program a few different MCUs, those concepts should help you figure out how to deal with others. In this chapter, I'll describe how to program I^2C communications on a pair of MCUs at the register (hardware) level. In particular, this chapter will explore I^2C programming on the Teensy 4.*x*'s NXP i.MX RT1062 MCU and the ATtiny84 MCU.

For the programming examples in this chapter, I use the Teensy 4.*x* modules and the SparkFun Atto84. The Teensy 4.0 and 4.1 modules share the same MCU IC, so their low-level I^2C programming is identical; the SparkFun Atto84 is based on the ATtiny84 MCU. All are low cost and commonly available, and they are used by many makers and hobbyists.

NOTE *The SparkFun Atto84 might be obsolete by the time you read this, but the code in this chapter should be usable on any ATtiny84-based MCU board.*

11.1 Teensy 4.x Controller Programming

The first example in this chapter will be I^2C controller programming on the Teensy 4.*x* modules using a driver written primarily by Richard Gemmell, with portions by Paul Stoffregen of PJRC. The discussion begins with a description of the Teensy's hardware registers that support I^2C communications, followed by the code (based on Gemmell's driver) that you'll need to program these registers to implement Arduino-like I^2C communication functions.

For more information on this driver and to download Gemmell's code, visit his GitHub page at *https://github.com/Richard-Gemmell/teensy4_i2c*. Gemmell's package includes both controller and peripheral code, but I'll focus solely on the controller portion. See the online chapters (particularly Chapter 18 at *https://bookofi2c.randallhyde.com*) for the corresponding discussion on programming the Teensy 4.*x* as an I^2C peripheral device.

When you work with low-level hardware on an MCU, the MCU's reference manual becomes an indispensable resource. See "For More Information" at the end of this chapter for the link to the NXP reference manual for the i.MX RT1060 MCU (which includes the i.MX RT1062) on the PJRC (Teensy) website. Chapter 47 in the manual describes the I²C interface.

11.1.1 i.MX RT1062 I²C Registers

The Teensy 4.0 and 4.1 modules use an NXP i.MX RT1062 MCU with an ARM Cortex M7 core. The ARM Cortex M7 core is the CPU, while the i.MX RT1062 is the MCU that consists of the CPU plus all the associated peripheral devices.

To understand the Teensy 4.x I²C code, you will need to learn about certain i.MX RT1062 registers, beginning with the I²C control register set. The *imx_rt1060.h* file that Gemmell's code uses contains the following declarations (annotations mine):

```
typedef struct
{
    const uint32_t VERID;
    const uint32_t PARAM;          // The "M" prefix stands
    const uint32_t unused1;        // for "Master" in the
    const uint32_t unused2;        // following names:
    volatile uint32_t MCR;         // 010 Control Reg
    volatile uint32_t MSR;         // 014 Status Reg
    volatile uint32_t MIER;        // 018 Int Enable Reg
    volatile uint32_t MDER;        // 01C DMA Enable Reg
    volatile uint32_t MCFGR0;      // 020 Config Reg 0
    volatile uint32_t MCFGR1;      // 024 Config Reg 1
    volatile uint32_t MCFGR2;      // 028 Config Reg 2
    volatile uint32_t MCFGR3;      // 02C Config Reg 3
    volatile uint32_t unused3[4];
    volatile uint32_t MDMR;        // 040 Data Match Reg
    volatile uint32_t unused4;
    volatile uint32_t MCCR0;       // 048 Clock Config Reg 0
    volatile uint32_t unused5;
    volatile uint32_t MCCR1;       // 050 Clock Config Reg 1
    volatile uint32_t unused6;
    volatile uint32_t MFCR;        // 058 FIFO Control Reg
    volatile uint32_t MFSR;        // 05C FIFO Status Reg
    volatile uint32_t MTDR;        // 060 Transmit Data Reg
    volatile uint32_t unused7[3];
    volatile uint32_t MRDR;        // 070 Receive Data Reg
    volatile uint32_t unused8[39];

                                   // The "S" prefix stands
                                   // for "Slave" in the
                                   // following names:
    volatile uint32_t SCR;         // 110 Control Reg
    volatile uint32_t SSR;         // 114 Status Reg
    volatile uint32_t SIER;        // 118 Int Enable Reg
    volatile uint32_t SDER;        // 11C DMA Enable Reg
```

```
        volatile uint32_t unused9;
        volatile uint32_t SCFGR1;        // 124 Config Reg 1
        volatile uint32_t SCFGR2;        // 128 Config Reg 2
        volatile uint32_t unused10[5];
        volatile uint32_t SAMR;          // 140 Address Match Reg
        volatile uint32_t unused11[3];
        volatile uint32_t SASR;          // 150 Address Status Reg
        volatile uint32_t STAR;          // 154 Transmit Ack Reg
        volatile uint32_t unused13[2];
        volatile uint32_t STDR;          // 160 Transmit Data Reg
        volatile uint32_t unused14[3];
        volatile uint32_t SRDR;          // 170 Receive Data Reg
} IMXRT_LPI2C_Registers;

// LPI2C2 is not connected to any
// pins on the Teensy 4.x.

#define LPI2C1      (*(IMXRT_LPI2C_Registers *)0x403F0000)
#define LPI2C2      (*(IMXRT_LPI2C_Registers *)0x403F4000)
#define LPI2C3      (*(IMXRT_LPI2C_Registers *)0x403F8000)
#define LPI2C4      (*(IMXRT_LPI2C_Registers *)0x403FC000)
```

The #define statements at the end of this listing define symbols that map this structure to different addresses in memory. Specifically, LPI2C1 corresponds to the registers associated with the Teensy 4's (SDA0, SCL0) pins, LPI2C3 corresponds to the (SDA1, SCL1) pins, and LPI2C4 corresponds to the (SCL2, SDA2) pins (note that the Teensy 4.x has only three I^2C ports brought out). You can read about these pin definitions in section 47.4 of the NXP manual.

NOTE *The* M *in various Teensy 4.x* I^2C *register names stands for* master, *and* S *stands for* slave. *Although this book prefers the terms* controller *and* peripheral, *the NXP documentation refers to these registers as* master *and* slave, *respectively, so for consistency I'll use NXP's language in this section.*

Although it's beyond the scope of this book to describe the uses of all of these registers in detail, it is worthwhile to describe several of them to understand the code in the sections that follow. See Chapter 47 of the NXP manual for more detail on all other registers.

Because the i.MX RT1062 is a 32-bit CPU, the registers are all 32 bits wide. Unlike CPU registers, whose addresses the ARM core encodes into the instruction opcodes, peripheral registers appear as memory locations to the processor—that is, LPI2C1 through LPI2C4. As the ARM supports byte, half-word (16-bit), and word (32-bit) memory accesses, you can access individual bytes or half-words in these peripheral registers (as well as in the whole 32-bit register, of course).

The Master Control Register (MCR)   The MCR is a collection of six flags (bits), spread out in the LO 10 bits of the register. Writing to these flags enables (1) or disables (0) I^2C features. Table 11-1 describes these flags.

Table 11-1: MCR Fields

Bit	Description
0	MEN (master enable): Enables or disables the controller aspects for a particular I²C port. Set to 1 to use the I²C port as a controller.
1	RST (software reset): A 1 in this bit resets the I²C controller. A 0 in this bit allows normal operation.
2	DOZEN (doze mode enable): A 1 in this bit enables operation in low-power doze mode. A 0 in this bit disables controller in doze mode (for normal operation).
3	DBGEN (debug enable): A 1 in this bit enables controller operation in debug mode. A 0 puts the I²C port in normal operational mode.
8	RTF (reset transmit FIFO [First-In, First-Out]): Writing a 1 in this bit resets the transmission FIFO; writing a 0 has no effect. This bit is write-only and always returns 0 when read.
9	RRF (reset receive FIFO): Writing a 1 in this bit resets the receive FIFO (writing a 0 does nothing). This bit is write-only and always returns 0 when read.

The Master Status Register (MSR)   The MSR is a collection of bits that specifies the current status of the I²C port. Table 11-2 lists the fields in this register.

Table 11-2: MSR Fields

Bit	Description
0	TDF (transmit data flag): Set whenever the number of bytes in the transmission FIFO is less than or equal to *TxWater*, the transmission low watermark.* TxWater is set in the MFCR. The purpose of this flag (and its corresponding interrupt) is to notify the system that the transmission FIFO needs more data. See Table 11-6 later in this chapter to set the TxWater value.
1	RDF (receive data flag): Set whenever the number of bytes in the receive FIFO is greater than *RxWater*, the receive high watermark. RxWater is set in the MFCR. The purpose of this flag (and its corresponding interrupt) is to notify the system that it needs to remove data from the receive FIFO. See Table 11-6 to set the RxWater value.
8	EPF (end packet flag): Set when a controller generates a *repeated* start condition or a stop condition (not set on the first start condition). Writing a 1 to this bit clears this flag.
9	SDF (stop detected flag): Set when the controller generates a stop condition. Writing a 1 to this bit clears this flag.
10	NDF (NAK detected flag): Set when the controller detects a NAK when transmitting an address or data. When this bit is 1, the system will not generate a start condition until the flag is cleared. If a NAK is expected after an address transmission, the hardware will set this flag if a NAK is not generated. Writing a 1 to this bit clears this flag.

*A watermark is a point in the buffer where some event will occur (such as setting the TDF or RDF).

(continued)

Table 11-2: MSR Fields *(continued)*

Bit	Description
11	ALF (arbitration lost flag): The controller will set this flag if it loses an arbitration battle on the I²C bus. Once set, the system will not initiate a new start condition until this flag is cleared. Writing a 1 to this bit clears this flag.
12	FEF (FIFO error flag): The controller sets this bit if it detects an attempt to transmit or receive data without a start, or repeated start, condition. Writing a 1 to this bit clears this flag.
13	PLTF (pin low timeout flag): Set if the controller detects that an SDA or SCL line is stuck low. Writing a 1 to this bit clears this flag, though it cannot be cleared as long as the low pin condition persists.
14	DMF (data match flag): Set if the controller determines that the received data has matched the MATCH0 or MATCH1 values (specified in MCFGR1). Writing a 1 to this bit clears this flag.
24	MBF (master busy flag): Set while the controller is busy.
25	BBF (bus busy flag): Set while the I²C bus is busy.

*A watermark is a point in the buffer where some event will occur (such as setting the TDF or RDF).

The Master Interrupt Enable Register (MIER)　The MIER allows you to enable or disable various I²C interrupts for a particular port. This is a collection of bits where a 1 indicates that the interrupt is enabled and a 0 indicates that the specific interrupt is disabled. Table 11-3 lists the fields in this register.

Table 11-3: MIER Fields

Bit	Description
0	TDIE: transmit data interrupt enable
1	RDIE: receive data interrupt enable
8	EPIE: end packet interrupt enable
9	SDIE: stop detected interrupt enable
10	NDIE: NAK detected interrupt enable
11	ALIE: arbitration lost interrupt enable
12	FEIE: FIFO error interrupt enable
13	PLTIE: pin low timeout interrupt enable
14	DMIE: data match interrupt enable

The Master Configuration Register 1 (MCFGR1)　The Teensy I²C code uses only the LO 3 bits of the MCFGR1. These 3 bits hold the clock prescaler value that divides the system clock by 2^{n+1}, where n is the 3-bit number passed in MCFGR1. For information on the other bits, see the NXP documentation.

The Master Configuration Register 2 (MCFGR2) The MCFGR2 contains bus idle timeout and glitch filter constants for the I²C bus. Table 11-4 describes the MCFGR2 fields.

Table 11-4: MCFGR2 Fields

Bits	Description
0 to 11	Bus idle timeout period in clock cycles. A 0 in this field disables bus idle checking.
16 to 19	SCL glitch filter. A 0 in this field disables the filter. Otherwise, pulses less than or equal to this many clock cycles long will be ignored on the SCL line.
24 to 27	SDA glitch filter. A 0 in this field disables the filter. Otherwise, pulses less than or equal to this many clock cycles long will be ignored on the SDA line.

The Master Configuration Register 3 (MCFGR3) The MCFGR3 holds the pin low timeout value. Bits 8 to 19 hold the pin low timeout constant (in clock cycles, times 256). Writing a 0 to these bits disables this feature. All other bits in MCFGR3 must be 0.

The Master Clock Configuration Register 0 (MCCR0) and 1 (MCCR1) The MCCR0 and MCCR1 specify various parameters concerning the I²C signal lines. Table 11-5 lists the fields held within this register. MCCR1 is the same as MCCR0, but it is used when operating in I²C high-speed mode.

Table 11-5: MCCR0 and MCCR1 Fields

Bits	Description
0 to 5	CLKLO: Minimum number of cycles (minus 1) that the SCL clock is driven low by the hardware.
8 to 13	CLKHI: Minimum number of cycles (minus 1) that the SCL clock is driven high by the hardware.
16 to 21	SETHOLD: Minimum number of cycles (minus 1) used by the controller as the hold time for a start condition. It is also used as the setup and hold time for a repeated start condition, and as the setup time for a stop condition.
24 to 29	DATAVD: Data valid delay. Minimum number of cycles (minus 1) used for the SDA data hold time. Must be less than CLKLO.

The Master FIFO Control Register (MFCR) The MFCR allows you to set the TxWater and RxWater watermarks. These are each 2-bit fields allowing you to set the watermark from 0 to 3 (the FIFOs hold 4 words each). The field positions appear in Table 11-6.

Table 11-6: MFCR Fields

Bits	Description
0 to 1	TxWater
16 to 17	RxWater

The Master FIFO Status Register (MFSR) The MFSR holds the current number of words in the transmit and receive FIFOs. The fields appear in Table 11-7. Although there are 3 bits associated with these fields, the FIFOs hold only four words.

Table 11-7: MFSR Fields

Bits	Description
0 to 2	Number of words in transmit buffer
16 to 18	Number of words in receive buffer

The Master Transmit Data Register (MTDR) The MTDR accepts commands and data bytes to control writing data onto the I^2C bus. It has two fields, shown in Table 11-8.

Table 11-8: MTDR Fields

Bits	Field
0 to 7	Data
8 to 10	Command

Any write to the LO 8 bits, be it by a byte write or a 16-bit (or 32-bit) write to this register, will insert the data byte at the end of the transmit FIFO and increment the FIFO pointer—assuming, of course, that the FIFO is not full. Also note that an 8-bit write to the LO 8 bits will zero-extend the write operation and write 0b000 to the command bits.

The command field is a 3-bit command code (see Table 11-9). Writing a single byte to bits 8 to 15 executes the command.

Table 11-9: MTDR Command Values

Command bits	Command
0b000	Transmit data (found in bits 0 to 7).
0b001	Receive data. Bits 0 to 7 specify the number of bytes to receive (plus 1).
0b010	Send stop condition.

Command bits	Command
0b011	Receive and discard bytes. Bits 0 to 7 specify the number of bytes to receive (plus 1).
0b100	Generate (repeated) start condition and transmit address in bits 0 to 7.
0b101	Generate (repeated) start condition and transmit address in bits 0 to 7. This transfer expects a NAK to be returned.
0b110	Generate (repeated) start condition and transmit address in bits 0 to 7 using high-speed mode.
0b111	Generate (repeated) start condition and transmit address in bits 0 to 7 using high-speed mode. This transfer expects a NAK to be returned.

Generally, the only command you'd write as a single byte (to bits 8 through 15) would to be to send a stop condition. All other commands have data associated with them.

Note that the FIFO holds commands as well as data. Therefore, the hardware associates the particular command it executes with the data as it pulls items from the transmit FIFO.

The Master Receive Data Register (MRDR) Data received by the I^2C hardware gets added to the receive FIFO. Reading the MRDR retrieves the next available byte from the FIFO (in bits 0 through 7). Bit 14 of the MRDR is set if the FIFO is empty. Note that you can also check to see if data is available in the FIFO by reading bits 16 through 18 in the MFSR.

11.1.2 Teensy 4.x Wire Code

The following sections describe the operations of Gemmell's Teensy 4 code directly associated with the Arduino I^2C functions. I won't provide the usual DAC output demonstration program in this section, since you can easily test Gemmell's code by downloading his library, including it in your Teensyduino IDE, and running the Arduino example in Listing 8-1 (don't forget to replace #include <Wire.h> with #include <i2c_driver_wire.h>). The results should prove nearly identical with possible slight differences in timing, as Gemmell's code is running on a much faster processor than the Teensy 3.2 I used to produce the oscilloscope output in Listing 8-1.

Gemmell's library provides drop-in code for the following Arduino I^2C functions:

- `Wire.begin()`
- `Wire.beginTransmission()`
- `Wire.endTransmission()`
- `Wire.write()`
- `Wire.requestFrom()`
- `Wire.read()`

The next sections describe the implementation of each of these functions.

When you study Gemmell's code, the best approach is to take a top-down look starting with the Arduino Wire objects. The *i2c_driver_wire.cpp* file declares the following three objects:

```
I2CDriverWire Wire( Master, Slave );
I2CDriverWire Wire1( Master1, Slave1 );
I2CDriverWire Wire2( Master2, Slave2 );
```

The Wire object corresponds to the standard Arduino I^{2}C Wire device and controls I^{2}C communication on the Teensy SDA and SCL lines. The Wire2 and Wire3 objects are extensions of the original Arduino I^{2}C library, supporting communication on the Teensy's (SDA1, SCL1) and (SDA2, SCL2) lines.

NOTE   *As a design pattern,* Wire *would normally be classified as a singleton. As there are three objects of class* I2CDriverWire, *I suppose the real term would be* tripleton. *In any case, you generally would not create any additional instances of* I2CDriverWire.

The Wire objects support both master and slave devices. (Again, I use the archaic terms *master* and *slave* in this section only for consistency with ARM documentation and Gemmell's code.) In this chapter I'll focus just on the master component.

11.1.2.1 The begin() Function

The begin() function replaces the standard Arduino Wire.begin() function. It is responsible for initializing the I^{2}C hardware and software before calling other I^{2}C functions. It initializes the appropriate Teensy pins for I^{2}C communication, resets any existing I^{2}C initialization, sets the I^{2}C clock frequency, sets up interrupt vectors, and initializes the iMXRT 1062 registers as necessary.

The Wire, Wire1, and Wire2 object declarations (in the *i2c_driver_wire.cpp* file) allocate storage but do little else. In the Arduino programming paradigm, object initialization does not take place in the constructor; instead, the initialization occurs during the call to the I2CDriverWire::begin() function:

```
void I2CDriverWire::begin()
{
    end();
    master.begin( master_frequency );
}
```

The begin() function stops any current activity by calling the end() function and then punts on the task to the I2CMaster class constructor (the master_frequency parameter is the default I^{2}C speed of 100 kHz). The I2CMaster class is just an abstract base class, overridden by the IMX_RT1060 _I2CMaster class, which provides the actual code.

Here is the overridden begin() function:

```
void IMX_RT1060_I2CMaster::begin( uint32_t frequency )
{
    // Make sure master mode is disabled before configuring it:

    stop( port, config.irq );

    // Set up pins and master clock:

    initialise_common( config, pad_control_config );

    // Configure and Enable Master Mode.
    // Set FIFO watermarks. Determines when the RDF and TDF
    // interrupts happen:

    port->MFCR = LPI2C_MFCR_RXWATER( 0 ) | LPI2C_MFCR_TXWATER( 0 );
    set_clock( frequency );

    // Set up interrupt service routine:

    attachInterruptVector( config.irq, isr );

    // Enable all the interrupts you use:

    port->MIER =
            LPI2C_MIER_RDIE | LPI2C_MIER_SDIE |
            LPI2C_MIER_NDIE | LPI2C_MIER_ALIE |
            LPI2C_MIER_FEIE | LPI2C_MIER_PLTIE;

    NVIC_ENABLE_IRQ( config.irq );
}
```

Before I discuss individual statements in this function, note that the identifier port is a class variable pointing at the register set for the I^2C port on which this function operates; config is also a class variable containing the port configuration.

The call to stop() in the begin() function in the previous code shuts down any activity on the I^2C port before this code initializes the system, which could happen, for example, if the programmer calls begin() twice. Here's the code for stop():

```
static void stop( IMXRT_LPI2C_Registers* port, IRQ_NUMBER_t irq )
{
    // Halt and reset Master Mode if it's running:

 ❶ port->MCR = (LPI2C_MCR_RST | LPI2C_MCR_RRF | LPI2C_MCR_RTF);
    port->MCR = 0;

    // Halt and reset Slave Mode if it's running:

 ❷ port->SCR = (LPI2C_SCR_RST | LPI2C_SCR_RRF | LPI2C_SCR_RTF);
```

```
    port->SCR = 0;

    // Disable interrupts:

 ❸ NVIC_DISABLE_IRQ( irq );
    attachInterruptVector( irq, nullptr );
}
```

Writing to the MCR using port->MCR ❶ does the following:

- LPI2C_MCR_RST does a software reset of the controller.
- LPI2C_MCR_RRF resets the receive FIFO memory buffer.
- LPI2C_MCR_RTF resets the transmit FIFO.

The write to SCR (by storing into port->SCR) does the same thing for peripheral (slave) mode ❷. Finally, the stop function ❶ turns off and disconnects any interrupts (and interrupt service routines).

The call to initialise_common() in the begin function initializes hardware common to the controller (master) and peripheral (slave) modes. Here's the code for that function:

```
static void initialise_common
(
 ❶ IMX_RT1060_I2CBase::Config hardware,
    uint32_t pad_control_config
){
    // Set LPI2C Clock to 24 MHz. This is required by
    // slaves as well as masters:

 ❷ CCM_CSCDR2 = (CCM_CSCDR2 & ~CCM_CSCDR2_LPI2C_CLK_PODF( 63 )) |
                   CCM_CSCDR2_LPI2C_CLK_SEL;

 ❸ hardware.clock_gate_register |= hardware.clock_gate_mask;

    // Set up SDA and SCL pins and registers:

 ❹ initialise_pin( hardware.sda_pin, pad_control_config );
    initialise_pin( hardware.scl_pin, pad_control_config );
}
```

IMX_RT1060_I2CBase::Config ❶ is a structure in the *imx_rt1060_i2c_driver.h* file (see the next box for its form). It defines Teensy pins and other information. CCM_CSCDR2 ❷ is a hardware definition on the MCU, the CCM Serial Clock Divider Register 2. The assignment to this hardware register sets up an internal clock divider needed to generate the I^2C clock. The PODF field is the clock divider, and the CCM_CSCDR2_LPI2C_CLK_SEL constant specifies that the I^2C clock gets derived from the system oscillator.

The assignment to hardware.clock_gate_register ❸ magically writes data to the CCM Clock Gating Register, because this variable overlays that register in the MCU's memory map. Finally, the last two assignment statements in this function ❹ initialize the appropriate (depending on the port) SDA and SCL lines so that they are used for I²C communications, rather than as, for example, digital I/O lines.

IMX_RT1060_I2CBASE::CONFIG STRUCTURE

The IMX_RT1060_I2CBase::Config structure takes the following form (see the imx_rt1060_i2c_driver.h file for more details and additional comments that were removed for formatting purposes):

```
class IMX_RT1060_I2CBase
{
public:
    typedef struct {
        const uint8_t pin;          // The Teensy 4.0 pin number
        const uint32_t mux_val;     // Value to set for mux
        volatile uint32_t* select_input_register;
        const uint32_t select_val;  // Value for that selection
    } PinInfo;

    typedef struct {
        volatile uint32_t& clock_gate_register;
        uint32_t clock_gate_mask;
        PinInfo sda_pin;            // The default SDA pin
        PinInfo scl_pin;            // The default SCL pin
        bool has_alternatives;
        PinInfo alternative_sda_pin;
        PinInfo alternative_scl_pin;
        IRQ_NUMBER_t irq;
    } Config;
};
```

The assignment port->MFCR in the begin() function defines when an interrupt occurs. This particular statement sets the interrupts to occur when the transmit FIFO is completely empty or when the receive FIFO contains at least one word. In the Arduino environment, 0 (empty FIFO) is probably a good value to use. In a multithreaded environment, you might get better throughput on the I²C bus by setting the transmit value to 1 or some other nonzero value to keep the FIFO not empty as long as there is data to transmit.

NOTE *The drawback to using a nonzero value in a multithreaded environment is that you will probably get more interrupts, thus reducing the overall system performance.*

The call to set_clock() sets the I²C bus to the frequency passed as an argument to this code. The parameter should be 100,000, 400,000, or 1,000,000.

You must call set_clock() before calling the begin() function. Here's the code for the set_clock() function:

```cpp
// Supports 100-kHz, 400-kHz, and 1-MHz modes.

void IMX_RT1060_I2CMaster::set_clock( uint32_t frequency )
{
    if( frequency < 400000 )
    {
        // Use Standard Mode (up to 100 kHz).

        port->MCCR0 = LPI2C_MCCR0_CLKHI( 55 ) |
                      LPI2C_MCCR0_CLKLO( 59 ) |
                      LPI2C_MCCR0_DATAVD( 25 ) |
                      LPI2C_MCCR0_SETHOLD( 40 );

        port->MCFGR1 = LPI2C_MCFGR1_PRESCALE( 1 );

        port->MCFGR2 = LPI2C_MCFGR2_FILTSDA( 5 ) |
                       LPI2C_MCFGR2_FILTSCL( 5 ) |
                       LPI2C_MCFGR2_BUSIDLE
                       (
                           2 * (59 + 40 + 2)
                       );

        port->MCFGR3 =
            LPI2C_MCFGR3_PINLOW
            (
                CLOCK_STRETCH_TIMEOUT * 12 / 256 + 1
            );

    }
    else if( frequency < 10000000 )
    {
        // Use Fast Mode - up to 400 kHz.

      ❶ port->MCCR0 = LPI2C_MCCR0_CLKHI( 26 ) |
                      LPI2C_MCCR0_CLKLO( 28 ) |
                      LPI2C_MCCR0_DATAVD( 12 ) |
                      LPI2C_MCCR0_SETHOLD( 18 );

      ❷ port->MCFGR1 = LPI2C_MCFGR1_PRESCALE( 0 );
      ❸ port->MCFGR2 = LPI2C_MCFGR2_FILTSDA( 2 ) |
                       LPI2C_MCFGR2_FILTSCL( 2 ) |
                       LPI2C_MCFGR2_BUSIDLE
                       (
                           2 * (28 + 18 + 2)
                       );

        port->MCFGR3 =
            LPI2C_MCFGR3_PINLOW
            (
                CLOCK_STRETCH_TIMEOUT * 24 / 256 + 1
            );
    }
```

```
    else
    {
        // Use Fast Mode Plus (up to 1 MHz).

        port->MCCR0 = LPI2C_MCCR0_CLKHI(9) |
                        LPI2C_MCCR0_CLKLO(10) |
                        LPI2C_MCCR0_DATAVD(4) |
                        LPI2C_MCCR0_SETHOLD(7);

        port->MCFGR1 = LPI2C_MCFGR1_PRESCALE(0);
        port->MCFGR2 = LPI2C_MCFGR2_FILTSDA(1) |
                        LPI2C_MCFGR2_FILTSCL(1) |
                        LPI2C_MCFGR2_BUSIDLE
                        (
                            2 * (10 + 7 + 2)
                        );

        port->MCFGR3 =
            LPI2C_MCFGR3_PINLOW
            (
                CLOCK_STRETCH_TIMEOUT * 24 / 256 + 1
            );
    }
 ❹ port->MCCR1 = port->MCCR0;
}
```

The MCCR0 ❶ contains several bit fields filled in by the macros after the assignment. The CLKLO field specifies the minimum number of clock cycles the system uses for a low clock signal on the I²C bus. The CLKHI field is similar but specifies how long the clock must be high (this value must be less than CLKLO). The DATAVD field specifies the amount of time the data must remain valid on the SDA line. The SETHOLD field specifies the time for a start or stop condition.

The MCFGR1 ❷ controls several fields (see the NXP documentation). The main value being set here is the clock divisor. For 100 kHz the divisor is 2; for other frequencies the divisor is 1.

The MCFGR2 register ❸ determines:

* The number of cycles used for SDA glitch filtering (LPI2C_MCFGR2_FILTSDA)
* The number of cycles used for SCL glitch filtering (LPI2C_MCFGR2_FILTSCL)
* The number of cycles to determine when the bus has gone idle (LPI2C_MCFGR2_BUSIDLE)

The MCCR1 register ❹ holds the clock configuration for I²C high-speed mode. See the discussion of MCCR0 a few paragraphs earlier for more details as, other than speed, it behaves similarly to MCCR1.

After setting the clock frequency, the begin() function attaches an ISR and enables interrupts. In theory, a nonthreaded system such as Arduino won't benefit as much from an interrupt-driven I²C device driver; all I²C calls are synchronous, so you still have to enter a busy-waiting loop until the transmission or reception is complete. Nevertheless, using interrupts can be useful if you're using the Teensy Threading Library, and an interrupt-driven system combined with the FIFOs can improve transmission and reception latency.

Each object gets its own instance of an ISR, which handles errors, nonempty receive FIFOs (meaning data has arrived), and empty transmission FIFOs (meaning you can send more data). Here's the source code for the ISR (cleaned up for publication):

```
void IMX_RT1060_I2CMaster::_interrupt_service_routine()
{
    uint32_t msr = port->MSR;

    // Check for the following errors (prioritized
    // in this order):
    //
    // NDF-  NAK detection flag.
    // ALF-  Arbitration lost flag.
    // FEF-  FIFO error flag.
    // PLTF- Pin low timeout flag.

❶ if
    (
        msr &
            (
                LPI2C_MSR_NDF |
                LPI2C_MSR_ALF |
                LPI2C_MSR_FEF |
                LPI2C_MSR_PLTF
            )
    ){

        // If you got a NAK, determine who caused
        // the NAK:

        if( msr & LPI2C_MSR_NDF )
        {
            port->MSR = LPI2C_MSR_NDF; // Clear the error
            if( state == State::starting )
            {
                _error = I2CError::address_nak;
            }
            else
            {
                _error = I2CError::data_nak;
            }
        }

        // If you got an arbitration lost error, that
        // takes precedence over NDF:

        if( msr & LPI2C_MSR_ALF )
        {
            port->MSR = LPI2C_MSR_ALF; // Clear the error
            _error = I2CError::arbitration_lost;
        }
```

```
            // FIFO empty error takes precedence over
            // earlier errors:

            if( msr & LPI2C_MSR_FEF )
            {
                port->MSR = LPI2C_MSR_FEF; // Clear error
                if( !has_error() )
                {
                    _error = I2CError::master_fifo_error;
                }

                // else FEF was triggered by another error.
                // Ignore it (and keep previous error status).
            }

            // If pin low timeout, clear error and set
            // error return value.

            if( msr & LPI2C_MSR_PLTF )
            {
                port->MSR = LPI2C_MSR_PLTF; // Clear error
                _error = I2CError::master_pin_low_timeout;
            }

            // On any of the above errors, put this in the
            // stopping state if it's not already there.

            if( state != State::stopping )
            {
                state = State::stopping;
                abort_transaction_async();
            }
            // else already trying to end the transaction.
        }

        // The following are "normal" conditions (not errors).
        //
        // Check for the "Stop Detected" flag, indicating end
        // of transmission has been received.

❷ if( msr & LPI2C_MSR_SDF )
    {
        // You don't want to handle TDF if you can avoid it,
        // so disable that interrupt.

        port->MIER &= ~LPI2C_MIER_TDIE;
        state = State::stopped;
        port->MSR = LPI2C_MSR_SDF; // Clear stop detected
    }

    // Check the received data flag. This bit gets set
    // whenever the number of bytes in the FIFO exceeds
    // the "high water" mark. Because this code sets
    // the HWM to 0, you get an interrupt whenever
```

```
                // any byte comes along.

        ❸ if( msr & LPI2C_MSR_RDF )
          {
              if( ignore_tdf )
              {
                  // Copy the byte out of the receive
                  // register into the memory buffer:

                  if( buff.not_started_reading() )
                  {
                      error = I2CError::ok;
                      state = State::transferring;
                  }
                  if( state == State::transferring )
                  {
                      buff.write( port->MRDR );
                  }
                  else
                  {
                      // Reset the receive FIFO if
                      // not expecting data.

                      port->MCR |= LPI2C_MCR_RRF;
                  }
                  if( buff.finished_reading() )
                  {
                      if( tx_fifo_count() == 1 )
                      {
                          state = State::stopping;
                      }
                      else
                      {
                          state = State::transfer_complete;
                      }

                      // Avoids triggering PLTF if
                      // you didn't send a STOP.

                      port->MCR &= ~LPI2C_MCR_MEN; // Master disable

                  }
              }
              else
              {
                  // This is a write transaction.
                  // Code shouldn't have gotten a read.

                  state = State::stopping;
                  abort_transaction_async();
              }
          }

        // Handle writing data to the I2C bus here.
```

```
        // Is data available (and code is not ignoring it)?

❹ if( !ignore_tdf && (msr & LPI2C_MSR_TDF) )
  {
      if( buff.not_started_writing() )
      {
          _error = I2CError::ok;
          state = State::transferring;
      }
      if( state == State::transferring )
      {
          // Fill the transmit buffer (FIFO).

          uint32_t fifo_space =
              NUM_FIFOS - tx_fifo_count();

          while
          (
                  buff.has_data_available()
              &&  fifo_space > 0
          ){
              port->MTDR =
                  LPI2C_MTDR_CMD_TRANSMIT | buff.read();
              fifo_space--;
          }

          // If writing is done, disable transmission
          // interrupts and clean up.

          if
          (
                  buff.finished_writing()
              &&  tx_fifo_count() == 0
          ){
              port->MIER &= ~LPI2C_MIER_TDIE;
              if ( stop_on_completion )
              {
                  state = State::stopping;
                  port->MTDR = LPI2C_MTDR_CMD_STOP;
              }
              else
              {
                  state = State::transfer_complete;
              }

              // Avoids triggering PLTF if
              // you didn't send a STOP.

              port->MCR &= ~LPI2C_MCR_MEN;
          }
      }
      // else ignore it. This flag is frequently
      // set in read transfers.
  }
}
```

The ISR begins by checking for possible errors ❶ and sets an appropriate error condition based on the type of error, if an error condition exists. If no error exists ❷, then the ISR checks to see if a stop condition has been detected and sets the appropriate stop flag if so. Next, the ISR checks to see if any data has been received ❸, in which case it adds the data to the receive buffer. It then checks to see if it is transmitting any data to the I^{2}C bus ❹, in which case it removes data from the transmit buffer to transmit, cleaning up and terminating the transmission if there is no data left to send in the buffer.

11.1.2.2 The beginTransmission() and endTransmission() Functions

In Arduino I^{2}C programming, the beginTransmission() function marks the beginning of a sequence to be transmitted across the I^{2}C bus, while the endTransmission() function marks the end of a write operation. These two functions bracket a sequence of write commands (described in the next section). The write commands simply place data in a buffer (initialized by the beginTransmission() call), and then the endTransmission() function transmits the data in the buffer across the I^{2}C bus.

The beginTransmission() function accepts a single argument, which is the I^{2}C device address. Here's its code:

```
void I2CDriverWire::beginTransmission( int address )
{
    write_address = (uint8_t)address;
    tx_next_byte_to_write = 0;
}
```

This function doesn't accomplish much. It saves the device address into a local (object) field for later use, initializes (to 0) a queue index for storing data to transmit, and then returns. Most of the real work happens in other functions.

Here's the code for the endTransmission() function:

```
uint8_t I2CDriverWire::endTransmission( int stop )
{
    master.write_async
    (
        write_address,
        tx_buffer,
        tx_next_byte_to_write,
        stop
    );
    finish();
    return toWireResult( master.error() );
}
```

The single parameter is a Boolean flag indicating whether the function transmits a stop condition after it completes transmitting the data in the buffer.

The write_async() function within endTransmission(), as its name suggests, asynchronously writes the data in the buffer (tx_buffer) across the I^2C bus. Because it is asynchronous, this function returns before the transmission is complete. Here's the write_async() code:

```
void IMX_RT1060_I2CMaster::write_async
(
    uint8_t address,
    uint8_t* buffer,
    size_t num_bytes,
    bool send_stop
){
  ❶ if( !start( address, MASTER_WRITE )) return;

    if( num_bytes == 0 )
    {
        // The caller is probably probing
        // addresses to find slaves.
        // Don't try to transmit anything.

        ignore_tdf = true;
      ❷ port->MTDR = LPI2C_MTDR_CMD_STOP;
        return;
    }

  ❸ buff.initialise( buffer, num_bytes );
    stop_on_completion = send_stop;
    port->MIER |= LPI2C_MIER_TDIE;
}
```

The start() function call ❶ within write_async() puts an I^2C start condition on the bus. It returns true if the operation was successful. If it fails, write_async() simply returns. If it succeeds, but there are no bytes to send, the write_async() function writes the appropriate bit to the MTDR to stop the whole transmission ❷. If start() succeeds and there is data to transmit, then write_async() initializes a transmission buffer ❸ and enables the transmit data interrupt enable bit.

Here's the code for the start() function within write_async():

```
bool IMX_RT1060_I2CMaster::start
(
    uint8_t address,
    uint32_t direction
){

{
  ❶ if( !finished() )
    {
        // Code hasn't completed the previous transaction yet.

        abort_transaction_async();

        _error = I2CError::master_not_ready;
```

```
        state = State::idle;
        return false;
    }

    // Start a new transaction.

❷ ignore_tdf = direction;
    _error = I2CError::ok;
    state = State::starting;

    // Make sure the FIFOs are empty before you start.

    if( tx_fifo_count() > 0 || rx_fifo_count() > 0 )
    {
        // This should never happen.

        error = I2CError::master_fifos_not_empty;
        abort_transaction_async();
        return false;
    }

    // Clear status flags.

    clear_all_msr_flags();

    // Send a START to the slave at "address."

❸ port->MCR |= LPI2C_MCR_MEN;
    uint8_t i2c_address = (address & 0x7F) << 1;
    port->MTDR =
        LPI2C_MTDR_CMD_START | i2c_address | direction;

    return true;
}
```

If the system is not finished with a previous transmission ❶, this function will terminate the previous transmission and set the state to idle. Then the start() function initializes a new I^{2}C bus transaction ❷ by clearing all FIFOs and status flags. Finally, this function places a start condition on the I^{2}C bus ❸. If this code is successful, it initializes the state field with State::starting.

STATE TYPE DEFINITION

Note that the State type has the following definition:

```
enum class State
{
        // Busy states:
        starting = 0,   // Waiting for START to be sent and ack'd
```

```
        transferring,    // In a transfer
        stopping,        // Transfer complete or aborted
                         // Waiting for STOP

        // "idle" and above mean that the driver has finished
        // whatever it was doing and is ready to do more work.

        idle = 100,        // Not in a transaction
        transfer_complete, // Transfer has finished and caller
                           // has not requested a STOP
        stopped            // Transaction has finished
                           // STOP sent
    };
```

The endTransmission() function is synchronous and does not return to the caller until the transmission is complete. To match those semantics, this version of the function calls the finish() function, which waits until the transmission is complete.

The finish() function is a simple little class method:

```
void finish()
{
    elapsedMillis timeout;
    while( timeout < timeout_millis )
    {
        if( master.finished() )
        {
            return;
        }
    }
}
```

This function is a short extension of the master.finished() function that adds a timeout capability, which looks like this:

```
inline bool IMX_RT1060_I2CMaster::finished()
{
    return state >= State::idle;
}
```

The state field is initialized in the call to start() within write_async() and then set by the ISR. If the state is transfer_complete or stopped, then the ISR is done transferring data. Otherwise, the ISR is still reading or writing data, and the endTransmission() function will wait until the ISR has completed transferring data after the write operation begins.

At the end of endTransmission(), the function calls toWireResult() to translate the error status bitmap returned by master.error() into an Arduino-compatible error code, and the function returns that value to the caller.

11.1.2.3 The write Functions

Between the beginTransmission() and endTransmission() calls, Arduino code calls the write() function to append data to the transmission buffer. There are two variants of the write() function: one that writes a single byte and one that writes a buffer.

NOTE *Keep in mind that these functions don't actually write data to the I^2C bus. They simply append data to the transmission buffer. The endTransmission() function handles the actual data transmission once the write operations are complete.*

Here's the source code for the two write() functions:

```
size_t I2CDriverWire::write( uint8_t data )
{
    if( tx_next_byte_to_write < tx_buffer_length )
    {
        tx_buffer[tx_next_byte_to_write++] = data;
        return 1;
    }
    return 0;
}

size_t I2CDriverWire::write( const uint8_t* data, size_t length )
{
    size_t avail = tx_buffer_length - tx_next_byte_to_write;
    if( avail >= length )
    {
        uint8_t* dest = tx_buffer + tx_next_byte_to_write;
        memcpy( dest, data, length );
        tx_next_byte_to_write += length;
        return length;
    }
    return 0;
}
```

The maximum buffer length (defined in the I2CDriverWire class) is 32 bytes. If an application attempts to transmit more than 32 bytes in a single I^2C transmission, this code will ignore all bytes beyond the size of the buffer.

11.1.2.4 The requestFrom(), read(), and available() Functions

Reading bytes from the I^2C bus is slightly less complex than writing data. There are three functions associated with reading: requestFrom(), read(), and available(). The requestFrom() function reads the data from a peripheral device and buffers the data up in memory, while the read() function retrieves bytes from the buffer and available() returns the number of bytes in the buffer.

Here's the source code for the requestFrom() function:

```
uint8_t I2CDriverWire::requestFrom
(
    int address,
    int quantity,
```

```
        int stop
){
    rx_bytes_available = 0;
    rx_next_byte_to_read = 0;
    master.read_async
    (
        (uint8_t)address,
        rxBuffer,
        min( (size_t)quantity, rx_buffer_length ),
        stop
    );
    finish();
    rx_bytes_available = master.get_bytes_transferred();
    return rx_bytes_available;
}
```

The first two statements in this function initialize the buffer index and count. The call to master.read_async() starts the actual read operation (it primes the system and notifies the ISR to start accepting data). As its name suggests, master.read_async() returns immediately, before the actual data is read. As with the endTransmission() function, requestFrom() calls the finish() function to wait until all the data has arrived from the peripheral device. Finally, requestFrom() returns the actual number of bytes read from the peripheral.

Here's the source code to the read_async() class function (which is called from requestFrom()):

```
void IMX_RT1060_I2CMaster::read_async
(
    uint8_t  address,
    uint8_t* buffer,
    size_t   num_bytes,
    bool     send_stop
){
❶ if( num_bytes > MAX_MASTER_READ_LENGTH )
    {
        error = I2CError::invalid_request;
        return;
    }

❷ if( !start( address, MASTER_READ ))
    {
        return;
    }
❸ if( num_bytes == 0 )
    {
        // The caller is probably probing addresses
        // to find slaves. Don't try to read anything.

      ❹ port->MTDR = LPI2C_MTDR_CMD_STOP;
        return;
    }

    buff.initialise( buffer, num_bytes );
```

```
    port->MTDR = LPI2C_MTDR_CMD_RECEIVE | (num_bytes - 1);

    if( send_stop )
    {
        port->MTDR = LPI2C_MTDR_CMD_STOP;
    }
}
```

The read_async() function begins with a quick validity check ❶ of the requested length. If the caller requested too many bytes (more than 32, the size of the internal buffer), the function returns an error.

Next, read_async() sends a start condition on the bus, along with the peripheral address and read command ❷. If that transmission is successful, the function checks to see if the caller is requesting 1 or more bytes to read ❸. If the caller specified 0 bytes, the function is done. Reading 0 bytes is a common way application code probes an address to see if there is a device present; read_async() will acknowledge the address byte transmission if it's there. If no device is present at the address, a NAK happens. The read_async() function transmits a stop condition ❹ if the caller specified a read of 0 bytes.

If the caller wants to read 1 or more bytes, read_async() calls the buffer initialization function to initialize the buffer associated with the calling IMX_RT1060_I2CMaster object. Then read_async() writes the receive command to the MTDR along with the number of bytes (minus 1) to receive. This particular write (32 bits) inserts the command into an on-chip command FIFO and increments the FIFO pointer. At this point, the on-chip hardware will begin processing this receive data request independently of code execution.

After writing the receive command to the MTDR, read_async() checks whether the caller wants to send a stop condition after receiving the data. If the caller does want to send a stop, read_async() writes a stop command to the MTDR register (placing it in the command FIFO to execute once the read command finishes).

Once the read_async() function returns, the MCU hardware takes over and handles the receive requests. The hardware notifies the software via interrupts as data arrives, and the ISR checks to see if the read request is complete, updating the class's state object as appropriate. The call to finish in the requestFrom() function returns once the read completes or a timeout occurs. Of course, this call to finish() completes the requestFrom() operation.

The read() function is straightforward: it just returns a byte from the buffer filled by a call to the requestFrom() function (or −1 if no data is available). Here's its source code:

```
int I2CDriverWire::read()
{
    if( rx_next_byte_to_read < rx_bytes_available )
        {
        return rxBuffer[rx_next_byte_to_read++];
    }
    return no_more_bytes;
}
```

Finally, the `available()` function is simple—it just returns the number of bytes available in the read buffer as the function result.

11.1.2.5 Beyond the Arduino Library

Gemmell's code was specifically written to support Teensyduino programming using the Arduino ("Wiring") programming paradigm. *Wiring programming* consists of some initialization code (the `setup()` procedure) followed by a main loop (the `loop()` function) that executes repeatedly. Wiring was designed to mimic the typical programming paradigm used for most noninterrupt-driven, non-RTOS embedded systems. Most MCUs that support hardware I^2C communication will also support RTOS environments by using interrupts, hardware FIFOs, and DMA. Indeed, Gemmell's code uses the NXP i.MX RT1062 MCU's interrupt and FIFO capabilities but returns to the Wiring paradigm via the `finish()` function (which effectively stops the program's execution until the data transfer is complete).

NOTE *Wiring is not to be confused with the Arduino Wire library; rather, the Arduino platform was based on the Wiring environment. For more information on Wiring, see* https://en.wikipedia.org/wiki/Wiring_(development_platform).

If you're running your code under some environment other than Arduino, especially a multithreaded environment, you can dramatically improve the performance of the system by replacing the `finish()` function with a wait-on-event–type API call. Such a call would suspend the thread until the ISR signals it and tells it that the transmission or reception is complete. Rather than burning CPU cycles in a busy-waiting loop, the thread would simply stop, and those CPU cycles would be available for other threads to use. Modifying Gemmell's code to support this would be easy: you'd simply replace the call to finish with an appropriate wait API call and modify the ISR to signal that thread when the I^2C operation is complete.

One issue with this current implementation is that an interrupt consumes CPU cycles every time a character is received or whenever the transmit FIFO empties and the system needs to add more characters in the output FIFO. Using DMA, you could spare the CPU from having to do this work. In a DMA-driven system, the application programs the CPU's DMA registers with an address and a count. Whenever an I^2C transmission needs more data or whenever an I^2C reception receives data, the DMA controller accesses memory without intervention of the CPU, saving all the work associated with an interrupt (saving machine state) and processing the interrupt. Although Gemmell's code does not use DMA, the i.MX RT1062 supports this for I^2C. For multithreaded RTOSs, this can make I^2C operations even more efficient. See the NXP documentation in "For More Information" for more details.

11.2 ATtiny Controller Programming

This section describes how to use the UART on an ATtiny84 MCU to create an I²C controller device. Chapter 3 originally described a software-based I²C controller on the ATtiny84; I moved that discussion to the online chapters because the code was largely redundant with respect to the Teensy code appearing in Chapter 3. See Chapter 17 online at *https://bookofi2c.randallhyde .com* for the software-based controller. This chapter describes a more efficient implementation using the universal serial interface hardware on the ATtiny84.

The code in this section is based on Adafruit's open source TinyWireM package, which is based on the Atmel AVR310 application note and was originally written by BroHogan and jkl (the names given in the source code). For the original code, visit *https://github.com/adafruit/TinyWireM*.

The ATtiny84 MCU—the MCU used on the Atto84 board from SparkFun—includes a hardware shift register known as the Universal Serial Interface (USI). You can employ the USI for any arbitrary shifting applications, including I²C, SPI, USB, or generic serial communication. Because the shifting is done in hardware, it is much more efficient than the bit-banging approach used in a software implementation of I²C. However, USI has a few limitations:

- It can be used for only one interface at a time, so it's a bit difficult to use if you need to control multiple serial buses concurrently (I²C and SPI, for example).
- It provides no glitch filtering or slew rate limiting, which I²C requires, so it can be a little noisier than hardware implementations.
- Clock generation (that is, SCL) must be done in software.
- It provides no buffering, so software must continuously monitor the shift register to retrieve data (or transmit new data) when the shift register is full or empty.

Generally, ATtiny84 MCUs are employed in low-cost, single-activity applications where they perform a single task, like transmitting or receiving data on the I²C bus. In these cases, their limitations aren't much of a problem.

The ATtiny84 has a few registers associated with the USI that you'll use for I²C communication: USDR, USISR, and USICR. USDR is the USI 8-bit data register (output data is written here and input data is read from here).

USISR is the USI status register, which contains information about the USI shift register's state. See Table 11-10 for a description of these bits.

Table 11-10: USISR Bit Definitions

Bit	Description
0 to 3	USICNT: 4-bit counter for the shift register.
4	USIDC: Data collision flag. Set to 1 when the data being transmitted to SDA does not match the value actually on the pin. Use this flag to detect lost arbitration.

Bit	Description
5	USIPF: Stop condition flag. Set when a stop condition occurs.
6	USIOIF: Counter overflow interrupt flag. Indicates that the 4-bit counter has overflowed. Must write a 1 to this bit position to clear this flag. If the overflow interrupt is enabled, an interrupt occurs on overflow.
7	USISIF: Start condition interrupt flag. Set (and an appropriate interrupt generated, if enabled) when a start condition is found on the I²C bus. Writing a 1 to this bit position clears this flag.

USICR is the USI control register. Bits written to this port affect the operation of the USI. See Table 11-11 for a description of these bits.

Table 11-11: USICR Bit Definitions

Bit	Description
0	USITC: Toggle clock pin. Writing a 1 to this bit position toggles the clock pin.
1	USICLK: Strobe clock. Writing a 1 to this bit increments the counter and shifts data in the shift register, but only if USICS0 and USICS1 are 0. If USICS1 is 1, then setting this bit to 1 will select the USITC as the clock (this is the state the software uses). See Table 11-12 for a description of this bit.
2 to 3	USICS0, USICS1: Clock select. See Table 11-12 for a description of these bits.
4 to 5	USIWM1, USIWM0: Wire mode. These bits control the SDA and SCL operation mode. For normal I²C operation, USIWM0 is 0 and USIWM1 is 1. Table 11-13 lists the meanings of these two bits.
6	Counter overflow interrupt enable.
7	Start condition interrupt enable.

Table 11-12 lists the clock source settings for bits 1 to 3 in the USICR register.

Table 11-12: USICR Clock Source Settings

USICS1	USICS0	USICLK	Clock source	4-bit counter clock source
0	0	0	No clock	No clock
0	0	1	Software clock strobe (USICLK)	Software clock strobe (USICLK)
0	1	X	Timer/Counter0 Compare Match	Timer/Counter0 Compare Match
1	0	0	External, positive edge	External, both edges
1	0	1	External, positive edge	Software clock strobe (USITC)
1	1	0	External, negative edge	External, both edges
1	1	1	External, negative edge	Software clock strobe (USITC)

Bits 4 and 5 in the USICR specify the mode of the USI pins on the ATtiny84. Table 11-13 specifies the various options for these bits.

Table 11-13: Pin Mode Settings

USIWM1	USIWM0	Description
0	0	Normal I/O pins (not connected to serial shift register).
0	1	Three-wire mode. Uses DO, DI, and USCK pins. This is for SPI bus operation.
1	0	Two-wire mode. Uses SDA (DI) and SCL (USCK) pins. This is the setting the software in this chapter uses for I^2C operation.
1	1	Two-wire mode. Uses SDA and SCL pins. Same as two-wire mode above, but the SCL line is held low when a counter overflow occurs and until the Counter Overflow Flag (USIOIF) is cleared.

In addition to the three USI ports, I^2C communication uses the ATtiny84's PORT A parallel port, on which the SDA and SCL lines appear (SCL on bit 4, SDA on bit 6). Three memory locations are associated with PORT A:

- PORTA: Output bits are written to this address.
- PINA: Input bits are read from this port.
- DDRA: I/O direction for PORTA is set here.

Because the I^2C SDA and SCL lines are bidirectional, the code is constantly setting the data direction bits in the DDRA register.

11.2.1 The Atto84 Triangle Wave Demonstration Program

The Atto84 triangle wave output program in Listing 11-1 provides the source code for the triangle wave output program for the Atto84, using the low-level ATtiny84 registers.

The first section of Listing 11-1 contains various constant declarations used throughout the code. In particular, it contains port address definitions, timing constants, and various bit patterns the code uses to initialize various registers:

```
// Listing11-1.ino
//
// Sample triangle wave output
// on an Atto84 board from SparkFun
// utilizing the ATtiny84 USI.

#include "Arduino.h"
#include <inttypes.h>
#include <avr/interrupt.h>
#include <avr/io.h>
```

```
#include <util/delay.h>

// From avr/io.h:
//
// PORTA output pins:
//
// PORTA    SFR_IO8(0x02)
// PORTA7   7
// PORTA6   6
// PORTA5   5
// PORTA4   4
// PORTA3   3
// PORTA2   2
// PORTA1   1
// PORTA0   0
//
// USI Control Register:
//
// USICR    SFR_MEM8(0xB8)
// USITC    0    Toggle clock port pin.
// USICLK   1    1 for software clk strobe.
// USICS0   2    0 for clk source select 0.
// USICS1   3    1 for clk source select 1.
// USIWM0   4    1 for I2C mode.
// USIWM1   5    0 for I2C mode.
// USIOIE   6    Cntr overflow int enable.
// USISIE   7    Start cond int enable.
//
// USI Status Register:
//
// USISR    SFR_MEM8(0xB9)
// USICNT0  0    4-bit counter value.
// USICNT1  1    4-bit counter value.
// USICNT2  2    4-bit counter value.
// USICNT3  3    4-bit Counter value.
// USIDC    4    Data output collision.
// USIPF    5    Stop condition flag.
// USIOIF   6    Cntr overflow int flag.
// USISIF   7    Start condition int flag.
//
// #define USIDR    SFR_MEM8(0xBA)
//
// DAC address:

#define DAC_ADRS 0x60 // 0x60 for SparkFun, 0x62 for Adafruit

// PORT A input pins:
//
// #define PINA     SFR_IO8(0x19)  Port A input pins:

#define DDR_USI         DDRA    // Data direction for port A
#define PORT_USI        PORTA   // Output pins on port A
#define PIN_USI         PINA    // Input pins on port A
```

```
#define PORT_USI_SDA     PORTA6  // Bit 6 on port A
#define PORT_USI_SCL     PORTA4  // Bit 4 on port A
#define PIN_USI_SDA      PINA6   // Bit 6 on port (pin) A
#define PIN_USI_SCL      PINA4   // Bit 4 on port (pin) A

#define TRUE (1)
#define FALSE (0)

// Time constants to pass to
// delay_us for clock delays:

#define T2_I2C           5 // >4.7 us
#define T4_I2C           4 // >4.0 us

#define I2C_READ_BIT     0
#define I2C_ADR_BITS     1
#define I2C_NAK_BIT      0

#define USI_I2C_NO_ACK_ON_ADDRESS    0x01
#define USI_I2C_NO_ACK_ON_DATA       0x02

static  unsigned char const USISR_8bit =
        (1 << USISIF)
    |   (1 << USIOIF)
    |   (1 << USIPF)
    |   (1 << USIDC)        // Clear flags
    |   (0x0 << USICNT0);   // Shift 8 bits

    unsigned char const USISR_1bit =
        (1 << USISIF)
    |   (1 << USIOIF)
    |   (1 << USIPF)
    |   (1 << USIDC)        // Clear flags
    |   (0xE << USICNT0);   // Shift 1 bit

union USI_I2C_state
{
  uint8_t allBits;
  struct
  {
    uint8_t addressMode : 1;
    uint8_t cntlrWriteDataMode : 1;
    uint8_t memReadMode : 1;
    uint8_t unused : 5;
  };
} USI_I2C_state;
```

Next, the USI_Initialize() function, as its name suggests, is responsible for initializing the USI. See the comments in the following code for the particular initializations this function provides:

```
// Listing11-1.ino (cont.)
//
// USI_Initialize-
```

```c
//
// Initializes the USI on the Atto84.

void USI_Initialize(void)
{
    // Enable pullup on SDA:

    PORT_USI |= (1 << PIN_USI_SDA);

    // Enable pullup on SCL:

    PORT_USI |= (1 << PIN_USI_SCL);

    // Enable SCL as output:

    DDR_USI |= (1 << PIN_USI_SCL);

    // Enable SDA as output:

    DDR_USI |= (1 << PIN_USI_SDA);

    // Preload data register with "bus released" data.

    USIDR = 0xFF;

    USICR = // Disable all interrupts
            (0 << USISIE)
        |   (0 << USIOIE)
        |   (1 << USIWM1)
        |   (0 << USIWM0)

            // Set USI in two-wire mode.

        |   (1 << USICS1)
        |   (0 << USICS0)

            // Software strobe as counter clock source.

        |   (1 << USICLK)
        |   (0 << USITC);

  USISR =
            (1 << USISIF) // Clear flags
        |   (1 << USIOIF)
        |   (1 << USIPF)
        |   (1 << USIDC)

            // Reset counter.

        |   (0x0 << USICNT0);

} // USI_Initialize
```

The USI_I2C_Cntlr_Start() and USI_I2C_Cntlr_Stop() functions put the start and stop conditions on the USI. In both functions, the code manually pulls the SCL and SDA lines low, as appropriate, with software-based timing to match the I^{2}C specifications:

```
// Listing11-1.ino (cont.)
//
// USI_I2C_Cntlr_Start-
//
// Function for generating an I2C start condition.

void USI_I2C_Cntlr_Start( void )
{
    // Release SCL to ensure that (repeated) start
    // can be performed:

    PORT_USI |= (1 << PIN_USI_SCL);

    // Verify that (wait until) SCL becomes high:

    while( !(PORT_USI & (1 << PIN_USI_SCL)) );

    // Delay for 1/2 bit time before generating
    // the start condition:

    _delay_us( T2_I2C );

    // Generate start condition. The SCL line has
    // been high for 1/2 bit time, pulling SDA
    // low generates the start:

    PORT_USI &= ~(1 << PIN_USI_SDA); // Force SDA low

    // Leave SDA low for at least 4 us:

    _delay_us( T4_I2C );

    // Okay, clean up after yourself. Start has
    // been generated, so release SDA and pull
    // SCL low (start of first bit's clock period):

    PORT_USI &= ~(1 << PIN_USI_SCL);
    PORT_USI |= (1 << PIN_USI_SDA);

    return;
}

// USI_I2C_Cntlr_Stop-
//
// Function for generating an I2C stop condition.
// Used to release the I2C bus.
// Returns true if it was successful.

void USI_I2C_Cntlr_Stop( void )
```

```
{
    // Stop condition consists of changing SDA from
    // low to high while the SCL line is high:

    PORT_USI &= ~(1 << PIN_USI_SDA); // Pull SDA low
    PORT_USI |= (1 << PIN_USI_SCL);  // Release SCL

    // Wait until the SCL line registers a high on
    // the SCL input pin:

    while( !(PIN_USI & (1 << PIN_USI_SCL)) );

    // Minimum setup time is 4 us:

    delay_us( T4_I2C );

    // Okay, raise the SDA line to signal the
    // stop condition:

    PORT_USI |= (1 << PIN_USI_SDA); // Release SDA

    // Minimum hold time is around 5 us:

    delay_us( T2_I2C );

    return TRUE;
}
```

The USI_I2C_Xcvr() function is responsible for transmitting and receiving data via the USI:

```
// Listing11-1.ino (cont.)
//
// USI_I2C_Xcvr-
//
// Transmits and receives data.

uint8_t USI_I2C_Xcvr
(
    uint8_t *msg,
    uint8_t msgSize
){
    uint8_t *savedMsg;
    uint8_t savedMsgSize;

    // Caller must clear before calling this function
    // so that memReadMode can be specified:

    USI_I2C_state.allBits = 0;        // Clear state bits
    USI_I2C_state.addressMode = TRUE; // True for first byte

    // Determine if this is a read (1) or write (0) operation
    // by looking at the LO bit of the first byte (the address
```

```
                // byte) in the message.

❶ if
  (
      !(
              *msg                  // The LSB in the address
          &   (1 << I2C_READ_BIT)   // byte determines if it
      )                             // is a cntlr Read or Write
  )                                 // operation
  {
      USI_I2C_state.cntlrWriteDataMode = TRUE;
  }

  // Save buffer pointer for later:

  savedMsg = msg;
  savedMsgSize = msgSize;

  // Send a start condition.

❷ USI_I2C_Cntlr_Start();

  // Write address and Read/Write data:

  do
  {
      // If cntlrWrite cycle (or initial address transmission):

    ❸ if
      (
              USI_I2C_state.addressMode
          || USI_I2C_state.cntlrWriteDataMode
      ){
          // Write a byte.
          // Pull SCL low.

          PORT_USI &= ~(1 << PIN_USI_SCL);

          // Set up data.

          USIDR = *(msg++);

          // Send 8 bits on bus.

          USI_I2C_Cntlr_Transfer( USISR_8bit );

          // Clock and verify (N)ACK from peripheral.

          // Enable SDA as input:

          DDR_USI &= ~(1 << PIN_USI_SDA);

          // If you get a NAK, not an ACK,
          // return an error code:
```

```
        if(
                USI_I2C_Cntlr_Transfer( USISR_1bit )
            &   (1 << I2C_NAK_BIT)
        ){

            if( USI_I2C_state.addressMode )
            {
                return USI_I2C_NO_ACK_ON_ADDRESS;
            }
            return USI_I2C_NO_ACK_ON_DATA;
        }

        if
        (
                (!USI_I2C_state.addressMode)
            &&   USI_I2C_state.memReadMode
        )
        {
            // Memory start address has been written.
            //
            // Start at peripheral address again:

            msg = savedMsg;

            // Set the Read Bit on peripheral address
            // (the first byte of the buffer):

            *(msg) |= (TRUE << I2C_READ_BIT);

            // Now set up for the Read cycle:

            USI_I2C_state.addressMode = TRUE;

            // Set byte count correctly:

            msgSize = savedMsgSize;

            // Note that the length should be peripheral
            // adrs byte + number of bytes to read + 1
            // (gets decremented below).

            USI_I2C_Cntlr_Start();

        }
        else
        {
            // Only perform address transmission once:

            USI_I2C_state.addressMode = FALSE;
        }
    }

    else    // cntlrRead cycle
    {
```

```
        // Enable SDA as input:

    ❹ DDR_USI &= ~(1 << PIN_USI_SDA);

        // Read a data byte:

        *(msg++) = USI_I2C_Cntlr_Transfer( USISR_8bit );

        // Prepare to generate ACK (or NAK
        // in case of End Of Transmission).

        if( msgSize == 1 )
        {
            // If transmission of last byte was performed,
            // load NAK to confirm End Of Transmission:

            USIDR = 0xFF;
        }
        else
        {
            // Load ACK.
            // Set data register bit 7 (output for SDA) low:

            USIDR = 0x00;
        }

        // Generate ACK/NAK:

        USI_I2C_Cntlr_Transfer( USISR_1bit );
    }
  }while( --msgSize ); // Until all data sent/received

// Usually a stop condition is sent here, but caller
// needs to choose whether or not to send it.
//
// Transmission is successfully completed.

return( 0 );
}
```

This code begins by determining if this is a read or write operation and setting the mode appropriately ❶. Then the code puts a start condition on the bus ❷. If this is a write operation or if the code is writing the peripheral address and R/W bit to the bus, the code transmits the appropriate byte via the USI ❸. If this is a read operation, the code switches SDA to become an input pin and reads the appropriate data from the USI ❹.

Next, the USI_I2C_Cntlr_Transfer() function is the generic function for reading or writing an array of bytes on the USI:

```
// Listing11-1.ino (cont.)
//
// USI_I2C_Cntlr_Transfer-
```

```c
//
// Core function for shifting data in and out from the USI.
// Data to be sent has to be placed into the USIDR before
// calling this function. Data read will be returned
// by the function.
//
// Status:
//     Data to write to the USISR.
//     In this code, this will be
//     USISR_8bit (for data transfers)
//     or USISR_1bit (for ACKs and NAKs).
//
// Returns the data read from the device.

uint8_t USI_I2C_Cntlr_Transfer( uint8_t status )
{
    USISR = status;         // Set USISR to status

    uint8_t control =       // Prepare clocking
            (0 << USISIE)   // Interrupts disabled
          | (0 << USIOIE)
          | (1 << USIWM1)   // Set USI in two-wire mode
          | (0 << USIWM0)
          | (1 << USICS1)
          | (0 << USICS0)
          | (1 << USICLK)   // Software clock as source
          | (1 << USITC);   // Toggle Clock Port

    do
    {
        // Wait for roughly 1/2 bit time (4.7-5 us):

        _delay_us( T2_I2C );

        // Toggle clock and generate positive SCL edge:

        USICR = control;

        // Wait for SCL to go high:

        while( !(PIN_USI & (1 << PIN_USI_SCL)) );

        // Leave SCL high for at least 4 us:

        _delay_us( T4_I2C );

        // Toggle clock to generate negative SCL edge:

        USICR = control;

    }while( !(USISR & (1 << USIOIF)) ); // Transfer complete?

    // Wait for 1/2 bit time so the clock is low for
```

```
// a full bit time:

_delay_us( T2_I2C );

uint8_t data = USIDR;           // Read out data
USIDR = 0xFF;                   // Release SDA

// Switch the SDA back to an output pin:

DDR_USI |= (1 << PIN_USI_SDA);

return data; // Return the data read from the USIDR
}
```

The I2C_rw() function is responsible for reading or writing an array of bytes on the USI and transmitting a stop condition at the completion of the transmission or reception:

```
// Listing11-1.ino (cont.)
//
// I2C_rw-
//
// Read or write a sequence of bytes from or to the I2C port.
// LO bit of buf[0] is 0 for write, 1 for read.

uint8_t I2C_rw( uint8_t *buf, size_t len, uint8_t stop )
{
    bool xferOK = false;
    uint8_t errorCode = USI_I2C_Xcvr( buf, len );

    // If there wasn't an error, see if code is
    // supposed to send a stop bit and transmit
    // it if you are:

    if( errorCode == 0 )
    {
        if( stop )
        {
            USI_I2C_Cntlr_Stop();
        }
        return 0;       // No error
    }
    return errorCode;   // There was an error
}
```

The "main program" (Arduino loop() function) is the code that actually transmits a triangle wave to the (Adafruit or SparkFun) DAC:

```
// Listing11-1.ino (cont.)
//
// Usual Arduino initialization function.

void setup( void )
```

```
{
    // Initialize the Atto84 I2C port:

    USI_Initialize();
}

// Arduino main loop function:

void loop( void )
{

    uint8_t writeBuf[3];

    // Transmit the rising edge of the triangle wave:

    for( uint16_t dac=0; dac<4096; ++dac )
    {
        // MCP4725 DAC at address DAC_ADRS (bits 1 to 7).
        // Create a write operation:

        writeBuf[0] = (DAC_ADRS << 1) | 0; // Write to DAC
        writeBuf[1] = (dac >> 8) & 0xff;   // HO byte
        writeBuf[2] = dac & 0xff;          // LO byte
        I2C_rw( writeBuf, 3, TRUE );
    }

    // Transmit the falling edge:

    for( uint16_t dac=4095; dac>0; --dac )
    {
        // MCP4725 DAC at address DAC_ADRS (bits 1 to 7).
        // Create a write operation:

        writeBuf[0] = (DAC_ADRS << 1) | 0; // Write to DAC_ADRS
        writeBuf[1] = (dac >> 8) & 0xff;   // HO byte
        writeBuf[2] = dac & 0xff;          // LO byte
        I2C_rw( writeBuf, 3, TRUE );
    }
}
```

The code in Listing 11-1 is relatively efficient, taking approximately 370 µsec per DAC transmission (3 bytes, about 120 µsec per byte). As the expected speed is about 100 µsec per byte (10 bits at 100 kHz), this is actually better than most of the other examples throughout this book, largely because of the streamlined code used to transmit the data. (Most of the other example programs execute considerable extra code between transmissions due to libraries, multitasking, and so on slowing them down.)

Figure 11-1 provides the oscilloscope output for the program in Listing 11-1.

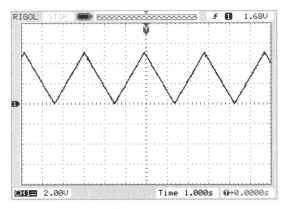

Figure 11-1: Atto84 I²C triangle wave output

Figure 11-2 shows the logic analyzer output for this program. As you can see, there is very little delay between bytes written in a single message and only a short delay between values (3 bytes) written to the MCP4725 DAC (at address 0x62).

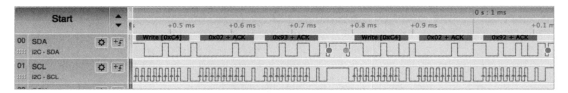

Figure 11-2: Logic analyzer output from Atto84 triangle wave output program

The program in Listing 11-1 is very straightforward; it just uses polling for everything (a typical Arduino paradigm). If you needed to do more than output a triangle wave from the Atto84, you would probably want to take advantage of the USI interrupts to allow other work to happen while waiting for I²C transmissions to take place. I'll demonstrate that ATtiny84 capability when describing bare-metal peripheral programming on the Atto84 later in this book (see section 16.1, "The ATtiny as an I²C Peripheral," in Chapter 16).

11.3 Chapter Summary

This chapter discussed I²C bus controller programming at the hardware level. Because each MCU provides a different mechanism for I²C communication, no general explanation will work with any MCU. Therefore, this chapter presents a couple of specific examples. In particular, it discusses two separate MCUs (the i.MXRT 1602 MCU used by the Teensy 4.*x*) and the ATtiny84 MCU. Each MCU section begins with a discussion of the appropriate MCU registers needed to control the bus, followed by some sample code to program those registers.

The section on the Teensy 4.*x* used an existing library from Richard Gemmell and Paul Stoffregen as the example code. This library is a drop-in replacement for the standard Arduino Wire library. The section on the ATtiny84 used code based on Adafruit's open source TinyWireM library. Both examples provided the basics for transmitting and receiving data on the I^2C bus.

FOR MORE INFORMATION

The NXP reference manual for the i.MX RT1062 MCU: *https://www.pjrc.com/teensy/IMXRT1060RM_rev2.pdf* (includes i.MX RT1062)

Another copy of the reference manual: *https://cdn.sparkfun.com/assets/d/a/f/c/9/IMXRT1060CEC.pdf*

Teensy 4 low-level library code: *https://github.com/Richard-Gemmell/teensy4_i2c*

Teensy 3 low-level library code: *https://github.com/nox771/i2c_t3/* and *https://github.com/heman4t/Ardino-I2C_T3*

Of course, the Teensyduino IDE contains the source code for the built-in I^2C library in source form as well.

ATtiny84 I^2C programming using the universal serial interface: *http://ww1.microchip.com/downloads/en/DeviceDoc/doc8006.pdf* (Chapter 14)

AVR310: Using the USI module as a TWI Master: *http://ww1.microchip.com/downloads/en/AppNotes/Atmel-2561-Using-the-USI-Module-as-a-I2C-Master_AP-Note_AVR310.pdf*

The following links lead to various libraries compatible with the ATtiny84:

   The Adafruit TinyWireM library: *https://github.com/adafruit/TinyWireM*

   The TinyI^2C library: *https://github.com/technoblogy/tiny-i2c*

   The Arduino TinyWire library: *https://github.com/svoisen/TinyWire*

   Original TinyWireM library: *https://github.com/JChristensen/TinyWireM*

PART IV

I^{2}C PERIPHERAL
PROGRAMMING EXAMPLES

12

THE TCA9548A
I²C BUS EXPANDER

The I^2C bus's 112 nonreserved peripheral addresses are more than enough for almost any system; you'll reach bus capacitance limits long before you put this many devices on the bus. However, since devices tend to hard-code their addresses into the hardware, only a limited number of identical devices can appear on the same I^2C bus. Furthermore, because hundreds or thousands of I^2C peripherals exist, there are often address conflicts between different I^2C devices. The 10-bit addressing scheme was created to alleviate this problem, but few devices and fewer controllers take advantage of this feature. If you want to put two devices with the same address on the I^2C bus, you'll need to use an I^2C bus expander.

I²C *bus expanders*, also known as *bus multiplexers* or *bus switches*, allow you to switch a single I²C bus between two, four, or eight separate I²C buses. In sum, you program one of these multiplexers to switch an incoming pair of I²C lines to one of the sets of lines the IC supports. Common I²C multiplexer ICs include:

- TCA9543A: Switches one I²C bus between two separate buses
- TCA9545A: Switches one I²C bus between four separate buses
- TCA9548A: Switches one I²C bus between eight separate buses

This chapter focuses on the TCA9548A IC, since it supports the greatest number of buses. Both Adafruit and SparkFun provide breakout boards for it, which this chapter also discusses.

12.1   The TCA9548A I²C Multiplexer

The TCA9548A is, perhaps, the most popular I²C multiplexer used by hobbyists because several manufacturers provide breakout boards for it. Therefore, the remainder of this chapter will discuss that particular device (the TCA9543A and TCA9545A devices provide a subset of the TCA9548A's capabilities, so studying the latter will tell you most of what you need to know concerning these other devices). The following subsections describe connecting devices, programming the register set, and programming the TCA9548A.

The TCA9548A contains nine (SDA, SCL) pairs on the chip. The datasheet names the main lines from the controller device (SDA, SCL) and names the other eight pairs (SD0, SC0), (SD1, SC1), . . . , (SD7, SC7).

12.1.1 Upstream and Downstream Devices

Devices on the same I²C bus as the TCA9548A are called *upstream devices* because they are on the main I²C bus before any of the switched I²C buses. Those switched buses are *downstream* from the TCA9548A. Upstream devices respond to addresses directly from the controller device, without any switching (or masking) on the part of the multiplexer. Therefore, if an upstream device shares the same address as a downstream device, the two devices will have an address conflict when the TCA9548A switches on the bus to which the downstream device is connected.

The TCA9548A is a device on the I²C bus, meaning it can appear on the same physical SDA and SCL lines as other devices (see Figure 12-1). I will refer to the main lines as the *upstream* pair and the remaining eight sets of lines as the *downstream* pairs.

Each of the downstream (SDA, SCL) pairs forms its own I²C bus, which can be operated independently of the other seven downstream pairs. By switching the upstream lines to one of the downstream pairs (under program control), a system with a TCA9548A can expand a single I²C bus into eight.

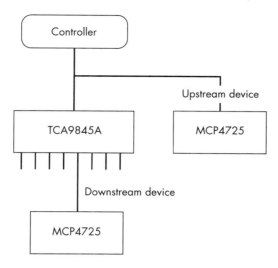

Figure 12-1: Upstream and downstream devices

12.1.2 The TCA9548A Selection Register

The TCA9548A is one of the simpler I^2C devices from a software perspective. The device has one 8-bit read/write register that appears at its I^2C address. Writing data to the device selects which output bus to use; reading from the device reads the last value written to it (0 is written to the register on power-up).

The register on the TCA9548A is a bit map used to select which downstream pairs connect to the upstream bus. A 1 in bit position 0 connects the upstream (SDA, SCL) lines to (SD0, SC0), a 1 in bit position 1 connects (SDA, SCL) to (SD1, SC1) and so on. A 1 in bit position 7 connects (SDA, SCL) to (SD7, SC7).

Though it's possible to write multiple 1 bits to various positions in the TCA9548A register, you normally wouldn't want to do this, since it could produce conflicts on the I^2C bus if it attempts to simultaneously access two different devices. One reason for writing multiple 1 bits to the register is to send a general call command to devices on all the downstream buses. However, most of the time, you should ensure that you write only a single 1 bit to the register. Note that writing all 0s to the register is reasonable: doing so turns off all the downstream pairs, in which case the controller can talk only to devices that are upstream of the TCA9548A (that is, on the main, or upstream, SDA and SCL lines).

12.1.3 TCA9548A Address and Reset Lines

The TCA9548A can respond to an I^2C address in the range 0x70 through 0x77. The chip has three address lines (A0, A1, and A2) that can be tied to Gnd or Vcc to select the address (the TCA9548A uses A0, A1, and A2 as the LO 3 bits of its address). This chapter will generally assume that the TCA9548A is configured for address 0x70, unless otherwise specified. To write to the on-board register, simply write a byte to the TCA9548A's address on the I²C bus.

In addition to the three address lines and the main (upstream) SDA and SCL lines, the TCA9548A has one other important input: reset. Briefly pulling the reset line low will reset the device (writing a 0 to the internal register). The datasheet claims that you can use this line to recover from a bus fault condition. Generally, you would connect this reset line to a digital I/O pin on your CPU or simply tie it high (typically through a 10-kΩ pullup resistor).

12.1.4 The TCA9548A Power Supply, Pullups, and Level Shifting

The TCA9548A operates off any voltage in the range 1.65 V to 5.0 V, so it works with 1.8-V, 2.5-V, 3.3-V, or 5-V logic. All the pins are 5-V tolerant regardless of the power supply voltage, meaning you can use the TCA9548A as an I²C level shifter.

NOTE *The datasheet limits the device to 3.6 V for extreme temperature use.*

Because the I²C bus is open drain, the actual voltage appearing on the SDA and SCL lines is determined by the pullup resistor connection for both upstream and downstream signals. If you have a 3.3-V system, then SDA and SCL (upstream) will likely be pulled up to 3.3 V. To be safe, you'd probably run the TCA8845A at 3.3 V as well. However, you can switch to a downstream channel (say, SD3 and SC3) and connect it to a 5-V device with 5-V pullup resistors on that downstream bus. The SD3 and SC3 pins on the TCA9548A will handle the 5-V signal just fine, without passing this voltage on to the controller device running at 3.3 V.

Conversely, if your controller is running at 5 V and you power the TCA9548A at 5 V, you can connect one of the downstream channels to a 3.3-V system by simply using pullups to 3.3 V on that channel's lines.

12.1.5 Reducing Bus Loading and Bus Speed

In addition to acting as a level shifter, the TCA9548A can reduce (capacitive) loading on the I²C bus. Suppose you have a dozen devices on an I²C bus and the loading is forcing you to run at 100 kHz instead of 400 kHz. You can use a TCA9548A to spread out those 12 devices across 8 or 9 buses, including the original upstream bus, to reduce capacitive loading. Even if there are no address conflicts, the TCA9548A is useful in this capacity.

The TCA9548A, by the way, can operate at normal (100 kHz) or fast (400 kHz) speed. It does not operate at fast mode plus (1 MHz) or faster.

12.1.6 Switching Between Buses

As I mentioned earlier, you activate a downstream bus by writing a 1 to the corresponding bit position in the TCA9548A register (and 0s to all the other bit positions). If you have three devices on downstream buses (SD0, SC0), (SD1, SC1), and (SD2, SC2) and you want to send data to each of these devices, use this process:

1. Write 0x01 (0b0000_0001) to the TCA9548A at address 0x70.
2. Write the data to the device on (SD0, SC0) by simply writing to SDA and SCL as though it were an upstream device.
3. Write 0x02 (0b0000_0010) to the TCA9548A to activate (SD1, SC1).
4. Write to the second device on (SD1, SC1), just treating it as if it were an upstream device.
5. Write 0x04 (0b0000_0100) to the TCA9548A to activate (SD2, SC2).
6. Write to the third device on (SD2, SC2), just treating it as if it were an upstream device.
7. (optional) Write 0x0 to the TCA9548A to disable all downstream buses.

As noted earlier, no upstream devices at any I^2C address should appear on a downstream bus. That would create a conflict between the device on the upstream and downstream buses.

12.1.7 Cascading TCA9548A Multiplexers

Because the TCA9548A has three address lines, you can place up to eight of them on the same I^2C bus. This gives you access to 64 (roughly) independent I^2C buses driving from the same pair of SDA and SCL lines on the controller; that's $112 \times 64 = 7,168$ independent addresses. If this isn't sufficient, you can cascade the multiplexers. Each downstream level needs a unique address, within a given level (that is, all TCA9548A devices connected to the outputs of the same TCA9548A can have the same address). In Figure 12-2, for example, the top TCA9548A could have address 0x70, the light gray ones could have address 0x71, and the dark gray ones could all have address 0x72.

To write to a device connected to the rightmost TCA9548A in Figure 12-2 (assuming channels from left to right are numbered 0 to 7), you'd start by writing 0x80 (0b1000_0000) to the TCA9548A at address 0x70 (the one connected directly to the controller). You would then write 0x80 to address 0x71 (corresponding to the rightmost light gray TCA9548A) and finally select the bus you wanted on the rightmost dark gray TCA9548A by writing the bus setting to address 0x72.

In practice, cascading TCA9548A devices in this manner is likely to create all types of timing and loading problems, so I wouldn't recommend it. The only good reason to cascade multiplexers would be because you need more than eight buses and there's only one open address in the range 0x70 through 0x77 on your upstream bus.

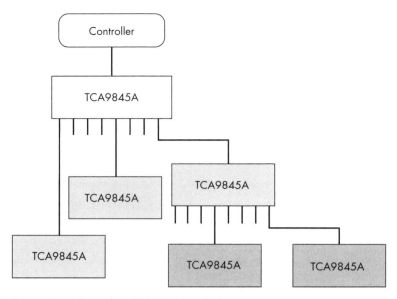

Figure 12-2: Cascading TCA9548A multiplexers

Because the TCA9548A is a surface mount device (SMD), it's a bit difficult to wire into a typical breadboard or prototype circuit. Fortunately, Adafruit, SparkFun, and other manufacturers provide breakout boards that make these devices easy to use. The following sections describe these breakout boards.

12.2 The Adafruit TCA9548A I²C Expander

The Adafruit TCA9548A I^{2}C Expander is a traditional breakout board, containing a single TCA9548A with the pins brought out on 0.1-inch centers (see the smaller breakout board in Figure 12-3). It also provides a bypass capacitor; pullup resistors for SDA, SCL, and reset; and three pulldown resistors that pull A0, A1, and A2 to Gnd so the device defaults to address 0x70. There are solder jumpers on the back of the PCB so you can cut the pullup resistors to SDA and SCL (in case you've already got pullups on the upstream bus) and also set the address.

NOTE *Because the address pins also come out on the connections on the edge of the board, you can set the address by wiring the A0, A1, and A2 PCB connectors to Vcc or Gnd.*

The Adafruit breakout board does not put pullup resistors on the downstream buses. Many breakout boards such as those from Adafruit and SparkFun include pullup resistors, so they wouldn't be necessary on the TCA9548A I^{2}C Expander. Even more importantly, if you want to use this board as a level shifter, you want to be able to control what voltage the pullup resistors connect to. However, don't forget that if you connect some I^{2}C IC directly to a downstream bus, you have to add the pullup resistors yourself.

Figure 12-3: The SparkFun I²C Mux and Adafruit TCA9548A I²C Expander

12.3 The SparkFun I²C Mux

SparkFun's I²C Mux device (see Figure 12-3) is handy if you work with Qwiic devices: it accepts an upstream Qwiic connector, routes it through the board if you want to connect other upstream devices, and then provides the eight downstream buses on Qwiic connectors.

There are some major differences between the SparkFun implementation and the Adafruit TCA9548A I²C Expander. First, because it's Qwiic based, the SparkFun expander is largely a 3.3-V device only (though see the next note). The SparkFun board provides pullup resistors for downstream and upstream buses at 3.3 V; you can remove the upstream pullups by cutting some traces, but you don't have this option with the pullups on the downstream buses.

NOTE *In theory, you could plug in a Qwiic connector with bare wires on the other end and stick pullup resistors with the appropriate voltage on them. However, when dealing with the Qwiic system, it's best to keep everything 3.3 V.*

The second major difference between the SparkFun and Adafruit boards is size. Because the SparkFun board includes 10 Qwiic connectors (2 for the upstream bus, 8 for the downstream buses), the board is quite a bit larger than the Adafruit device (see Figure 12-3).

Beyond these issues, the functionality of the SparkFun and Adafruit boards is exactly the same. Personally, if I were using Qwiic system parts, I'd use the SparkFun board; otherwise, I'd probably use the Adafruit board.

12.4 Chapter Summary

This chapter discussed three different I^2C multiplexers: the TCA9543A, TCA9545A, and TCA9548A. These ICs allow you to expand a single I^2C bus to two, four, or eight independent buses. This chapter discussed making device connections (upstream and downstream) to the multiplexers, programming the multiplexer, and connecting the multiplexer to an I^2C bus. It also described how to use the TCA9548A as a level shifter and commented on the operating frequency of the device. This chapter concluded the generic discussion of the TCA9548A by describing how to cascade devices to support more than eight additional I^2C buses.

Finally, this chapter described two breakout boards manufactured by Adafruit and SparkFun. The Adafruit I^2C Expander board is a traditional breakout board, bringing out the pins on a TCA9548A IC to 0.1-inch–centered pins on a small PCB. The SparkFun I^2C Mux provides eight Qwiic connectors (rather than pins) for expanding the bus.

FOR MORE INFORMATION

TCA9548A datasheet: *https://www.ti.com/lit/ds/symlink/tca9548a.pdf*

Adafruit TCA9548A I^2C Expander: *https://www.adafruit.com/product/2717*

SparkFun I^2C Mux: *https://www.sparkfun.com/products/16784*

MIKROE four-channel TCA9543 Mux: *https://www.mouser.com/datasheet/2/272/I2C_MUX_4_Click-1901422.pdf*

13

THE MCP23017 AND MCP23008 GPIO EXPANDERS

Most SBCs and MCUs provide anywhere from three to a couple dozen digital I/O pins. Sometimes, you'll need more digital I/O than the standard complement. Even on those MCUs that provide a couple dozen pins or more, most of them are multifunction. If you use them for their alternate purposes, you may find that you don't have enough remaining pins for digital I/O. This is where a GPIO expander comes in handy.

While there are many different ICs you can purchase to provide GPIO expansion on the I^{2}C bus, the MCP23008 and MCP23017 (collectively MCP230*xx*) are popular; they're available in DIP (through-hole) packages, and there's considerable library code available for them. The MCP23008 supports 8 GPIO pins while the MCP23017 supports 16, but these 2 ICs are otherwise identical.

Unlike many of the other devices this book describes, you generally won't find many breakout boards available for the MCP230xx parts. That's because they are available in breadboard-friendly DIP packages (though Adafruit recently added a STEMMA/Qwiic breakout board; see https://www.adafruit.com/product/5346*).*

This chapter describes the MCP23017 and MCP23008 devices, their electrical connections, and how to program them. It describes the internal device registers (and how to use them). It also provides some sample programs to demonstrate the ICs' operation.

13.1   The MCP23017 and MCP23008 Pinouts

The MCP23017 has the pinout depicted in Figure 13-1.

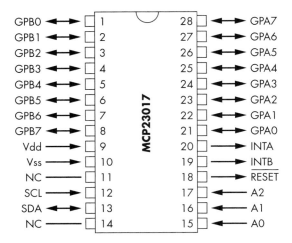

Figure 13-1: MCP23017 pinout

The MCP23008 has the pinout shown in Figure 13-2.

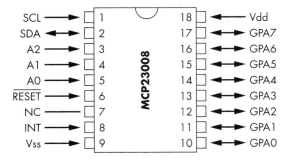

Figure 13-2: MCP23008 pinout

Table 13-1 shows what the pins on each device mean.

Table 13-1: MCP230xx Pin Functions

Pin	MCP23008	MCP23017
1	SCL (I^{2}C clock)	GPIO 0, port B
2	SDA (I^{2}C data)	GPIO 1, port B
3	A2 (address selection)	GPIO 2, port B
4	A1 (address selection)	GPIO 3, port B
5	A0 (address selection)	GPIO 4, port B
6	Reset (active low)	GPIO 5, port B
7	NC (no connection)	GPIO 6, port B
8	INT (interrupt on input)	GPIO 7, port B
9	Vss (ground)	Vdd (1.8 V, 3.3 V, or 5 V)
10	GPIO 0	Vss (ground)
11	GPIO 1	NC (no connection)
12	GPIO 2	SCL (I^{2}C clock)
13	GPIO 3	SDA (I^{2}C data)
14	GPIO 4	NC (no connection)
15	GPIO 5	A0 (address selection)
16	GPIO 6	A1 (address selection)
17	GPIO 7	A2 (address selection)
18	Vdd (1.8 V, 3.3 V, or 5 V)	Reset (active low)
19	n/a	INTB (interrupt on port B)
20	n/a	INTA (interrupt on port A)
21	n/a	GPIO 0, port A
22	n/a	GPIO 1, port A
23	n/a	GPIO 2, port A
24	n/a	GPIO 3, port A
25	n/a	GPIO 4, port A
26	n/a	GPIO 5, port A
27	n/a	GPIO 6, port A
28	n/a	GPIO 7, port A

The Vdd pin is the power supply (positive voltage) to the IC. The MCP230xx can operate at several different logic levels ranging from 1.8 V to 5.5 V (typically 1.8 V, 3.3 V, or 5.0 V). The Vss pin is the ground connection.

The SCL and SDA are the I^{2}C bus pins. As usual, these are open-drain pins. The bus voltages (held via I^{2}C pullup resistors) should be close to Vdd. Note that the MCP230xx are capable of operating at 100 kHz, 400 kHz, or as high as 1.7 MHz.

The GPIOx pins provide the general-purpose I/O expansion. The MCP23008 has 8 expansion I/O pins, while the MCP23017 has 16 (named *port A* and *port B* with 8 pins each). When operating as an input, these pins accept voltages up to Vdd. When operating as output pins, they produce Vdd on their outputs.

The A0, A1, and A2 pins specify the LO 3 bits of the device address. These should be wired to Vdd or Vss to set the device address. The MCP230*xx* ICs support up to eight different devices (selected by A0, A1, and A2 as the LO address bits) on the I²C bus. Note that the HO 4 address bits are always 0b0100, so the full device address falls in the range 0x20 to 0x27 (0x40 to 0x4E when shifted into the output byte).

The Reset signal is an active low signal that resets the device. This pin, when low, will configure all the pins as inputs and configure the device in *safe mode* (least likely to cause hardware problems). Note that the MCP230*xx* devices automatically reset themselves when power is applied, so unless a circuit absolutely needs to be able to reset the MCP230*xx* during operation, you'll normally find this pin connected to Vdd.

The MCP23008 INT and the MCP23017 INTA and INTB pins signal an interrupt. An *interrupt* is an asynchronous signal that alerts the CPU to take some action (generally pausing the current execution stream and running a special interrupt service routine to handle the event). You can program the INT, INTA, and INTB pins to pulse or to be set to some level whenever a change occurs on the MCP230*xx*, which is useful for detecting input changes when the system can't poll the input pins on a frequent basis.

13.2 MCP230xx Registers

The MCP230*xx* ICs are feature-rich devices. Unfortunately, this feature set comes at a cost: programming complexity. To program these ICs, you read and write various registers. The MCP23008 has 11 internal registers (see Table 13-2).

Table 13-2: MCP23008 Registers

Register number	Name	Function
0	IODIR	I/O data direction register
1	IPOL	Input polarity
2	GPINTEN	GPIO interrupt enable register
3	DEFVAL	Default comparison value (for interrupts)
4	INTCON	Interrupt control register
5	IOCON	I/O configuration register
6	GPPU	GPIO pullup register
7	INTF	Interrupt flag register
8	INTCAP	Interrupt capture register
9	GPIO	GPIO I/O port register
10 (0xA)	OLAT	Output latch register

The MCP23017 has 22 internal registers (see Table 13-3).

Table 13-3: MCP23017 Registers

Register number, BANK = 0	Alternate register number, BANK = 1	Name	Function
0	0	IODIRA	Port A I/O data direction register
1	16 (0x10)	IODIRB	Port B I/O data direction register
2	1	IPOLA	Port A input polarity
3	17 (0x11)	IPOLB	Port B input polarity
4	2	GPINTENA	Port A GPIO interrupt enable register
5	18 (0x12)	GPINTENB	Port B GPIO interrupt enable register
6	3	DEFVALA	Port A default comparison value (for interrupts)
7	19 (0x13)	DEFVALB	Port B default comparison value (for interrupts)
8	4	INTCONA	Port A interrupt control register
9	20 (0x14)	INTCONB	Port B interrupt control register
10 (0xA)	5	IOCON	I/O configuration register (only single IOCON)
11 (0xB)	21 (0x15)	IOCON	I/O configuration register (same as register 10/5)
12 (0xC)	6	GPPUA	Port A GPIO pullup register
13 (0xD)	22 (0x16)	GPPUB	Port B GPIO pullup register
14 (0xE)	7	INTFA	Port A interrupt flag register
15 (0xF)	23 (0x17)	INTFB	Port B interrupt flag register
16 (0x10)	8	INTCAPA	Port A interrupt capture register
17 (0x11)	24 (0x18)	INTCAPB	Port B interrupt capture register
18 (0x12)	9	GPIOA	Port A GPIO
19 (0x13)	25 (0x19)	GPIOB	Port B GPIO
20 (0x14)	10 (0xA)	OLATA	Port A output latch register
21 (0x15)	26 (0x1A)	OLATB	Port B output latch register

The MCP23017 supports two sets of register numbers, standard and alternate (or "special"). The register number is selected by bit 7 in the IOCON (control) register. If this bit is 0 (the power-up/reset state), then the MCP23017 uses the standard register numbering. If bit 7 is 1, then the MCP23017 uses the alternate register numbering, which separates the two ports into separate register banks (0 to 0xA for port A and 0x10 to 0x1A for port B).

13.2.1 Accessing MCP230xx Registers

Because the MCP230*xx* devices have multiple registers, writing and reading data to and from these devices are a little more complex than with simpler devices like the MCP4725. The (typical) protocol for writing a single byte to a register is as follows:

1. Put a start condition on the I^{2}C bus.
2. Transmit the I^{2}C address byte (a value in the range 0x40 to 0x46). This is always a write operation, so the LO bit of the address byte will always be 0.
3. Write the register address to the I^{2}C bus.
4. Place the register data (to write to the MCP230*xx* register) on the I^{2}C bus.
5. Put a stop condition on the bus to terminate the transfer.

The (typical) protocol for reading a single byte from a register is as follows:

1. Put a start condition on the I^{2}C bus.
2. Transmit the I^{2}C address byte (a value in the range 0x40 to 0x46). This is always a write operation, so the LO bit of the address byte will always be 0.
3. Write the register address to the I^{2}C bus.
4. Put a (re)start condition on the I^{2}C bus.
5. Transmit the I^{2}C address byte (a value in the range 0x41 to 0x47). This is a read operation, so the LO bit of the address byte will be 1.
6. Read the register data from the I^{2}C bus.
7. Put a stop condition on the bus to terminate the transfer.

This chapter discusses additional forms of this protocol for block reads and writes; see section 13.2.6, "Sequential Register Operations," later in this chapter.

13.2.2 MCP230xx Initialization

At power-up, the MCP230*xx* devices enter the following state:

*   IOCON bit 7 is set to 0 to select standard register numbers on the MCP23017.
*   All GPIO pins are programmed as inputs (see section 13.2.3, "Programming the Data Direction").
*   All pullup resistors are turned off (see section 13.2.4, "Programming Input Pullup Resistors").

- All interrupts are disabled (see section 13.5.5, "Enabling Interrupts on the MCP230xx").

- On the MCP23017, port A and B interrupts will be handled independently (should they be enabled).

- The MCP230xx is programmed for sequential register operations (see section 13.2.6, "Sequential Register Operations").

- SDA slew rate control is enabled (see section 13.2.7, "Slew Rate Control").

- The INTx pin(s) are active outputs (not open drain; see section 13.2.8, "Reading General-Purpose Input/Output Pins on the MCP230xx").

- Interrupt output pins are active-low (low signal when an interrupt occurs; see section 13.5.5, "Enabling Interrupts on the MCP230xx").

The IOCON register (I/O configuration) handles most of this initialization. Table 13-4 lists the bits in IOCON and their functions.

Table 13-4: IOCON Register Functions

Bit	Default on power-up or reset	Name	Function
7	0	BANK	MCP23017 only. Selects standard register numbering (BANK = 0) or alternate register numbering (BANK = 1).
6	0	MIRROR	MCP23017 only. INTA/B mirror function. If MIRROR = 0, then the INTA and INTB pins operate independently. If MIRROR = 1, then the two pins are internally wired together. See "INTx Pin Polarity" under section 13.5.2 for more information.
5	0	SEQOP	If SEQOP = 1, then successive data read/write operations read and write the same register number. If SEQOP = 0, then the register number is incremented after each operation (mainly for MCP23017).
4	0	DISSLW	Slew rate control for SDA pin. If DISSLW = 0, then slew rate control is enabled. If DISSLW = 1, then slew rate control is disabled.
3	0	N/A	Used only by SPI version of the MCP23Sxx GPIO expander.
2	0	ODR	Open drain control. If ODR = 1, then the INTx pins are open-drain outputs. If ODR = 0, then the INTx pins are active logic outputs. See section 13.5.5, "Enabling Interrupts on the MCP230xx" for more information.
1	0	INTPOL	Sets the polarity of the INT pins. If INTPOL = 0, then the INTx pins are active low. If INTPOL = 1, then the INTx pins are active high. This bit sets the polarity only if ODR = 0. See section 13.5.4, "Open-Drain INTx Output," for more information.
0	0	N/A	Not used.

If you decide you want to initialize the MCP230*xx* with something other than the default value, you will need to write an appropriate value to the IOCON register. Do so immediately after your program begins execution. While it is possible to change the configuration during execution, this is rare; most of the time you'll configure the MCP230*xx* once and then not touch the register thereafter.

NOTE   *An exception to rarely changing the IOCON register is the SEQOP bit, which you might want to change under program control. See section 13.2.6, "Sequential Register Operations," for more details.*

To program the IOCON register, you will need to write 3 bytes to the I^2C bus (see Figure 13-3):

1. Put a start condition on the I^2C bus.
2. Write the device address (0x40 to 0x46) with the LO bit set to 0 (write operation).
3. Write the IOCON register number 0x0A (or 0x05, if using alternate register numbers) to the bus.
4. Write the new IOCON register value to the I^2C bus.
5. Put a stop condition on the I^2C bus.

Figure 13-3: Example IOCON initialization sequence

On power-up or after a reset operation, the register addresses default to the standard register numbers. If you intend to use the alternate register numbers, you must write an IOCON value with bit 7 equal to 1 to address 0x0A, the power-on/reset IOCON address. After that, any writes to IOCON must happen at register number 0x05.

Note that if external hardware can reset the MCP230*xx*, then the IOCON register will switch back to address 0x0A. This can be a problem if the software isn't aware that the reset operation took place. This is a good argument for leaving the MCP230*xx* in standard register number mode.

13.2.3 Programming the Data Direction

The GPIO pins on the MCP230*xx* are individually programmable as inputs or outputs. The *data direction registers (DDRs)* control the input or output state of each pin. The MCP23008 has a single (8-bit) IODIR (register 0), and the MCP23017 has two (IODIRA is register 0, and IODIRB is register 1 or 16).

Each bit position in an IODIR*x* register controls the I/O state of the corresponding GPIO pin. That is, bit 0 in IODIRA (IODIR on the MCP23008) controls GPA0, bit 1 in IODIRA controls GPA1, and so on. Likewise, bit 0 in IODIRB controls GPB0, bit 1 controls GPB1, and so on. A 1 in a given bit position programs the corresponding GPIO pin as an input; a 0 in the bit position programs the corresponding GPIO pin as an output.

When the MCP230*xx* powers up or when the reset line is brought low, the IC programs all GPIO pins as inputs (that is, it initializes the IODIR*x* registers with all 1 bits). This is the safest initial configuration, as it prevents programming a GPIO pin as an output, which might produce an electrical conflict if that pin is connected to a line with an active signal.

Because of the MCP230*xx*'s IODIR flexibility, you can program arbitrary bits as inputs or outputs. In practice, it's most convenient (at least on the MCP23017) to program each bank of 8 bits as either all inputs or all outputs. Doing so makes it more convenient to program the MCP230*xx* ICs. Of course, if your hardware design requires that you mix and match I/O directions on a single port, that's perfectly acceptable; the cost is slightly more complex programming requirements.

To send the data direction value to the MCP230*xx* ICs, transmit the sequence shown in Figure 13-4.

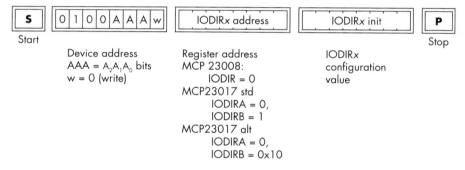

Figure 13-4: IODIRx initialization sequence

The third byte of the sequence appearing in Figure 13-4 is the data direction initialization value.

13.2.4 Programming Input Pullup Resistors

Input pins on the MCP230*xx* are often connected to *dry contact inputs*: switches, relay contacts, or other devices that connect two different signal lines. A typical dry contact might be a push button, DIP switch, or other SPST switch or relay.

Usually, a dry contact will connect an input pin on an MCP230*xx* to ground. Closing the contact shunts the input to ground so that a 0 input value appears on the corresponding bit in the GPIO*x* register. When the contact is open, the input signal *floats*, which is never good; the electronics might interpret a floating input as either a logic 0 or 1. To avoid floating inputs, designers typically put a pullup resistor on the input pin. This raises the voltage pin to the voltage connected to the pullup resistor (typically Vdd) when the dry contact is in the open position. When the dry contact is in the closed position, this shunts the input to ground, providing a logic 0 input.

NOTE   *Non-dry contact inputs generally consist of logic-level voltage signals.*

The only problem with pullup resistors is that you'll need to find space for them on a printed circuit or prototype board, as well as time and energy to install them. For convenience, the MCP230*xx* parts provide *programmable pullup resistors* that allow you to programmatically enable or disable pullup resistors on input pins. The GPPU*x* registers provide this capability. Programming a GPPU*x* bit with a 1 (and programming that same bit position in IODIR*x* with a 1) will connect a 100-kΩ pullup resistor to that pin. Conversely, programming a 0 bit disconnects the pullup resistor.

You should program only pullup resistors on GPIO pins connected to dry contact inputs. If a logic-level signal connects to a GPIO pin, programming a pullup resistor on that same pin might damage the MCP230*xx* or the logic device at the other end of the connection. Even if it doesn't damage the electronics, it could interfere with the input signal.

To set the pullup value on the MCP230*xx* ICs, transmit the sequence shown in Figure 13-5.

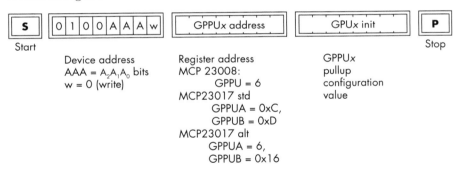

Figure 13-5: GPPUx pullup initialization

The last byte in the sequence in Figure 13-5 is the bitmap value for the pullup initialization.

13.2.5 Programming the Input Polarity

If you've been reading closely, you may have noticed that reading a dry contact switch with a pullup resistor in the previous section produced a 0 input when the switch was closed (pressed) and a 1 input when the switch was open (unpressed). This logic, *active low logic*, is opposite of what you might expect in software. Intuition suggests you should get a logic 1 when you press (close) the switch and a logic 0 when you release (open) it—that is, you expect *active high logic.* Although it is easy enough to invert the signal once you've read it from the GPIO pin, the MCP230*xx* devices provide a special *polarity register* that lets you select active high or active low logic signals.

The MCP23008 IPOL and the MCP23017 IPOLA and IPOLB registers let you control the polarity of an input pin. If a bit in IPOL*x* is 0, then the corresponding bit in the GPIO*x* register will reflect the current state of the input pin. If a bit in IPOL*x* is 1, then the corresponding bit in GPIO*x* will reflect the inverted state of the input pin.

If an actual input is active low but you want to read it as though it were active high, simply program the corresponding bit in IPOL*x* with a 1 to invert the signal when you read it. Inverting dry contacts, for example, makes them active high inputs so that their logic matches logic-level input signals.

To set the input pin polarities on the MCP230*xx* ICs, transmit the sequence shown in Figure 13-6.

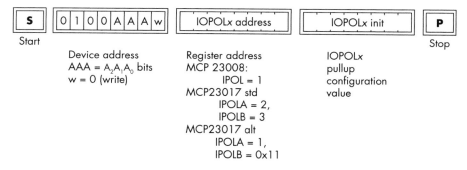

Figure 13-6: IPOLx input pin polarity sequence

The third byte in the sequence appearing in Figure 13-6 is the polarity initialization value.

13.2.6 Sequential Register Operations

Reading or writing a register value on the MCP230*xx* requires a minimum of three 1-byte transmissions on the I^{2}C bus: an I^{2}C address byte, a register number, and a data transmission to or from the register. Because I^{2}C transmissions are relatively slow (especially when operating at 100 kHz), the MCP230*xx* provides a special *sequential register access mode* to reduce the number of I^{2}C bus transactions. The SEQOP bit in IOCON (bit 5) controls this mode. If SEQOP contains 0, then the MCP230*xx* automatically increments the register number after each data transmission and reception on the I^{2}C bus. If SEQOP contains 1, then the MCP230*xx* disables the auto-increment mode.

When the autoincrement mode is active, the controller device can read or write multiple data bytes after transmitting a single pair of I^2C address and register bytes. As long as the controller device does not put a stop condition on the bus, successive clock pulses on SCL will continue to read or write successive registers on the MCP230*xx*.

This autoincrement feature is especially useful on the MCP23017 when the registers are in standard (non-banked) mode. In standard mode, the port A and port B registers appear in successive locations. This allows you to successively read and write registers from both ports as a 16-bit operation. For example, if you want to initialize IODIRA and IODIRB at the same time, you would use the following sequence (assuming SEQOP is 0, which is the power-on/reset condition):

1. Place the start condition on the I^2C bus.
2. Write the address to the I^2C bus (0x40 to 0x46) with the LO bit 0 (for write).
3. Write 0 to the I^2C bus (IODIRA register address).
4. Write the data direction bits for IODIRA to the I^2C bus.
5. Write the data direction bits for IODIRB to the I^2C bus.
6. Place the stop condition on the I^2C bus.

Between steps 4 and 5 in this sequence, the MCP23017 automatically incremented the register number so that step 5 writes the data direction bits to register one (IODIRB), as shown in Figure 13-7.

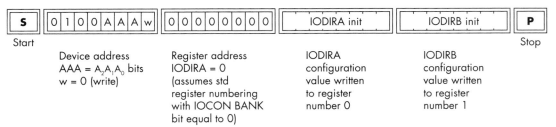

Figure 13-7: Autoincrementing register numbers

This sequence requires writing only 4 bytes to the I^2C bus. This is two less than the 6 bytes that would have been required to individually write to the IODIRA and IODIRB registers using independent transactions.

You're not limited to writing just two values using the autoincrement mode. You could, for example, write the direction and polarity initialization values all at once:

1. Place the start condition on the I^2C bus.
2. Write the address to the I^2C bus (0x40 to 0x46) with the LO bit 0 (for write).

3. Write 0 to the I²C bus (IODIRA register address).

4. Write the data direction bits for IODIRA to the I²C bus.

5. Write the data direction bits for IODIRB to the I²C bus.

6. Write the polarity bits for IPOLA to the I²C bus.

7. Write the polarity bits for IPOLB to the I²C bus.

8. Place the stop condition on the I²C bus.

In theory, you could also write interrupt initialization values in this sequence, though it's uncommon to use all the interrupt initialization features, so sequential writing isn't always possible. Sadly, the pullup registers don't appear sequentially in a common initialization list, so you wind up having to write their address and register values independently.

Of course, you're unlikely to write the initialization bits more often than once in a typical application, so the savings for a single initialization won't be that great. However, it is common to read all 16 input bits from the MCP23017 or to write all 16 output bits. The autoincrement mode is useful for those operations, which occur frequently in common applications.

Register autoincrement mode is not always useful, though. Perhaps you want to quickly write the GPIO, GPIOA, or GPIOB register to put some waveform onto the output pins, and you:

1. Put a start condition on the bus.

2. Write the I²C address to the bus with the LO (read) bit equal to 1.

3. Write the register number to the bus (for example, 12/0xC for GPIOA).

4. Write a byte to the bus.

5. Repeat step 4 for each different value to be written to the output pins.

6. Place a stop condition on the bus.

This code would require SEQOP to be set to 1 to disable autoincrementing the register number after step 4.

NOTE *Keep in mind that certain library functions might limit the number of successive bytes that can be written in one I²C bus transaction.*

You'll have to decide whether it's better to operate with the autoincrement feature turned on or off (by default) in your code. If you're constantly switching between the two modes, it may be more efficient just to operate in non-autoincrement mode.

13.2.7 Slew Rate Control

Bit 4 of the IOCON register (DISSLW) controls the I²C SDA slew rate. When enabled (0), the slew rate control reduces the speed at which the SDA line rises from low to high or falls from high to low (see Figure 13-8). By default, this bit is 0, which reduces the signal's rise and fall time.

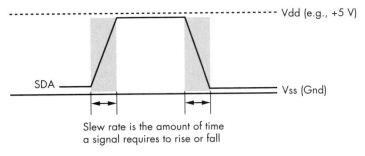

Figure 13-8: Slew rate

Reducing the slew rate can reduce noise (due to *ringing*, noise caused by the signal temporarily bouncing up and down after a change) on the SDA line. However, at higher speeds, reducing the slew rate can introduce errors on its own. You would typically enable slew rate control at 100 kHz and disable it at 1 MHz. At 400 kHz, you would enable it or disable it as necessary, depending on the signal noise, which you would have to verify with an oscilloscope. As the MCP230*xx* devices enable slew rate control by default, you should turn it off only if there are noise problems in your system.

13.2.8 *Reading General-Purpose Input/Output Pins on the MCP230xx*

Reading the GPIO*x* register(s) on the MCP230*xx* is probably the most common software activity. Reading these registers returns the current state of the GPA*x* and GPB*x* pins. If the pins were programmed as output, then reading the GPIO*x* registers returns the last value written (or default reset state) to the output pins, which is the current state of those pins.

Reading data from the GPIO*x* registers requires two I^2C bus transactions. First, write the GPIO*x* register address, and second, read the register value(s):

1. Place a start condition on the I^2C bus.
2. Write the device address with the LO bit 0 (write operation).
3. Write the GPIO, GPIOA, or GPIOB register address (GPIO = 9 on MCP23008, GPIOA = 9 or 0x12, and GPIOB = 0x19 or 0x13 on MCP23017).
4. Place a (repeated) start condition on the I^2C bus.
5. Write the device address with the LO bit 1 (read operation) to the I^2C bus.
6. Read the GPIO bits from the I^2C bus.
7. (optional on MCP23017) Read the second set of GPIO bits (GPIOB) from the I^2C bus (see Figure 13-9).
8. Place a stop condition on the bus.

Step 7 assumes SEQOP bit in IOCON is 0 and the register address written in step 3 was GPIOA (address 0x12 in standard mode).

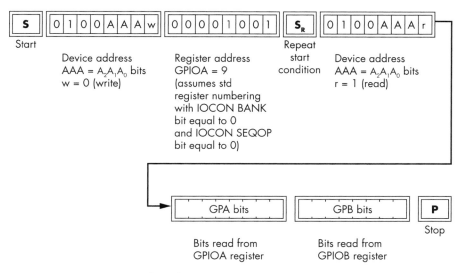

```
| S || 0 1 0 0 A A A w | 0 0 0 0 1 0 0 1 | S_R || 0 1 0 0 A A A r |
```

Start

Device address
AAA = $A_2A_1A_0$ bits
w = 0 (write)

Register address
GPIOA = 9
(assumes std
register numbering
with IOCON BANK
bit equal to 0
and IOCON SEQOP
bit equal to 0)

Repeat
start
condition

Device address
AAA = $A_2A_1A_0$ bits
r = 1 (read)

```
| GPA bits | GPB bits | P |
```

Stop

Bits read from
GPIOA register

Bits read from
GPIOB register

Figure 13-9: GPIO sequential read operation

Note that if SEQOP in IOCON has been programmed as a 1 (no auto-incrementing register address), then you can reread the GPIOx bits over and over again.

13.3 Writing General-Purpose Input/Output Pins on the MCP230xx

There are two ways to write data to output pins on the MCP230xx: write the data to the GPIOx register(s) or write the data to the OLATx register(s). Writing to either set of registers will place the output data on the output pins.

For output purposes, there is no real difference between writing to the GPIOx and OLATx registers. Internally, the MCP230xx converts a write to GPIOx into a write to OLATx. The two register sets differ when you read from them. Reading from GPIOx, of course, reads the current state of the GPAn and GPBn input pins. Reading from OLATx returns the last value written to the OLATx (or GPIOx) registers. This will produce differing results if any pins were programmed as inputs.

Writing to the OLATx (or GPIOx) registers is slightly less complex than reading from the GPIOx registers. Here are the steps:

1. Place a start condition on the I²C bus.

2. Write the device address with the LO bit 0 (write operation).

3. Write the OLAT, OLATA, or OLATB register address (OLAT = 0xA on MCP23008, OLATA = 0xA or 0x14, and OLATB = 0x1A or 0x15 on MCP23017).

4. Write the OLAT bits to the I^{2}C bus.

5. Write the second set of OLAT bits (OLATB) to the I^{2}C bus (see Figure 13-10). This is optional on MCP23017 (SEQOP = 0, only).

6. Place a stop condition on the bus.

This sequence is less complex than reading because you don't have to do a repeated start condition and write a second device address to the bus.

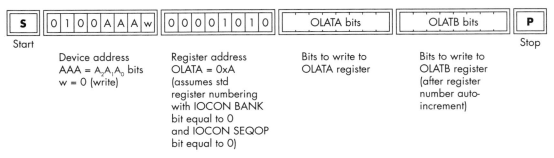

| S | 0 1 0 0 A A A w | 0 0 0 0 1 0 1 0 | OLATA bits | OLATB bits | P |

Start   Stop

Device address   Register address   Bits to write to   Bits to write to
AAA = A$_2$A$_1$A$_0$ bits   OLATA = 0xA   OLATA register   OLATB register
w = 0 (write)   (assumes std   (after register
                                register numbering   number auto-
                                with IOCON BANK   increment)
                                bit equal to 0
                                and IOCON SEQOP
                                bit equal to 0)

Figure 13-10: GPIO (OLAT) 16-bit sequential write operation

Note that the output pins on the MCP230*xx* ICs are not capable of driving much current. Each pin is capable of sourcing or sinking 25 mA—barely enough to light an LED. The entire package is further limited to 150 mA, meaning you cannot connect 16 LEDs and run them all at 25 mA. To handle more current, you will need to connect a transistor or other current amplifier to the output pin. The ULN2308 Darlington array—8 Darlington amplifiers in an 18-pin package, each capable of sinking 500 mA—is a perfect device for this purpose.

13.4   Demonstrating Input/Output on an MCP23017

By now you've learned enough to actually program the MCP230*xx* devices in polled (non-interrupt) mode. The sample Arduino program in this section writes some output data to port B on an MCP23017 and reads this data from port A on the same device. This program is relatively trivial in terms of functionality, but it demonstrates most of what you need to program the device.

The program uses the circuit shown in Figure 13-11. The SDA and SCL lines on the MCP23017 are wired to the corresponding pins on an Arduino Uno Rev3 (or other Arduino-compatible device). Pins A0, A1, and A2 are wired to Gnd, so the 7-bit device address will be 0x20. The reset pin is wired to +5 V or +3.3 V, depending on whether you're running a 3.3-V or 5.0-V system. The port A pins are wired to the reversed port B pins. Finally, if your SBC does not provide appropriate pullup resistors on the SDA and SCL lines, you will need to put a pair of 4.7-kΩ resistors between these two lines and Vdd (+5 V or +3.3 V).

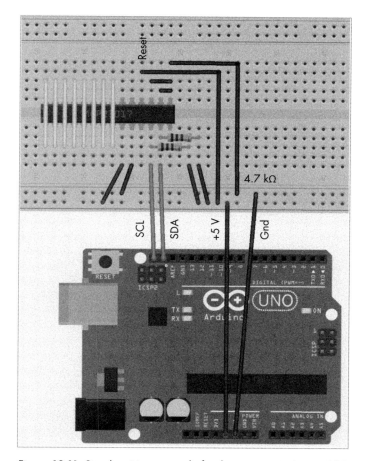

Figure 13-11: Simple wiring example for the program in Listing 13-1

Note in Figure 13-11 that GPB0 is connected to GPA7, GPB1 is connected to GPA6, . . . , and GPB7 is connected to GPA0. So the output bits will be reversed when read as inputs. This was done to simplify wiring; the bit reversal can be fixed in software.

The program in Listing 13-1 does not use interrupts, so you can leave the INTA and INTB pins floating. Also, don't forget to wire the Vdd (pin 9) and Vss (pin 10) pins to +5 V (or +3.3 V) and Gnd, respectively.

```
// Listing13-1.ino
//
// A simple program that demonstrates
// MCP23017 programming.
//
// This program writes a value to port B, reads
// a value from port A, and verifies that the
// value sent to port B was properly read on port A.

#include <Wire.h>
#define mcp23017    (0x20)
```

```
// MCP23017 registers:

#define IODIRA (0)
#define IOCON  (0x0A)
#define GPPUA  (0x0C)
#define GPIOA  (0x12)
#define OLATB  (0x15)

void setup( void )
{

    Serial.begin( 9600 );
    delay( 1000 );
    Serial.println( "Test reading and writing MCP23017" );

    Wire.begin(); // Initialize I2C library

    // Initialize the MCP23017:
    //
    // - Sequential port A/B registers (BANK = 0)
    // - Don't mirror INT pins (MIRROR = 0)
    // - Autoincrement register numbers (SEQOP = 0)
    // - Slew rate control on (DISSLW = 0)
    // - ODR in open-drain mode (ODR = 1)
    // - Interrupt polarity is active low (INTP = 0)

    #define initIOCON (4)    // ODR = 1

    Wire.beginTransmission( mcp23017 );
    Wire.write( IOCON );
    Wire.write( initIOCON );
    Wire.endTransmission(); // Sends stop condition

    // Set port A to input, port B to output,
    // and polarity noninverting.

    Wire.beginTransmission( mcp23017 );
    Wire.write( IODIRA );
    Wire.write( 0xff );      // Port A = inputs
    Wire.write( 0 );         // Port B = outputs
    Wire.write( 0 );         // Port A noninverting
    Wire.endTransmission(); // Sends stop condition

    // Disable pullup resistors on port A.

    Wire.beginTransmission( mcp23017 );
    Wire.write( GPPUA );
    Wire.write( 0 );         // Port A = no pullups
    Wire.endTransmission(); // Sends stop condition

}

void loop( void )
```

```
{
    static byte outputValue    = 0;
    static byte expectedValue = 0;

    ++outputValue;

    // You simplified the wiring and connected
    // GPB0 to GPA7, GPB1 to GPA6, ..., GPB7 to GPA0.
    // So you need to reverse the bits in the
    // expected value.

    expectedValue =    ((outputValue & 0x01) << 7)
                    | ((outputValue & 0x02) << 5)
                    | ((outputValue & 0x04) << 3)
                    | ((outputValue & 0x08) << 1)
                    | ((outputValue & 0x10) >> 1)
                    | ((outputValue & 0x20) >> 3)
                    | ((outputValue & 0x40) >> 5)
                    | ((outputValue & 0x80) >> 7);

    // Write the byte to the output (port B).

    Wire.beginTransmission( mcp23017 );
    Wire.write( OLATB );
    Wire.write( outputValue );
    Wire.endTransmission(); // Sends stop condition

    // Read a byte from the input (port A).

    Wire.beginTransmission( mcp23017 );
    Wire.write( GPIOA );                 // Send register address
    Wire.endTransmission( false );       // No stop condition

    Wire.requestFrom( mcp23017, 1 );     // Read from portA
    while( !Wire.available() ){}         // Wait for byte

    byte b = Wire.read();                // Get input byte

    if( b != expectedValue)
    {
        Serial.print
        (
            "Error writing and reading MCP23017, value=0x"
        );
        Serial.print( b, 16 );
        Serial.print( ", output 0x" );
        Serial.print( outputValue, 16 );
        Serial.print( ", expected 0x" );
        Serial.println( expectedValue, 16 );
    }
    else
{
        static uint32_t count = 0;

        if( ++count & 0x3f )
```

```
                Serial.print( "." );
        else
                Serial.println( "." );
    }
}
```

The setup() function initializes the MCP23017 device as appropriate for this sample program. Most importantly, it initializes port A pins as inputs and port B pins as outputs. It also disables the pullup resistors on the port A input pins, because port B is connected directly to port A, and port B's pins provide TTL (5-V) signals.

The loop() function simply writes a sequence of byte values to port B, reads a byte value from port A, and verifies that the value read is equal (with bit reversal due to wiring) to the value that was written (to port B). This function prints an error message to the serial port if the two values do not match.

13.5   Interrupts on the MCP230xx

Most programmers using the MCP230*xx* on an Arduino system don't bother using the interrupt facilities on those devices. It's often less work to simply poll the device to determine if any input bits have changed rather than to create an ISR and program the interrupts on the MCP230*xx*. If you're programming a system that can poll the MCP230*xx* at a sufficiently high frequency without impacting the performance of other activities on your system, polling is a reasonable approach. However, if real-time concerns mean polling is not an option, the interrupt facilities on the MCP230*xx* can be a lifesaver.

13.5.1   Interrupt Actions on the MCP230xx

The program in Listing 13-1 continuously wrote and read data. Because this program was responsible for both writing the data (to port B) and reading the data (at port A), the application always knows when data will be available on port A (specifically, data will be available immediately after the loop() function writes the data to port B). In the majority of real-world systems, the incoming data usually comes from some external hardware, and the loop() function wouldn't intrinsically know when new data has arrived on port A. One solution might be to have the loop() function continuously read port A and compare the value read against the previous reading. When the two values are different, the function can assume that external hardware has transmitted a new value and deal with it appropriately. This scheme is known as *polling*.

One problem with polling is that it consumes CPU time (to read and compare the port B value) even when the external hardware is not transmitting new values. During polling, the CPU cannot be used for other operations. A better solution would be to have the external hardware notify the CPU that new data is available; this notification would interrupt the current CPU's activities so it can briefly deal with the changed data and then resume the interrupted operation after handling the new data. The question is, how can the external hardware interrupt the CPU whenever it applies new data to port B?

You can program the MCP230*xx* devices to produce a signal on the MCP23008 INT or the MCP23017 INTA or INTB pins whenever a change in state occurs. A change in state, known as an *interrupt-on-change (IOC)*, is noted in one of two programmable situations:

- A pin changes state (from low to high or from high to low).
- A pin changes state when compared against the corresponding bit in the DEFVAL register.

The INT*x* pins reflect the current interrupt state. You would normally connect the INT*x* pins to an interrupt input on your SBC. Different SBCs support interrupts on different pins. Of course, if you are using a different SBC or a different RTOS, you will have to check the documentation for the SBC or RTOS to determine which pins are suitable for use as interrupt inputs. This section will assume you are using the Arduino libraries; see your SBC or RTOS documentation when using a different system.

13.5.2 Interrupt Service Routines

When an interrupt causes the CPU to halt the current program execution, it transfers control to a special function: the ISR. The ISR quickly does whatever is necessary to handle the hardware event and then returns control to the system, which resumes the original, interrupted code. To support ISRs in an application, you'll need to address a few questions. Answers vary by system; the following sections give answers for the Arduino.

How and where is the electronic signal input to the system?

In most systems, Arduino included, interrupts are digital logic signals input on specific CPU or system pins. On the Arduino, selected digital I/O pins can serve as interrupt inputs. (See "For More Information" for information on Arduino-brand pin selections for interrupts.) For example, the Arduino Uno Rev3 supports interrupts on digital I/O pins 2 and 3, and the Teensy 3.1 supports interrupts on any digital I/O pin. Not all Arduino devices support pin 2 as an interrupt pin; check your documentation when using a different device.

What type of input signals the interrupt?

Because digital I/O signals can be low (0) or high (1), you might think that interrupts can occur only on these two conditions. In fact, most Arduino systems will invoke an interrupt on one of the following conditions:

- A low-to-high transition on the interrupt pin
- A high-to-low transition on the interrupt pin

- Any change (low-to-high or high-to-low) on the interrupt pin
- A low signal on the interrupt pin

Some, but not all, Arduino devices can also invoke an interrupt when the interrupt pin is high.

How do you specify the ISR function?

Arduino systems use the `attachInterrupt()` function to associate a particular digital I/O pin with an interrupt. The call takes the following form:

```
attachInterrupt( digitalPinToInterrupt( pin ), ISR, mode );
```

In this call, *pin* is a digital I/O pin number, `ISR` is the name of a void function with no parameters that serves as the interrupt service routine, and *mode* is one of the following identifiers:

`LOW`   Triggers the interrupt whenever the pin is low

`CHANGE`   Triggers the interrupt whenever the pin changes value

`RISING`   Triggers when the pin goes from low to high

`FALLING`   Triggers when the pin goes from high to low

`HIGH`   Triggers the interrupt whenever the pin is high

Only some Arduino-compatible boards allow `HIGH`, so check your board's documentation to see if it supports active high interrupt signaling (for example, the Uno Rev3 does not support `HIGH`).

To use interrupts on other systems, see the documentation for your library, OS, or SBC.

What are the constraints on the ISR function?

Most operating systems place constraints on ISRs. Generally, you should assume the following:

- Any global variables an ISR modifies should be declared as `volatile`.
- ISR functions should be short, and execution time should be as minimal as possible.
- Many systems do not allow interrupts to be nested (that is, they don't allow one interrupt signal to interrupt an executing ISR).
- Many systems limit the type of library function calls that you can make in an ISR.

Please consult your particular OS's reference manuals for additional information about interrupt service routines.

The Arduino library, for example, places a couple of additional constraints on ISRs. In particular, you cannot use the `delay()` or `millis()` functions within an ISR. See "For More Information" for links to Arduino interrupt documentation.

INTx pin polarity

When the MCP230xx detects a pin change that would cause an interrupt, it will set the INTx pin high or low. The INTPOL bit (bit 1) in the IOCON register determines the interrupt polarity. If INTPOL is 1, then the interrupt signal is active high—that is, the INTx pin will go high when an interrupt occurs. If INTPOL is 0, then the interrupt signal is active low and goes low on an interrupt.

You can select the appropriate interrupt polarity either by using the Arduino attachInterrupt() mode parameter or by setting the interrupt polarity on the MCP230xx. However, it is important to ensure that the polarity you specify by mode matches the polarity you specify with the INTPOL bit. The common convention is to use active low interrupts and specify either LOW or FALLING as the mode parameter value.

13.5.3 Mirroring INTx Pins (MCP23017 Only)

The MCP23017 provides two independent interrupt pins for port A (INTA pin) and port B (INTB pin). This allows you to quickly determine the source of an interrupt if both ports A and B can generate interrupts, though at the cost of requiring two separate interrupt pins on the CPU. If you want to use only a single pin as an interrupt line on your CPU and are willing to use some software to differentiate port A and port B interrupts, you can program the MCP23017 to wire the INTA and INTB pins together so that an interrupt on either port will send a signal to the INTA and INTB pins.

Programming the MIRROR bit (bit 6) with a 1 in the IOCON register achieves this. Conversely, programming the MIRROR bit with a 0 (the default condition) routes all port A interrupts to INTA and all port B interrupts to INTB.

13.5.4 Open-Drain INTx Output

Bit 2 of the IOCON register (ODR) controls the INTx line open-drain interface. If this bit is programmed as a 1, open-drain output is enabled; if it is programmed as a 0 (the default), the active logic output in the INTx lines is enabled.

The open-drain form allows you to connect the INT lines from multiple MCP230xx devices together. This mode requires a pullup resistor on the output line. In open-drain mode, an interrupt signal will pull the INTx pin low, which, presumably, signals an interrupt on the controller. The controller will have to poll the various MCP230xx devices to determine the source of the interrupt.

The active logic output mode puts a logic signal directly on the INTx output pin. In this mode, the INTx pin must exclusively connect to an interrupt on the controller device; you cannot tie the interrupt pins together since that would create an electrical fault. This mode is best when you have a single MCP230xx device or if you need separate interrupts for each MCP230xx (so you don't have to poll the devices to determine the source of the interrupt).

Active logic mode is the default interrupt mode, a design error in MCP230xx devices. Tying multiple devices' INTx lines together and forgetting to program the ODR bit in open-drain mode could create an electrical conflict that could damage the MCP230xx parts. Moral of the story: always program the ODR bit in IOCON correctly! Many designers stick a transistor (such as a 2N7000 MOSFET) on the INTx pins to force open-drain (open-collector) mode and program ODR in active logic mode to drive the transistor. This avoids the possibility of a programming error that would damage the MCP230xx.

13.5.5 Enabling Interrupts on the MCP230xx

By default, the MCP230xx parts do not generate any interrupts; you must explicitly enable interrupts for the INTx pins to become active. You can do so with the MCP23008 GPINTEN and MCP23017 GPINTENA and GPINTENB registers.

The MCP230xx devices allow you to enable or disable interrupts on a pin-by-pin basis. Each bit in a GPINTENx register matches one of the GPIO pins: GPINTENA matches GPIOA pins, and GPINTENB matches GPIOB pins on the MCP23017. If a bit in GPINTENx contains 0, then interrupts are disabled for that particular I/O pin. If the bit contains 1, then interrupts are enabled for that bit, and interrupts are generated based on the bit settings in the INTCON and DEFVAL registers.

If interrupts are enabled for a particular I/O pin, then the INTCON and DEFVAL registers allow you to program the MCP230xx to generate an interrupt on a pin change or on a particular level. If a specific INTCON bit is 0, then the MCP230xx will generate an interrupt any time the input bit changes (that is, it will generate an interrupt on a low-to-high or on a high-to-low transition). In this case, the MCP230xx ignores the corresponding bit in DEFVAL. If a specific INTCON bit is 1, then the MCP230xx will generate an interrupt any time the input bit differs from the value of the corresponding bit in DEFVAL. This allows you to create level-sensing interrupts. If the corresponding bit in DEFVAL is 0, then the MCP230xx generates interrupts when the input pin is high; if the bit in DEFVAL is 1, then the MCP230xx generates interrupts when the input pin is low. Note that if the corresponding bit in INTCON is 0, or if that bit in GPINTENx is 0, the system ignores the bit in DEFVAL.

Although it is possible to modify the GPINTENx, INTCONx, and DEFVALx registers throughout program execution in complex systems, most commonly you initialize these registers just once when your program first begins execution. To prevent race conditions, you should initialize interrupts in the following order:

1. Initialize the DEFVALx register(s), if necessary.
2. Initialize the INTCONx register(s), if necessary.
3. Read the GPIO pins to clear any existing interrupts.
4. Initialize the GPINTENx register(s), if necessary.
5. Attach an ISR to the particular pin using `attachInterrupt()`.

A sequence like this helps prevent any inadvertent interrupts resulting from pre-existing conditions on the input pins or conditions that change during initialization. This particular sequence is for an Arduino system, but all other systems have a comparable one.

13.5.6 Testing and Clearing Interrupts

The INT*x* pin(s) on the MCP230*xx* indicate only that an interrupt has occurred on one (or both) banks. When the system invokes the ISR, you don't know which pin—or pins, if multiple pins change simultaneously—is responsible for the interrupt. To determine the exact source(s) of the interrupt, you will need to read the MCP23008 INTF or MCP23017 INTFA or INTFB register(s).

The bits in the INTF*x* register indicate which bits are responsible for an interrupt. When the ISR begins execution, it should read the INTF*x* register(s), where a 1 bit in a bit position indicates that the interrupt resulted from a change in the specified input bit. The ISR can then read the appropriate GPIO pin to determine the state of that pin when the interrupt occurred. For example, if interrupts are enabled for any change, reading the GPIO pin will tell you whether a rising or falling edge on the pin called the interrupt.

In theory, the CPU will invoke the ISR almost immediately after the interrupt pin changes state. In practice, it is possible for the ISR invocation to be slightly delayed after the interrupt condition occurs; for example, some other high-priority code (ISR) could be executing with the interrupts disabled. In that case, the ISR will be called only when the current high-priority code re-enables interrupts. During this time, it is possible for the state of the I/O pin to change. Therefore, by the time the ISR reads the signal on the input pin, the input data could have changed, and whatever the ISR reads might be wrong (a common race condition). To prevent this from happening, the MCP230*xx captures* the state of the pins when the interrupt occurs. The MCP230*xx* puts this snapshot of the pins in the MCP23008 INTCAP or MCP23017 INTCAPA and INTCAPB registers. Therefore, the ISR should actually read the contents of the appropriate INTCAP*x* register to determine the pin state that produced the interrupt.

By reading GPIO data (GPIO*x* or INTCAP*x* port), the ISR unfreezes the INTCAP*x*. This prepares it to capture the next interrupt pin set. You should always read the INTCAP*x* register(s) first in an ISR, since it's possible to lose captured information if another interrupt is pending and you read the GPIO*x* port first instead. Typically, there is no real need to read the GPIO*x* register(s) in an ISR—the INTCAP*x* register(s) usually provide all the information you need.

Pins configured for interrupt-on-change (in the INTCON*x* registers) will change the state that causes the next interrupt after you read the corresponding INTCAP*x* register. For example, if an interrupt occurred because a pin changed from high to low, the new interrupt condition (low to high) will not be active until you clear the interrupt by reading GPIO*x* or INTCAP*x*. If the pin actually toggles from high to low, then low to high and high to low again, the MCP230*xx* will signal a single interrupt only if the system has not cleared the interrupts between these level changes on the input pin.

Pins configured for interrupt-on-level—that is, pins configured to cause an interrupt based on the value appearing in a DEFVAL*x* register—continuously generate an interrupt signal as long as that level condition exists on the input pin. Reading or writing the GPIO*x* or INTCAP*x* register(s) does not reset that particular interrupt state until the interrupt condition ceases to exist.

13.6   A Sample Interrupt-Driven MCP230xx

Reading rotary shaft encoders is a common way to demonstrate interrupt programming on MCP230*xx* devices. As it turns out, twisting a rotary encoded at a high speed can easily result in data loss if the CPU is often busy doing other work, like displaying the values read from the rotary encoders. Using an ISR to quickly capture the encoder data and make it available for some main thread to process can eliminate data loss. This section provides some simple library code that demonstrates how to read and display the data from a SparkFun rotary encoder with red and green LEDs (*https://www.sparkfun.com/products/15140*).

NOTE   *You could also use SparkFun's RGB rotary encoder (*https://www.sparkfun.com/ products/15141*) or shaft encoder (*https://www.sparkfun.com/products/9117*) for the example in this section, with a few modifications.*

The SparkFun rotary encoder breakout (*https://www.sparkfun.com/products/ 11722*) makes it easy to breadboard one of these devices into a circuit, as shown in Figure 13-12.

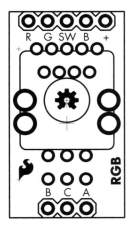

Figure 13-12: SparkFun rotary encoder breakout board

SparkFun rotary encoders have two digital I/O pins labeled A and B, which specify rotational changes (see Figure 13-13). You wire these pins through a 10-kΩ resistor to +5 V and wire the pin labeled C to Gnd. (If you connect the rotary encoder to an MCP230*xx* device, you can use the built-in programmable pullup resistor in place of the 10-kΩ resistor.) As you rotate the shaft on the encoder, it selectively connects pins A and B to pin C, that is, to Gnd. The pins labeled 1, 2, 3, and 4 in Figure 13-13 connect to the red and green LEDs, a pushbutton switch, and a common for these pins.

Connecting pins A and B to inputs on your SBC allows you to read the state of the two pins (high or low). By observing the state of these two pins over time, you can tell which direction the shaft is rotating, and at what speed, if you are timing the changes.

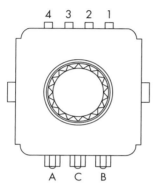

Figure 13-13: SparkFun
Red/Green rotary encoder

If you turn the shaft clockwise (CW) at a fixed speed, you will get the waveform shown in Figure 13-14 on pins A and B.

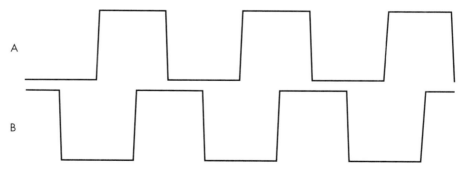

Figure 13-14: Rotary encoder output when rotating shaft clockwise

The output in Figure 13-14 is known as a *quadrature output*, where two out-of-phase signals determine the rotation direction, producing binary outputs similar to those shown in Table 13-5 over time.

Table 13-5: Clockwise Rotary Encoder Output

Output A	0	0	1	1	0	0	1	And so on
Output B	1	0	0	1	1	0	0	And so on

If you treat the input pairs as a 2-bit binary value, turning the encoder clockwise produces the repeating binary sequence 01 00 10 11 01 00 10 11 . . . over time. This is an example of a 2-bit *gray code*, a binary counting sequence where no more than a single bit changes between any two successive values (see "For More Information"). Gray codes are useful when working with multibit mechanical inputs because they are more immune to noise than regular binary codes are.

If you turn the shaft counterclockwise (CCW) at a fixed speed, you will get the waveform in Figure 13-15 on pins A and B.

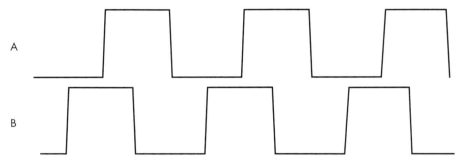

Figure 13-15: Rotary encoder output when rotating shaft counterclockwise

This also produces outputs similar to those shown in Table 13-6 over time.

Table 13-6: Counterclockwise Rotary Encoder Output

Output A	0	0	1	1	0	0	1	1	0	And so on
Output B	0	1	1	0	0	1	1	0	0	And so on

The gray code output is the binary sequence: 00 01 11 10 00 01 . . .

Another way to interpret the A and B inputs is to use a change in A to indicate a rotation of the encoder shaft and then read the B input to determine the direction of the rotation:

• A high-to-low transition on A with B low during the transition indicates a CCW rotation.

• A low-to-high transition on A with B high also indicates a CCW rotation.

• A high-to-low transition on A with B high during the transition indicates a CW rotation.

• A low-to-high transition on A with B low also indicates a CW rotation.

A NOTE ABOUT CONTACT BOUNCING

The contacts on a rotary switch are mechanical and subject to a phenomenon known as keybounce (or just bouncing). Bouncing occurs when the contacts switch from on to off or off to on. During this transition is a brief amount of time (typically a few milliseconds) when the contact rapidly switches between the two states. In a mechanical switch (for example, a pushbutton), the metallic contacts are literally bouncing on and off one another. If software is rapidly scanning this switch contact on an input port (usually at microsecond-level scanning times), the software will see several switch closures and opens until the contacts finally settle in an open or closed position. This can create problems if the software is looking for a single closure or open of the switch.

Keybounce can be fixed in hardware or software. The hardware solution is to use resistor-capacitor (RC) timing circuit to reduce the rise or fall time of the switch closure. A 10-kΩ resistor and 0.1-μF capacitor, for example, produce a 1 msec time constant (you would also feed this into a Schmidt trigger device, such as a 74HC14 inverter, to add hysteresis to the circuit). You can also solve this problem in software by reducing the scanning rate of the input (say, to less than once every 10 msec).

Using gray codes on a rotary encoder can reduce noise problems due to keybounce. Physically, the keybounce is still present, but the bouncing switches the inputs between two consecutive numbers in the gray code (as only 1 bit changes at a time on the rotary encoder, and if only 1 bit changes, the resulting numbers are consecutive). This introduces a small amount of jitter in the reading from the rotary encoder, which may be acceptable when using rotary encoders. Of course, if the jitter is unacceptable, you can use hardware (or software) debouncing to resolve the problem.

An MCP23008 GPIO expander would allow you to connect up to four of the SparkFun Illuminated Red/Green rotary encoders to a system. The encoder used in this section, however, connects a single rotary encoder to pins GP0 and GP1 on an MCP23008. Specifically, the encoder's A pin connects to GP1, and the B pin connects to GP0 through optional debouncing circuitry. If you also want to control the red and green LEDs on the encoder from the MCP23008, you can add some resistors between pins on MCP23008 to be programmed as outputs, along with the pins 2 and 3 on the rotary encoder. You will also need to connect the pin labeled 1 to Gnd. The resistors should probably be between 470 Ω and 1 kΩ. You can turn the red and green LEDs on or off by programming those output pins with logic 1s or 0s; programming both pins produces a yellow output. The example in this section will ignore the LED outputs, but you can easily add code to control them if you want.

The rotary encoder A and B pins are dry contacts. To read logic signals from these pins, you would normally add pullup resistors to the circuit (to +5 V or +3.3 V, whichever is appropriate). Rather than explicitly adding these resistors, the software will enable the GP0 and GP1 pins to use the MCP23008 programmable pin pullup resistors.

The program in Listing 13-2 uses a change on the A pin to cause an interrupt. The ISR will read the A and B pin values on GP1 (A) and GP0 (B) and increment or decrement a global counter based on the previous and current readings of these pins. The main program (that is, the code outside the ISR) uses the value of this global variable to determine how many "clicks" the encoder has been turned in the clockwise or counterclockwise direction since the application began execution.

NOTE *For familiarity, the program in Listing 13-2 is encoded in the Arduino IDE and written specifically for a Teensy 3.2 (or later) module. This code reads the INTCAP register within the ISR. As noted already in this chapter, ISR code must be fast, and certain system (library) calls may not be allowable. This code does not run on an Arduino Uno Rev3 but does seem to work okay on a Teensy 3.2. Whether this is due to the speed difference between the two CPUs or because the Teensy Wire library code is better written is a good question. Generally, I would recommend using a better operating system (FreeRTOS, Mbed, or NetBurner OS) rather than using this scheme in Arduino code. Treat the program in Listing 13-2 as a "demonstration only" product. The online chapters contain example code for the ESP32 using FreeRTOS if you'd like to see a better implementation.*

For the program in Listing 13-2, the MCP23008 SCL and SDA lines (pins 1 and 2) connect to the Teensy 3.2 SDA0 and SCL0 pins (pins D18 and D19). The INT line (pin 8) connects to the Teensy D2 pin. The RESET (pin 6) and Vdd (pin 18) pins connect to +3.3 V. The address lines and Vss (pins 3, 4, 5, and 9) connect to Gnd. Finally, GP1 connects to the rotary encoder A pin, and GP0 connects to the rotary encoder B pin (the rotary encoder C pin connects to ground).

Listing 13-2 programs the MCP23008 to generate an interrupt (active low) whenever there is a change on the GPA1 pin. When the ISR reads the INTCAP register, GP1 will reflect the value of the A pin *after* the rising or falling transition. Therefore, if the ISR reads 0 in the LO 2 bits of INTCAP, there has been a falling edge (GP1 is 0) and B is 0. This indicates a counterclockwise rotation. Likewise, if the LO 2 bits of INTCAP are 3 (0b11), then there has been a rising edge and B is 1, which also indicates a CCW rotation.

On a CW rotation, if the ISR reads a 1 in the LO 2 bits of INTCAP, this indicates a falling edge on A while B is 1. If the ISR reads a 2 (0b10) in the LO 2 bits of INTCAP, this indicates a rising edge on A while B is low (also a CW rotation).

The ISR simply increments or decrements a global variable (rotaryPosn) on a CW or CCW rotation, respectively. The main program checks this global variable and displays its value whenever it changes.

```
// Listing13-2.ino
//
// Demonstrate reading a rotary encoder
// using an MCP23008 with interrupts.
//
// Assumptions:
//
// - MCP23008 INT line connected to
//   digital I/O line 2.
//
// - SparkFun illuminated R/G rotary
//   encoder output A connected to
//   GP1 on MCP23008.
//
// - SparkFun illuminated R/G rotary
//   encoder output B connected to
//   GP0 on MCP23008.
//
// - MCP23008 wired to use address
//   0x20 (A0, A1, A2 = 0, 0 0).

#include <Wire.h>

#define led          (13)
#define mcp23008     (0x20)

#define IODIR        (0)
#define IOPOL        (1)
#define GPINTEN      (2)
#define DEFVAL       (3)
#define INTCON       (4)
#define IOCON        (5)
#define GPPU         (6)
#define INTF         (7)
#define INTCAP       (8)
#define GPIO         (9)
#define OLAT         (10)

// The following variable tracks
// rotations on the rotary encoder.
// This variable is negative if there
// have been more clockwise rotations
// than counterclockwise (likewise,
// it's positive if there have been
// more counterclockwise rotations).

volatile int rotaryPosn = 0;

// Write a value to an MCP23008 register:

❶ void writeReg( int reg, int val )
```

```
    {
        Wire.beginTransmission( mcp23008 );
        Wire.write( reg );
        Wire.write( val );
        Wire.endTransmission();
    }

    // Read a value from an MCP23008 register:

❷ int readReg( int reg )
    {
        Wire.beginTransmission( mcp23008 );
        Wire.write( reg );
        Wire.endTransmission( false );
        Wire.requestFrom( mcp23008, 1 );
        return Wire.read();
    }

    // Reset the MCP23008 to a known state:

❸ void mcpReset( void )
    {
        // I2C General Call is not mentioned in
        // the manual so do this the hard way.

        // INTF   is read only.
        // INTCAP is read only.

        // Disable interrupts
        // and clear any pending.

        writeReg( GPINTEN, 0 );
        readReg( INTCAP );

        // Set remaining registers
        // to POR/RST values.

        writeReg( IODIR,    0xFF );
        writeReg( IOPOL,    0 );
        writeReg( GPINTEN,  0 );
        writeReg( DEFVAL,   0 );
        writeReg( INTCON,   0 );
        writeReg( IOCON,    0 );
        writeReg( GPPU,     0 );
        writeReg( GPIO,     0 );
        writeReg( OLAT,     0 );
    }

    // Interrupt service routine that gets
    // called whenever the INT pin on the
    // MCP23008 goes from high to low.
    // This function needs to be *fast*.
    // That means minimizing the number
```

```
    // of I2C transactions.

❹ void ISRFunc( void )

  {
      // Read the INTCAP register.
      // This reads the GPIO pins at
      // the time of the interrupt and
      // also clears the interrupt flags.
      //
      // Note: A rotary encoder input in GPA1,
      // B rotary encoder input in GPA0.

      int cur = readReg( INTCAP ) & 0x3;

      // You have CCW rotation if:
      //
      //      A:0->1 && B==1  (cur=3)
      // or   A:1->0 && B==0  (cur=0)

      if( cur == 0 || cur == 3 )
      {
          ++rotaryPosn;
      }
      else if( cur == 1 || cur == 2 )
      {
          --rotaryPosn;   // CW rotation
      }
      // else illegal reading . . .
  }

  // Usual Arduino initialization code:

❺ void setup( void )
  {
      Serial.begin( 9600 );
      delay( 1000 );
      Serial.println( "Rotary Encoder test" );

      pinMode( 0, INPUT_PULLUP );
      pinMode( 1, INPUT_PULLUP );
      pinMode( 2, INPUT );
      pinMode( led, OUTPUT );
      digitalWrite( led, 0 );

      Wire.begin();

      // Reset the MCP23008 to a known state.

      mcpReset();

      // Initialize the MCP23008 (this is the default
```

```
    // state, so just defensive coding). Note that
    // SEQOP = 0 is autoincrementing registers and
    // INTPOL = 0 yields active low interrupts.

    writeReg( IOCON, 0 );

    // Set data direction to input and
    // turn pullups on for GPA0/GPA1.
    // Set polarity to inverting for GPA0/GPA1.

    writeReg( IODIR, 0xff );
    writeReg( IOPOL, 3 );
    writeReg( GPPU, 3 );

    // Initialize MCP23008 interrupts.

    writeReg( INTCON, 0 );      // GPA1 int on change
    writeReg( GPINTEN, 0x2 );   // Enable GPA1 interrupt

    attachInterrupt( digitalPinToInterrupt(2), ISRFunc, FALLING );
    interrupts();               // Ensure CPU interrupts enabled
}

// Main Arduino loop:

❻ void loop( void )
{
    static int lastRP = 0;

    if( rotaryPosn != lastRP )
    {
        Serial.print( "Posn=" ); Serial.println( rotaryPosn );
        lastRP = rotaryPosn;
    }
}
```

Listing 13-2 contains two functions, writeReg() ❶ and readReg() ❷, that write data to and read data from an MCP23008 register. These functions transmit the appropriate I²C bytes to accomplish this. The mcpReset() ❸ function initializes the MCP23008 to the power-on reset state, which is useful if the code is rerun without powering down the MCP23008. The code also includes an interrupt service routine, ISRFunc() ❹, along with the usual Arduino setup() ❺ and loop() ❻ functions.

When a change occurs on the GP1 pin (because the shaft has rotated), this triggers an interrupt, causing the system to call the ISRFunc() function. This function determines if the shaft has rotated clockwise or counterclockwise and adjusts the value of the rotaryPosn variable accordingly.

The following is some sample output from the program in Listing 13-2 obtained by twisting the encoder knob back and forth.

```
Posn=0
Posn=-1
Posn=-2
Posn=-3
Posn=-4
Posn=-5
Posn=-6
Posn=-7
Posn=-8
Posn=-7
Posn=-6
Posn=-5
Posn=-4
Posn=-3
Posn=-2
Posn=-1
Posn=0
Posn=1
Posn=2
Posn=3
Posn=4
```

As you can determine from the output, the shaft was rotated counterclockwise for a short period, decrementing the output value, and then it was turned clockwise for a bit, incrementing the output value.

13.7 MCP230xx Library Code

Because of the complexity, many programmers prefer to use calls to existing library code rather than writing directly to the hardware themselves. Arduino provides an MCP230xx library package to help you out with this. See "For More Information" for the links to these libraries.

If you'd prefer to program the MCP230xx on a Raspberry Pi, Adafruit has also ported its library to the Pi; see "For More Information" for details. Likewise, those links describe where to find an MCP23008 library for Mbed. A quick web search will turn up several example Mbed libraries for the MCP23017 (mostly adaptations of the Adafruit library). You can also easily search for the dozens of examples of MCP230xx code scattered across the internet for a wide variety of CPUs, operating systems, and programming languages.

13.8 I²C Performance

Although digital I/O functions, like reading a pushbutton, don't require blazing performance, many such activities do require fast processing to properly read or write high-frequency digital signals. Unfortunately, high-performance operation and I^{2}C bus connections are often mutually exclusive. Because it can sometimes take three or four bus transactions to read or write digital data via an MCP230xx device, it might require 400 μsec to 500 μsec for a single I/O operation at 100 kHz, yielding a 2-kHz sample rate. This can be too slow for certain operations.

Fortunately, the MCP230xx devices can run at 400 kHz and up to 1.7 MHz as well as 100 kHz. At 400 kHz, you can achieve (at least) an 8-kHz sample rate, and 10 kHz to 20 kHz is not unreasonable with carefully written code. If you're willing to operate the bus at 1 MHz or more, you could even get the sample rate up to around 100 kHz, which is suitable for most applications. If you need higher performance, you'll probably want to use something other than the I^{2}C bus, like SPI versions of the MCP230xx.

13.9   MCP23Sxx Parts

When searching for information about the MCP23008 and MCP23017 parts, you may come across references to the MCP23S08 and MCP23S17 devices. These GPIO expanders are nearly identical to the MCP230xx parts, except that they were designed for use on the SPI bus rather than the I^{2}C bus. Most code written for the MCP23Sxx parts will work fine on the MCP230xx devices with minimal modifications: essentially, you'd change the code to call I^{2}C library functions rather than SPI library functions to write and read data to and from the devices.

Because the SPI bus operates at a higher frequency than the I^{2}C bus, SPI variants can read input data at a higher sampling frequency. For more information, see the MCP23xxx documentation (which covers both the SPI and I^{2}C parts). Links appear in "For More Information."

13.10   Chapter Summary

This chapter covered the MCP23017 and MCP23008 GPIO expansion ICs. It described the on-chip registers, including the data, data direction, pullup, and polarity registers. It described how to read and write digital data via the pins on the MCP230xx. This chapter also discussed interrupt-driven I/O using the MCP230xx devices; it presented a short sample program to read a SparkFun rotary encoder using an ISR to help avoid missing any pulses from the encoder. Finally, this chapter ended by discussing the use of open-software libraries available for the MCP230xx.

FOR MORE INFORMATION

Some interesting online tutorials for the MCP230xx: *https://www.best-micro controller-projects.com/mcp23017.html*

MCP23017 datasheet: *https://ww1.microchip.com/downloads/en/ devicedoc/20001952c.pdf*

MCP23008 datasheet: *https://ww1.microchip.com/downloads/en/ devicedoc/21919e.pdf*

Arduino libraries for MCP230xx devices: *https://www.arduino.cc/reference/en/ libraries/mcp23017*

Adafruit libraries for MCP230xx devices: *https://github.com/adafruit/ Adafruit-MCP23017-Arduino-Library*

Sming libraries for MCP230xx devices: *https://sming.readthedocs.io/en/latest/ _inc/Sming/Libraries/MCP23017/index.html*

An Mbed MCP23008 library: *https://os.mbed.com/users/dewyatt/code/ MCP23008/docs/tip/classMCP23008.html*

Arduino documentation: *https://www.arduino.cc/reference/en/language/functions/ external-interrupts/attachinterrupt*

Information on Arduino interrupts: *https://gammon.com.au/interrupts*

Information on gray codes: *https://en.wikipedia.org/wiki/Gray_code*

Programming MCP230xx devices on the Raspberry Pi: *https://learn.adafruit.com/ mcp230xx-gpio-expander-on-the-raspberry-pi*

Wiring MCP23008 library on the Raspberry Pi: *http://wiringpi.com/extensions/ i2c-mcp23008-mcp23017*

14

THE ADS1015 AND ADS1115 ANALOG-TO-DIGITAL CONVERTERS

Although digital I/O is probably the most popular form of input/output on embedded computer systems, analog input is also popular. Converting a real-world analog signal (typically a voltage in the range 0 V to 3.3 V or 5 V) to numeric (digital) form allows an application to use real-world continuous measurements rather than the simple on or off from a digital input device. To perform such conversions, you'll need an ADC.

Many types of ADCs are available. The vast majority of them convert an input voltage to an n-bit number, though some convert other physical measurements into numeric form. For the most part, real-world sensors produce a voltage output rather than producing a digital number directly. You would use an ADC to convert this voltage level to a digital value. Therefore, to read common sensor outputs, an ADC is a critical item in your toolbox.

This chapter discusses two popular ADCs: the ADS1015 and the ADS1115. Both devices convert voltages between 0.0 V and some upper bound (such as 4.095 V) into numeric form: the ADS1015 produces a 12-bit result, and the ADS1115 produces a 16-bit result. The ADS1015 is faster, supporting 3,300 samples per second versus the ADS1115 at 860 samples per second (a classic trade-off of bits for speed). Although other I^2C ADCs are available, the ADS1x15 devices are popular because Adafruit has created a pair of breakout boards that support these two ICs. The original Adafruit designs were open hardware, and over time, low-cost clones of these boards have appeared on Amazon and other places. These devices are easy to interface to any system that has an I^2C bus. Adafruit, for example, provides library code for Arduino and Raspberry Pi systems, though it's easy enough to interface these devices to any RTOS or system. However, the purpose of this book is to teach you how to directly program I^2C peripherals, so the next section provides the necessary background information on the ADS1x15 so you can program it.

NOTE   *This chapter typically uses a Teensy 3.2 for testing purposes. The reported timing values may vary from numbers you get if you're using an Arduino Uno Rev3 or other Arduino-compatible SBC.*

14.1   Analog-to-Digital Converter Specifications

ADCs have several important specifications that affect their use. Table 14-1 lists some of the more common specifications.

Table 14-1: Typical ADC Features

Feature	Units	Description
Resolution	Bits	The size of the integer value produced by the conversion
Channels	Integer	Number of independent converters available on the device
Polarity	Unipolar or bipolar	Determines whether an ADC supports negative voltages (bipolar or differential)* or only non-negative voltages (unipolar)
Range	Volts	Supported voltage range for inputs to the ADC
Input type	Differential or single-ended	Specifies whether the input(s) are differential or single-ended (common ground)
Sample frequency	Hz	Number of readings per second the ADC is capable of making (also known as *samples per second* or *sps*)

*The ADS1x15 devices do not accept actual negative voltages; rather, they accept a differential input where the difference between two positive voltage inputs is negative. See the discussion of differential inputs in section 14.1.5, "Differential vs. Single-Ended Modes," later in this chapter.

The following subsections will describe each of these items and discuss the actual ADC1x15 specifications.

14.1.1 Analog-to-Digital Converter Resolution

The resolution of an ADC is the number of bits the ADC produces for a conversion. Low-end ADCs have an 8- or 10-bit resolution (10 bits is typical for the analog pins on a typical Arduino-class SBC), while mid-range ADCs commonly have 12-, 14-, or 16-bit resolution. Higher-end ADCs support 20- or 24-bit resolution. For differential inputs, the ADS1015 device provides a 12-bit resolution, and the ADC1115 provides 16 bits of resolution. For single-ended applications on either device, you lose a bit (see section 14.1.5, "Differential vs. Single-Ended Modes," for more details on differential versus single-ended mode).

The resolution determines the smallest difference between two voltages an ADC can detect. For example, in full-scale mode both the ADS1015 and ADS1115 ADCs support voltages in the range of 0 V to 4.095 V. The resolution of the device divides this range by the maximum value. A 12-bit resolution divides the input range into 4,096 steps, so in theory, the ADS1015 is capable of resolving a difference of 0.001 V. The ADS1115, being a 16-bit converter, breaks up the input range into 65,536 steps. In theory, it's capable of resolving a difference of 0.0000625 V—substantially better. The single-ended inputs have 11-bit and 15-bit resolution, respectively, producing 0.002-V and 0.000125-V steps.

As a general rule, more is better when it comes to ADC resolution. The higher the resolution, the more accurate the reading will be. However, extra resolution comes at a cost: all other things equal, higher-resolution ADCs are generally more expensive and slower than lower-resolution ADCs. Using a higher-resolution ADC also does not guarantee that you'll get more precise readings. System noise and other effects may render the extra resolution meaningless in actual applications. For most typical SBC applications, 12 bits are sufficient. The presence of 0.0001 V of noise often completely obliterates the small readings possible with a 16-bit ADC.

14.1.2 Analog-to-Digital Converter Channel Count

Many ADC devices provide multiple analog inputs. This allows you to connect several analog sources to a single ADC device, thus reducing the count and cost of parts. The ADS1015 and ADS1115 devices, for example, provide four input channels. ADS1013, ADS1113, ADS1014, and ADS1114 devices provide fewer inputs.

Having multiple input channels does not imply that the device has multiple ADCs on board. Instead, most multichannel ADCs have an analog multiplexer, a switch that connects a single input to the ADC at a time. This is an important distinction: if you have multiple ADCs, they can all convert an input from analog to digital concurrently, but a multiplexer switches between inputs, allowing only one conversion at a time. The ADS1015 and ADS1115 use internal multiplexers to feed a single ADC, so they must perform analog-to-digital conversions for each channel serially.

14.1.3 Analog-to-Digital Converter Polarity

ADCs can be unipolar or bipolar. *Unipolar* ADCs can convert only non-negative voltages to digital form. This is typical of the ADC found on common SBCs; for example, Arduino-class SBCs typically convert voltages in the range of 0 V to 3.3 V or 5 V. Unipolar ADCs cannot handle negative voltages—in fact, a negative input voltage might damage the device. Bipolar ADCs can handle positive and negative input voltages.

Bipolar ADCs are usually programmable to operate as a bipolar or unipolar device. The reason for operating a bipolar device in unipolar mode is resolution. Being able to handle positive and negative voltages eats up a bit of resolution. For example, if you operate a 16-bit ADC in bipolar mode, you get a 15-bit range for the negative voltages and a 15-bit range for the positive voltages. If you feed the device only positive voltages, you lose a bit of resolution. However, if you program the device for unipolar operation, you get the full 16 bits of resolution, allowing you to resolve smaller positive voltages.

The ADS1x15 devices aren't true bipolar ADCs. Pin input voltages must always be positive with respect to ground. See section 14.1.5, "Differential vs. Single-Ended Modes," for details on how the ADS1x15 handle negative inputs.

14.1.4 Analog-to-Digital Converter Range

ADC range is the range of minimum and maximum voltages an ADC can handle. For example, a typical Arduino-class ADC will handle a range of 0 V to 3.3 V or 0 V to 5 V. Other common ADCs can handle 3.3 V, 4.095 V, 5 V, or 10 V.

A given ADC might have two different range specifications. One is the span of voltages over which the ADC will produce distinct readings—for example, 0 V to 5 V. The other range is the maximum permissible voltage the inputs will accept without damaging the device, which might be −0.5 V to 5.5 V for a typical ADC that supports a normal range of 0 V to 5 V. Generally, though, when discussing the range of an ADC, I'm talking about the range of inputs that produce distinct readings. Voltages outside this range but still within the maximum permissible range tend to clip their readings to the minimum or maximum values.

Unipolar devices almost always have a range from 0 V to some maximum voltage n V. Bipolar devices typically have a range that is $\pm n$ V (n is typically some value such as 3.3 V, 5 V, or 10 V).

The ADS1015 and ADS1115 are unipolar in single-ended mode and bipolar in differential mode (see the next section for a discussion of differential versus single-ended operation). They have a programmable gain stage that limits the range to ±5 V (actually 6.144 V, though the pins are limited to 5-V inputs), ±4.095 V, ±2.047 V, ±1.023 V, ±0.511 V, or ±0.255 V in differential/bipolar mode. For single-ended/unipolar mode, cut the range in half with a minimum voltage of 0 V.

14.1.5 Differential vs. Single-Ended Modes

ADCs commonly operate in one of two modes: differential or single-ended. Single-ended inputs are easier to wire, less complex, and compatible with just about any voltage source. Differential inputs may require special differential driver voltage sources and are therefore more complex to use.

In *single-ended mode*, the ADC has a single input with a common ground (for all channels, if the ADC supports multiple input channels). Most Arduino-class analog inputs fall into this category, with the conversion measuring the voltage between the A*n* analog input pin and the common-to-all-analog-inputs analog ground pin.

In *differential mode*, an ADC conversion takes two inputs, generally labeled + and −, and computes the difference between the voltages on those inputs. It then converts this difference to digital form. Differential inputs are generally fed from *differential line drivers*, which typically put one half of a single-ended voltage on the + output and negative one half of that voltage on the − output. Measuring the voltage between the + and − lines gives you the original input voltage.

The main advantage to using differential inputs is that they reduce noise induced by the system. A voltage spike (noise) in the system is often summed onto input signal lines, such as the inputs to an ADC. On a single-ended input, that noise spike might produce a temporary increase or decrease of the input voltage, resulting in a momentary deviant reading from the ADC. That noise spike induces the same temporary voltage change on a set of differential inputs. However, the spike produces roughly the same increase or decrease on both of the differential inputs. When the differential input computes the difference between the two inputs, any value added to or subtracted from both differential inputs is eliminated from the conversion because the value added to the + line matches the value added to the − line. This means differential inputs are much less noisy than single-ended inputs, so you should use them whenever possible when working with high-resolution (16-bit or higher) ADCs.

There are two problems with differential inputs. First, most multichannel ADCs that support differential inputs use one channel for the + input and a second input channel for the − output. Therefore, using differential inputs cuts the number of available ADC channels in half. Differential inputs also require the added expense and complexity of special differential driver circuitry to convert a standard voltage (single-ended input) to differential form.

NOTE *It's technically possible to feed a single-ended input to the + input and connect the − input to Gnd, but if you do so, you'll lose many of the benefits of using a differential circuit.*

The ADS1*x*15 devices are programmable to operate in single-ended or differential mode. Differential mode uses two input channels for each differential input, so you wind up with two differential inputs per device (rather than four single-ended input channels). Nevertheless, if you're using an ADS1115 with 16-bit precision, you really should operate it in differential mode to take advantage of that extra precision and not swamp the LO bits of the reading in noise.

The ADS1x15 devices also support three differential inputs where AN0, AN1, and AN2 all share the same (–) input (AN3).

The ADS1x15 devices do not allow negative voltages on their input pins, which affect their differential performance. If your differential line driver converts the single-ended input voltage to a positive and negative voltage pair, that negative voltage could damage the ADS1x15. Instead, assuming you're using the range of 0 V to 4.095 V, you must devise a differential driver circuit that puts out 2.047 V on both pins when you want a zero reading. It drives the + pin above 2.047 V and the – pin below 2.047 V for positive readings; for negative readings, it drives the + pin below 2.047 V and the – pin above 2.047 V. The ADS1x15 produces the maximum (positive or negative) reading when 0 V is on one pin and 4.095 V is on the other. If you're using one of the other voltage ranges on the ADS1x15, then substitute one half the maximum voltage for 2.047 V and the maximum voltage for 4.095 V in this description.

Also note that a range of 0 V to 4.095 V produces only a 15-bit result (0 V to 32,767 V). Although the ADS1115 allows only positive voltage on its input pins, it is a bipolar device and produces 16-bit signed integer conversions (–32,768 to +32,767). The ADS1115 produces negative outputs when the – input has a higher voltage than the + input. For example, if the + input is at 0 V and the – input is at 4.095 V, then the ADS1115 produces –32,768 for the conversion.

14.1.6 Sample Frequency

Analog-to-digital conversion is not an instantaneous process. Some ADCs are relatively slow, while others are much speedier (and more expensive). Different ADCs also have different *sample frequencies*, or readings made per second.

An ADC's sample frequency has a direct bearing on its applicability. The ADS1x15 devices are not particularly fast. The ADS1115 is capable of 860 samples per second (sps) at most; the ADS1015 is a little better, at 3,300 sps. The famous *Nyquest theorem* states that you must be able to sample an analog signal at least twice its highest frequency in order to create a reasonable digital waveform. This means that the ADS1115 is capable of digitizing up to 430-Hz waveforms, while the ADS1015 can capture 1,650-Hz waveforms. These devices definitely won't allow you to capture digital audio, which requires at least a 40-kHz sample rate for 20-Hz to 20,000-Hz capture. Nevertheless, the ADS1x15 parts are perfectly acceptable for capturing slowly changing signals, like those from human-controlled potentiometers, thermocouples, resistive temperature detectors (RTDs), power supply measurement, light sensing circuitry, and so on.

NOTE *If you're interested in capturing digital audio, there are ADCs capable of 50 kHz to 200 kHz (and at 24-bit resolution) specifically intended for this purpose.*

In some respects, the ADS1x115's slow sample speed isn't a major problem—the I^{2}C bus data transfers provide their own limit on how fast conversions can take place. However, these slow conversion rates can also impact the overall application performance, especially with Arduino single-thread code.

14.1.7 Miscellaneous ADS1x15 Features

The ADS1x15 devices have the following unique built-in features:

I^{2}C bus speed   The ADS1x15 devices fully support standard speed mode (100 kHz), fast mode (400 kHz), and high-speed mode (up to 3.4 MHz).

General call support   The ADS1x15 devices support the I^{2}C general call-reset command, where the first byte is 00h and the second byte is 06h.

Programmable gain amplifier   The ADS1x15 devices feature a programmable gain amplifier (PGA), which allows you to set the gain to one of six different levels. The gain is selected by 3 bits in the configuration register using the values appearing in Table 14-5 in section 14.3.2.3, "Programmable Gain Amplifier Control Bits." See section 14.3, "ADS1x15 Analog-to-Digital Converter Registers," for information about programming the configuration register gain settings.

Programmable comparator   The ADS1x15 devices provide two 16-bit comparator registers that automatically compare the current conversion against a low threshold value and a high threshold value. When active, the IC will assert the ALRT pin whenever the conversion value is less than the low or higher than the high threshold value ("windowed" mode) or whenever the conversion value is greater than the high threshold value ("traditional" mode).

Continuous (one-shot) mode   The ADS1x15 devices can be programmed to constantly perform ADC conversions or operate in a *one-shot mode* where they perform a conversion only in response to a command over the I^{2}C bus.

14.2   Analog Conditioning

ADC input ranges are often different from the signals you obtain in the real world. A range of 0 V to 5 V is common, both as an input to an ADC and as a single voltage in the real world. However, ADC ranges and input signals don't often match. The ADS1x15 ADCs are a good example; in their full resolution mode, they support an input range of only 0 V to 4.095 V, something you rarely see in real life.

The most common voltage ranges of industrial equipment output are probably 0 V to 5 V, ±5 V, 0 V to 10 V, or ±10 V. While some ADCs, such as the LTC1859 series, support these ranges, you will often need to translate the signal you have to a signal your ADC will accept. This—along with other activities such as converting currents to voltages—is known as *analog conditioning* (or *signal conditioning*).

Figure 14-1 shows a schematic for an opamp circuit that provides two functions: signal amplification or reduction, and conversion from single-ended input to differential output. The top half of the figure (opamps at pins 1, 2, and 3, and 5, 6, and 7) is an amplifier circuit that will take a voltage in the range of ±10 V and translate it to some other voltage in the range of ±10 V. Two potentiometers, ZERO and SPAN, control the offset and gain of the amplifier. The ZERO (offset) pot adds a voltage in the range of −10 V to +10 V to the input, while the SPAN (gain) pot adjusts the amplification (gain) from around 0.05 to about 20, with a limit of ±10 V on the output.

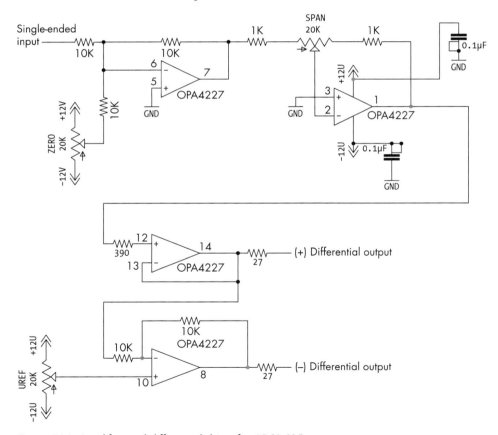

Figure 14-1: Amplifier and differential driver for ADS1x115

The bottom half of the circuit takes the output from the amplification stage and converts it to a differential signal. The top opamp in this differential driver is a noninverting amplifier with a gain of one, which simply outputs its input voltage as the + differential output. The bottom opamp in this circuit is an inverting amplifier, also with a gain of one (0 dB). If the VREF pot is set to 0 V (middle position), this amplifier inverts the input. Therefore, this circuit will produce the positive output from the top half of the circuit on the + output and the negative output from the top half of the circuit on the – output. Overall, this circuit has a gain of two (6 dB) because the difference between the + and – outputs is actually twice the output from the top half of the circuit. Correct for this by reducing the gain in the top amplifier circuit.

Some comments about the quality of the parts in the Figure 14-1 circuit are in order, because sticking inexpensive components into this circuit may produce less-than-desirable results.

First, if you care about long-term stability and lack of drift, you will want to use instrumentation-quality OPA4227 or OPA2227 opamps. These aren't cheap, but they are very good. If you don't mind recalibrating the circuit on a regular basis, you can use cheaper (jellybean) LM324 opamps.

Using high-precision, low-TCR resistors in this circuit will also help to ensure long-term stability and lack of drift. In particular, the 10-kΩ and 1-kΩ resistors should be 0.1 percent 15 PPM/C resistors, which I've found for less than $0.50 each in batches of 100 (at the time this was written). The 20-kΩ pots should be 10 percent and 50 PPM/C or less; these are not at all cheap, typically $15 to $20 each. If you don't mind recalibrating the circuit on a regular basis, you can use cheap resistors and pots—it's safer to use lower-TCR pots if you need to save money.

The two 1-kΩ resistors in this circuit are optional. They are there to prevent the gain from going crazy as the SPAN pot approaches one end or the other. Larger values like 4.7 kΩ will make gain adjustments smoother, at the expense of a more limited gain range. If you pick different resistors, make sure they are low-TCR (PPM/C) resistors. The precision isn't as important because of the pot, but it's usually going to be 0.1 percent for reasonably priced, low-TCR resistors.

The circuit's 27-Ω resistors are also optional and exist just to prevent a complete meltdown if the opamp outputs are shorted. If you decide to install these resistors, use 1-percent, metal-film resistors. The 390-Ω resistor can also be a 1-percent, metal-film resistor; it's not that important to the circuit.

Finally, if you are using single-ended inputs on your ADC, you can drop the bottom half of the circuit and feed the output from pin 1 on the OPA4227 directly into the ADC. Of course, given the cost, you should probably substitute an OPA2227 dual opamp in place of the OPA4277 quad opamp if you do this.

Before using this circuit, you will need to calibrate it. The following steps describe the calibration for an ADS1x15 ADC device. You'll need to modify this procedure by changing the output voltage the circuit produces when using a different ADC. *Do not connect this circuit to the ADS1x15 during calibration.* Doing so may damage the ADC.

1. Try to put all the pots in approximately their middle position. The position doesn't have to be accurate, but you want the pot wipers away from either end of the terminals.

2. Put 0 V on the single-ended input and apply power to the circuit (±12 V).

3. Measure the voltage on pin 7 of the OPA4277 and adjust the ZERO pot until the output is as close to zero as possible.

4. Now, measure the voltage at pin 1 of the OPA4277 and, again, adjust the ZERO pot until the output voltage is as close to zero as possible.

5. Change the input voltage to match the maximum voltage you're going to allow (say, 5 V).

6. Measuring the voltage on pin 1 of the OPA4277, adjust the SPAN pot until you get an output as close to 4.095 V as possible. This assumes you will be using an ADS1x15 programmed to accept 0 V to 4.095 V. If using a different ADC or an ADS1x15 programmed for a different range, adjust this number accordingly.

7. Repeat steps 4 through 6 until you don't have to make any changes to the ZERO or SPAN pots. Adjusting one may affect the other, so repeating this process fine-tunes the calibration.

At this point, you've calibrated the amplifier stage. If you're not using a differential output, you're done; you can feed pin 1 on the OPA4277 to the ADC input. If you're using a differential output, further adjustment is necessary. The following steps will warp the calibration of the amplification stage; that's okay, since calibrating the amplifier in steps 1 through 7 just verifies the circuit is behaving properly before calibrating the differential driver.

1. Measure the voltage on pin 10 of the OPA4277 and adjust the VREF pot to get the voltage as close to zero as possible.

2. Apply 0 V to the single-ended input and measure the + differential output with respect to Gnd. You should see 0 V at this point. Otherwise, adjust the offset using the ZERO pot.

3. While still applying 0 V to the single-ended input, measure the − differential output with respect to Gnd. You should see 0 V. Otherwise, adjust the offset using the VREF pot.

4. Change the voltage on the single-ended input to the maximum value you expect (say, 5 V) and measure the + differential output with respect to Gnd. You should see 4.095 V at this point. Otherwise, adjust the gain using the SPAN pot.

5. Repeat steps 2 through 4 until further adjustments are unnecessary. Ideally you're seeing −4.095 V, or something very close, on the − differential output at step 11. If there is any major deviation (for example, more than 0.01 V), the 10-kΩ resistors in the differential driver circuit must have problems.

At this point, there are a couple of problems with the current calibration: first, it outputs negative voltages, which you cannot apply to an ADS1x15 input. Second, the gain is off by a factor of two. The following steps rectify that.

1. Set the voltage on the single-ended input to your maximum voltage (for example, 5 V). Measure the voltage between the + and − terminals on the differential outputs; it should be about 8.191 V. Reduce the gain using the SPAN pot until the output voltage is 4.095 V.

2. Set the voltage on the single-ended input to 0 V. Measure the voltage between the + differential output and Gnd. Adjust the ZERO pot until it reads +2.047 V.

3. Set the voltage on the single-ended input to the maximum expected voltage (for example, 5 V). Measure the voltage between the + differential output and Gnd. Adjust the SPAN pot until the voltage is +4.095 V.

4. Repeat steps 2 and 3 until no further adjustments are needed.

5. Apply the maximum voltage to the single-ended input. Measure the voltage between the − differential output and ground; it should be somewhere near 0 V. Adjust the VREF pot until it's as close as possible to 0 V.

6. Repeat steps 2 through 5 until no further adjustments are necessary.

At this point your circuit should be calibrated for use with an ADS1x15 operating in differential mode. You should be able to input ±5 to the single-ended input and, with appropriate software, read −32768 to +32,767 from the device.

14.3   ADS1x15 Analog-to-Digital Converter Registers

The ADS1x15 devices have five internal registers: the 8-bit pointer register (write only), the 16-bit conversion register (read only), the 16-bit configuration register (read/write), the 16-bit low threshold register, and the 16-bit high threshold register.

The LO 2 bits of the pointer register select one of the other four registers (00: conversion, 01: configuration, 10: low threshold, and 11: high threshold). The HO 6 bits of the pointer register value should always be 0. Pointer register selection always occurs after a start condition and an address byte with the LO bit equal to 0 (a write operation). The next byte after the address transmission is the pointer register value (see Figure 14-2).

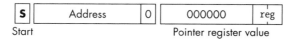

Figure 14-2: Pointer register value follows a write command

When writing to the configuration or threshold registers, you follow the sequence in Figure 14-2 with the 2-byte value to write to the register specified by the reg bits. The HO byte of the 16-bit value follows the pointer register value, and the LO byte follows, usually with an ending stop condition. See Figure 14-3 for details.

Figure 14-3: Writing a value to a 16-bit register

Reading from a 16-bit register is slightly more complex than writing to the register, as it requires sending 2 address bytes—one with the write command and a pointer register value and one with a read command (with an intervening restart condition). Figure 14-4 shows the sequence needed to read 16 bits from a register. Note that the system must send a restart condition between the register pointer value and the second address, and that the second address has the LO bit set to 1 to indicate a read operation.

Figure 14-4: Reading a 16-bit register

The last 2 bytes of the sequence contain the 16-bit value read from the ADC. This consists of the HO byte followed by the LO byte.

14.3.1 The Conversion Register

The conversion register (register pointer value 0) is a read-only register that holds the value of the last analog-to-digital conversion. This is a two's complement signed binary integer in the range of −32768 to +32,767. On the ADS1015 device (which is only a 12-bit ADC), the LO 4 bits of this register always contain 0, meaning the range is actually −32,760 to +32759.

In continuous mode, the ADS1x15 automatically fills this register with the last conversion it makes. In one-shot mode, the ADS1x15 places the last requested conversion into this register. See section 14.3.2.5, "Operational Status Bit," later in this chapter for information about starting a conversion.

14.3.2 The Configuration Register

Most of the activity required to perform an analog-to-digital conversion takes place in the configuration register (register pointer value 1). Table 14-2 catalogs the meanings of the 16 bits in the configuration register.

Table 14-2: Configuration Register Bits

Bit	Read operation	Write operation
0	Read comparator queue state	00: assert ALRT after 1 conversion 01: assert ALRT after 2 conversions 10: assert ALRT after 4 conversions 11: disable comparator
1		
2	Read ALRT latch setting	0: non-latching ALRT; 1: latching ALRT
3	Read ALRT pin polarity	0: active low ALRT; 1: active high ALRT
4	Read comparator mode	Write mode. 0: traditional; 1: windowed
5	Read conversion rate	Set conversion rate (see details below)
6		
7		
8	Read device mode	Set device mode. 1: one shot; 0: continuous
9	Read PGA setting	Set PGA value
10		
11		
12	Read mux selection	Write mux selection
13		
14	Read input control	Set input control. 0: differential; 1: single-ended
15	0: device is busy doing a conversion; 1: device is ready	Writing a 1 to this location begins a conversion from power-down mode

The following subsections go into more detail concerning these register configuration bits.

14.3.2.1 Comparator Control Bits

Bits 0 through 4 in the configuration register control the operation of the comparator on the ADS1x15. These control whether the comparator is active, and they control the ALRT pin polarity and latch, and the type of comparator.

Bits 0 and 1 enable and disable the comparator and control the alert logic. If these bits are 0b11 (the default state on power-up/reset), then the comparator circuitry is disabled. If the comparator control bits are 0b00, 0b01, or 0b10, then the comparator will be enabled and assert the ALRT pin when the conversion value exceeds the threshold register range for one reading, two readings, or four readings, respectively. Increasing the number of readings before asserting ALRT helps filter out noise spikes.

Bit 2 in the configuration register controls the latching mode on the ALRT pin. In the default state (0), the ADS1x15 asserts the ALRT pin only while the last conversion exceeds the threshold range. Should the conversion value drop back below the low threshold range, the IC will deassert the ALRT pin. In the latching mode, once a conversion value is outside the threshold range (for the specified number of conversions), the ALRT pin is latched in the asserted condition. To clear the latch, you have to read the conversion register.

Bit 3 in the configuration register controls the ALRT pin polarity. A 0 in this bit position (default on power-up/reset) sets an active low signal; a 1 in this position sets an active high signal.

Bit 4 sets the traditional or window (range) comparator mode. In the traditional mode, the ADS1x15 compares the last conversion value against the high threshold register (with hysteresis, deasserting the ALRT pin when the input falls below the low threshold value). In the window (range) mode, it compares the last conversion value against the low and high threshold registers and generates an ALRT if the conversion is outside this range.

In addition to the comparator control bits, you also control the comparator using the low and high threshold registers. See the discussion of those registers in section 14.3.4, "The Low and High Threshold Registers," for more details, especially concerning the definition of the ALRT pin as an alert or a ready function.

14.3.2.2 Device Mode Configuration Bit and Conversion Rate

Bit 8 of the configuration register specifies whether the ADS1x15 operates in "one-shot" conversion mode (1, the default on power-up/reset) or in continuous conversion mode (0). In one-shot mode, the ADC will perform a conversion only in response to a command arriving over the I^2C bus (writing a 1 to bit 15 of the configuration register). In continuous mode, the ADC begins a new conversion when the current one completes. Bits 5 through 7 determine the sample frequency. The ADS1015 sample frequencies appear in Table 14-3.

Table 14-3: ADS1015 Sample Frequencies

Configuration bits 5–7	Sample frequency
000	128 sps
001	250 sps
010	490 sps
011	920 sps
100	1600 sps
101	2400 sps
110	3300 sps
111	3300 sps

The ADS1115 sample frequencies appear in Table 14-4. Note that the sample frequencies are different for the two ICs.

Table 14-4: ADS1115 Sample Frequencies

Configuration bits 5–7	Sample frequency
000	8 sps
001	16 sps
010	32 sps
011	64 sps
100	128 sps
101	250 sps
110	475 sps
111	860 sps

If the ALRT pin is programmed as the "ready" signal, then the ADS1x15 will pulse the ALRT (or RDY) pin after each conversion when operating in continuous mode. When operating in one-shot mode, the ADS1x15 will assert the ALRT/RDY pin after the conversion is complete if the COMP_POL bit is set to 0. See section 14.3.3, "The Low and High Threshold Registers," later in this chapter for more on how to set the ALRT pin to act as the alert or ready signal.

14.3.2.3 Programmable Gain Amplifier Control Bits

Bits 9 through 11 in the configuration register specify the gain to apply to the incoming analog signal. Table 14-5 lists the possible gain values and voltage ranges.

Table 14-5: Programmable Gain Amplifier

Config settings	Gain	Input voltage range
000	2/3	±6.144 V
001	1	±4.095 V
010	2	±2.047 V
011	4	±1.023 V
100	8	±0.511 V
101, 110, 111	16	±0.255 V

In no case may the voltage ranges in Table 14-5 exceed Vdd. This means that if you select configuration value 0b000, the input voltage is still limited to 5 V (assuming Vdd is 5 V) even though the range is 0 V to 6.144 V.

In this mode, the maximum value you will read from the conversion registers is about 26,666 rather than 32,767.

Additionally, voltages on input pins must never drop below 0 V. Negative values are valid for differential mode only when the + input is less than the − input; both inputs must be positive with respect to Gnd.

Keep in mind, when you look at Table 14-5, that the voltage ranges are further limited by Vdd, regardless of the PGA setting. For example, if you're running the ADS1x15 at 3.3 V and you've programmed the PGA with 0b001 (±4.095 V), the maximum voltage input will still be 3.3 V. This means that the readings will be in the range of −26399 to +26399, rather than the usual −32768 to +32767.

You'll most often program the PGA just once (I most commonly use 0b001, for the ±4.095-V range). However, if you dynamically modify the PGA during operation—for example, to use a different gain setting for each input channel—this may affect the operation of the comparator circuitry. All input channels share the same analog-to-digital converter circuitry. If you set the comparator threshold(s) for one channel and then switch the input multiplexer to a different channel with a different gain, the comparator will trip at different voltages for the two channels. The moral of the story is that it's generally best to use the same gain settings for all active input channels when working with the comparator circuit.

14.3.2.4 Multiplexer Control Bits

Bits 12 through 13 in the configuration register select the input, and bit 14 controls differential or single-ended mode. If bit 14 is 0 (default on power-up/reset), the ADC operates in differential mode. If bit 14 is 1, the ADC operates in single-ended mode.

Bits 12 through 13 select an appropriate input, or pair of inputs, as shown in Table 14-6.

Table 14-6: Input Multiplexer Selection

Configuration bits 12 and 13	If bit 14 is 0 (differential mode)		If bit 14 is 1 (single-ended mode)
	+ Terminal	− Terminal	+ Terminal (− terminal is Gnd)
00	A0	A1	A0
01	A0	A3	A1
10	A1	A3	A2
11	A2	A3	A3

The peculiar 0b01 and 0b10 settings in differential mode allow you to use up to three differential inputs, if the three inputs (A0, A1, and A2) all share the same – terminal. This usually isn't the case, so differential inputs typically use 0b00 or 0b11 for bits 12 and 13. In single-ended mode (bit 14 = 1), bits 12 and 13 select one of the four single-ended input channels.

14.3.2.5 Operational Status Bit

When reading the configuration register, bits 0 through 14 reflect the last values written to those bits. Bit 15, however, performs different duties on read and write operations.

Reading the configuration returns the current *ready* status in bit 15. If this bit returns 1, the ADS1x15 is not currently performing a conversion, so you can begin a new conversion. If bit 15 returns 0, the ADS1x15 is in the middle of a conversion, and you cannot begin another. Once you begin a conversion in one-shot mode, you can test this bit to determine when that conversion is complete. In continuous mode, you don't really care, as the conversion register contains the value of the last conversion made.

To begin a conversion in one-shot mode, write a 1 to bit 15 in the conversion register. Keep in mind that you must also rewrite the other 15 configuration bits when writing to the configuration register. You typically set up a 16-bit value that defines how you want the conversion to proceed and set bit 15 equal to 1 (to begin the conversion). To write to the configuration register without beginning a new conversion, just put a 0 in bit 15.

Note that you can write a 1 to bit 15 only when operating in one-shot mode, which is also known as *power-down* mode. If the ADS1x15 is currently operating in continuous mode, you must first put it in one-shot mode by writing a 1 to bit 8. You can then programmatically start new conversions by writing a 1 to bit 15.

14.3.3 The Low and High Threshold Registers

The ADS1x15 devices provide two 16-bit threshold registers, low (pointer register value is 0b10) and high (0b11). The ADS1115 allows you to write the full 16 bits to these registers. As the ADS1015 ADCs are 12-bit devices, you should always write 0s into the LO 4 bits of these registers.

When operating as a traditional comparator, the ADS1x15 compares the conversion register against the value in the high threshold register and asserts the ALRT pin if the conversion value is greater than the high threshold. The ADS1x15 uses the low threshold register to determine when to deassert the ALRT signal. When the input conversion value falls below the value in the low threshold, the ADS1x15 deasserts ALRT.

In window comparator mode (range mode), the ADS1x15 asserts the ALRT pin whenever the conversion value is below the low threshold register value or above the high threshold value. If you want to assert the pin while the conversion value is between the two thresholds, you can simply invert the ALRT pin using bit 3 of the configuration register.

In nonlatching mode (see section 14.3.2.1, "Comparator Control Bits," earlier in this chapter), the ADS1x15 will automatically assert and deassert the ALRT pin as the conversion value goes in and out of range. In latching mode, once the IC asserts the ALRT pin, that pin stays active until the software reads the conversion register—that is, assuming the conversion value is back within range at that point.

The threshold registers provide one additional hidden feature: control of the ALRT pin. If the HO bit of the high threshold register is 1 and the HO bit of the low threshold register is 0, then the ADS1x15 outputs the ready condition (configuration register bit 15) on the ALRT pin (which should be called RDY in this configuration). Because the values in the threshold registers are two's complement signed binary integers, this particular situation means that the value in the high threshold register is less than the value in the low threshold register. This is usually an illegal combination; except for this special case, the value in the high threshold must always be greater than the value in the low threshold register.

This concludes the discussion of the internal architecture of the ADS1x15 IC. To program it, however, you'll need some actual hardware you can wire into a circuit containing a controlling CPU. Because of their size, you wouldn't normally try to hook an ADS1x15 directly onto a breadboard. The next section describes the solution to this problem.

14.4 The Adafruit ADS1x15 Breakout Boards

The ADS1x15 ICs are tiny SMDs that are difficult for all but the most experienced of electronic technicians or circuit assembly houses to use. Adafruit solves this issue by putting the IC on a small PCB, a "breakout board" with a set of 0.1-inch headers that make it easy to use this IC as part of some other circuit.

Figure 14-5 shows the Adafruit ADS1115 breakout board. For what it's worth, the ADS1015 board is identical to the ADS1115 board, except for the silkscreen and the actual IC placed on the board.

NOTE *As Adafruit sells breakout boards for the ADS1015 and ADS1115 ADCs, it's not surprising to find that they also provide library code for Arduino and Raspberry Pi systems. See "For More Information" for links to these libraries.*

The ADS1015 and ADS1115 have identical pinouts consisting of 10 holes into which you'd normally solder a 1×10 pin header, as described in Table 14-7.

Figure 14-5: The Adafruit ADS1115 breakout board

Table 14-7: Adafruit ADS1x15 Pinout

Pin (name)	Function
Vdd	Power supply (2 V to 5 V)
Gnd	Digital and analog ground
SCL	I²C clock line
SDA	I²C data line
ADDR	Address selection line
ALRT	Alert (comparator out of range) or conversion complete
A0	Analog input channel 0 (+ differential input 0)
A1	Analog input channel 1 (– differential input 0)
A2	Analog input channel 2 (+ differential input 1)
A3	Analog input channel 3 (– differential input 1)

The Vdd, Gnd, SCL, and SDA pins have the usual connections. However, remember that although the power supply can be in the range of 2 V to 5 V, the analog input pins must never exceed Vdd. If you power the ADS1x15 from 3.3 V, the analog inputs are limited to 3.3 V.

The Adafruit ADS1x15 breakout boards include 10-kΩ pullup resistors on the SCL and SDA lines (to Vdd). While it's convenient to not have to add the pullups yourself, if you connect a large number of such devices (with their own pullups) to the same I²C bus, the parallel resistance might be an issue. You'll have to desolder the SMD chip resistors from the breakout board if this is the case.

The ADDR pin is an input that the ADS1x15 uses to select one of four different I²C addresses. Connecting ADDR to Gnd, Vdd, SDA, or SCL specifies the I²C address as shown in Table 14-8—a particularly clever way to get four separate addresses from a single address pin.

Table 14-8: Address Selection on ADS1x15

ADDR connected to	I²C address
Gnd	0x48
Vdd	0x49
SDA	0x4A
SCL	0x4B

Now refer back to Table 14-7; the ALRT pin serves two purposes on the ADS1x15: when used with the built-in comparator, it can signal when a conversion is out of some programmable range. This pin can also be used to indicate that a conversion is complete—for example, to generate an interrupt, so the CPU doesn't have to constantly poll the device to see when the conversion is done. The ALRT pin is an open-drain output pin. The Adafruit ADS1x15 breakout boards automatically include a pullup resistor on this line so you can treat the ALRT pin as a standard logic output.

The A0, A1, A2, and A3 are the single-ended input pins (the other signal connection goes to Gnd). In differential mode 0b000 (configuration register bits 12 through 14 are 0b000), pins A0 and A1 correspond to channel zero + and – inputs, respectively, and pins A2 and A3 correspond to channel 1 + and – inputs. In differential modes 0b001, 0b010, and 0b011 (bits 12 through 14 in the configuration register), there are three differential inputs using pins (A0, A3), (A1, A3), and (A2, A3), with A3 being the common (–) differential signal.

14.5 An ADS1x15 Programming Example

Basic ADS1x15 programming consists of writing an appropriate configuration value to the configuration register (including a "start conversion" bit in one-shot mode), waiting for the conversion to complete, and then reading the converted value from the conversion register. In a typical system, that's all there is to using the ADS1x15.

As a test, hook up an Adafruit ADS1115 breakout board to an Arduino, as shown in Figure 14-6. You can also use an ADS1015 if you prefer; the code works with either device, and I provide sample output for both devices later in this section. Note that the ADDR line is wired to Gnd; this sets the I²C address to 0x48. Vdd is wired to +5 V on the Arduino. The sample program in this section will read only the A0 input, so connect an appropriate voltage source to the A0 pin (0 V to 4.095 V). For quick tests, I just connected A0 to ground and the 3.3-V supply.

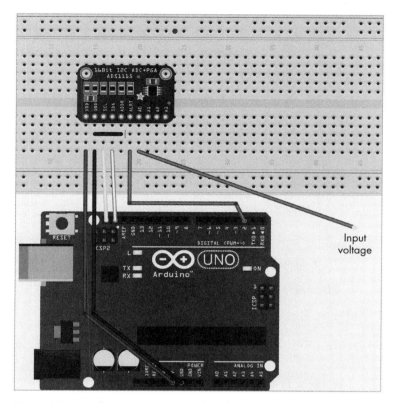

Figure 14-6: Hooking up an ADS1115 breakout board to an Arduino

The program in Listing 14-1 demonstrates reading input channel A0 and displaying the result in the Arduino serial monitor window.

```
// Listing14-1.ino
//
// A simple program that demonstrates
// ADS1115 programming.
//
// This program constantly reads the A0
// ADC channel and displays its values.

#include <Wire.h>
#define ads1115 (0x48) // Connect ADDR to Gnd

// ADS1x15 registers:

#define conversion  (0)
#define config      (1)
#define lowThresh   (2)
#define highThresh  (3)
```

```
// Usual Arduino initialization code:

void setup( void )
{
    Serial.begin( 9600 );
    delay( 1000 );
    Serial.println( "Test reading ADS1115" );
    Wire.begin(); // Initialize I2C library

    adsReset();
}

// adsReset-
//
// Reset the ADS1x115 to a known state:

void adsReset()
{
    // Use the I2C General Call with a reset command:

    Wire.beginTransmission( 0 );
    Wire.write( 6 );
    Wire.endTransmission();
}

// adsWrite-
//
// Writes a 16-bit value to one
// of the ADS1x115 registers:

void adsWrite( int adrs, int reg, int value )
{
    Wire.beginTransmission( adrs );
    Wire.write( reg );                    // Pointer register value

    // Split the output value into 2 bytes
    // and write them to the ADS1x15. Note that
    // this is written immediately after the
    // pointer register byte.

    Wire.write( (value << 8) & 0xff );
    Wire.write( value & 0xff );
    Wire.endTransmission();
}

// adsRead-
//
// Reads a (signed) 16-bit value from one
// of the ADS1x15 registers.

int adsRead( int adrs, int reg )
{
    unsigned char LOByte;
    unsigned char HOByte;
```

```
    Wire.beginTransmission( adrs );
    Wire.write( reg );              // Pointer register value
    Wire.endTransmission( false );  // No stop condition

    // Must send a new start condition and address
    // byte with the LO bit set to 1 in order to
    // the 2 bytes (Wire.requestFrom does this).

    Wire.requestFrom( adrs, 2 );    // Read two bytes from
    HOByte = Wire.read();           // the conversion register
    LOByte = Wire.read();

    // Convert the 2 bytes read from the conversion
    // register to a signed integer and return.

    return (int) ((short) (HOByte << 8) | LOByte);
}

// wait4Ready-
//
// Polls bit 15 of the configuration register ("ready" bit)
// until it contains a 1 (conversion complete).

void wait4Ready( void )
{
  ❶ while( (adsRead( ads1115, config ) & 0x8000) == 0 )
    {
        // Wait for conversion to complete.
    }
}

// Arduino main loop.

void loop( void )
{
    uint16_t startConv;

    // Create value to write to the configuration
    // register that will start a conversion on
    // single-ended input A0:

    startConv =
        ❷ (1) << 15        // Start conversion
    ❸ |   (0b100) << 12   // A0, single-ended
    ❹ |   (0b001) << 9    // PGA = 4.095 V
    ❺ |   (1) << 8        // One-shot mode
    ❻ |   (0b111) << 5    // 860 sps (ADS1115), 3300 (ADS1015)
        |   (0) << 4        // Comparator mode (not used)
        |   (0) << 3        // Comparator polarity (not used)
        |   (0) << 2        // Non-latching (not used)
    ❼ |   (0b11);          // Comparator disabled

    // First, wait until any existing conversion completes:

    wait4Ready();
```

```
    // Start a conversion:

❽ adsWrite( ads1115, config, startConv );

    // Wait for it to complete:

❾ wait4Ready();

    // Read the ADC value:

    int16_t adcValue = adsRead( ads1115, conversion );

    // Display result:

    Serial.print( "ADC: " );
    Serial.println( adcValue );
}
```

For testing purposes, the simplest code will set up the configuration register as follows:

- Program bits 0 to 4 with 0b00011 (disable the comparator) ❼
- Program bits 5 to 7 with 0b111 (860 sps, though this value is irrelevant) ❻
- Program bit 8 with 1 (one-shot mode) ❺
- Program bits 9 to 11 with 0b001 (PGA = 4.095 V range) ❹
- Program bits 12 to 14 with 0b100 (single-ended, select A0) ❸
- Program bit 15 with 1 (start conversion) ❷

After writing this value (0xC3E3) to the configuration register ❽, the ADS1115 will begin converting the voltage appearing on A0 to digital form. The software must wait around 1.2 msec for this conversion to complete before it reads the result from the conversion register. Of course, a software delay of 1.2 msec is completely inappropriate; the right way to wait for the conversion to complete is to test bit 15 of the configuration register (the operational status bit) until it is 1 (❶ and ❾).

When executing the code in Listing 14-1, connecting the A0 line to ground should produce output like this:

```
ADC: -2
ADC: 3
ADC: -1
ADC: -2
ADC: -1
ADC: 1
ADC: -1
ADC: 0
ADC: 0
ADC: 0
ADC: -1
ADC: -1
```

```
ADC: 1
ADC: -2
ADC: 0
ADC: -1
ADC: 0
ADC: -1
```

You can see the tiny amount of noise present during 16-bit conversions (remember, each integer unit represents 0.0000625 V). This particular sequence is very clean indeed, ranging from −2 to +3—a variance of only about 0.00003 V, an artifact of connecting A0 directly to a power supply pin.

This software also works fine with an Adafruit ADS1015 12-bit ADC breakout board. Here's some output from that board:

```
ADC: 0
ADC: 0
ADC: 0
ADC: 0
ADC: 0
ADC: 0
ADC: -16
ADC: 0
ADC: 0
ADC: 16
ADC: 0
ADC: 0
ADC: 0
```

Although the error looks much greater than with the ADS1x15, it's actually better. Remember from "The Conversion Register" earlier in this chapter that the LO 4 bits of the conversion register are always 0 and the 12-bit conversion appears in bits 4 through 15, so what you're seeing in the previous output is an occasional 1-bit error. This is one advantage to using a 12-bit rather than a 16-bit ADC: less noise.

14.6   Improving Polling Performance

The program in Listing 14-1 polled bit 15 of the configuration register until it became 1, indicating the conversion was complete and the ADS1x15 was ready to do another conversion. This might not seem like a big deal, but keep in mind that reading the configuration register requires five I^2C bus transactions: two to set the pointer register value and three to read the actual conversion register. At 100 kHz, this could take longer than 500 μsec—almost half the time of the conversion!

Of course, you could reduce time lost to polling by running the ADS1x15 at a higher clock frequency, but not all SBCs or CPUs support this; some, as you've seen in this book, don't even run at a full 100 kHz. Fortunately, if you have a spare input pin on your SBC, there is a much faster solution: program the ALRT pin as a RDY pin and test for conversion complete by reading that pin.

To program the ALRT pin as RDY, write a 0 to bit 15 of the low threshold register and a 1 to bit 15 of the high threshold register, turn off comparator latching (write a 0 to bit 2 of the configuration register), set the ALRT polarity to 0 (bit 3 of the configuration register), and enable the comparator. This enables reading the RDY status on the ALRT pin. You may have noticed that the ALRT pin in Figure 14-6 is wired to the D2 digital I/O pin on the Arduino. The program in Listing 14-1 ignored pin D2, but the program in Listing 14-2 will use this connection to test for when the conversion is complete.

The program in Listing 14-2 is just a minor modification of the program in Listing 14-1. As such, I won't reprint the repeated portions of Listing 14-1 but will simply highlight the parts of the code that are new. I begin with the usual #define statements at the beginning of the file:

```
// Listing14-2.ino
//
// A simple program that demonstrates
// ADS1115 programming.
//
// This program constantly reads the A0
// ADC channel and displays its values.
// It reads the ALRT/RDY pin to determine
// when the conversion is complete (connect
// ALRT to D2 on Arduino).

  #include <Wire.h>
  #define ads1115 (0x48) // Connect ADDR to Gnd
❶ #define rdy (2)        // RDY is on pin 2
```

The main addition to this section is the definition of the rdy pin ❶.

Next, I turn to the wait4Ready() function, rewritten from the code in Listing 14-1:

```
// Listing14-2.ino (cont.)
//
// wait4Ready-
//
// Polls digital I/O pin 2 to see
// if the conversion is complete.

void wait4Ready( void )
{
❷ while( digitalRead( rdy ) != 0 )
    {
        // Wait for conversion to complete.
    }
}
```

This wait4Ready() function reads the ready status from digital input pin D2 ❷ rather than reading the configuration register (which is slow) and testing bit 15 of that register.

We next turn to the setup() function:

```
// Listing14-2.ino (cont.)

void setup( void )
{
    Serial.begin( 9600 );
    delay( 1000 );
    Serial.println( "Test reading ADS1115" );
    Wire.begin(); // Initialize I2C library
    pinMode( 2, INPUT );

    // Write a 1 to the HO bit of the
    // high threshold register and a 0
    // to the HO bit of the low threshold
    // register to program the ALRT pin
    // to behave as the RDY pin.

    adsReset();
    adsWrite( ads1115, config, 0x43E0 );
 ❸ adsWrite( ads1115, lowThresh, 0x0 );
 ❹ adsWrite( ads1115, highThresh, 0x8000 );
}
```

The setup() function needs to initialize the threshold registers so that the low threshold register has a 0 in its HO bit ❸ and the high threshold register has a 1 in its HO bit ❹. This code also activates the comparator circuit so it can pass the ready status on to the ALRT pin on the ADS1x15.

The final change is to the code that writes to the configuration in the main loop:

```
// Listing14-2.ino (cont.)

void loop( void )
{
    uint16_t startConv;

    // Create value to write to the configuration
    // register that will start a conversion on
    // single-ended input A0:

    startConv =
            (1) << 15        // Start conversion
        |   (0b100) << 12    // A0, single-ended
        |   (0b001) << 9     // PGA = 4.095 V
        |   (1) << 8         // One-shot mode
        |   (0b111) << 5     // 860 sps
        |   (0) << 4         // Comparator mode (not used)
        |   (0) << 3         // Comparator polarity (used)
        |   (0) << 2         // Non-latching (not used)
     ❺ |   (0b00);          // Comparator enabled
```

While the code in Listing 14-1 disables the comparator on each pass of the loop, the code in Listing 14-2 needs to keep the comparator enabled ❺.

These changes to Listing 14-1 produce noticeably faster output. Figure 14-7 shows the output on the ALRT pin (input to the digital I/O D2 pin). When this signal is high, the ADC is busy doing a conversion. When it is low, the ADC is ready to do another conversion. As Figure 14-7 shows, the conversions take slightly more than 1 msec when using a Teensy 3.2 (remember, the ADS1115, on which this was measured, is capable of about 860 sps). The low portion of the oscilloscope trace is the time spent sending the conversion command to the ADS1115 plus outputting data to the Arduino Serial terminal.

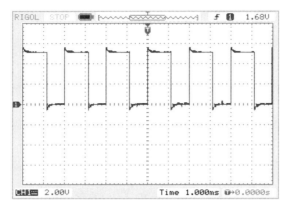

Figure 14-7: Oscilloscope output from Listing 14-2

Remember that I ran the code that produced the output in Figure 14-7 on a 96-MHz Teensy 3.2, not a 16-MHz Arduino Uno Rev3. On an Arduino, the bottom portion of the cycle might be a bit wider.

READING MORE THAN ONE CHANNEL

The programs up to this point have read data only from a single analog input channel (A0). Reading multiple channels is relatively straightforward: simply modify the value in the multiplexer control bits (12 through 14) in the configuration register that the code writes in the main loop. By sequencing values 0b100 through 0b111, you can read all four channels, one channel per loop execution.

Of course, there is only one actual ADC on the ADS1x15. The multiplexer control allows you to select a different input on each conversion, but it will take four separate conversions (and therefore, four times as long) to read all four channels. Obviously, this reduces the maximum sampling frequency for each channel by four.

Using the RDY pin is not the only way to improve A/D conversion performance. The next section looks at another way to speed up the sampling rate.

14.7   Improving Performance Using Continuous Scanning

In Figure 14-7, just a little more than half the execution time is spent doing an analog-to-digital conversion (that is, when the ALRT [RDY] pin is high). Between conversions, there are three activities going on in the main Arduino loop function: writing to the configuration register to start the conversion, reading the conversion value from the ADS1115, and printing the results to the Arduino Serial terminal. Writing the results to the Serial terminal is not a blazing fast process, but writing the configuration register and reading the conversion register require nine I^2C bus transactions—probably around 900 µsec on a 100-kHz bus.

NOTE   *The conversion performance would have been worse had the code that produced the output in Figure 14-7 actually run on a 16-MHz Arduino Uno Rev3 rather than a 96-MHz Teensy 3.2.*

Nothing can be done to improve the performance of reading the conversion register—that's the only way to get data out of the ADS1115. However, you can save the expense of writing the configuration register on each loop (around 400 µsec) by putting the ADS1115 in continuous conversion mode. In this mode, the CPU can request the data from the ADS1115 whenever it wants, without having to check if a conversion is complete; the ADS1115 will always return the value of the last conversion and will automatically update that value as each new conversion takes place. Listing 14-3 provides the code that puts the ADS1115 in continuous conversion mode. Again, I won't reprint any code shared with the previous two listings.

```
// Listing14-3.ino
//
// A simple program that demonstrates
// ADS1115 programming.
//
// This program constantly reads the A0
// ADC channel and displays its values
// using continuous conversion mode.
// It reads the ALRT/RDY pin to determine
// when a new conversion occurs (so it can
// output data to the Serial terminal).
//
// adsReset-
//
// Reset the ADS1x115 to a known state:

void adsReset()
```

```
{
    // Use the I2C General Call with a reset command:

    Wire.beginTransmission( 0 );
    Wire.write( 6 );
    Wire.endTransmission();
}

// wait4Conversion-
//
// Polls digital I/O pin 2 to see if the
// conversion is complete.

void wait4Conversion( void )
{
    // Wait for the falling edge that
    // indicates a conversion has occurred.

  ❶ while( digitalRead( rdy ) == 0 )
    {
        // Wait for conversion to complete.
    }

    // Wait for the rising edge so that
    // the next loop doesn't mistakenly
    // think a new conversion occurred.

  ❷ while( digitalRead( rdy ) == 1 )
    {
        // Wait for conversion to complete.
    }
}
```

The wait4Conversion() function in Listing 14-3 replaces wait4Ready() in the previous two listings. This function waits until the RDY line (digital input D2) goes low ❶, indicating that a conversion has just completed. The ADS1115 will pulse RDY low for slightly less than 10 μsec and then automatically set it high again. This is plenty long enough for the Arduino (or Teensy, in my case) to detect that the conversion has completed. However, the code also has to wait for this line to go back high ❷ so that the loop function won't repeat while the signal is still low and think another conversion has completed.

```
// Listing14-3.ino (cont.)
//
// Usual Arduino initialization code.

void setup( void )
{

    Serial.begin( 9600 );
```

```
        delay( 1000 );
        Serial.println( "Test reading ADS1115" );
        Wire.begin(); // Initialize I2C library
        pinMode( 2, INPUT );

        // Write a 1 to the HO bit of the
        // high threshold register and a 0
        // to the HO bit of the low threshold
        // register to program the ALRT pin
        // to behave as the RDY pin. Also
        // put a 0 in bit 8 to turn on the
        // continuous conversion mode.

        adsReset();
   ❸ adsWrite( ads1115, config, 0x42E0 );
        adsWrite( ads1115, lowThresh, 0x0 );
        adsWrite( ads1115, highThresh, 0x8000 );
    }
```

The only real modification to the setup function from the previous examples is that it programs bit 8 of the configuration register with 0 ❸, putting the device in continuous conversion mode:

```
// Listing14-3.ino (cont.)
//
// Arduino main loop.

void loop( void )
{

    // Wait for a conversion to complete:

 ❹ wait4Conversion();

    // Read the ADC value:

    int16_t adcValue = adsRead( ads1115, conversion );

    // Display result:

    Serial.print( "ADC: " );
    Serial.println( adcValue );
}
```

In the loop() function, the code to write the configuration register is gone. Because the ADS1115 is operating in continuous mode, there is no longer a need to start a new conversion by writing to the configuration register. The wait4Conversion() function ❹ is very fast (it's all digital I/O with no I^{2}C transactions). This leaves only reading the conversion register to slow down the main loop.

Figure 14-8 shows the oscilloscope output for the program in Listing 14-3. The first thing to note is that the time scale is one half that of the previous figure's (500 µsec instead of 1 msec). The period for each pulse is just a little more than 1.2 msec (versus about 2 msec in Figure 14-7), meaning this code runs almost twice as fast as the code in the previous listings.

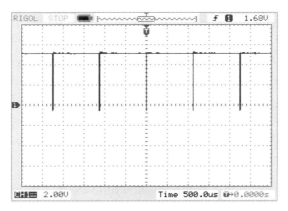

Figure 14-8: Oscilloscope output for Listing 14-3

The only drawback to using the continuous mode to speed up the application is that you can read from only one ADC channel (ignoring the power-saving aspects of one-shot/power-down mode). To change multiplexer channels, you have to write to the configuration register, which eats up all the time saved by removing that call in the first place.

14.8 Interrupts and the ADS1x15

In theory, it's possible to connect the ALRT (RDY) pin to an interrupt input on the Arduino—D2 is an interrupt pin on the Arduino Uno Rev3, for example. Whenever an interrupt occurs (due to a conversion complete or a comparison out-of-range signal), the interrupt service routine can read the data or process the comparison fault and pass that information along to the main program.

In practice, however, using interrupts in Arduino code is dubious at best. I^2C communications, which would have to take place inside the ISR, are extremely slow, and ISRs need to be really fast. Maybe it would work with a high-speed–mode I^2C clock; you'd have to test that and see.

On the other hand, if you are using a multithreaded RTOS with good interrupt support (that is, with an interrupt-driven I^2C library), interrupts become very practical. The ISR would simply signal a thread when a conversion is complete, and that thread could talk to the ADS1115, blocking while I^2C transmissions (and conversion) are taking place. This would consume little CPU time compared to polling and would allow other threads to run with little performance loss.

14.9   Filtering Noise

In the real world—as opposed to the simple test circuits I've used in this chapter, where I've wired an analog input directly to a power supply pin—noise can be a big issue when reading analog signals. Sources of noise include the environment, the circuitry, and the analog sensors themselves. Fortunately, you can digitally filter out some of this noise with some simple software techniques.

One of the most common such techniques is to take several readings—say, three to nine—and take the median of those values. This scheme picks the middle of a bunch of readings and has the advantage of eliminating outlier values. A slightly more efficient technique is to take several readings and compute the arithmetic mean of those values. This is usually faster than computing the median but has the disadvantage of incorporating outliers into the average.

However, both median and mean are based on a fixed set of values, while analog readings tend to be a continuous stream. Therefore, the most appropriate solution is to create a *windowed average*. To do so, maintain a list of the last n readings, where n is the window size, and compute the average based on those values. Each time a new ADC reading comes along, you add it to the window list and throw out the oldest reading from the list.

In relatively noisy environments, I usually use *both* techniques to filter out the noise. I keep the last seven or nine readings from the ADC and compute the median of those values. Then I keep the last 4 to 20 median values (depending on the application) and compute the arithmetic mean of those values. For example, if I'm computing the median of 9 values and the arithmetic mean of 10 values, I'm actually averaging a total of 90 ADC readings at any one given time. In the next section, I'll describe how to do this.

The price of filtering out noise using averaging is that your results will only slowly reflect any sudden changes in the analog readings. For example, if your input voltage suddenly jumps from 0 V to 5 V, it may take several hundred readings before your average shows a solid 5 V.

14.9.1   Computing Means and Medians

Computing the arithmetic mean is relatively simple: just sum all the values and divide by the number of values. Choosing a window size that is a power of two can improve performance, as division by n (normally a slow operation) becomes a simple shift-right operation. Normally, the window size is sufficiently small that summing all the elements in the window is no big deal; however, if you have a large number of items, you can save a small amount of time by subtracting the oldest element in the window and then adding in the latest reading.

The generic algorithm for computing a median is to sort the data and pick the middle element (or take the mean of the middle two elements if there is an even number of elements). The quickselect algorithm does much better (see *https://en.wikipedia.org/wiki/Quickselect*). However, for very small windows (say, three, seven, or nine elements), a brute-force approach is probably the most efficient. For example, the common way to compute the median of three elements is to use code like the following:

```
int medianOfThree( int a, int b, int c )
{
    if( (a > b) != (a > c) )
        return a;
    else if( (b > a) != (b > c) )
        return b;
    else
        return c;
}
```

Code like this is often used to create a pivot element for the quicksort algorithm; see "For More Information" for details.

Here's a generic function that computes the median of an array of any size (not just three elements) and is faster for certain array sizes. You'll normally work with a fixed window size in any given application. Simply pull out the code from the appropriate case in this function to get an algorithm that works for your particular window size.

```
#include <string.h>

#define ever ;;
#define breakif(exp) if (exp) break

// Find the median element of an int16_t array.
//
// This Quickselect routine is based on the algorithm
// described in "Numerical recipes in C," Second Edition,
// Cambridge University Press, 1992, Section 8.5,
// ISBN 0-521-43108-5.
//
// This code was originally written by Nicolas Devillard - 1998
// Public domain.
//
// Code was modified to use macros (straight-line code) for
// arrays with 9 or fewer elements (an optimization).

#define ELEM_SORT(a,b) { if((a)>(b)) ELEM_SWAP( (a), (b) ); }
#define ELEM_SWAP(a,b) { register int16_t t=(a);(a)=(b);(b)=t; }
#define ainReadings_c 32  // Maximum number of readings

int16_t quick_select(int16_t array[ainReadings_c], int n)
{
    int low;
    int high;
    int median;
    int middle;
    int ll;
    int hh;
```

```
// Make temporary copy here because you will modify array.

int16_t arr[ainReadings_c];

// Macros to handle special cases as fast as possible.

switch( n )
{
    case 1:
        return array[0];

    case 2:

        // If just two elements, return their
        // arithmetic mean:

        return (array[0] + array[1]) / 2;

    case 3:
        arr[0] = array[0];
        arr[1] = array[1];
        arr[2] = array[2];

        ELEM_SORT( arr[0], arr[1] );
        ELEM_SORT( arr[1], arr[2] );
        ELEM_SORT( arr[0], arr[1] );
        return(arr[1]) ;

    case 4:
        arr[0] = array[0];
        arr[1] = array[1];
        arr[2] = array[2];
        arr[3] = array[3];

        ELEM_SORT( arr[0], arr[1] );
        ELEM_SORT( arr[2], arr[3] );
        ELEM_SORT( arr[0], arr[2] );
        ELEM_SORT( arr[1], arr[3] );

        // arr[1] and arr[3] may be out of order,
        // but it doesn't matter.

        // Return the mean of the upper and lower medians:

        return( (arr[1] + arr[2]) / 2 );

    case 5:
        arr[0] = array[0];
        arr[1] = array[1];
        arr[2] = array[2];
        arr[3] = array[3];
        arr[4] = array[4];

        ELEM_SORT( arr[0], arr[1] );
        ELEM_SORT( arr[3], arr[4] );
```

```
        ELEM_SORT( arr[0], arr[3] );
        ELEM_SORT( arr[1], arr[4] );
        ELEM_SORT( arr[1], arr[2] );
        ELEM_SORT( arr[2], arr[3] );
        ELEM_SORT( arr[1], arr[2] );
        return( arr[2] );

    case 6:
        arr[0] = array[0];
        arr[1] = array[1];
        arr[2] = array[2];
        arr[3] = array[3];
        arr[4] = array[4];
        arr[5] = array[5];

        ELEM_SORT( arr[1], arr[2] );
        ELEM_SORT( arr[3], arr[4] );
        ELEM_SORT( arr[0], arr[1] );
        ELEM_SORT( arr[2], arr[3] );
        ELEM_SORT( arr[4], arr[5] );
        ELEM_SORT( arr[1], arr[2] );
        ELEM_SORT( arr[3], arr[4] );
        ELEM_SORT( arr[0], arr[1] );
        ELEM_SORT( arr[2], arr[3] );
        ELEM_SORT( arr[4], arr[5] );
        ELEM_SORT( arr[1], arr[2] );
        ELEM_SORT( arr[3], arr[4] );

        // ELEM_SORT( arr[2], arr[3] ) results in lower
        // median in  arr[2] and upper median in  arr[3].
        // "Median" of an even number of elements is the
        // mean of the two middle elements in this code.

        return (  arr[2] +  arr[3] ) / 2;

    case 7:
        arr[0] = array[0];
        arr[1] = array[1];
        arr[2] = array[2];
        arr[3] = array[3];
        arr[4] = array[4];
        arr[5] = array[5];
        arr[6] = array[6];

        ELEM_SORT( arr[0], arr[5] );
        ELEM_SORT( arr[0], arr[3] );
        ELEM_SORT( arr[1], arr[6] );
        ELEM_SORT( arr[2], arr[4] );
        ELEM_SORT( arr[0], arr[1] );
        ELEM_SORT( arr[3], arr[5] );
        ELEM_SORT( arr[2], arr[6] );
        ELEM_SORT( arr[2], arr[3] );
        ELEM_SORT( arr[3], arr[6] );
        ELEM_SORT( arr[4], arr[5] );
```

```
            ELEM_SORT( arr[1], arr[4] );
            ELEM_SORT( arr[1], arr[3] );
            ELEM_SORT( arr[3], arr[4] );
            return ( arr[3] );

    case 8:
            arr[0] = array[0];
            arr[1] = array[1];
            arr[2] = array[2];
            arr[3] = array[3];
            arr[4] = array[4];
            arr[5] = array[5];
            arr[6] = array[6];
            arr[7] = array[7];

            // No convenient macro to get the median
            // of eight elements, so resorted to an
            // ugly insertion sort here:

            ELEM_SORT( arr[0], arr[1] );
            ELEM_SORT( arr[6], arr[7] );
            ELEM_SORT( arr[1], arr[2] );
            ELEM_SORT( arr[5], arr[6] );
            ELEM_SORT( arr[2], arr[3] );
            ELEM_SORT( arr[4], arr[5] );
            ELEM_SORT( arr[3], arr[4] );
            ELEM_SORT( arr[4], arr[5] );
            ELEM_SORT( arr[2], arr[3] );
            ELEM_SORT( arr[5], arr[6] );
            ELEM_SORT( arr[1], arr[2] );
            ELEM_SORT( arr[6], arr[7] );
            ELEM_SORT( arr[0], arr[1] );
            ELEM_SORT( arr[1], arr[2] );
            ELEM_SORT( arr[5], arr[6] );
            ELEM_SORT( arr[2], arr[3] );
            ELEM_SORT( arr[4], arr[5] );
            ELEM_SORT( arr[3], arr[4] );
            ELEM_SORT( arr[4], arr[5] );
            ELEM_SORT( arr[2], arr[3] );
            ELEM_SORT( arr[5], arr[6] );
            ELEM_SORT( arr[1], arr[2] );
            ELEM_SORT( arr[2], arr[3] );
            ELEM_SORT( arr[4], arr[5] );
            ELEM_SORT( arr[3], arr[4] );
            ELEM_SORT( arr[2], arr[3] );
            return( (arr[3] + arr[4]) / 2);

    case 9:
            arr[0] = array[0];
            arr[1] = array[1];
            arr[2] = array[2];
            arr[3] = array[3];
            arr[4] = array[4];
            arr[5] = array[5];
```

```
        arr[6] = array[6];
        arr[7] = array[7];
        arr[8] = array[8];

        ELEM_SORT( arr[1], arr[2] );
        ELEM_SORT( arr[4], arr[5] );
        ELEM_SORT( arr[7], arr[8] );
        ELEM_SORT( arr[0], arr[1] );
        ELEM_SORT( arr[3], arr[4] );
        ELEM_SORT( arr[6], arr[7] );
        ELEM_SORT( arr[1], arr[2] );
        ELEM_SORT( arr[4], arr[5] );
        ELEM_SORT( arr[7], arr[8] );
        ELEM_SORT( arr[0], arr[3] );
        ELEM_SORT( arr[5], arr[8] );
        ELEM_SORT( arr[4], arr[7] );
        ELEM_SORT( arr[3], arr[6] );
        ELEM_SORT( arr[1], arr[4] );
        ELEM_SORT( arr[2], arr[5] );
        ELEM_SORT( arr[4], arr[7] );
        ELEM_SORT( arr[4], arr[2] );
        ELEM_SORT( arr[6], arr[4] );
        ELEM_SORT( arr[4], arr[2] );
        return( arr[4]) ;

// Handle the general case (not one of the above) here:

default:

    // The quick_select algorithm modifies the array.
    // Therefore, you need to make a copy of it prior
    // to use.

    memcpy( arr, array, n*sizeof( int16_t ) );
    low = 0;
    high = n-1;
    median = (low + high) / 2;
    for( ever )
    {
        if (high <= low)      // One element only
        {
            return arr[median];
        } // endif

        if (high == low + 1) // Two elements only
        {
            return (arr[low] + arr[high]) / 2;
        } // endif

        // Find median of low, middle, and high items;
        // swap into position (low).

        middle = (low + high) / 2;
        if (arr[middle] > arr[high])
```

```
                    {
                        ELEM_SWAP(arr[middle], arr[high]);
                    } // endif
                    if (arr[low] > arr[high])
                    {
                        ELEM_SWAP(arr[low], arr[high])
                    } // endif
                    if (arr[middle] > arr[low])
                    {
                        ELEM_SWAP(arr[middle], arr[low]);
                    } // endif

                    // Swap low item (now in position middle)
                    // into position (low+1).

                    ELEM_SWAP(arr[middle], arr[low+1]) ;

                    // Nibble from each end towards middle,
                    // swapping items when stuck.

                    ll = low + 1;
                    hh = high;
                    for( ever )
                    {
                        do ll++; while (arr[low] > arr[ll]);
                        do hh--; while (arr[hh]  > arr[low]);

                        breakif (hh < ll);

                        ELEM_SWAP(arr[ll], arr[hh]);
                    } // endfor

                    // Swap middle item (in position low) back
                    // into correct position.

                    ELEM_SWAP(arr[low], arr[hh]);

                    // Reset active partition.

                    if (hh <= median)
                    {
                        low = ll;
                    } // endif
                    if (hh >= median)
                    high = hh - 1;

            } // endfor
        } // end switch
} // quick_select

#undef ELEM_SWAP
```

Insertion into an already sorted list takes time equal to O(lg n), where n is the number of elements in the list. If you keep a sorted list of the last n readings, you can compute the median more efficiently (though removing the oldest element might be tricky). However, this is a book on I^{2}C programming, not algorithm development, so I will leave further optimizations to interested readers.

14.10 Chapter Summary

This chapter covered the programming and use of the ADS1015 and ADS1115 analog-to-digital converters. It began with a discussion of the specifications and features of generic ADCs with some specific features of the ADS1x15 devices to provide an appropriate background for the discussion in this chapter.

Because most ADCs have a limited range of voltage inputs they can process, you will often need to add additional analog circuity to *condition* real-world signals, that is, convert the incoming signal to something that is appropriate for the ADC. Because the ADS1x15 ICs are limited to the (somewhat) unusual range of 0 V to 4.095 V (in full-range mode), this chapter provided an opamp circuit that will convert voltages within the range of ±10 V to a range acceptable to the ADS1x15 ICs.

After discussing analog conditioning, this chapter then did a deep dive into the registers present on the ADS1x15 devices and how to program them via the I^{2}C bus. The chapter described all the various bits in the registers and how to initialize and use the ADS1x15.

Because the ADS1x15 parts are surface-mount devices, they're a bit difficult to wire onto a typical prototyping breadboard. So this chapter briefly described the Adafruit breakout boards for the ADS1015 and ADS1115 ICs. Adafruit is also kind enough to provide sample library code for Arduino and Raspberry Pi systems, for which this chapter provided links.

Although you can use the Adafruit libraries to read analog data using the ADS1x15 devices, the goal of this chapter was to teach you how to program the ADS1x15 parts directly. Therefore, this chapter also provided sample programs that program the chips directly and obtain the analog data. It also discussed how to improve the performance of the (rather slow) ADC parts, and it briefly touched on using interrupts with the ADS1x15.

This chapter concluded by pointing out that ADC inputs tend to have a bit of noise associated with them. It then described a filtering algorithm (using arithmetic mean and median averages) to produce a quieter input.

FOR MORE INFORMATION

ADS1015 datasheet: *https://cdn-shop.adafruit.com/datasheets/ads1015.pdf*

ADS1115 datasheet: *https://cdn-shop.adafruit.com/datasheets/ads1115.pdf*

ADS1x15 information on the web: *https://thecavepearlproject.org/2020/05/21/ using-the-ads1115-in-continuous-mode-for-burst-sampling*

ADS1x15 Arduino library code:

    Adafruit GitHub site: *https://github.com/adafruit/Adafruit_ADS1X15*

    Another GitHub site: *https://github.com/addicore/ADS1115*

    Adafruit documentation: *https://learn.adafruit.com/adafruit-4-channel -adc-breakouts/arduino-code*

    Original library: *https://github.com/jrowberg/i2cdevlib/blob/master/Arduino/ ADS1115/ADS1115.cpp*

    Python versions: *https://github.com/adafruit/Adafruit_CircuitPython_ADS1x15*

ADS1x15 Raspberry Pi library code:

    University of Cambridge code: *http://openlabtools.eng.cam.ac.uk/Resources/ Datalog/RPi_ADS1115*

    Adafruit GitHub site: *https://github.com/hallgrimur1471/Adafruit_ADS1X15_RPi*

Adafruit breakout boards:

    Adafruit ADS1015: *https://www.adafruit.com/product/1083*

    Adafruit ADS1115: *https://www.adafruit.com/product/1085*

    Computing medians: *https://rcoh.me/posts/linear-time-median-finding*

    More on medians: *https://stackoverflow.com/questions/7559608/ median-of-three-values-strategy*

15

THE MCP4725 DIGITAL-TO-ANALOG CONVERTER

Chapter 14 described an ADC, the ADS1x15. This chapter describes the converse function: the DAC. Although DACs appear less frequently in systems than ADCs, understanding how to program them is still essential. This chapter describes the MCP4725 DAC used in software examples throughout this book, filling in several details that were unnecessary for coding examples up to this point.

The MCP4725 DAC is a common device for which both Adafruit and SparkFun produce breakout boards. It is a single 12-bit converter, translating integers in the range of 0 to 4095 to a voltage between 0 V and Vdd, the power supply pin on the DAC.

This DAC works with a power supply ranging from 2.7 V to 5.5 V. That means that its output will also be in this range. With a 3.3-V power supply, this corresponds to 0.81 mV per unit; with a 5-V power supply, this is 1.22 mV per unit.

If you need to produce some other voltage range, you can always take the output from this DAC and feed it into an opamp circuit, as in Figure 15-1. That circuit will translate the output from the DAC to any voltage in the range ±10 V (adjustable).

Since the majority of this book has used the MCP4725 in its example code, I'll spare you the redundancy of providing new demonstrations here. Check out Listings 8-2 or 8-3 in Chapter 8 to review some earlier examples.

15.1 MCP4275 Overview

The MCP4725 supports a single address pin allowing you to select one of two addresses. Internally, the MCP4725 actually supports 3 address bits; however, 2 of those bits are hard-coded during manufacturing. You can order up to four different parts with base address 0x60, 0x62, 0x64, or 0x66. The address pin on the MCP4725 allows further differentiation between addresses 0x60 and 0x61, 0x62 and 0x63, 0x64 and 0x65, and 0x66 and 0x67.

NOTE *Adafruit's MCP4725 breakout boards come preprogrammed for addresses 0x62 and 0x63. SparkFun's breakout boards come preprogrammed for addresses 0x60 and 0x61. If you purchase a set of boards from SparkFun and Adafruit, you can put four of these breakout boards on the same I^2C bus.*

The MCP4725 includes an on-board, 14-bit EEPROM from which it loads a power-down mode and initial output setting on power-up/reset. This allows you to force the DAC output to a particular voltage on startup. To see why the default shouldn't just be 0 V, imagine you're driving an opamp circuit like that in Figure 15-1 (copied from Figure 14-1) calibrated to produce an output of –10 V to +10 V based on an input of 0 V to 5 V. This means the DAC would have to output +2.5 V to yield 0 V on the opamp circuit's output, which would be the appropriate power-up reset voltage. Of course, another purpose for the EEPROM is to allow a system to restore the DAC voltage to the last power-down value—so, for example, it would disable DAC outputs on startup.

The MCP4725 is capable of running at standard speed (100 kHz), fast speed (400 kHz), or high speed (up to 3.4 MHz). If your CPU or SBC supports high-speed operation, this will allow you to update waveforms at nearly 200 kHz.

The MCP4725 is easy to program, which is why this book has used it in most of the generic examples. There are three basic command formats:

- A Fast Write command with three bus transactions (extensible)
- A Write command with four bus transactions (extensible)
- A Read command with six bus transactions

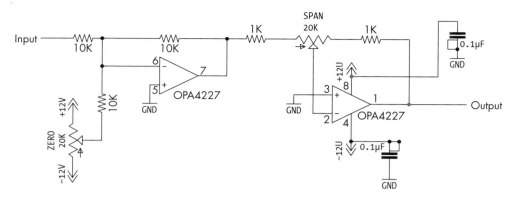

Figure 15-1: Opamp circuit providing span (gain) and zero (offset) capabilities

Write commands, as usual, begin with a start condition and an I^2C address byte with the LO bit containing 0. The byte following the address contains a command in the HO 2 or 3 bits (see Figure 15-2).

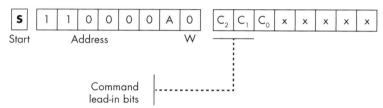

Figure 15-2: First 2 bytes of a Write command

Table 15-1 lists the commands to which the MCP4725 responds.

Table 15-1: MCP4725 Commands

$C_2 C_1 C_0$	Command
00x*	Fast Write command
010	Write DAC register
011	Write DAC and EEPROM
1xx	Reserved for future use

*x/xx = don't care

If C_2 and C_1 in Table 15-1 are both 0 (the Fast Write command), then C_0 is used as one of the power-down bits. I'll explain this further in the next section.

There is only one Read command. Sending an address byte with the LO bit containing 1 invokes the Read command (see section 15.5, "The Read Command," later in this chapter).

15.2 The Fast Write Command

Since writing a value to the DAC register is the most common operation on the MCP4725, the IC supports a command that lets you write a new DAC value with as few as three I²C bus transactions (see Figure 15-3). The second byte of the transaction contains three pieces of information: the command (0b00) in the HO 2 bits, a power-down select code in bits 4 and 5 (see section 15.4, "Power-Down Modes," later in this chapter), and the HO 4 bits of the 12-bit DAC value. The third byte contains the LO 8 bits of the DAC value.

As you can see in Figure 15-3, the DAC value is an unsigned 12-bit binary number. 0xFFF produces the largest voltage from the DAC (Vdd), and 0x000 produces 0 V.

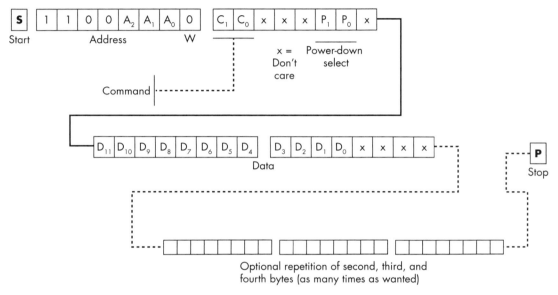

Figure 15-3: Fast Write command format

As Figure 15-3 shows, you can send a sequence of commands to the DAC register with the Fast Write command. You can specify an arbitrary number of pairs of 16-bit values between the first three transactions and the stop condition (though many libraries limit the number of bytes you can write at a time to the I²C bus; the Arduino libraries, for example, limit this to about 32 bytes). This allows you to create a faster waveform by writing two words per voltage change rather than three words, though there might be an occasional blip when you're forced to send a new start condition along with a new address byte.

15.3 The Write Command

The standard MCP4725 Write command has two forms: write DAC register (a long form of the Fast Write command, with $C_2C_1C_0 = $ 0b010) and write

DAC register and EEPROM ($C_2C_1C_0$ = 0b011). This form requires a minimum of 4 bytes to do its job, one more than the Fast Write command (see Figure 15-4).

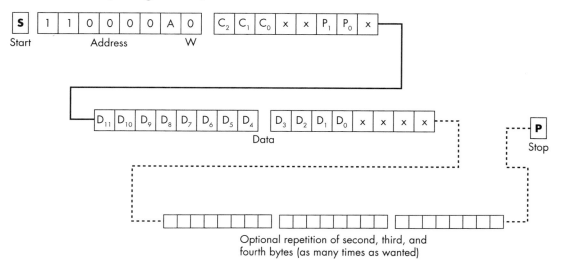

Figure 15-4: Write command format

For the most part, you wouldn't use the standard Write command to write data to the DAC register, as it's always quicker to do so with the Fast Write command. The only argument for using this command to write DAC data is that the data format is different: it conveniently places the data in the HO 12 bits of the 2 bytes, which is compatible with the 12-bit ADS1015 ADC, for example. However, given the extra cost of an I^2C bus transaction, it's far more efficient to shift the data into the correct location for the Fast Write operation.

The main reason for this command (arguably the only reason) is that you can use it to program the EEPROM data on the MCP4725. This allows you to set the power-on/reset voltage when the system first comes up. The EEPROM holds 12 data bits plus 2 power-down mode bits.

Note that it takes around 50 msec to program the EEPROM. During this time, the MCP4725 will ignore any new Write commands. You can determine when the EEPROM write operation is complete by polling the busy bit in the status register (see section 15.5, "The Read Command").

The EEPROM has a life of about one million write cycles. While this is probably more than the average designer will need, constantly writing to the EEPROM will wear it out. In general, write to the EEPROM only during explicit initialization or when powering off your system. If you do the latter, the DAC will come up at the last output voltage when power comes back on.

15.4 Power-Down Modes

The P_1 and P_0 bits allow you to place the MCP4725 in a special power-down mode or normal mode. Table 15-2 shows what these bits accomplish.

Table 15-2: Power-Down Bits

P_1P_0	DAC output	Pull-down resistor
00	Enabled	None
01	Off	1 kΩ
10	Off	100 kΩ
11	Off	500 kΩ

During normal operation, when you're expecting the DAC to produce an output voltage, you'd program these 2 bits with 0b00. If you're not using the DAC output, you can program these bits with 0b01, 0b10, or 0b11; in all three cases, this disconnects the DAC output from the V_{out} pin on the IC and break-out board. These power-down values also connect a pull-down resistor to the V_{out} pin so that it outputs 0 V to the outside world rather than floating, which often generates noise. The amount of pull-down to use varies based on the circuitry that follows the DAC. Generally, the lower the resistance, the more noise immunity you will have, though lower resistances can create impedance problems too. The correct choice depends on your circuit design.

As the name suggests, power-down modes exist to reduce power consumption in very low-power environments. If you are not concerned about power usage, leave the device in normal mode.

15.5 The Read Command

A DAC is intrinsically an output-only device, so reading DACs isn't common. You'll read data from the MCP4725 in just four cases:

- To determine the last value you (or some other thread) wrote to the DAC register
- To determine the last value written to the MCP4725's EEPROM
- To determine when the MCP4725 has finished its power-on/reset cycle so you can start sending Write commands to it
- To read the status of the busy bit to determine when the MCP4725 is done writing data to the EEPROM

As shown in Figure 15-5, the Read command begins with the usual start condition and an address byte whose LO bit contains a 1. After the controller places this command on the bus, the MCP4725 responds with a sequence of 5 bytes. The first byte is a status byte describing the system state and power-down settings. The next 2 bytes contain the current DAC register data (appearing in the HO 12 bits of these 2 bytes). The last 2 bytes contain the EEPROM data (power-down bits and power-on/reset DAC register value). You can see that the DAC register data appears in different locations in the second and third, and fourth and fifth bytes received.

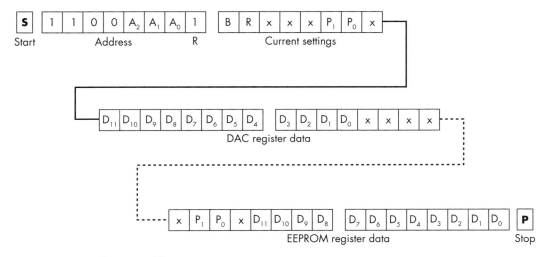

Figure 15-5: Read command format

The HO bit of the settings byte is the RDY (BUSY) bit. This bit is 0 while the MCP4725 is busy writing data to the EEPROM. The DAC will not accept a Write command while this bit is low. After writing data to the EEPROM, you should continuously loop, testing this bit until it comes back with a 1.

Bit 6 of the current settings is the power-on reset bit. This bit will contain a 0 while the system is busy resetting, either from power on or from a general call reset function. Don't execute any Write commands during the reset operation.

Bits 1 and 2 of the current settings byte provide the current power-down settings. This is different from those same 2 bits in the EEPROM register data bytes, which specify what the power-down bits will be initialized with during a power-on/reset operation.

15.6   Chapter Summary

This chapter described the use of the MCP4725 digital-to-analog converter. Of course, this should be familiar to you by now, as it has been the I^2C peripheral of choice for most of the examples in this book.

This chapter began by filling in details on the MCP4725 that haven't been present in the examples throughout the book. It provided an overview of the device and then described the Fast Write and standard Write commands as well as writing to the on-board EEPROM. Then it discussed the power-down modes. Finally, this chapter discussed the Read command, used to read the contents of the on-chip EEPROM and the current DAC settings and to test the DAC busy bit.

FOR MORE INFORMATION

MCP4725 datasheet: *https://cdn.sparkfun.com/datasheets/BreakoutBoards/MCP4725_2009.pdf*

SparkFun MCP4725 breakout board: *https://www.sparkfun.com/products/12918*

Adafruit MCP4725 breakout board: *https://www.adafruit.com/product/935*

16

BARE-METAL PERIPHERAL PROGRAMMING

Chapter 11 described how to program an
I²C controller device at the register level.
This chapter provides the complement to
that information, showing how to program an
MCU as an I²C peripheral at the machine register
level, allowing you to create your own I²C peripherals.
To do so, it explores a fairly comprehensive example
of such programming running on the ATtiny84 MCU, a
SparkFun Atto84 board.

Creating a software-based (bit-banging) I²C peripheral on such an MCU
as simple and slow as the ATtiny84 is next to impossible (see Chapter 3,
which punted on this task). Fortunately, the ATtiny84 provides hardware

support that enables the peripheral programming covered in this chapter, fulfilling the promise in Chapter 3 to provide support for an I^2C peripheral on the ATtiny84.

16.1   The ATtiny as an I^2C Peripheral

The ATtiny84—and, in fact, most of the members of the Atmel ATtiny family—provides a couple of pieces of hardware that dramatically reduce the burden on software when processing I^2C bus transactions. The first and arguably most important is the *Universal Serial Interface (USI)*, a generic shift register than can handle up to 8 data bits before overflowing (though it can be programmed for fewer bits). On the ATtiny84, you can use the USI port to implement I^2C, SPI, serial, USB, and other types of communication (hence the word *Universal* in its name).

You can either program the USI to accept data from an external pin and make that serial data available as an 8-bit byte (serial to parallel mode) or use the USI to accept an 8-bit data value and shift it out serially on some pin. By connecting the input and output on the USI to the SDA pin, you can enable the USI to receive data from the I^2C bus or transmit data onto the I^2C bus. You can also select the USI's clock source, using either an internal timer or an external pin. This is useful for I^2C operation—if you choose the external option and use the SCL pin at the clock source, you can shift data into the USI synchronized to the SCL clock signal.

Beyond the USI, the ATtiny84 also provides a start condition detector and a shift-register overflow interrupt that allow you to quickly handle important I^2C conditions that are difficult to manage on an 8-MHz CPU's software.

The USI and other support hardware are not a true I^2C interface; indeed, Atmel often refers to this as the two-wire interface, since they don't fully support the I^2C standard. For example, the USI does not support glitch filtering or slew rate control. You'll have to live with other compromises as well (such as having to do considerable work in software), because the USI was not designed specifically for I^2C communications. It's a jack of all trades, master of none.

The information in this chapter comes from two main sources. The first is the Atmel AVR312 application note, "Using the USI Module as a I^2C Slave," which describes how to implement I^2C communication using the USI. The second and biggest source is the TinyWire library (see "For More Information" at the end of this chapter). This site lists many contributors, including BroHogan, Don Blake, Jochen Toppe, and Suovula; see the source code for complete details.

This chapter will not repeat the discussion of the ATtiny84 MCU registers appearing in Chapter 11. Please refer to section 11.2, "ATtiny Controller Programming," in Chapter 11 for information concerning the registers and the USI.

16.2   Introducing the Memory Peripheral

With a generic microcontroller like the ATtiny84, you can create a wide variety of different peripheral lines. For example, you could easily use the device to build a small port expander or ADC, given the on-board digital I/O and analog input pins. Alternatively, you could create something fancier like a NeoPixel driver (see "For More Information") or just about anything else you could connect to an Atto84 (minus two pins, needed for the SDA and SCL lines).

   This chapter will show you how to create a simple 4-byte memory peripheral, something you probably won't have any real-world use for. However, working with this almost trivial device has some advantages:

- Because it's simple, it's easy to understand. You won't waste time trying to figure out how the device works in addition to the intended challenge: learning how to create an I^2C peripheral device.

- It reduces the amount of code you have to read (and the number of pages in this book you need to pay for).

- It provides a framework for creating more complex devices: you can easily strip out the trivial memory device code and insert code for your own real-world device.

   This memory device supports four memory locations. You can read and write any number of these locations with a single operation. You can also specify a starting offset into the array; if the length you specify would go beyond the end of the array, the index simply wraps back around to the beginning.

   The I^2C write command takes the form shown in Figure 16-1.

Start   Address = 0x20   Command   0 to 4 data bytes   Stop

Figure 16-1: Peripheral write command

The write command actually serves two purposes: as you would expect by its name, it allows you to write data to the four memory locations (registers). It also lets you specify the memory address (register number) from which subsequent read commands will retrieve their data along with the amount of data to fetch.

Read commands take the form shown in Figure 16-2.

Start   Address = 0x20   0 to 4 data bytes   Stop

Figure 16-2: Peripheral read command

Notice that a command byte immediately follows the I^2C address byte in an I^2C write transaction. The LO 3 bits (sss) specify a data transfer length that must be in the range 0 to 4; larger values are clipped to 4. Bits 3 and 4 (rr) specify the starting offset into the register array (the register number). Bit 5 (d) specifies a data direction: a 0 means that the rrsss bits apply to the data that immediately follow the command byte, which will be written to the register, while a 1 tells the peripheral to ignore any further data (until a stop condition comes along) and use the rrsss bits for the next I^2C read operation.

Consider the following I^2C bus sequences:

```
40 04 01 02 03 04
40 24
41 ww xx yy zz
```

The first byte of the first line is an I^2C write operation to the device at address 0x20 (the memory peripheral). The command byte specifies d = 0 (memory write), rr = 0, and sss = 4. This writes the following 4 bytes (1, 2, 3, and 4) to memory locations 0 through 3.

The second line is also an I^2C write operation. The command byte specifies d = 1 (memory read), rr = 0, and sss = 4. When the d bit is 0, there is no data payload after the command byte. This write operation appears to be specifying a memory read operation, which might seem odd; in reality, however, it's just setting the peripheral's read parameter registers in preparation for a data read.

The third line in this example is an I^2C read operation (LO bit of the address byte contains 1). Immediately after the controller puts this address byte on the bus, the peripheral responds by returning 4 bytes (the number of bytes specified by the previous write command on line two). In this case, *ww*, *xx*, *yy*, and *zz* will actually be 01, 02, 03, and 04, as the command on the first line previously wrote those values to the registers.

This memory peripheral has some additional semantics, but you should now understand the core of what is happening in the code. I'll refer you to the source code for more specific issues, such as address wraparound, multiple read operations, and so on.

16.3 The Memory Peripheral Software Architecture

The memory peripheral software has four main components:

- Initialization code
- Interrupt service routines
- Callbacks to the main program (from the ISRs)
- The main loop

The program is broken up into two pieces: the main file containing the Arduino setup() and loop() functions, as well as the callback functions, and a second file containing the library code that handles I^{2}C operations—specifically, the ISRs and utility functions (which the following paragraphs briefly describe).

The setup() function calls the ISR library initialization function and sets up pointer addresses to the callback functions. The main Arduino loop is empty (the CPU just idly spins when interrupt processing isn't happening) because the ISRs handle all the work. In a more complex peripheral design, you'd probably handle background activities in the main loop.

There are three callback functions in this program, which the ISRs call in three situations:

- Before transmitting any data from the peripheral to the controller in response to an I^{2}C read request
- After transmitting the data from the peripheral to the controller in response to an I^{2}C read request, when an ACK or a NAK is expected from the controller
- Upon receiving data from the controller in response to an I^{2}C write request

These callbacks are generally responsible for supplying data to send to the controller (for an I^{2}C read operation) or dealing with data arriving from a controller (for an I^{2}C write operation).

The two main ISRs in the system handle two events: the presence of a start condition and the completion of a data byte transaction (receipt or transmission) on the I^{2}C bus. Because these events happen infrequently and don't demand too much processor time, I^{2}C transactions don't swamp the CPU as they did in the bit-banging approach (see Chapter 3 for the bit-banging approach).

16.3.1 The Main File

This section walks through *attiny84_Periph.ino*, the main program for the memory peripheral device. Because of the size and complexity of this source file, I will break it up into pieces and describe each piece separately.

The first section covers the comments and #include statements you find in a typical C or C++ program:

```
// attiny84_Periph.ino
//
// Implements a simple I2C peripheral
// running on a SparkFun Atto84 (ATtiny84).
//
// I2C protocol for this device:
//
// For I2C write operations:
//
//   |adrs+W| cmd | optional Data |
//
//   cmd:
//       00drrsss
//
// where d is 0 for write operation and 1 for read,
// rr specifies a "register number" (which is an index
// into "i2c_regs" array below), and sss is a size (0-4).
//
// For write operations (d = 0) then, there will be sss
// additional bytes (max 4) following the cmd byte.
// These bytes will be written to i2c_regs starting
// at offset rr (wrapping around to the beginning
// of the array if sss+rr >= 4).
//
// For read operations (d = 1), any additional data beyond
// the cmd byte is ignored (up to the stop condition).
//
// For I2C read operations:
//
//   |adrs+R| Data |
//
// where "Data" is the number of bytes specified by the
// last I2C write operation with d = 1 (number of bytes will
// be sss). Data transferred is from i2c_regs starting at
// location rr (from the last write operation).
//
// Consecutive I2C read operations, without intervening
// writes, will read the same locations from the registers.

#define I2C_PERIPH_ADDRESS 0x20 // The 7-bit address

#define __AVR_ATtiny84__
```

```
extern "C" {
  #include <inttypes.h>
  #include "usiI2CPeriph.h"
  #include <avr/interrupt.h>
  }

#include "Arduino.h"
```

Next, the memory peripheral program stores the 4 bytes in the `i2c_regs` variable:

```
// attiny84_Periph.ino (cont.)
//
// 4-byte R/W register area
// for this sample program:

volatile uint8_t i2c_regs[4] =
{
    0xDE,
    0xAD,
    0xBE,
    0xEF,
};

// Tracks the current register pointer position
// for read and write operations.
//
// *_position holds the index into i2c_regs
// where I2C reads and writes will begin.
//
// *size holds the number of bytes for
// the read/write operation.

volatile byte reg_position;    // For writes
volatile byte size;            // For writes

volatile size_t read_position; // For reads
volatile size_t read_size;     // For reads

const byte reg_size = sizeof( i2c_regs );

// Command byte bits:

#define cmdSizeMask (0b000111)
#define cmdRegMask  (0b011000)
#define cmdDirMask  (0b100000)
```

This section of the program also contains the global variables that track the rr and sss values in the last command byte. There are two sets of these variables—one for memory read operations (d = 1) and one for memory write operations (d = 0). This section also includes some defines for command bit masks.

The next section begins the callback routines. The interrupt service routines call the requestHandledEvent() function once it's done transmitting a byte to the controller in response to an I^{2}C read command:

```
// attiny84_Periph.ino (cont.)
//
// requestHandledEvent-
//
// Called after data has been shipped
// to the controller.

void requestHandledEvent()
{
}
```

At this point, the code expects an ACK or a NAK from the controller. Normally, this function would handle cleanup (such as clearing buffers, turning off electronic signals, and so on). However, since the memory peripheral requires no cleanup, this function simply returns. For this project, you technically could have skipped initializing the pointer to this function, since the library's default condition is to do nothing; I've included it just so you're aware of its presence in the system.

Next comes the requestEvent() callback function. The ISRs call this function when an I^{2}C read command has arrived, before actually transmitting any data to the controller.

```
// attiny84_Periph.ino (cont.)
//
// requestEvent-
//
// Called before data has been shipped
// to the controller.

void requestEvent()
{
        for( size_t i=0; i < read_size; ++i )
        {
            size_t index = (read_position+i) %  reg_size;
            usiI2CTransmitByte( i2c_regs[index] );
        }
}
```

In theory, you could use this function to initialize the output stream with the data that the ISRs will transmit to the controller, but this code uses usiI2CTransmitByte() for that purpose. Like the Arduino Wire.write() function, requestEvent() doesn't actually transmit the data; the function just appends it to an internal buffer. The ISRs will handle the actual data transmission later. In this source code, this buffer has a limited length of 16 bytes. If you attempt to insert more than 16 bytes into the buffer, the code will block until space becomes available. For the memory peripheral device, requestEvent() just fetches the number of bytes specified by the read_size variable (filled in by the sss field of the command byte from the previous write operation), starting at the offset specified by the read_position global (from the rr field).

Next, the callback function receiveEvent() handles the data stream received from the controller during an I^{2}C write operation.

```
// attiny84_Periph.ino (cont.)
//
// receiveEvent-
//
// Called when data has been received
// from the controller.
//
// Parse the received data and set up the
// position and size variables as needed.
// If optional data arrives, store it into
// the i2c_regs array.
//
// rcvCnt parameter specifies the
// number of bytes received.

void receiveEvent( uint8_t rcvCnt )
{
    byte cmd;

    // Punt if controller sent too
    // much data...

    if( rcvCnt > I2C_RX_BUFFER_SIZE )
    {
        return;
    }

    // ...or too little:

    if( rcvCnt > 0 )
    {
        cmd             = usiI2CReceiveByte();
        size            = cmd & cmdSizeMask;

        // cmdSizeMask is 3 bits, but
        // the maximum size is 4.
        // Enforce that here:

        if( size > 4 )
        {
            size = 4;
        }
        reg_position    = cmd & cmdRegMask;
        reg_position    >>= 3;

        // Determine if the controller is
        // specifying a read operation or a
        // write operation. This is not the
```

```
// R/W bit in the address byte (you
// got here on an I2C write). The
// direction bit specifies whether
// whether you can expect an I2C
// read operation after this command
// to read the specified data.

if( cmd & cmdDirMask )
{
    // A read command, just set up
    // the count and pointer values
    // for any upcoming reads.

    read_size = size;
    read_position = reg_position;
}
else // A write command
{
    // Copy any additional data the
    // controller sends you to the
    // i2c_regs array. Note that
    // this code ignores any bytes
    // beyond the fourth one the
    // controller sends.

    byte maxXfer = 4;
    while( --rcvCnt && maxXfer-- )
    {
        i2c_regs[reg_position] = usiI2CReceiveByte();
        reg_position++;
        if( reg_position >= reg_size )
        {
            reg_position = 0;
        }
    }
}
}
}
```

The receiveEvent() function is responsible for stripping out the bits from the command byte, parsing the command, and dealing with any additional data appearing beyond the command byte (that is, writing that data to the i2c_regs array).

Next, the setup() function calls the ISR library code's initialization function usiI2CPeripheralInit(), which does most of the real work, and then sets up the address of the callback functions.

```
// attiny84_Periph.ino (cont.)
//
// Usual Arduino initialization code
// even for an I2C peripheral application.

void setup()
```

```
{
    // Initialize the peripheral code:

    usiI2CPeripheralInit( I2C_PERIPH_ADDRESS );

    // Set up callbacks to local functions:

    usi_onReceiverPtr = receiveEvent;
    usi_onRequestPtr = requestEvent;
    usi_afterRequestPtr = requestHandledEvent;
}
```

The setup() function must also initialize the pointers to the callback functions. Since the ISRs do all the real work, the main Arduino loop is empty:

```
// attiny84_Periph.ino (cont.)
//
// The main loop does nothing but spin its
// wheels. All the work in this sample
// program is done inside the ISRs and
// callback functions. If this peripheral
// were a little more complex, background
// activities could be taken care of here.

void loop()
{
    // Do nothing.
}
```

If this peripheral device were a little more complex, the main() function could handle some background tasks while waiting for I²C commands to arrive.

16.3.2 The Interrupt Service Routine Library

This section will discuss *usiI2CPeriph.c*, the source code for the ISR module. This is a modification of the original AVR two-wire peripheral code written by Donald Blake and modified by Jochen Toppe. I have made further modifications to adjust for the sample application in *attiny84_Periph.ino*.

As in the previous section, I'll describe this code piece by piece. As this code is an implementation of the architecture that Atmel's AVR312 application note describes, it wouldn't hurt to have a copy of the application note available so you can reference it while reading this code (see "For More Information").

As usual, the first part of the source file contains introductory comments, header file includes, and some important defines and macros:

```
// usiI2CPeriph.c
//
// USI I2C Peripheral driver.
//
// Created by Donald R. Blake, donblake at worldnet.att.net.
// Adapted by Jochen Toppe, jochen.toppe at jtoee.com.
```

```
// Further modifications by Randall Hyde for "The Book of I2C."
//
// ------------------------------------------------------------
//
// Created from Atmel source files for Application Note
// AVR312: Using the USI Module as an I2C peripheral.

#include <avr/io.h>
#include <avr/interrupt.h>

#include "usiI2CPeriph.h"

#define breakif(x) if(x) break

// Device dependent defines:

#define DDR_USI              DDRA
#define PORT_USI             PORTA
#define PIN_USI              PINA
#define PORT_USI_SDA         PORTA6
#define PORT_USI_SCL         PORTA4
#define PIN_USI_SDA          PINA6
#define PIN_USI_SCL          PINA4
#define USI_START_COND_INT   USISIF
#define USI_START_VECTOR     USI_START_vect
#define USI_OVERFLOW_VECTOR  USI_OVF_vect

// These macros make the stop condition detection code
// more readable.

#define USI_PINS_SCL_SDA          \
    (                             \
          ( 1 << PIN_USI_SDA )    \
        | ( 1 << PIN_USI_SCL )    \
    )

#define USI_PINS_SDA    ( 1 << PIN_USI_SDA )
#define USI_PINS_SCL    ( 1 << PIN_USI_SCL )
```

The DDRA, PORTA, PORTA6, PINA6, PINA4, USISIF, USI_START_vect, and USI_OVF_vect definitions appear in the *avr/io.h* header file.

The USI Overflow ISR (from AVR312, ISR(USI_OVERFLOW_VECTOR) in this code) implements a state machine, as per AVR312. The ISRstate_t type definition provides meaningful names for each of the states this function implements. See the code comments for a description of each of these states:

```
// usiI2CPeriph.c (cont.)
//
/***********************************************************

                   typedef's

***********************************************************/
```

```
// ISRstate_t are the different states possible for
// the ISR state machine that handles incoming
// bytes from the controller.

typedef enum
{
    // Address byte has just arrived:

    USI_PERIPH_CHECK_ADDRESS                 = 0x00,

    // Peripheral is transmitting bytes to
    // the controller (I2C read transaction).

    USI_PERIPH_SEND_DATA                     = 0x01,

    // Receive an ACK from controller after sending
    // a byte to it.

    USI_PERIPH_REQUEST_REPLY_FROM_SEND_DATA = 0x02,

    // Deals with ACK or NAK received from
    // controller after sending a byte
    // to the controller (I2C read).

    USI_PERIPH_CHECK_REPLY_FROM_SEND_DATA   = 0x03,

    // Handle data coming to the peripheral
    // (I2C write operation).

    USI_PERIPH_REQUEST_DATA                 = 0x04,
    USI_PERIPH_GET_DATA_AND_SEND_ACK        = 0x05
} ISRstate_t;
```

Next up are some global variables (local to this source file):

```
// usiI2CPeriph.c (cont.)
//
/**********************************************************

                   local variables

**********************************************************/

// periphAddress holds the 7-bit I2C address.

static uint8_t              periphAddress;
static uint8_t              sleep_enable_bit;
static uint8_t              in_transaction;
static volatile ISRstate_t  ISRstate;


static uint8_t          rxBuf[I2C_RX_BUFFER_SIZE];
static volatile uint8_t rxHead;
static volatile uint8_t rxTail;
```

```
static volatile uint8_t rxCount;

static uint8_t        txBuf[I2C_TX_BUFFER_SIZE];
static volatile uint8_t txHead;
static volatile uint8_t txTail;
static volatile uint8_t txCount;
```

These variables are used as follows:

periphAddress   Holds the peripheral device's I²C address (for example,
0x20 for the memory peripheral device)

sleep_enable_bit   Saves the state of the SE bit in the MCUCR register as
this bit gets overwritten by changes to the MCUCR in the ISRs

in_transaction   A Boolean variable that tracks whether you're in the
middle of an I²C transaction (that is, you haven't yet seen a stop condition) while entering and leaving the overflow ISR

ISRstate   Holds the current state value (ISRstate_t) for the overflow ISR
state machine

rx* variables   Receive buffer variables

tx* variables   Transmit buffer variables

usi_onRequestPtr   Pointer to callback function that the overflow ISR
calls after receiving the address byte but before returning any data to
the controller device

usi_onReceiverPtr   Pointer to the callback function that the overflow
ISR calls after receiving the address byte but before reading any additional data sent by the controller device on an I²C write operation

usi_afterRequestPtr   Pointer to callback function that the overflow ISR
calls after processing all the bytes received from the controller on an
I²C read operation

There are also three function pointers appearing in the global declarations: usi_afterRequestPtr, usi_onRequestPtr, and usi_onReceiverPtr. In addition
to these variables, this section defines two empty functions with which it initializes the callback pointers. Pre-initializing these function pointers spares
the code from having to check if these pointers contain NULL.

```
// usiI2CPeriph.c (cont.)
//
// Dummy functions so you don't have to check if
// usi_afterRequestPtr or usi_onReceiverPtr are NULL.

static void dummy1( void ){}
static void dummy2( uint8_t d ){}


void    (*usi_afterRequestPtr)( void )   = dummy1;
void    (*usi_onRequestPtr)( void )      = dummy1;
void    (*usi_onReceiverPtr)( uint8_t )  = dummy2;
```

Next are a couple of utility support functions private to this source file.

```
// usiI2CPeriph.c (cont.)
//
/***********************************************************

                    Local functions

***********************************************************/

// Flushes the I2C buffers.

static void flushI2CBuffers( void )
{
  rxTail = 0;
  rxHead = 0;
  rxCount = 0;
  txTail = 0;
  txHead = 0;
  txCount = 0;
} // End flushI2CBuffers
```

The startSetConditionMode() function initializes the ATtiny84's interrupt system to disable the USI overflow interrupt and enable the start condition interrupt. This happens, for example, when an I^{2}C transaction is complete and the peripheral is waiting for another start condition to come along. Once the code initializes these interrupts, it can do something else (currently just spinning in the empty loop function) until the next start condition.

```
// usiI2CPeriph.c (cont.)
//
// startSetConditionMode-
//
// This initializes the interrupt system so that
// the code waits for the arrival of a start
// condition (and generates an interrupt when
// one arrives).

static void setStartConditionMode( void )
{
    USICR =
            // Enable Start Condition Interrupt.

            ( 1 << USISIE )

            // Disable Overflow Interrupt.

        |   ( 0 << USIOIE )

            // Set USI in two-wire mode.

        |   ( 1 << USIWM1 )
```

```
                    // No USI Counter overflow hold.

            |   ( 0 << USIWMO )

                    // Shift Register Clock Source = external,
                    // positive edge.

            |   ( 1 << USICS1 )
            |   ( 0 << USICS0 )

                    // 4-Bit Counter Source = external,
                    // both edges.

            |   ( 0 << USICLK )

                    // No toggle clock-port pin.

            |   ( 0 << USITC );

        // Clear all interrupt flags, except Start Cond.

        USISR =
                ( 0 << USI_START_COND_INT )
            |   ( 1 << USIOIF )
            |   ( 1 << USIPF )
            |   ( 1 << USIDC )
            |   ( 0x0 << USICNT0 );
}
```

See section 11.2, "ATtiny Controller Programming," in Chapter 11 for an explanation of the USICR and USISR registers that appear in this code.

The next section of the program introduces public functions that the main application can call, beginning with the main ISR initialization function. This programs the SDA and SCL lines as outputs, programs them high (the quiescent state), and sets up the system to wait for a start condition interrupt.

```
// usiI2CPeriph.c (cont.)
//
/*********************************************************

                    Public functions

*********************************************************/

// Initialize USI for I2C peripheral mode.

void usiI2CPeripheralInit( uint8_t ownAddress )
{
    // Initialize the TX and RX buffers to empty.

    flushI2CBuffers( );
```

```
periphAddress = ownAddress;

// In two-wire (I2C) mode (USIWM1, USIWM0 = 1X),
// the peripheral USI will pull SCL low when a
// start condition is detected or a counter
// overflow (only for USIWM1, USIWM0 = 11). This
// inserts a wait state. SCL is released by the
// ISRs (USI_START_vect and USI_OVERFLOW_vect).
//
// Set SCL and SDA as output.

DDR_USI |= ( 1 << PORT_USI_SCL ) | ( 1 << PORT_USI_SDA );

// Set SCL high.

PORT_USI |= ( 1 << PORT_USI_SCL );

// Set SDA high.

PORT_USI |= ( 1 << PORT_USI_SDA );

// Set SDA as input.

DDR_USI &= ~( 1 << PORT_USI_SDA );

USICR =
        // Enable Start Condition Interrupt.

        ( 1 << USISIE )

        // Disable Overflow Interrupt.

    |   ( 0 << USIOIE )

        // Set USI in two-wire mode.

    |   ( 1 << USIWM1 )

        // No USI Counter overflow hold.

    |   ( 0 << USIWM0 )

        // Shift Register Clock Source = external,
        // positive edge.
        // 4-Bit Counter Source = external, both edges.

    |   ( 1 << USICS1 )
    |   ( 0 << USICS0 )
    |   ( 0 << USICLK )

        // No toggle clock-port pin.

    |   ( 0 << USITC );
```

```
        // Clear all interrupt flags and reset overflow counter.

        USISR =
                ( 1 << USI_START_COND_INT )
            |   ( 1 << USIOIF )
            |   ( 1 << USIPF )
            |   ( 1 << USIDC );

        // The in_transaction variable remembers if the
        // usiI2CPeriph driver is in the middle of
        // an I2C transaction. Initialize it to 0.

        in_transaction = 0;

} // end usiI2CPeripheralInit
```

Up next are various functions for testing the presence of data in the transmit and receive buffers, as well as inserting data into, and extracting data from, these buffers:

```
// usiI2CPeriph.c (cont.)
//
// usiI2CDataInTransmitBuffer-
//
// Return 0 (false) if the transmit buffer is empty, true
// (nonzero) if data is available in the transmit buffer.

bool usiI2CDataInTransmitBuffer( void )
{
    return txCount; // Actual count is nonzero
                    // if data available :)
} // End usiI2CDataInTransmitBuffer

// usiI2CTransmitByte-
//
// Adds a byte to the transmission buffer,
// wait for bytes to be transmitted
// if buffer is full.
//
// Race condition warning: As this function
// modifies txCount, it should be called only
// from the USI_OVERFLOW_VECTOR ISR or code
// called from it. Otherwise, there could
// be problems with the updates of the global
// txBuf, txHead, and txCount variables (which
// are unprotected).
//
// In particular, it is safe to call this
// function from whomever usi_afterRequestPtr,
// usi_onRequestPtr, or usi_onReceiverPtr
// point at, but you must not call this
// code from the main Arduino loop or
```

```
// setup function.

void usiI2CTransmitByte( uint8_t data )
{

    // Wait for free space in buffer.

    while( txCount == I2C_TX_BUFFER_SIZE ) ;

    // Store data in buffer.

    txBuf[txHead] = data;
    txHead = ( txHead + 1 ) & I2C_TX_BUFFER_MASK;
    txCount++;

}   // End usiI2CTransmitByte

// usiI2CReceiveByte-
//
// Return a byte from the receive
// buffer, wait if buffer is empty.
// As above, call this only from the
// USI_OVERFLOW_VECTOR ISR or code
// called by it.

uint8_t usiI2CReceiveByte( void )
{
    uint8_t rtn_byte;

    // Wait for Rx data.

    while( !rxCount );

    rtn_byte = rxBuf[rxTail];

    // Calculate buffer index.

    rxTail = ( rxTail + 1 ) & I2C_RX_BUFFER_MASK;
    rxCount--;

    // Return data from the buffer.

    return rtn_byte;

}   // End usiI2CReceiveByte

// usiI2CAmountDataInReceiveBuffer-
//
// Returns the number of bytes in the
// receive buffer.

uint8_t usiI2CAmountDataInReceiveBuffer( void )
{
    return rxCount;
}
```

Next comes the ISR that handles the arrival of a start condition on the I²C bus. Special hardware inside the ATtiny84 detects the presence of a start condition and triggers the interrupt that calls the following code:

```
// usiI2CPeriph.c (cont.)
//
/*******************************************************

                USI Start Condition ISR

*******************************************************/

// USI_START_VECTOR interrupt service routine.
//
// This ISR gets invoked whenever a start condition
// appears on the I2C bus (assuming the USISIE/start
// condition interrupt is enabled in USICR).
//
// The global variable "in_transaction" is nonzero if
// this is a repeated start condition (that is, haven't
// seen a stop condition since the last start).

ISR( USI_START_VECTOR )
{
    uint8_t usi_pins;

    // Notes about ISR. The compiler in the Arduino IDE handles
    // some of the basic ISR plumbing (unless the "ISR_NAKED"
    // attribute is applied):
    //
    //    * The AVR processor resets the SREG.I bit
    //      when jumping into an ISR.
    //    * The compiler automatically adds code to save SREG.
    //    * < user's ISR code goes here >
    //    * The compiler automatically adds code to restore SREG.
    //    * The compiler automatically uses the RETI instruction
    //      to return from the ISR.
    //
    //      The RETI instruction enables interrupts after the
    //      return from ISR.
    //
    // cli() call is not necessary. Processor disables
    // interrupts when calling to an ISR.
    //
    // No need to save the SREG. The compiler does this
    // automatically when using the ISR construct without
    // modifying attributes.

  ❶ if( !in_transaction )
    {
        // Remember the sleep enable bit when entering the ISR.

        sleep_enable_bit = MCUCR & ( 1 << SE );
```

```
            // Clear the sleep enable bit to prevent the CPU from
            // entering sleep mode while executing this ISR.

            MCUCR &= ~( 1 << SE );
        }

        // Set default starting conditions for new I2C packet.

❷  ISRstate = USI_PERIPH_CHECK_ADDRESS;

        // Program SDA pin as input.

        DDR_USI &= ~( 1 << PORT_USI_SDA );

        // The start condition is that the controller pulls SDA low
        // (while SCL is high).
        //
        // Wait for SCL to go low to ensure the start condition
        // has completed (the start detector will hold SCL low);
        // if a stop condition arises, then leave the interrupt to
        // prevent waiting forever. Don't use USISR to test for
        // stop condition as in Application Note AVR312, because
        // the stop condition flag is going to be set from the last
        // I2C sequence.

❸  while
    (
            ( usi_pins = PIN_USI & USI_PINS_SCL_SDA )
        ==  USI_PINS_SCL
    ){
        // While SCL is high and SDA is low.
    }

        // If SDA line was low at SCL edge, then start
        // condition occurred.

❹  if( !( usi_pins & USI_PINS_SDA ) )
    {
        // A stop condition did not occur.

        // Execute callback if this is a repeated start.

        if( in_transaction )
        {
            if( usiI2CAmountDataInReceiveBuffer() )
            {
                usi_onReceiverPtr
                (
                    usiI2CAmountDataInReceiveBuffer()
                );
            }
        }

        // Now that you've seen a start condition,
```

```
                // you need to dynamically enable the
                // overflow interrupt that tells you when
                // you've received a byte of data.

        ❺ USICR =
                        // Keep start condition interrupt
                        // enabled to detect RESTART.

                        ( 1 << USISIE )

                        // Enable overflow interrupt.

                    |   ( 1 << USIOIE )

                        // Set USI in two-wire mode, hold SCL
                        // low on USI Counter overflow.

                    |   ( 1 << USIWM1 )
                    |   ( 1 << USIWM0 )

                        // Shift register clock source = external,
                        // positive edge.

                    |   ( 1 << USICS1 )
                    |   ( 0 << USICS0 )

                        // 4-Bit Counter Source = external, both edges.

                    |   ( 0 << USICLK )

                        // No toggle clock-port pin.

                    |   ( 0 << USITC );

            // Remember that the USI is in a valid I2C transaction.

            in_transaction = 1;
        }
        else // SDA was high
        {
            // A stop condition did occur; reset
            // the interrupts to look for a new
            // start condition.

        ❻ USICR =
                        // Enable start condition interrupt.

                        ( 1 << USISIE )

                        // Disable overflow interrupt.

                    |   ( 0 << USIOIE )
```

```
                    // Set USI in two-wire mode.

            |   ( 1 << USIWM1 )

                    // No USI counter overflow hold.

            |   ( 0 << USIWM0 )

                    // Shift register clock source = external,
                    // positive edge.

            |   ( 1 << USICS1 )
            |   ( 0 << USICS0 )

                    // 4-Bit counter source = external,
                    // both edges.

            |   ( 0 << USICLK )

                    // No toggle clock-port pin.

            |   ( 0 << USITC );

        // No longer in valid I2C transaction.

        in_transaction = 0;

        // Restore the sleep enable bit.

        MCUCR |= sleep_enable_bit;

    }  // end if

    USISR =
            // Clear interrupt flags - resetting the Start
            // Condition Flag will release SCL.

            ( 1 << USI_START_COND_INT )
        |   ( 1 << USIOIF )
        |   ( 1 << USIPF )
        |   ( 1 << USIDC )

            // Set USI to sample 8 bits (count 16
            // external SCL pin toggles).

        |   ( 0x0 << USICNT0);

} // End ISR( USI_START_VECTOR )
```

The USI_START_VECTOR interrupt service routine begins by turning off
the sleep mode ❶. This prevents the CPU from sleeping while processing a byte coming in on the I^{2}C pins. Next, the ISR set the state so that
the code will process an address byte immediately following the start
condition ❷.

The while loop waits until the SCL line goes low (the end of the start condition) ❸, and then the code checks to see if this is an actual start condition (SDA line is low) or a stop condition (SDA line is high). If it's a start condition, the ISR checks to see if this is a restart condition, meaning there was no stop condition since the last start ❹. Once the ISR has properly seen a start (or restart) condition, it enables the overflow interrupt to trigger when the USI receives the next full byte ❺. In the event a stop condition arrived, the code resets the interrupts to look for a new start condition ❻.

The USI Overflow interrupt service routine processes the bytes that arrive from the USI:

```
// usiI2CPeriph.c (cont.)
//
// USI Overflow ISR-
//
// Invoked when the shift register is full (programmable
// size, usually 1 or 8 bits). Because the byte coming
// in could be any part of an I2C transmission, this ISR
// uses a state machine to track the incoming bytes. This
// ISR handles controller reads and writes (peripheral
// writes and reads).
//
// Note that this ISR is disabled when waiting for a
// start condition to arrive (incoming bytes at that
// point are intended for a different device).

ISR( USI_OVERFLOW_VECTOR )
{
  uint8_t finished;
  uint8_t usi_pins;

  // This ISR is only ever entered because the
  // ISR(USI_START_VECTOR) interrupt routine ran
  // first. That routine saved the sleep mode and
  // disabled sleep.
  //
  // ISRstate is the state machine variable for
  // the overflow.

  // Most of the time this routine exits, it has set up the
  // USI to shift in/out bits and is expected to have re-entered
  // because of the USI overflow interrupt. Track whether or
  // not the transaction is completely finished.

  finished = 0;
```

Because each byte can have a different meaning, the overflow ISR tracks the arrivals with a state machine (and the ISRstate variable). The first byte to arrive after the start condition is the address-R/W byte. The LO bit (R/W) determines whether the state machine will handle memory read operations (R/W = 1, state = USI_PERIPH_SEND_DATA) or memory write operations (R/W = 0, state = USI_PERIPH_REQUEST_DATA).

The following code is the start of the actual state machine, controlled by the ISRstate variable:

```
// usiI2CPeriph.c (cont.)

  switch ( ISRstate )
  {

    // Address mode:
    // Check address and send ACK (and next
    // USI_PERIPH_SEND_DATA) if OK, else reset USI.

    case USI_PERIPH_CHECK_ADDRESS:
        if(
                ( USIDR == 0 )
            || (( USIDR >> 1 ) == periphAddress )
        ){
            if( USIDR & 0x01 ) // Controller read request?
            {
                ISRstate = USI_PERIPH_SEND_DATA;
                usi_onRequestPtr();

            }
            else    // Must be controller write operation
            {
                ISRstate = USI_PERIPH_REQUEST_DATA;
            }        // end if

            // Acknowledge the start frame.
            // Sets up the USI to pull SDA low
            // and clock 1 bit (two edges).

            USIDR = 0; // Prepare ACK, acknowledge is a single 0

            // Set SDA data direction as output.

            DDR_USI |= ( 1 << PORT_USI_SDA );

            // Clear all interrupt flags, except start cond.

            USISR =
                    ( 0 << USI_START_COND_INT )
                |   ( 1 << USIOIF )
                |   ( 1 << USIPF )
                |   ( 1 << USIDC )
                |   ( 0x0E << USICNT0 ); // Shift 1 bit
        }
        else    // I2C transaction for some other device
        {
            setStartConditionMode();
            finished = 1;
        }
        break;
```

The first state appearing in this code is USI_PERIPH_CHECK_ADDRESS, which corresponds to the arrival of a start condition. This state checks the incoming I²C address byte and R/W bit. If the address doesn't match, the code turns off the overflow interrupt enable, because the code will ignore all incoming bytes until a new start condition comes along; the current bus transactions are intended for some other device. If the address matches, however, this code changes the state based on the R/W bit. One state handles additional incoming bytes (an I²C write operation), while another handles outgoing bytes (an I²C read operation).

Next, the USI_PERIPH_CHECK_REPLY_FROM_SEND_DATA state verifies that an ACK or a NAK came from the controller after the peripheral has transmitted a byte to the controller (an I²C read operation).

```
// usiI2CPeriph.c (cont.)
//
// USI_PERIPH_CHECK_REPLY_FROM_SEND_DATA-
//
// State that executes when you've received
// an ACK or a NAK from the controller after
// sending it a byte.
// Check reply and go to USI_PERIPH_SEND_DATA
// if OK, else reset USI.

case USI_PERIPH_CHECK_REPLY_FROM_SEND_DATA:

    // Execute request callback after each byte's
    // ACK or NAK has arrived.

    usi_afterRequestPtr();

    if( USIDR )
    {
    // If NAK, the controller does not want more data.

        setStartConditionMode();
        finished = 1;
    break;
    }

    // From here you just drop straight
    // into USI_PERIPH_SEND_DATA if the
    // controller sent an ACK.
```

If a NAK arrived, you're done transmitting data back to the controller; if an ACK arrived, the program continues transmitting more data. If this code were to receive an ACK from the controller, it would normally set the state to USI_PERIPH_SEND_DATA. However, this code simply falls down into that state and immediately transmits the next byte to the controller without changing the state (it will be set back to USI_PERIPH_CHECK_REPLY_FROM_SEND_DATA, anyway).

Next, the USI_PERIPH_SEND_DATA state transmits a byte of data to the controller in response to a read operation. After transmitting a byte, it also sets the state to USI_PERIPH_REQUEST_REPLY_FROM_SEND_DATA to handle the ACK or NAK from the controller.

```c
// usiI2CPeriph.c (cont.)
//
// Controller read operation (peripheral write operation).
//
// Copy data from buffer to USIDR and set USI to shift byte
// next USI_PERIPH_REQUEST_REPLY_FROM_SEND_DATA.

case USI_PERIPH_SEND_DATA:

    // Get data from buffer.

    if( txCount )
    {
        USIDR = txBuf[ txTail ];
        txTail = ( txTail + 1 ) & I2C_TX_BUFFER_MASK;
        txCount--;

        ISRstate =
            USI_PERIPH_REQUEST_REPLY_FROM_SEND_DATA;

        DDR_USI |= ( 1 << PORT_USI_SDA );

        // Clear all interrupt flags, except start cond.

        USISR    =
            ( 0 << USI_START_COND_INT )
            | ( 1 << USIOIF )
            | ( 1 << USIPF )
            | ( 1 << USIDC)
            | ( 0x0 << USICNT0 ); // Shift 8 bits
    }
    else
    {
        // The buffer is empty.

        // Read an ACK:
        //
        // This might be necessary sometimes. See
        // http://www.avrfreaks.net/index.php?name=
        // PNphpBB2&file=viewtopic&p=805227#805227.

        DDR_USI &= ~( 1 << PORT_USI_SDA );
        USIDR = 0; // Must ship out a 0 bit for ACK

        USISR =
                // Clear all interrupt flags,
                // except start cond.

                ( 0 << USI_START_COND_INT )
            | ( 1 << USIOIF )
            | ( 1 << USIPF )
```

```
            |   ( 1 << USIDC )

                // Set USI ctr to shift 1 bit.

            |   ( 0x0E << USICNT0 );

        setStartConditionMode();
    } // end if
    break;
```

Next, the USI_PERIPH_REQUEST_REPLY_FROM_SEND_DATA state sets up the USI to wait for a single bit, either the ACK or NAK, to arrive in the USI. This state also changes the state variable to USI_PERIPH_CHECK_REPLY_FROM_SEND_DATA, which will process the ACK or NAK when it arrives.

```
// usiI2CPeriph.c (cont.)
//
// This state sets up the state machine
// to accept an ACK from the controller
// device after sending a byte to the
// controller (an I2C read operation).
//
// Set USI to sample reply from controller
// next USI_PERIPH_CHECK_REPLY_FROM_SEND_DATA.

case USI_PERIPH_REQUEST_REPLY_FROM_SEND_DATA:

    ISRstate =
        USI_PERIPH_CHECK_REPLY_FROM_SEND_DATA;

    // Read an ACK:

    DDR_USI &= ~( 1 << PORT_USI_SDA );
    USIDR = 0; // Must ship out a zero bit for ACK
    USISR =
            // Clear all interrupt flags,
            // except Start Cond.

            ( 0 << USI_START_COND_INT )
        |   ( 1 << USIOIF )
        |   ( 1 << USIPF )
        |   ( 1 << USIDC )

            // Set USI ctr to shift 1 bit.

        |   ( 0x0E << USICNT0 );

    break;
```

Next, the USI_PERIPH_REQUEST_DATA state sets up the system to expect the arrival of a byte from the controller (that is, an I^2C write operation). This state gets set after the address byte or after an arbitrary byte is read from the controller (that is, some byte in a stream of bytes the controller is transmitting). This code delays until the SCL line goes high and then looks for a possible stop condition. If no stop condition occurs, then the system sets the state to USI_PERIPH_GET_DATA_AND_SEND_ACK and waits for the next byte to arrive:

```
// usiI2CPeriph.c (cont.)
//
// Controller-send / peripheral-receive-
//
// Set USI to sample data from controller,
// next: USI_PERIPH_GET_DATA_AND_SEND_ACK.

case USI_PERIPH_REQUEST_DATA:

    ISRstate = USI_PERIPH_GET_DATA_AND_SEND_ACK;

    // Set USI to read data.
    //
    // Set SDA as input.

    DDR_USI &= ~( 1 << PORT_USI_SDA );

    // Clear all interrupt flags, except start cond.

    USISR   =
        ( 0 << USI_START_COND_INT )
    |   ( 1 << USIOIF )
    |   ( 1 << USIPF )
    |   ( 1 << USIDC )
    |   ( 0x0 << USICNT0 ); // Read 8 bits

    // With the code above, the USI has been set to catch the
    // next byte if the controller sends one. While that's
    // going on, look for a stop condition here when the
    // SDA line goes high after the SCL line.
    //
    // Wait until SCL goes high.

    while
    (
        !(
                ( usi_pins = PIN_USI & USI_PINS_SCL_SDA )
            &   USI_PINS_SCL
        )
    );

    // If SDA line was high at SCL edge,
    // then not a stop condition.

    breakif( usi_pins & USI_PINS_SDA );
    while
    (
            ( usi_pins = PIN_USI & USI_PINS_SCL_SDA )
        ==  USI_PINS_SCL
```

```
)  {
        // Wait until SCL goes low or SDA goes high.
};

// If both SCL and SDA are high, then stop
// condition occurred.

if( usi_pins == USI_PINS_SCL_SDA )
{
    if( usiI2CAmountDataInReceiveBuffer() )
    {
        usi_onReceiverPtr
        (
            usiI2CAmountDataInReceiveBuffer()
        );
    }
    setStartConditionMode();
    finished = 1;
}

break;
```

If a byte has arrived from the controller, the following state fetches that byte from the USI and adds it to the receive buffer. This code also sends the controller an ACK in response to the received byte:

```
// usiI2CPeriph.c (cont.)
//
// This state sends an ACK to the
// controller after receiving a byte
// from the controller (I2C write).
//
// Copy data from USIDR and send ACK
// next USI_PERIPH_REQUEST_DATA.

case USI_PERIPH_GET_DATA_AND_SEND_ACK:

    // Put data into buffer and
    // check buffer size.

    if( rxCount < I2C_RX_BUFFER_SIZE )
    {
        rxBuf[rxHead] = USIDR;
        rxHead = ( rxHead + 1 ) & I2C_RX_BUFFER_MASK;
        rxCount++;
    }
    else
    {
        // Overrun, drop data.
    }

    // Next: USI_PERIPH_REQUEST_DATA
    // (keep accepting bytes from
    // the controller until a stop
```

```
// condition happens).

ISRstate = USI_PERIPH_REQUEST_DATA;

// Send acknowledge.

USIDR = 0; // Prepare ACK, acknowledge is a single 0

// Set SDA data direction as output.

DDR_USI |= ( 1 << PORT_USI_SDA );

// Clear all interrupt flags, except start cond.

USISR =
        ( 0 << USI_START_COND_INT )
    |   ( 1 << USIOIF )
    |   ( 1 << USIPF )
    |   ( 1 << USIDC )
    |   ( 0x0E << USICNT0 ); // Shift 1 bit

break;

}       // End switch

if(finished)
{
        // No longer in valid I2C transaction.

        in_transaction = 0;

        // Restore the sleep enable bit.
        // This allows sleep but does
        // not cause sleep; must execute
        // the "sleep" instruction to
        // actually put MCU in sleep mode.

        MCUCR |= sleep_enable_bit;
}
} // End ISR( USI_OVERFLOW_VECTOR )
```

This concludes the code to handle I^{2}C peripherals on an ATtiny84. In addition to the code appearing in *attiny84_Periph.ino* and *usiI2CPeriph.c*, the full memory peripheral software has a small header file (*usiI2CPeriph.h*). I will not reproduce that header file here as it simply replicates information appearing in these two listings. See the online source files for the full source code.

It should be straightforward to modify the code in *attiny84_Periph.ino* to implement whatever peripheral you desire on the Atto84 device (assuming, of course, it's powerful enough for the job). You could, for example, program it as an ADC—only 10 bits, because the Atto84 built-in ADC is a 10-bit ADC—or as a small GPIO expander. With a little more work, you could use it to create an I^{2}C NeoPixel controller. Your imagination is limited only by the ATtiny84's capabilities.

16.3.3 A Sample Controller Application

If you compile the code in *attiny84_Periph.ino* and *usiI2CPeriph.c* and program it into a SparkFun Atto84 SBC, that code will happily start execution after power-up and . . . do nothing (nothing observable, anyway). Because that Atto84 becomes an I²C peripheral, you must connect it to an I²C controller device that is programmed to talk to the Atto84. Listing 16-1 is a simple Arduino program that you can use to exercise the memory peripheral.

```
// Listing16-1.ino
//
// A very simple Arduino application
// that exercises the Atto84 memory
// peripheral device.

#include <Wire.h>
#define periph (0x20) // Peripheral address

// Usual Arduino initialization code.

void setup( void )
{

    Serial.begin( 9600 );
    delay( 1000 );
    Serial.println( "Test reading ATTO84" );
    Wire.begin();    // Initialize I2C library

    // Initialize the four registers on the
    // memory device with 0x12, 0x34, 0x56,
    // and 0x78.

    Wire.beginTransmission( periph );

    // cmd byte; d=0 (W), rr=00, sss=100 (4)

    Wire.write( 0b000100 );

    // Register initialization data.

    Wire.write( 0x12 );
    Wire.write( 0x34 );
    Wire.write( 0x56 );
    Wire.write( 0x78 );
    Wire.endTransmission();
}

// Arduino main loop.

void loop( void )
```

```
{
    static int value =0;

    // Send a command to the
    // memory peripheral to set
    // the read address and length:
    //
    // d = 1 (R), rr = 00, sss = 100 (4)

    Wire.beginTransmission( periph );
    Wire.write( 0b100100 );
    Wire.endTransmission();

    delayMicroseconds( 25 );

    // Read the 4 bytes from
    // the memory peripheral and
    // display them in the
    // Arduino Serial window.

    Wire.requestFrom( periph, 4 );
    uint8_t b = Wire.read();
    Serial.print( b, 16 );
    b=Wire.read();
    Serial.print( b, 16 );
    b=Wire.read();
    Serial.print( " " );
    Serial.print( b, 16 );
    b=Wire.read();
    Serial.println( b, 16 );

    delay( 25 );
}
```

If you run this program on an Arduino-compatible system and connect its SDA and SCL lines to the Atto84 from the previous sections, this program will exercise the memory capabilities of that Atto84 I^{2}C peripheral.

16.4   Chapter Summary

This chapter covered how to program a SparkFun Atto84 (ATtiny84) as an I^{2}C peripheral. It began with a brief discussion of the ATtiny84 Universal Serial Interface that it used to implement I^{2}C communication in hardware. It then described a simple device implemented as an I^{2}C peripheral: an I^{2}C memory device. The meat of this chapter was the actual implementation of the I^{2}C memory peripheral on the Atto84. Finally, the chapter concluded with a simple I^{2}C controller application for an Arduino-compatible system that exercises the memory peripheral.

FOR MORE INFORMATION

Atmel AVR ATtiny84 datasheet: *https://ww1.microchip.com/downloads/en/devicedoc/Atmel-7701_Automotive-Microcontrollers-ATtiny24-44-84_Datasheet.pdf*

TinyWire library: *https://github.com/rambo/TinyWire*

AVR312 Application Note: *https://ww1.microchip.com/downloads/en/AppNotes/Atmel-2560-Using-the-USI-Module-as-a-I2C-Slave_ApplicationNote_AVR312.pdf*

SparkFun Atto84: *https://www.sparkfun.com/products/14804*

More information on the SparkFun Atto84: *https://learn.sparkfun.com/tutorials/atto84-hookup-guide?_ga=2.165544824.614200035.1610263644-640834246.1610134206*

NeoPixel library information: *https://learn.adafruit.com/adafruit-neopixel-uberguide*

EPILOGUE

This concludes the treeware version of *The Book of I²C*. However, this is only the beginning of your journey toward learning how to program I²C devices. There are hundreds of different I²C devices in the real world, with more appearing all the time. No matter how many devices I describe in this book, it will eventually become out of date as manufacturers create new devices.

Indeed, as this book was being edited, two new and important devices arrived: the MCP4728 quad DAC and the Raspberry Pi Pico. That's in addition to the many common devices already on the market, with boards produced by Adafruit, SparkFun, Seeed Studio, and others.

As discussed in the introduction, to keep the page count and cost of this book reasonable, I've chosen to move the discussion of several devices onto my website at *https://www.randallhyde.com/bookofi2c*. Chapters 17 and beyond of this book will appear on that site, making them easy to update and extend as time permits and new devices become popular. Appendix B in this book describes currently planned online chapters, but I intend to add more in the future. Please visit the website to find additional support material, expanded example code, and links to other information on I^2C programming.

Even without the online materials, this book has taught you almost everything you need to know to begin using I^2C peripherals. At this point, you should be able to read through a device's datasheet and use that information to program any I^2C device out there. Good luck, and happy programming!

A

THE ADAFRUIT I^{2}C ADDRESS COMPILATION

This appendix contains a list of common I^{2}C peripherals, organized by address and primarily drawn from the Adafruit I^{2}C Address Compilation. I've added a few entries of my own for parts I've used or encountered in the past. It is, by no means, a complete listing of all I^{2}C devices available, but it covers those commonly used by hobbyists—specifically, devices for which breakout boards or DIP (through-hole) packages are available.

The information gathered in Table A-1 is from Limor "Lady Ada" Fried's list on the Adafruit website (*https://learn.adafruit.com/i2c-addresses/the-list*). It was taken from the source in early 2022. Please visit Adafruit's site to check for any updates.

Table A-1: Adafruit I²C Address List

Start address or single address	End address	Devices
0x00	0x07	I²C reserved addresses
0x00		General call address
0x01		Reserved for CBUS compatibility
0x02		Reserved for I²C-compatible variants
0x03		Reserved for future compatibility
0x04	0x7	Reserved for high-speed mode controller (master)
0x0B	0x0B	LC709203F fuel gauge and battery monitor
0x0C	0x0F	MLX90393 3-axis magnetometer
0x0E		MAG3110 3-axis magnetometer
0x0F		
0x10	0x1F	
	0x10	VEML6075 UV sensor VEML7700 ambient light sensor
0x11		Si4713 FM transmitter with RDS (0x11 or 0x63)
0x12		PMSA0031 gas sensor
0x13		VCNL40x0 proximity sensor
0x18		MPRLS pressure sensor
0x18		LIS3DH 3-axis accelerometer (0x18 or 0x19)
0x18		LIS331 3-axis accelerometer (0x18 or 0x19)
0x18	0x1F	MCP9808 temperature sensor (0x18–0x1F)
0x19		LSM303 accelerometer and magnetometer (0x19 for accelerometer and 0x1E for magnetometer)
0x1C		LIS3MDL magnetometer (0x1C and 0x1E)
0x1C	0x1D	MMA845x 3-axis accelerometer (0x1C or 0x1D)
0x1C	0x1D	MMA7455L (0x1C or 0x1D)
0x1C	0x1F	FXOS8700 accelerometer and magnetometer (0x1C, 0x1D, 0x1E or 0x1F)
0x1D		ADXL343 3-axis accelerometer (0x1D or 0x53)
0x1D		ADXL345 3-axis accelerometer (0x1D or 0x53)
0x1D	0x1E	LSM9DS0 9-axis IMU (0x1D or 0x1E for accelerometer and magnetometer, 0x6A or 0x6B for gyroscope)
0x1E		HMC5883 magnetometer (0x1E only)

Start address or single address	End address	Devices
0x1E		LIS2MDL magnetometer
0x1E		LIS3MDL magnetometer (0x1C and 0x1E)
0x1E		LSM303 accelerometer and magnetometer (0x19 for accelerometer and 0x1E for magnetometer)
0x20	0x2F	
0x20		Chirp! water sensor (0x20)
0x20	0x21	FXAS21002 gyroscope (0x20 or 0x21)
0x20	0x21	PCAL6408A 8-bit GPIO expander
0x20	0x21	PCAL6416A 16-bit GPIO expander
0x20	0x23	PCAL6524 I^2C 24-bit GPIO expander
0x20	0x23	PCAL6534 I^2C 34-bit GPIO expander
0x20	0x27	MCP23008 I^2C 8-bit GPIO expander
0x20	0x27	MCP23017 I^2C 16-bit GPIO expander
0x20	0x27	PCA9555A I^2C 16-bit GPIO expander
0x23		BH1750 light sensor (0x23 or 0x5C)
0x24		PCA9570 4-bit GPIO expander
0x26		MSA301 triple axis accelerometer
0x28	0x29	BNO055 IMU (0x28 or 0x29)
0x28	0x29	TSL2591 light sensor
0x28	0x2B	DS1841 I^2C digital logarithmic potentiometer (0x28–0x2B)
0x28	0x2B	DS3502 I^2C digital 10K potentiometer (0x28–0x2B)
0x28	0x2D	CAP1188 8-channel capacitive touch (0x28–0x2D)
0x28	0x2E	PCT2075 temperature sensor (0x28–0x2E, 0x48–0x4F, or 0x70–0x77)
0x29		TCS34725 color sensor (0x29 only)
0x29		TSL2561 light sensor (0x29, 0x39, or 0x49)
0x29		VL53L0x ToF distance (0x29, software selectable)
0x29		VL6180X ToF sensor (0x29)
0x30	0x3F	
0x33		MLX90640 IR thermal camera
0x36	0x3D	Adafruit I^2C QT rotary encoder with NeoPixel
0x38		AHT20 temperature sensor

(continued)

Table A-1: Adafruit I²C Address List *(continued)*

Start address or single address	End address	Devices
0x38		FT6x06 capacitive touch driver
0x38	0x39	TSL2561 light sensor
0x38	0x39	VEML6070 UV index
0x39		AS7341 color sensor
0x39		APDS-9960 IR, color, and proximity sensor
0x39		TSL2561 light sensor (0x29, 0x39, or 0x49)
0x3C	0x3D	SSD1305 monochrome OLED
0x3C	0x3D	SSD1306 monochrome OLED
0x40	0x4F	
0x40		Si7021 humidity and temperature sensor
0x40		HTU21D-F humidity and temperature sensor
0x40	0x41	HTU31D-F humidity and temperature sensor
0x40	0x43	HDC1008 humidity and temperature sensor
0x40		MS8607 temperature, barometric, and humidity sensor (0x40 for humidity and 0x76 for barometric and temperature)
0x40	0x47	TMP006 IR temperature sensor
0x40	0x47	TMP007 IR temperature sensor
0x40	0x4F	INA219 high-side DC current and voltage sensor
0x40	0x4F	INA260 precision DC current and power sensor
0x40	0x7F	PCA9685 16-channel PWM driver default address (can actually use addresses in the range 0x40 to 0x7F)
0x41		STMPE610 or STMPE811 resistive touch controller (0x41 or 0x44)
0x42	0x49	STMPE1600 16-bit GPIO expander
0x44		STMPE610 or STMPE811 resistive touch controller (0x41 or 0x44)
0x44		SHT40 humidity and temperature sensor
0x44	0x45	SHT31 humidity and temperature sensor
0x44		ISL29125 color sensor
0x44		STMPE610 or STMPE811 resistive touch controller (0x41 or 0x44)
0x48		PN532 NFC and RFID reader
0x48	0x4B	ADS1115 4-channel 16-bit ADC
0x48	0x4B	ADT7410 temperature sensor
0x48	0x4B	TMP102 temperature sensor

Start address or single address	End address	Devices
0x48	0x4B	TMP117 temperature sensor
0x48	0x4F	PCF8591 quad 8-bit ADC and 8-bit DAC
0x48	0x4F	PCT2075 temperature sensor (0x28–0x2E, 0x48–0x4F, or 0x70–0x77)
0x49		TSL2561 light sensor (0x29, 0x39, or 0x49)
0x49		AS7262 light and color sensor
0x4A	0x4B	BNO085 9-DoF IMU
0x4C		EMC2101 fan controller
0x50	0x5F	
0x50	0x57	MB85RC I²C FRAM
0x52		Nintendo Nunchuck controller
0x53		ADXL343 3-axis accelerometer (0x1D or 0x53)
0x53		ADXL345 3-axis accelerometer (0x1D or 0x53)
0x53		LTR390 UV sensor
0x57		MAX3010x pulse and oximetry sensor
0x58		AW9523 GPIO expander and LED driver (0x58–0x5B)
0x58		TPA2016 I²C-controlled amplifier
0x58		SGP30 gas sensor
0x59		SGP40 gas sensor
0x5A		DRV2605 haptic motor driver
0x5A		MLX9061x IR temperature sensor
0x5A		DRV2605 haptic motor driver
0x5A	0x5B	CCS811 VOC sensor
0x5A	0x5D	MPR121 12-point capacitive touch sensor
0x5C		AM2315 humidity and temperature sensor
0x5C		BH1750 light sensor (0x23 or 0x5C)
0x5C		AM2320 humidity and temperature sensor
0x5C	0x5D	LPS22 pressure sensor
0x5C	0x5D	LPS25 pressure sensor
0x5C	0x5D	LPS33HW ported pressure sensor
0x5C	0x5D	LPS35HW pressure sensor
0x5E		TLV493D triple-axis magnetometer

(continued)

Table A-1: Adafruit I²C Address List *(continued)*

Start address or single address	End address	Devices
0x5F		HTS221 humidity and temperature sensor
0x60	0x6F	
0x60		ATECC608 cryptographic coprocessor
0x60		MCP4728 quad DAC
0x60		MPL115A2 barometric pressure
0x60		MPL3115A2 barometric pressure
0x60		Si1145 light and IR sensor
0x60		TEA5767 radio receiver
0x60		VCNL4040 proximity and ambient light sensor
0x60	0x61	Si5351A clock generator
0x60	0x61	MCP4725A0 12-bit DAC
0x60	0x67	MCP9600 temperature sensor
0x61		SCD30 humidity, temperature, and gas sensor
0x62	0x63	MCP4725A1 12-bit DAC
0x63		Si4713 FM transmitter with RDS (0x11 or 0x63)
0x64	0x65	MCP4725A2 12-bit DAC
0x66	0x67	MCP4725A3 12-bit DAC
0x68		This address is really popular with real-time clocks; almost all of them use 0x68!
0x68		DS1307 RTC
0x68		DS3231 RTC
0x68		PCF8523 RTC
0x68	0x69	AMG8833 IR thermal camera breakout
0x68	0x69	ICM-20649 accelerometer and gyroscope
0x68	0x69	ITG3200 gyroscope
0x68	0x69	MPU-9250 9-DoF IMU
0x68	0x69	MPU-60X0 accelerometer and gyroscope
0x6A	0x6B	LSM9DS0 9-axis IMU (0x1D or 0x1E for accelerometer and magnetometer, 0x6A or 0x6B for gyroscope)
0x6A	0x6B	ICM330DHC 6-axis IMU
0x6A	0x6B	L3GD20H gyroscope
0x6A	0x6B	LSM6DS33 6-axis IMU

Start address or single address	End address	Devices
0x6A	0x6B	LSM6DSOX 6-axis IMU
0x70	0x7F	
0x70		SHTC3 temperature and humidity sensor
0x70	0x77	HT16K33 LED matrix driver
0x70	0x77	PCT2075 temperature sensor (0x28–0x2E, 0x48–0x4F, or 0x70–0x77)
0x70	0x77	TCA9548 1-to-8 I²C multiplexer
0x74	0x77	IS31FL3731 144-LED CharliePlex driver (0x74, 0x75, 0x76, or 0x77)
0x76		MS8607 temperature, barometric, and humidity sensor (0x76 for barometric and temperature)
0x76	0x77	BME280 temperature, barometric, and humidity sensor
0x76	0x77	BME680 temperature, barometric, and humidity sensor
0x76	0x77	BMP280 temperature and barometric sensor
0x76	0x77	BMP280 temperature and barometric sensor
0x76	0x77	BMP388 temperature and barometric sensor
0x76	0x77	BMP390 temperature and barometric sensor
0x76	0x77	DPS310 barometric sensor
0x76	0x77	MS5607 and MS5611 barometric pressure
0x77		BMA180 accelerometer
0x77		BMP180 temperature and barometric sensor
0x77		BMP085 temperature and barometric sensor
0x78	0x7B	Reserved for 10-bit I²C addressing
0x7C	0x7F	Reserved for future purposes

B

ONLINE CHAPTERS

There is far too much information about I^2C controllers and peripheral devices to include in a single book. Even if it were possible, new I^2C devices will undoubtedly appear during and after the publication of this book. To resolve this issue, this book is paired with several online chapters freely available at *https://bookofi2c .randallhyde.com*.

The following online chapters are currently planned for inclusion. At the time of printing, some may already be available, while others may be "in the works." As time permits (and as new devices appear), I will attempt to add additional chapters not listed here.

Chapter 17: A Software Implementation on the Atto84   This chapter contains overflow information from Chapter 3, describing a software implementation of the I^2C on the Atto84 (ATtiny84) MCU.

Chapter 18: Teensy 4.x Low-Level I^{2}C Peripheral Device   This chapter provides a low-level peripheral driver for the Teensy 4.x MCUs.

Chapter 19: The MCP4728 Quad Digital-to-Analog Converter Chapter 15 described the MCP4725 12-bit DAC. This chapter covers its big brother, the MCP4728 quad DAC.

Chapter 20: The Maxim DS3502 Digital Potentiometer   This chapter describes the DS3502 digital potentiometer, which allows you to implement a 7-bit resistive pot in software.

Chapter 21: The DS3231 Precision RTC   This chapter describes the DS3231 high-precision real-time clock—one of the more popular choices for real-time timekeeping on the I^{2}C bus.

Chapter 22: The MCP9600 Thermocouple Amplifier   This chapter describes the MCP9600 I^{2}C-based thermocouple amplifier and converter. By connecting a thermocouple to this device, you can measure high temperatures (depending on the thermocouple, well over 1,000°C).

Chapter 23: I^{2}C Displays   This chapter discusses various I^{2}C-based displays (LED and LCD) and display drivers. This chapter also describes an open source display library capable of controlling various displays.

Chapter 24: The SX1509 GPIO Expander   The SX1509 is another 16-bit GPIO expander (similar to, but less complex than, the MCP23017). This chapter describes programming the GPIO pins on that part.

Chapter 25: The PCA9685 PWM Driver   The PCA9685 is a 16-channel, 12-bit, pulse-width modulation driver. Typically, you would use this for LED dimming and motor speed control (or PWM analog output). This chapter describes programming this part.

Chapter 26: The INA169 and INA218 Current Sensors   The INA169 and INA218 ICs are current sensors that allow you to track the power used in a circuit. This is useful for battery monitoring and other circuits where you need to track the current through the system. This chapter discusses how to program each of these parts.

Chapter 27: The MPR121 Capacitive Touch Sensor   The MPR121 is a 12-channel capacitive touch controller that allows you to turn any marginally conductive item into a switch. This chapter describes how to program the MPR121 to read "button presses" using the capacitive controller.

Chapter 28: The Alchitry FPGA   SparkFun sells a nifty FPGA kit by Alchitry that provides I^{2}C in hardware (no CPU required). This chapter provides examples on programming the Alchitry FPGAs to act as a peripheral.

Chapter 29: The Raspberry Pi Pico   The Raspberry Pi Pico is a popular microcontroller unit produced by the Raspberry Pi folks. Because of its inexpensive price tag, it has become extremely important. This chapter discusses programming I^{2}C on this device.

Chapter 30: The ESP32   The ESP32 (along with the ESP 8266) is probably the most popular IoT controller used by hobbyists and professional embedded programmers. This chapter discusses using I^{2}C on this MCU.

In addition to these chapters, *https://bookofi2c.randallhyde.com* contains useful information such as sample builds (pictures and schematics) for many of the examples appearing throughout this book. It will also contain links to useful information concerning programming I^{2}C controllers and peripherals. Check the website for the latest updates.

GLOSSARY

A

Active high logic
A digital logic signal that is 1 (high) when asserted and 0 (low) when unasserted.

Active low logic
A digital signal that is asserted when the signal is 0 (low) and unasserted when it is 1 (high).

A/D
Analog-to-digital.

ADC
Analog-to-digital converter.

API
Application programming interface.

B

Bus expander
A device that multiplexes multiple I^2C buses onto a single actual bus.

C

CCW
Counterclockwise.

Clock stretching
A peripheral can hold the I^2C SCL line to add wait states to an I^2C transmission. This is known as clock stretching.

COTS
Commercial off-the-shelf.

CPU
Central processing unit.

CW
Clockwise.

D

D/A
Digital-to-analog.

DAC
Digital-to-analog converter.

Debouncing
The process of converting a noisy switch input into a clean signal by eliminating rapid changes in state after the first such change (in some time period).

DIP
Dual in-line package.

Dispatcher
A special kind of function that serves as an entry point for many different functions. One of the dispatcher's arguments specifies the actual function to call. Dispatchers provide the basic implementation of many different APIs.

DMA

Direct memory access.

DMM

Digital multimeter (see also *DVM*).

Dry contact input

A passive (switched, not active logic) input signal. Generally this is a switch, relay contact, or other similar nonpowered switching device.

DSI

Display serial interface (Raspberry Pi).

DVM

Digital voltmeter.

E

EEPROM

Electrically erasable programmable read-only memory.

F

FET

Field-effect transistor.

Floating input

An input signal that is not connected to an active signal source.

G

GPIO

General-purpose I/O.

Gray code

A binary code (sequence) where only 1 bit changes between any two numbers in the sequence.

H

HAT

Stands for "hardware attached on top," a hardware add-on board for a Raspberry Pi.

I

I2C
Inter-integrated circuit, a low-speed bus for connecting ICs in embedded systems.

I^2C
See *I2C*.

IC
Integrated circuit.

IDE
Integrated development environment.

IIC
See *I2C*.

IoT
Internet of Things.

ISR
Interrupt service routine.

J

JFET
Junction field-effect transistor.

L

LKM
Loadable kernel module (Raspberry Pi OS).

LSB
Least significant bit.

M

Master device
Archaic term for an I^2C controller device.

MCU

Microcontroller unit (a CPU or MPU specifically designed for embedded applications).

MOSFET

Metal-oxide semiconductor field-effect transistor.

MPU

Microprocessor unit (same as CPU, but specifying a microprocessor as the central processing unit).

MSB

Most significant bit.

O

OSHWA

Open Source Hardware Association.

P

PCB

Printed circuit board.

Peripheral

A device connected to a computer system (or bus), typically for performing input or output operations.

PGA

Programmable gain amplifier (also: *pin grid array*, depending on context).

Pullup resistor

A resistor attached to some power supply (usually 3.3 V or 5 V) that weakly pulls up the voltage on the circuit connected to the other end of the resistor. The circuit side of the resistor can force that signal to Gnd (0 V) by providing a lower-resistance path to Gnd.

R

Race condition

An errant calculation in a program due to the timing or sequence of operations in a code (whose results can vary based on when the code executes).

RTD

Resistance temperature detector.

S

SBC
Single-board computer.

SCL
Serial clock line (I^2C).

SDA
Serial data line (I^2C).

Singleton class object
A singleton class that only ever has one object instance created for it.

Slave device
Archaic term for an I^2C peripheral device.

SMBus
System management bus.

SMD
Surface mount device.

Snippets
Small code fragments that demonstrate some concept but might not be compilable or runnable.

T

TWI
Two-wire interface.

U

USI
Universal Serial Interface (ATtiny84).

INDEX

Feather SBCs, 102, 117
Feather specifications, 117
FeatherWings, 117, 120
filtering analog input noise, 331
four-wire mode, 5
FreeRTOS, 175, 189
FTDI, 112

G

general call, 21
glitch filtering, 221, 234
GPINTENA register (MCP23017), 265
GPINTENB register (MCP23017), 265
GPINTEN register (MCP23008), 264
GPINTEN*x* register (MCP230*xx*), 284
GPIOA register (MCP23017), 265
GPIOB register (MCP23017), 265
GPIO pins (MCP230*xx*), 263
GPIO register (MCP23008), 264
GPPUA register (MCP23017), 265
GPPUB register (MCP23017), 265
GPPU register (MCP23008), 264
GPPU*x* register (MCP230*xx*), 270
Grand Central M4 Express, 102
Grove bus, 115, 125
Grove bus pinouts, 126
guaranteed response time (ISR), 176

H

hardware general calls, 23
HATs, 116, 148
HDMI, 89
high-speed mode, 10, 24
high threshold register (ADS1*x*15), 315
host (I^2C, SMBus), 82

I

I^2C
    addresses, 5, 10, 19
    bus bit order, 17
    bus speed, 5, 9
    bus start sequence, 12
    clock frequency on the
        Raspberry Pi, 152
    clock stretching, 13
    controller devices, 4
    driver, 70
    host, 82

PC support, 112
peripheral devices, 4
peripheral programming, 349
PiOS kernel function calls for, 162
PiOS programming, 158
programming on the Arduino, 134
protocol, 15
support on a PC, 112
I^2C bus
    arbitration, 12
    clocking data to, 16, 28
    writing data to, 19
i2cdetect utility (Linux), 155
i2c-dev functions (Linux/PiOS), 163
i2cdump utility (Linux), 155
i2cget utility (Linux), 155
i2cput utility (Linux), 155
i2c_smbus_read_block_data
        function, 169
i2c_smbus_read_byte_data function, 166
i2c_smbus_read_byte function, 165
i2c_smbus_read_word_data function, 168
i2c_smbus_write_block_data
        function, 170
i2c_smbus_write_byte_data
        function, 168
i2c_smbus_write_byte function, 166
i2c_smbus_write_quick function, 164
i2c_smbus_write_word_data
        function, 169
illegal command code (general call
        operation), 22
input polarity (MCP230*xx*), 270
INTCAPA register (MCP23017), 265
INTCAPB register (MCP23017), 265
INTCAP/INTCAPA/INTCAPB
        registers (MCP230*xx*), 285
INTCAP register (MCP23008), 264
INTCONA register (MCP23017), 265
INTCONB register (MCP23017), 265
INTCON register (MCP23008), 264
INTCON register (MCP230*xx*), 284
internal pullup resistors on
        MCP230*xx*, 269
interrupt polarity (MCP230*xx*), 283
interrupt service routine, 142, 176, 281
interrupt signal, 176
interrupts on the MCP230*xx*, 280

The Book of I²C is set in New Baskerville, Futura, Dogma, and TheSansMono Condensed. The book was printed and bound by Sheridan Books, Inc. in Chelsea, Michigan.